The Eyes of the People

The Eyes of the People

Democracy in an Age of Spectatorship

Jeffrey Edward Green

OXFORD
UNIVERSITY PRESS
2010

OXFORD
UNIVERSITY PRESS

Oxford University Press, Inc., publishes works that further
Oxford University's objective of excellence
in research, scholarship, and education.

Oxford New York
Auckland Cape Town Dar es Salaam Hong Kong Karachi
Kuala Lumpur Madrid Melbourne Mexico City Nairobi
New Delhi Shanghai Taipei Toronto

With offices in
Argentina Austria Brazil Chile Czech Republic France Greece
Guatemala Hungary Italy Japan Poland Portugal Singapore
South Korea Switzerland Thailand Turkey Ukraine Vietnam

Published by Oxford University Press, Inc.
198 Madison Avenue, New York, New York 10016
www.oup.com

Oxford is a registered trademark of Oxford University Press

Library of Congress Cataloging-in-Publication Data

Green, Jeffrey E. (Jeffrey Edward)
The eyes of the people : democracy in an age of spectatorship /
Jeffrey E. Green.
p. cm.
Includes bibliographical references and index.
ISBN: 978-0-19-537264-9
1. Representative government and representation. 2. Collective
behavior—Political aspects. 3. Democracy. 4. Plebiscite.
5. Political participation. I. Title.
JF1051.G74 2009
321.8—dc22   2009011326

3 5 7 9 8 6 4 2

Printed in the United States of America
on acid-free paper

For Amy

ACKNOWLEDGMENTS

This is my first book, and it could not have been written without my teachers. First mention must be made of Nancy Rosenblum, whose gentle yet forceful luminosity showed me the way on innumerable occasions, and Dennis Thompson, whose wonderfully demanding criticism has been an education in itself. Both read many earlier versions of the manuscript and provided guidance of inestimable worth. Sharon Krause has been an extraordinary mentor for almost a decade; this book owes much to her and her example, as well as to countless critical comments she made along the way. Michael Sandel offered encouragement and penetrating insight at key junctures. Other teachers, though not directly involved in this project, nonetheless have been indispensable as sources of inspiration and exemplary scholarship. Bruce Ackerman, Mark Barr, David Bromwich, Gunnar Falkemark, Robert Forbes, Paul Kahn, Tony Kronman, Sven-Eric Liedman, Harvey Mansfield, Russell Muirhead, and Richard Tuck made a lasting impact for which I am grateful.

Friends, colleagues, and other informal advisors also played an essential role. It is difficult to exaggerate my gratitude to Aziz Rana and the conversations we had just as the project was getting off the ground. I am no less indebted to Brendhain Diamond, whose friendship and pre-Socratic philosophical style enriched both the book and my life beyond it. It has been a privilege to complete this work at the University of Pennsylvania, and I would like to thank my colleagues in Penn's Political Science Department—especially Avery Goldstein, Nancy Hirschmann, Ellen Kennedy, Anne Norton, and Rogers Smith—who have been supportive to the highest degree and offered suggestions and criticism that were crucial to the final stage of the writing process. A debt of gratitude is owed to many others who took time to read the manuscript, offer feedback, or point me to key sources: Jon Argaman, Bryan Garsten, Murad Idris, Johan Karlsson, Odette Lienau, Paul Linden-Retek, Michael Nitsch, Andrew Norris, Göran Duus-Otterström, Jonathan Schroeder, Josh Stanfield, Marty West, Elizabeth Wingrove, and John Zaller.

I also benefited from three outstanding research assistants—Meike Schallert, Aaron Ross, and Joe Datko—each of whom dedicated great care to this project.

Generous financial support was provided by Penn's Provost Office, a Fulbright scholarship from the U.S. State Department, a Graduate Society Fellowship from Harvard, research grants from two exceptionally supportive Swedish foundations, the Herbert and Karin Jacobssons Stiftelse and the Mary von Sydow f. Wijks Stiftelse, and the Program on Constitutional Government at Harvard.

Earlier versions of various portions of this book were presented at Berkeley's Jurisprudence and Social Policy Program, Columbia's Political Theory Workshop, Penn's Political Science Department, the Institute for Humane Studies, and Gothenburg University's Political Theory Workshop. Earlier drafts of parts of the book were also presented at the annual meetings of the American Political Science Association, the New England Political Science Association, and the Northeastern Political Science Association. Feedback from these venues helped to refine and strengthen the book's main claims.

A good deal of chapter 5 was previously published in my essay "Max Weber and the Reinvention of Popular Power," *Max Weber Studies*, 8. 2, 2008, pp. 187–224. I owe thanks to Sam Whimster and the rest of the journal's editorial board for permission to reprint parts of the essay here.

I am deeply grateful to David McBride, my editor at Oxford University Press, for believing in this project and to the two anonymous reviewers for their critical suggestions. Susan Ecklund, Alexandra Dauler, Paul Hobson, and Brendan O'Neill also provided excellent editorial assistance.

Finally, I am indebted beyond measure to my family. My parents, Joan and Franklin Green, and sister, Julie, have provided a lifetime of love and support without which this book surely would never have been undertaken. My extended family in Sweden—Helen, Oscar, Ebba, and August—have given me a second home from which so much of the book was written. My daughter, Kitty, has been a source of joy and a healthy reminder of the world beyond literacy. To Amy—who has read over hundreds of my pages during the last many years, as well as helped me through the mountain of microdecisions pertaining to the book's development—I can only proclaim how fortunate I am to have such a patient, kind, beautiful, and talented wife. I dedicate this book to her.

JEG
Philadelphia, PA
June 2009

CONTENTS

The Eyes of the People

1

Ocular Democracy

As our case is new, so we must think anew, and act anew.
We must disenthrall ourselves.

—Abraham Lincoln

1.1 The Eyes of the People

Democracy hitherto has been conceived as an empowerment of the People's voice. This book is a call to consider the People's *eyes* as an organ that might more properly function as a site of popular empowerment.

The dominance of a metaphorics of voice when contemplating the People and the nature of its power within democracy is readily observed. Since as early as the eighth century political theory has been informed by the doctrine *vox populi, vox dei*: the voice of the People is the voice of God. And if few have ever followed this doctrine to the utmost extent, the inclination to understand popular power in terms of voice is so firmly established as to be an almost universal tenet within the modern tradition of democratic thought. Not only do the best-known democratic institutions—elections and public opinion—easily lend themselves to a metaphorics of voice, but among otherwise diverse approaches within democratic theory there is a pronounced tendency to theorize democracy from the perspective of the People's voice. Deliberative democrats look at how politicians, advocates, jurists, and other public figures ought to talk with each other and how their deliberations can refine and enlarge the People's voice. Pluralists have reminded us that there is no single sovereign voice in modern democracy, but a multiplicity of voices that compete and cooperate to produce the harmony that prevails within stable democratic systems. And aggregationists, who focus on the mechanics of voting, choose for their analyses the one moment when the People—or, to be much more accurate, the majority of those who vote—formally expresses itself through voicing a preference about who should hold power.

The perspective of this book is not that the focus on voice is wrong—at least not as it pertains to the political activities of particular individuals and groups—but that, by itself, this focus is too narrow and too productive of a democratic theory out of touch with the way politics is experienced by

3

most people most of the time and by the People itself (the mass of every-day, non-office-holding citizens in their *collective* capacity) all of the time. The fact is that for most of us, our political voice is something we exercise rarely ... : in periodic votes, the occasional poll, and perhaps also in pursu... ...rticular issue that galvanizes us. And should our voice actually b... ...–if our candidate wins or our particular issue is resolved favorably ... ...ually a conceit to think the People is speaking and not some majo... ...ell-organized minority that has won. In any case, the key point is ... ...st majority of our political experience, whether voter or nonvoter, i... ...t engaged in such action and decision making, but rather watching ... stening to *others* who are themselves actively engaged. Such spectato... ...hip is inscribed in the very nature of political action itself. When a politician makes a speech, there are thousands who tune in to hear what he or she has to say. When public interest organizations engage in public protest, the very logic of their efforts assumes a nonacting but watching broader public who might be inspired to join the cause. And when something goes wrong—when a terrorist attack or natural disaster threatens the life of the polity—most can only stand by and hope that those with decision-making authority use their power wisely and to the benefit of the broader populace consigned to watch the crisis unfold. That is to say, most citizens most of the time are not decision makers, relating to politics with their voices, but *spectators* who relate to politics with their eyes. The ambition of this book is to consider the meaning of democratic ideals in light of this fact.

Political spectatorship is not simply the normal correlate of political action, but a *problem* that indicates the distinctive difficulties besetting democratic life at the dawn of the twenty-first century. On the technological level, the problem of spectatorship is reflected in the rise of mass communication technologies, especially television, that have fundamentally altered the conduct of political life by cementing spectatorship into the very structure of daily political experience. The organization and resources required to express oneself meaningfully through the mass media have made it so that there is little rotation between actor and spectator, but rather a semipermanent spectating class that watches a much smaller group of political elites. Whereas in the past, as in Athens, the spectating citizen could easily step forward and become a political actor, today most political spectators are addressed by political messages in ways that make it impossible to respond directly and extremely difficult to respond at all. The relationship between actor and spectator, in its current form, threatens the political equality prized by democracy. Richard Bernstein is surely correct when he declares that the "search to find some reconciliation between the actor and the spectator continues to be one of the deepest problems of our time."[1] In bringing politics before the eyes of the People to an unprecedented degree, the mass media has also normalized a set of political practices—the photo op, the sound bite, the press leak, and, more generally, the issueless politics of personality—that have undermined the rationality of public discourse, thus further alienating everyday citizens from the sense that they are a party to genuine political decision making and the reasoning on which it is based. Confronting democracy from the perspective of the spectator means, then, doing democratic theory in light of the specific pathologies and dysfunctions that have accompanied democratic development over the course of the last century.

In pursuing a political theory that takes into account this problem of spectatorship—that is informed by the fact that most people engage with politics primarily with their eyes,[2] rather than their voice, and that approaches the collective concept of the People from an ocular rather than vocal perspective—my method will be to revive and develop a forgotten alternative within democratic theory: the school of thought known as *plebiscitary democracy*. To refer to plebiscitary democracy as a school of thought, to suggest that one might be a plebiscitarian in the same way that one can be a deliberative democrat, pluralist, or participationist, is already to give plebiscitarianism more credit than it normally receives. In its current form, plebiscitary democracy is something of a curse word in democratic theory, indicating a sham or simply bad democracy—a democracy in which political elites' strategic political marketing through the mass media has crowded out the deliberation and popular participation required for meaningful popular decision making. In the work of leading democratic theorists like Jürgen Habermas in Germany and Bruce Ackerman and James Fishkin in the United States, for example, plebiscitary democracy designates a politics of spectacle, dominated by manipulative elites, in which genuine popular decision making has been corrupted and most citizens are consigned to play the role of spectator. But this strictly pejorative rendering of plebiscitary democracy is too narrow. Plebiscitary democracy is not just a condition, but also a theory. It does not simply name a democracy inundated by spectatorship, but offers a way of reasoning about and pursuing democracy from the spectator's perspective. By going back to the earliest theorist of plebiscitary democracy, Max Weber, by examining the contributions of his two most influential successors, Carl Schmitt and Joseph Schumpeter, and by turning to a variety of other authors sensitive to the importance of spectatorship in politics, such as Aristotle, Shakespeare, and Benjamin Constant, I intend to reconstruct a theory of plebiscitary democracy, rehabilitating it as a viable paradigm within democratic thought.

To be clear, a theory of plebiscitary democracy does not affirm that it is better to be a spectator than a political actor, but only that it is possible to do democratic theory from the spectator's perspective: that there are understandings of citizenship, popular power, and democratic progress that can be worked out from the standpoint of the political spectator.

But if spectatorship is not better than acting, if the spectator is a problematic figure who upsets traditional democratic values of equality and autonomy, why bother with a democratic theory devoted to the interest of the spectator? Why not, instead, seek to find ways to transform spectators into actors? One reason, which has already been alluded to, is that spectatorship is definitive of the way ordinary people relate to politics in their ordinary lives. While political philosophy need not be interested in the way most people most of the time engage with politics, political philosophy of a democratic stamp has a special obligation to develop political principles in a manner that respects the everyday structure of political experience. Taking spectatorship seriously is a way of respecting the political lives of ordinary people. A second reason, also alluded to, is that spectatorial processes are more truly communal than vocal ones and thus serve as a more appropriate foundation for the collective notion of the People. While it is true that all citizens in mass democracy possess a common right to exercise their voices in occasional elections, the actual usage of this right prevents ordinary citizens from obtaining a collective consciousness insofar as electoral results divide the citizenry between voter and nonvoter, between opposing partisan attachments, and ultimately between a sense of having vicariously won or lost the contest itself. Because it values the concept of the People—everyday citizens conceived in their collective capacity— plebiscitary democracy grounds itself on the condition of spectatorship that all ordinary citizens bear toward their government by virtue of their shared lack of office.

Finally, another justification for a theory of plebiscitary democracy is that the unideal circumstance of spectatorship on which it is grounded actually recommends its importance and its value. As democracy has spread across the globe over the last century, there has emerged a growing sense that democracy has not—and perhaps can never—live up to the high idealism that surrounded its modern rebirth in the eighteenth and nineteenth centuries. This disappointment, which is not at all the same thing as antidemocratic sentiment, has been expressed in different ways. Winston Churchill's quip that democracy is the worst form of government except for all the others is probably the most famous in this regard. And the Italian political theorist Norberto Bobbio's delineation of democracy's "broken promises" and "unforeseen obstacles" is probably the most important.[3] What is needed, and what in large part has yet to be attempted, is a democratic theory that productively responds to this sense of disappointment—a democratic theory that can maneuver between the twin pitfalls of relying on perfect ideals (like undominated discourse, pluralist equilibrium, or one-person-one-vote) that mask the way disappointment has become a part of the phenomenology of democratic experience and, from the other side, becoming so committed to exposing dysfunction within today's democratic systems that all ideals, and with them all political hope, are seen as illusory. A theory of plebiscitary democracy aims to navigate this middle path. By grounding itself on the People's eyes rather than the People's voice, and thus on an organ that carries with it the problems of inequality and passivity rather than the perfection of autonomy and representation, the plebiscitary model I shall defend strives for ideals especially suitable to the fallen conditions that shape the way democracy has come to be experienced today.

The details of this theory are spelled out in the pages that follow, but the broad principles that inform it can be outlined here at the outset. In the remainder of this chapter, my aim is to introduce in a preliminary way the main features of a theory of plebiscitary democracy whose elaboration and defense will be the purpose of the succeeding chapters. In section 1.2, I argue that, in spite of both moral and intellectual suspicion of spectatorship as a legitimate topic of political study, it is after all possible to pursue democracy from the perspective of the political spectator: that there is such a thing as an *ocular model of popular empowerment* and that it is precisely plebiscitary democracy's embrace of this model that makes it an important alternative within political thought. Further, not only is an ocular model of popular empowerment possible, but its pursuit would lead to a meaningfully different account of the types of public goods at stake in the quest for a more democratic society. Plebiscitary democracy is not merely an alternate interpretation of familiar democratic processes, but represents a novel ethical paradigm that would reshape the way the moral meaning of democracy is approached and pursued. Sections 1.3 to 1.6 review the specific intellectual, aesthetic, egalitarian, and solidaristic values that would be realized by a theory of plebiscitary democracy and its ocular paradigm of popular empowerment. The concluding section 1.7 details the overall plan for the book's remaining chapters.

1.2 Two Models of Popular Power: Vocal versus Ocular

It might seem that a theory of plebiscitary democracy, with its ambition to pursue democracy from the perspective of the eyes of the spectator rather than the voice of the actor, sets out to accomplish the impossible. Political science, after all, is hardly accustomed to treating the faculty of vision as a suitable foundation for political empowerment. The normal assumption is that the eyes are outside of power: that spectatorship, if it signifies anything, indicates domination (the subordination of the many who watch to the few who are watched on the public stage) and that, accordingly, empowerment occurs only through taking up speech, action, and deci-sion—which of course is precisely what the spectator does not do.

Underlying this sense that spectatorship is a theoretical dead end—that the spectator as such is powerless and that a theory of democracy grounded on spectatorship is therefore without critical purchase—is a widespread assumption about the form popular empowerment must take in a democracy. I call this traditional and still dominant model of popu-lar power the *vocal model*. Although its features will be elaborated in the following chapters, its three central elements can be summarized here: it holds that the *object* of popular power is *law* (defined broadly as the stat-utes and norms shaping public life), that the *organ* of popular power is the *decision* (expressive determinations, like voting and public opinion, that pertain to what a polity should do), and that the *critical ideal* of democracy is therefore *autonomy* (the People's ability to live under laws it has helped to author). A reader skeptical that there is such a thing as traditional demo-cratic theory—or who doubts that it takes the form of a vocal model of popular power—will find these claims substantiated in chapter 3. For now, however, the point is simply that it is not difficult to see that when power is conceived according to the vocal paradigm, spectatorship can only appear powerless. As a nonparticipant who only watches politics, the spectator does not decide, does not shape laws, and hence remains outside processes of collective authorship and self-legislation. Under the dominance of the vocal model of popular power, then, political science can only find in spec-tatorship—and by extension in vision itself—a form of experience outside of politics, bereft of power, and without any application to a progressive theory of democracy.

In theorizing democracy from the perspective of the spectator, the theory of plebiscitary democracy I shall defend looks to overcome the confines of the vocal model. It challenges each of the elements of the vocal model and refashions popular power according to an ocular paradigm. This ocular paradigm is best understood in terms of three shifts vis-à-vis the vocal model.

First, when politics concerns the spectator who watches rather than the actor who decides, the object of popular empowerment must shift to the *leaders* who are watched, away from its traditional basis in the *laws* that are written, debated, and enacted. To be sure, conventional democratic ideology, under the influence of the vocal model, often insists upon the need for the cultivation of robust leadership, but such leadership is under-stood not as the end of democracy, but as a means toward accomplishing the People's will or helping form and educate citizens' preferences about laws, norms, and policies. What the ocular model calls for is a concep-tion of popular empowerment more immediately linked to the conduct of leadership. The measure or index of popular empowerment on the ocular account no longer resides in the laws that are ratified but rather depends on the People's relationship to the leaders who are seen. Unlike the vocal model, which understands leaders as a means to the ultimate end of legislation, under the ocular paradigm it is the leaders who function as the ultimate site on which democracy is realized.

By itself, this first shift no doubt will seem abstract. If the ocular model calls for giving center stage to the People's relationship to its leaders, as opposed to the traditional elevation of the People-law relationship, there is still the key question of what form the People-leadership relationship ought to take. This leads to the second difference between the ocular and vocal paradigms. Normally, as conceived according to a vocal model, the People exercises control over leaders through its voice: through such devices as choosing whom to support, expressing the preferences, opinions, and values toward which leaders ought to be responsive, and making judgments in elections as well as in public opinion that hold leaders accountable for their actions. The vocal model thus assumes that the organ of popular power is the *decision*: an empowered form of voice by which the People identifies its will—or wills—and brings this will to bear upon political life through elections, instructions, delegation, or other processes that might communicate opinions, values, and concerns.

The ocular model, by contrast, is grounded on the People's eyes and its capacity for vision, rather than on the People's voice and its capacity for speech. Popular empowerment under the ocular model does not involve the crystallization of the People's voice into an authoritative decision, but rather refers to the elevation of the People's spectatorship into the status of a *gaze*. It is the gaze—that hierarchical form of visualization that inspects, observes, and achieves surveillance—that functions as the chief organ of popular empowerment under the ocular model. What the plebiscitarian committed to an ocular paradigm of democracy seeks, then, is not an empowered form of speaking (the decision), but an empowered form of looking (the gaze).

This notion of the gaze as an empowered form of looking is almost entirely unfamiliar to democratic theory in its current state, but it is an important aspect of disciplines outside the study of politics, including theology, psychology, philosophy, art, and cultural studies. One of the ambitions of my defense of a theory of plebiscitary democracy, therefore, is to make relevant for democracy the concept of the gaze and the understanding of ocular power upon which it rests. While there is a great deal of diversity regarding treatment of the gaze, five variations are of particular relevance in both inspiring and helping to define any invocation of the *popular gaze*. First, deist theology, which of course so influenced the generation that oversaw the rebirth of democracy at the end of the eighteenth century, upholds the importance of the *divine gaze* even as it denies the reality of the divine voice. The deist God does not speak—does not communicate to humankind via scripture, prophecy, or miracles—but watches. It is the great "superintending power," as Jefferson described it.[4] Even divine judgment in an afterlife is minimized in deist theology, so that it is primarily the this-worldly internalization of the divine gaze in the form of one's gaze of oneself, or conscience, rather than any fear of future retribution, that stands as the most important ethical consequence of this theology.[5] Second, a secularized version of this theology can be found in the psychoanalytic tradition in which the sense of being watched by another is deemed fundamental to the inner architecture of psychic life. With Freud and especially Lacan, there is an important distinction between the ideal ego (the person I wish to become) and the ego ideal (the person whose gaze functions as the imagined audience before whom the events of my life are hypothetically performed).[6] With this concept of the gaze of the ego ideal, psychoanalysis recognizes that not only are we usually seeing ourselves from the perspective of some other, but who this other is tends to be relatively stable—so that it becomes quite meaningful for an individual to identify just whose hypothetical spectatorship has been empowered to play this disciplinary role. Third, the most ambitious philosophical attempt to come to grips with ocular power is undoubtedly Sartre's notion of the *existential gaze*, or *le regard*. For Sartre, the spectator is no merely passive figure but, as the holder of the gaze, someone with the power, albeit a perverse one, to undermine the agency of another. The sense that one is being watched turns the individual from a subject to an object, generating shame, pride, or a sense of danger—all three of which dislodge a free being from his or her authentic path.[7] Fourth, Foucault's notion of disciplinary power—the power that trains and forms individual subjectivities as opposed to the sovereign power commanding them to fight, pay taxes, and obey the law—is inseparable from Foucault's concept of the *disciplinary gaze*. The key mechanism of disciplinary power is "compulsory visibility" of the subject. As Foucault explains in his study of the modern prison, "It is the fact of being constantly seen, of being able always to be seen, that maintains the disciplined individual in his subjection." Disciplinary power is effected, then, neither by commands nor by drawing attention to itself in ostentatious displays of its potency, but rather is "a power . . . manifested only by its gaze."[8] Finally, from feminist theory there has come the notion of the *male gaze*. For Laura Mulvey, who coined the term, the male gaze signifies a state of affairs, common within Hollywood films, in which men dominate not simply as the protagonists of a film, but as the implied spectator for whose sake the film is being shown. Even when women are at the forefront of the narrative, they tend to be presented in a manner that oscillates between sadistic voyeurism and hagiographic fetishism—that is, in a manner that both assumes and enforces a male perspective. By imposing a male frame of reference, then, traditional Hollywood movies make it so that female spectators must adapt to an identity that is not their own. There has been much debate about Mulvey's thesis, particularly her essentialist rendering of the male and female forms of identity. But what seems especially important and enduring about Mulvey's analysis is that she interprets spectatorship as a position of power: "In a world ordered by sexual imbalance, pleasure in looking has been split between active/male and passive/female. The determining male gaze projects its phantasy on to the female figure which is styled accordingly."[9] That is to say, on Mulvey's reading, patriarchal power is not simply the power to dominate the world of action (what is done, who gets to do it, who shares in the profits), but also includes the power to shape the nature of the gaze by which action (both political and cultural) is understood.

Despite their manifest differences, what all of these examples share is that they recognize the spectator as potentially occupying a position of power vis-à-vis the individual who is being seen. All suggest that there is a difference between empowered and unempowered forms of looking and that, accordingly, it is possible to seek empowerment in ocular terms. To be sure, there is a key tension within this body of thought—a tension as to whether the gaze exerts independent power by virtue of the intrinsic properties of looking at someone, or whether the gaze is best understood as the reflection of a power that has its base in some nonocular terrain. It is the former case—which finds support not only in the long tradition of folklore surrounding the evil eye, but in certain social norms (like the impoliteness of staring) and in the way the gaze of an otherwise harmless infant can unnerve us—that is clearly affirmed by Sartre's account.[10] In the other examples, however, the gaze is less the main cause of a hierarchical power relation than it is a field in which some underlying hierarchy— divine-human, prison-inmate, patriarchal society-female—reveals itself in an ocular way. But even in this more modest understanding of ocular power, in which the gaze, as an empowered form of looking, owes its power to nonocular sources, it is still the case that one can distinguish relative degrees of ocular empowerment. God might or might not be watching. A prison might or might not engage in panoptical surveillance. A patriarchal society might or might not impose a male perspective as the implied spectator of cultural productions. At the very least, then, the ocular field offers a venue in which power might manifest itself, suggesting that it ought to be possible to interpret the power of the People—the core moral meaning of democracy—in an ocular direction.

In employing the concept of the *popular gaze*, it is this more modest meaning—an empowered form of looking available to the People, characterized by genuine and literal surveillance of its leaders, *that may in*

fact depend on nonocular sources (such as elections)—that I will employ
when defending a theory of plebiscitary democracy and the ocular model
of popular power on which this theory depends. This choice seems justified
not simply because any claims about the intrinsic power of looking suggested by Sartre seem too speculative, but because it is after all a clear
feature of modern mass democracy that ocular obligations imposed
on leaders—their felt compulsion to appear on the public stage and potentially submit themselves to rigorous forms of observation and surveillance—are underwritten by nonocular sources, such as the threat of losing
an election or, if called to testify, the threat of physical punishment. But
lest it be thought that the ocular model's dependence on nonocular sources of authority should somehow disqualify it vis-à-vis the vocal paradigm,
it should be recognized that the vocal model is itself dependent on
extravocal sources. The long-standing celebration and theorization of the
People's voice is rarely interpreted as a claim about the intrinsic power of
speaking—as if merely by using words and voicing preferences citizens
empowered themselves—but, rather, is taken to mean that electoral
institutions (the desire of candidates for electoral victory) and the coercive
force of the state, both of which are themselves silent, might be used to
enforce otherwise ineffectual popular articulations about policies, laws,
and other substantive determinations of the common good. The choice
between ocular and vocal methods of popular empowerment—and, specifically, between seeking to empower the People's eyes in the form of a
gaze, rather than its voice in the form of an authoritative decision—is less
a debate about the origins of popular power than a question about how
that power should be applied.

It is a core claim of this book that it matters whether one privileges
the gaze or the decision and that there is good reason to privilege the ocular understanding of democracy when thinking about the People and the
nature of its power. The ocular model thus rejects the vocal approach to
the extent the latter interferes with the former—and to the extent that a
false belief in the perfectibility of the latter seems to obviate the need for
the former. But this is as far as the hostility goes. In many cases, vocal and
ocular mechanisms intersect. It is not simply that, as I have discussed,
ocular requirements that leaders appear will tend to rely on leaders' desire
to win a majority of the electorate's voice, but that elections, far from being
only occasions for exercising voice, greatly facilitate and expand ocular
processes of mass spectatorship. This is not only because elections usually
relate most directly to who will hold power (and thus who must be watched
and listened to) and not to what ought to be done, but because the electoral
process demands a never-ending series of public appearances by leaders—
both among candidates who must campaign for the electorate's support
well in advance of the actual election and among elected leaders who, once

in office, feel compelled to engage in a continual process of orchestrated public events designed to extract support from the portions of the People that vote.

The question about what should be the organ of popular empowerment—the gaze or the decision—is a question about which features of a common set of electoral institutions should be privileged: their ocular or their vocal ones? Whereas most democratic theory finds the ocular norm that candidates and political leaders must appear in public as secondary if not altogether incidental to the primary focus on the substantive decisions leaders reach, it is precisely within the sphere of public appearances that the plebiscitarian approach to democracy I defend grounds and orients itself. Thus, in privileging the People's gaze (an empowered form of popular looking) vis-à-vis the People's decision (an empowered form of popular voice), a theory of plebiscitary democracy does not so much assert the independence of ocular power from vocal power, but rather insists that it is in the ocular realm of public appearances by leaders, rather than in the vocal realm of legislative and electoral decisions, that progressive demands for greater popular empowerment are most properly, most favorably, and most constructively sought. Because vocal processes on a mass scale tend to be rare, inarticulate, uncertain in their capacity to hold leaders responsive and accountable, and never truly collective (but belonging only to a subset of the People), I argue that it makes sense to understand the collective concept of the People—and, specifically, the organ of popular empowerment—in terms of a gaze instead of a decision.

These first two features of the ocular model—its relocation of the object of popular power in the leader rather than the law, and its relocation of the organ of popular power in the popular gaze rather than the decision—raise an important set of questions. What are the criteria that separate an empowered form of looking from a disempowered one? What is the difference between the People's genuine surveillance of its leaders and its mere ability to see them? What, in short, is the principle that would guide a plebiscitarian reformer seeking to empower the people in an ocular, rather than a vocal, way? These questions point toward the third line of difference between the ocular and the vocal models: that pertaining to the *critical ideal* that defines and guides the pursuit of democratic progressivism. Whereas traditional democratic theory, informed by the vocal model, appeals to the critical ideal of autonomy (the People's ability to engage in processes of self-legislation), plebiscitary democracy's ocular paradigm of popular empowerment understands the critical ideal to be *candor*—by which I mean not primarily the individual norm that leaders be sincere, but rather the institutional requirement that leaders not be in control of the conditions of their publicity. Leaders are candid to the extent their public appearances are neither rehearsed, preplanned, nor managed from above, but rather contain all the risk and uncertainty of spontaneous public events.

Although not usually theorized, the criterion of candor ought to be familiar to any observer of contemporary politics. On the one hand, as is usually the case, a leader can control his or her publicity in numerous ways: determining when to appear, for how long, in what venue, with whom, and under what circumstances. Indeed, with unprecedented technological and organizational resources, leaders and their political machines can control public appearances to the point that they are prepackaged, scripted, and even micromanaged to the smallest detail, including the angle of the camera shot, the background scenery, and, increasingly, the reactions of an allegedly independent assembled audience. On the other hand, however, we are equally aware that this control is not total and that in certain instances leaders are relatively less in command of the conditions of their publicity—as when their public appearances are live rather than prerecorded, free-flowing rather than scripted, compelled rather than discretionary, and subjected to questioning and probing from others rather than insulated in a monologic form.

Examples of candor within contemporary mass democracy include rare instances of extemporaneous cross-examination by candidates of one another in presidential debates (a practice that until recently was banned in the United States);[11] press conferences in which heckling or an unusually persistent journalist overcomes the devices whereby leaders or high officials control the event (e.g., picking on whom to call, not granting follow-ups, refusing to comment); and occasions when leaders themselves voluntarily agree to subject themselves to a candid form of publicity, as when they grant public interviews to unsympathetic journalists, permit unprecedented surveillance of their inner circle (as in the movie *The War Room*), or appear before public gatherings in ways that do not preclude the risk of harsh criticism and abuse. The British practice of question time, which is also employed by a handful of other nations, is one of the few political institutions that seeks to regularize candor as an everyday feature of democracy.

Whereas traditional democratic theories oriented around the ideal of autonomy seek to give the People control of the means of lawmaking, plebiscitary democracy, in pursuing candor, seeks to bestow upon the People *control of the means of publicity*. This control, to be sure, is negative, since it involves wresting control from leaders rather than the People itself determining the precise way in which a public presentation should be conducted. But this negativity ought not obscure the primary point: that the principle of candor introduces the criterion of whether, and to what degree, political spectacles are under the control of the leaders

whose public appearances constitute them. What the principle of candor
insists upon, therefore, is that any wholesale rejection of the visual nature
of contemporary mass politics—its tendency toward spectacle, image,
and spectatorship—is too broad. Within the ocular realm it is possible to
distinguish better and worse outcomes—that is, better and worse experiences of viewership. The most influential critics of spectatorship have
been so taken by the inferiority of all spectacles vis-à-vis a deliberative
politics of inclusive rational discourse that they have overlooked the key
fact that, within the ocular realm, it is still possible to differentiate morally
superior and inferior forms of spectacles.[12] What these critics have forgotten, and what my defense of a theory of plebiscitary democracy with its
ideal of candor aims to address, is that the ocular relation between leaders
and spectators is susceptible to its own moral analysis. Such an approach
may be considered as parallel to the deduction of ethical duties implicit
in the speech act—a deduction at the heart of communicative ethics and
deliberativist approaches to democracy. Just as Apel and Habermas have
argued, albeit in slightly different ways, that the very act of communicative speech presupposes certain normative criteria (reciprocity, sincerity,
respect, and a telos of mutual understanding) so can we say that the very
act of political spectatorship carries within itself its own implicit ideal—
that the public appearances of political elites show themselves to be *worthy of being watched*—and that the principle of candor best defines what
worthy of being watched means.[13] Candor thus serves as the critical ideal
on the basis of which democratic *imagery* can be assessed, developed, and
reformed.

These, then, are the main lines of difference between the ocular and
vocal models of popular empowerment. The ocular model understands
the object of popular power to be the leader rather than the law, the organ
of popular power to be the gaze rather than the decision, and the critical
ideal of popular power to be candor rather than autonomy. This threefold
shift provides the basic template for distinguishing an ocular model of
popular power from a traditional, vocal one; I shall return to it throughout the book as a way to elaborate the meaning of a theory of plebiscitary
democracy.

It must be reiterated, however, that the plebiscitarian ideal of candor,
while different from the traditional value of autonomy, is not diametrically
opposed to it—and that, by extension, the ocular model is not absolutely
hostile to the vocal model in every case. The two paradigms are best considered as cousins that are related in numerous respects. For one thing,
it may be, as I have suggested, that ocular power is underwritten by the
vocal one: that without elections, leaders would have little obligation to
make public appearances, let alone candid ones. Further, insofar as electoral decisions are increasingly bound up with the personality of leaders

and less tied to predefined partisan allegiances, candor is a principle that, by insisting leaders appear in public under conditions they do not orchestrate and manage, would facilitate the exposure of leaders' characters and thus enable voters to make a better-informed decision about personality.[14] In this sense, ocular, spectatorial processes would help improve vocal, decisional ones. Most of all, values dear to popular autonomy and the vocal paradigm—such as deliberation (that decisions be reached through processes of rational discourse) and transparency (that the electorate maximize its access to information regarding governmental activities in order to best exercise its decision-making function)—would very often be aided by candor, at least up to a point. It is difficult, after all, to conceive of a genuine deliberative exchange that did not also require an element of candor; one can equally say that, ceteris paribus, candor would surely aid rather than inhibit governmental transparency. For these reasons, candor is a commitment that is not altogether novel, but consonant to some extent with more familiar values and goals.

And yet a core assertion of this book is that candor—and, by extension, a theory of plebiscitary democracy centered on an ocular rather than a vocal model of popular power—does present a novel ethical paradigm for the pursuit of democracy. Although cousins, the two paradigms are not the same, and in many cases they will imply contrasting recommendations for the way different democratic commitments should be balanced and for the way specific institutions and reforms should be designed. Chapters 6 and 7 detail some of the specific institutional and ethical consequences of privileging an ocular politics of candor over a traditional vocal politics of autonomy. But in advance of this discussion, given that a plebiscitarian reformer will pursue democracy in ways irreducible to traditional concerns about strengthening, empowering, and obeying the People's voice, it no doubt will be asked: What good is candor? What good is the ocular model of popular empowerment? Why should a democratic reformer privilege the control of the means of publicity over the control of the means of lawmaking?

In answering these questions it must be remembered, first and foremost, that the raison d'être of the ocular model is that it provides a democratic theory suitable to democratic citizens in their everyday capacity as spectators. In chapter 2, I shall elaborate on the phenomenon of spectatorship—arguing that it defines the way most people experience politics most of the time, and that democracy, as a form of government uniquely concerned with everyday citizens, ought to be interpreted in a way that respects and responds to the everyday character of ordinary political experience—but for now it is enough to reiterate that, at the most elemental level, the ocular model of popular empowerment is justified because its mechanics do not assume that everyday citizens are what they clearly are not (choice-making, speech-making, legislating, active deciders of public affairs) but, on the contrary, acknowledge the passive, nonparticipatory, *spectatorial* nature of everyday political life. However, this elemental feature of the ocular paradigm is less a justification for plebiscitary democracy's ocular model of popular power than it is the starting point upon which all other justifications are grounded. A plebiscitarian politics of candor is justified not simply because it respects and is responsive to the political spectator, but because, in doing so, other important values are thereby realized— of which *four* are particularly important and worthy of elaboration in the remainder of this opening chapter. These are, first, on the *intellectual* level, a plebiscitarian politics of candor presents a promising path by which democratic theory might exit the increasingly contested, always obscure, rubric of representation. Second, from the *aesthetic* standpoint, plebiscitarianism, with its central ideal of candor, promises to inject eventfulness into a political culture inundated by what Daniel Boorstin aptly named "pseudo-events." Third, a politics of candor possesses an *egalitarian* value, insofar as it imposes special risks and obligations on political elites as a form of compensation for their disproportionate, never fully legitimate hierarchical authority. Finally, there is a clear *solidarity* value in plebiscitary democracy which, by redefining the People as an ocular rather than a vocal being, rescues the very notion of the People from its recent demise, revitalizes it, and thus makes it possible for everyday citizens to understand themselves as members of a meaningful and effective collective. In what follows, I will discuss each of these four values, explaining how they are maximized by the plebiscitarian pursuit of candor, as opposed to the traditional concern with autonomy.

1.3 The Intellectual Value of the Ocular Model: A Postrepresentational Theory of Democracy

What is special about the ocular model of popular empowerment and its ideal of candor, on a purely theoretical level, is that it is a political value that is novel insofar as it is outside the normative rubric of representation: it does not depend on citizens having preexisting preferences, interests, or opinions that they hope government might incorporate into legislation. In fact, it does not depend on citizens deciding at all. In these respects, candor indicates a postrepresentational or nonrepresentational theory of democracy.

The reasons for wanting to escape a representational paradigm are many. They include, first of all, the opposition to political representation that occurs as part of a larger critique of representation in postmodern theories of philosophy, literature, art, and history. Representation is

considered metaphysically objectionable insofar as it relies on the subject-
object dichotomy, positing both subjectivity (a coherent, unified, selfsame
subject, such as an expressive People looming behind government) and
objectivity (the capacity of government to reflect the represented faithfully
and without distortion).[15] Second, since Rousseau, critics of representation
have objected to its predemocratic, feudal provenance and to its mystical,
ultimately unverifiable character.[16] Guizot, for example, one of the first
formal students of representation, acknowledged that the question of what
constitutes adequate representation is ultimately a matter of taste.[17] More
recently, Ankersmit, though a defender of the concept of representation,
has conveyed a similar criticism: "Correct representation will always be
a matter of dispute and can never be objectively ascertained in the way
we can ascertain the factual truth of a statement."[18] Third, social choice
theory has exposed numerous types of irrationalities besetting the representative system, leading to doubt about the capacity of individual preferences to be nonarbitrarily and meaningfully aggregated into a collective
outcome.[19] Finally, at the most pedestrian level—although perhaps also at
the most relevant and applicable one—representation has been challenged
by those who call into question its central building blocks. Either the existence of inputs from the People on the basis of which government might be
held responsible and accountable is challenged,[20] or the capacity of existing
electoral machinery to meaningfully and consistently realize responsiveness and accountability in the conduct of elected leaders is doubted.[21] In
both cases the suggestion would be that representation is a political idea
whose currency in both academic and everyday parlance exceeds its actual
functionality as a regulative norm of political behavior in contemporary
mass democracy.

In reciting these challenges to representation I do not mean to get
caught up in the debate about whether and to what extent existing liberal
democracies really do satisfy a meaningful standard of representation. This
question is under intense debate and in many respects lies at the heart of
contemporary political science. Clearly, insofar as a belief in representation is still the norm among most political scientists as well as journalists
and lay critics, it would be misguided to disrespect the concept. What can
be said, however, is that among those who do challenge the representative
system—that is, the ideal of democracy as a regime in which government
supposedly carries out the aims, policies, and interests of the electorate
through the central vehicle of periodic elections for leadership—there has
been a substantial difficulty in explaining what other type of democratic
ideals should take the place of representation. Among some of the best
known and otherwise diverse critics of representation, for example, there
is a common deficit in the political-moral imagination: that is, a shared
difficulty in trying to think through what democracy might mean if not

the People's self-legislation through the choice of its representatives in
an election. Either democracy is redefined in positivistic terms as being
altogether bereft of ideals (as in Schumpeter's definition of democracy as
method);[22] or democracy is minimized so that it now means simply that
leaders or parties can be removed from power[23] (a goal that does not so
much abandon representation as limit its applicability); or the critique
of representation occurs without a clearly conceived alternative (so that
there is critique without construction);[24] or the moral kernel of representation—self-legislation—is reaffirmed in a way that bypasses the election
of representatives (as in the defense of direct democracy by exponents of
participatory democracy).[25] There seems to be, then, a normative lacuna
among those who challenge representation: a profound difficulty in imag-
ining "the rule of people" as something other than a *decisional* power by
which the People governs itself or chooses its governors. A plebiscitary
politics grounded on the ocular ideal of candor, however, does suggest
an alternate moral universe that can potentially satisfy critics who worry
about the feasibility of representation and popular autonomy. Centered on
sight rather than *voice*, and focused on the behavioral constraints placed
upon *leaders* rather than *laws*, a plebiscitarian politics of candor breaks free
from the hegemony of representation and the ideal of self-legislation—a
hegemony that for the most part has confined even those critics who have
desired to escape it.

1.4 The Aesthetic Value of the Ocular Model: Eventfulness

As a political ideal suitable to the position and the place of the political
spectator, one of the clear consequences of the principle of candor—the
principle that leaders not control the conditions of their publicity—would
be to maximize the eventfulness of everyday political life and discourse.
A previous age may have found the criterion of eventfulness difficult to
comprehend and insisted, legitimately perhaps, that all occurrences were
equally eventful. But the transaction of politics through the mass media,
especially through the post-nineteenth-century technologies of radio,
television, and internet, has made this distinction between more or less
authentic events a matter of course. When Boorstin coined the term
pseudo-event in the 1960s, he was not so much inventing a new idea as
conceptualizing what virtually any participant in modern life already
knew: that not all happenings are equally entitled to call themselves
events. Among the features that distinguish pseudo-events from genuine
events, Boorstin argued, were their lack of spontaneity (pseudo-events
are carefully orchestrated productions managed from above), their lack of
meaning (pseudo-events are either routine and automatic, or they relay

information that has already been disseminated ahead of time), and their
tendency toward the celebration of their organizers (pseudo-events extract
loyalty from onlookers rather than subject what is being presented to critique). Bereft of spontaneity, predictable, and acclamatory, pseudo-events
are like real ones in asking for our attention, but, unlike real ones, they
leave the observer empty, perhaps manipulated, and with a sense of having
wasted one's time.[26]

Like Boorstin's distinction between genuine events and pseudo-events,
the plebiscitarian principle of candor also makes a distinction regarding the
watchability of what is being watched. Further, the principle of candor
also interprets the distinction in roughly the same way as Boorstin—by
opposing as uncandid public appearances that are managed, predictable,
and riskless for the participants. Yet, whereas Boorstin was skeptical of
virtually all political spectacles for being artificial and constructed—even
the first televised presidential debates in 1960—and tended to model the
genuine event on spontaneous social or natural processes, like a train wreck
or earthquake, the principle of candor provides a way of distinguishing,
within politics, between more or less eventful events. That is to say, rather
than reject categorically all political spectacles—all media productions
where leaders are brought before the public eye—the plebiscitarian politics of candor I defend seeks to refine and improve such occurrences so
that they can better attain their potential as genuine events. The central
claim is that if leaders do not control the conditions of their publicity, then
their public appearances will tend to shift away from the pathologies typical of pseudo-events and come to contain the spontaneity, meaningfulness,
and risks that distinguish genuine events. A candid event is, by definition,
spontaneous in the sense that it cannot be managed or staged or rehearsed
from above. Nor can candid events be predictable. Because those on stage
are not in control of the meaning of the event, how the event will be interpreted is uncertain and thus up to the independent judgment of the spectator. And while the celebration of the leader might still follow, it is not built
in to the event itself. It is definitive of candid events that leaders are forced
to act and earn their acclaim, not receive it passively and without effort. In
these respects candor tries to make political happenings—even those that
are constructed spectacles—worthy of being watched. In watching candid
events, we do not observe merely what we already know or what someone
else wants us to know, but rather something that is revealed in the course
of the happening itself.

Of course, a theory of plebiscitary democracy does not simply commit itself to the distinction between genuine events and pseudo-events,
but asserts that there is an intrinsic value in a politics that generates the
former and diminishes the latter. In validating eventfulness as a specifically
democratic value, plebiscitary democracy follows in a nascent, yet growing,

tradition of democratic thought that links democracy to the cultivation and institutionalization of spontaneity. The greatest exponent of this tradition to date is Hannah Arendt, who celebrated political life for its capacity to break free from the automatic and repetitive processes of nature, to generate new and historical events in a world otherwise inundated by cyclicality and, as a result, "to make the extraordinary an ordinary occurrence of everyday life."[27] A theory of plebiscitary democracy builds on this Arendtian foundation, emphasizing a key claim that is never entirely explicit in her thought: namely, that eventfulness is a value to be enjoyed, not simply by the political actors who perform the event, but even more by spectators who behold it—and that, further, the call for greater eventfulness in politics is a *democratic* aspiration precisely because it seeks a political life that will satisfy not only the few who enjoy the fame and responsibility of self-disclosure on the public stage but the many who routinely watch such figures as they appear. Although Arendt's theatrical model of politics generally has been interpreted from the perspective of the actor, she herself was clearly aware that the eventfulness promised by her ideal democracy would be of interest to the great spectating majority. Arendt's recognition of the intrinsic satisfaction of witnessing spontaneous events is indicated by her own status as a nonacting theorist celebrating political action, by her favorite metaphor of *the miracle* when describing the promise of eventfulness (since the miracle is miraculous only to the onlooker of the miracle, not its performer), and most of all by the fact that in her later work especially she recognized that spontaneous action, far from being politics' gift to its practitioners, was the standard by which political leaders might be criticized from without by those who only watched and did not participate. Politics, it turned out, even if it escaped the automatism of nature and other nonhistorical processes, was still subject to its own internal form of automatism.[28] The speech act, which constitutes the practice of politics in its authentic, event-generating form, could disintegrate into two different uneventful pathologies: speech without deeds (as in propaganda) and deeds without speech (as in violence, mere technology, and clandestine politics).[29] In calling for a politics that was free of these pathologies, Arendt was not simply celebrating the life of political action, but seeking a political world that would be accessible to and appreciated by the political spectator. What Arendt seems to say, and what a theory of plebiscitary democracy more explicitly affirms, is that in addition to the traditional value of turning to politics to achieve freedom—whether defined broadly as any kind of collective action or more specifically as self-authorship of the laws—there is also a value, probably lesser but for this no less real, of *seeing freedom*: witnessing political events that are spontaneous, unscripted, and genuine portrayals of historical individuals under conditions of pressure and intensity.

Just as the *plebiscitarian value* of candor is a principle that can both comprehend and guide the amelioration of Boorstin's lament about the pseudo-event, so can candor similarly address the Arendtian concern about a politics in which speech and deed have separated to the detriment of eventfulness. The principle of candor—which calls for taking from leaders the control of their publicity—undermines propaganda to the extent that leaders' public appearances become contested, subject to critique, and thus less likely to propagate lies, contradictions, and empty rhetoric. Likewise, candor, whose first and most fundamental requirement is that leaders appear and appear often, would alleviate the problem of speechlessness by forcing power holders out onto the public stage—or at least by theorizing any nonappearance as itself undemocratic, no matter how valuable the deeds being achieved. A politics guided by the principle of candor would thus seek to bring decision makers before the public eye, where they might be compelled to join words to their actions and actions to their words.

In sum, a plebiscitarian politics devoted to the maximization of candor contributes to the theorization of democracy in terms of eventfulness in two ways. First and foremost, it provides a device for distinguishing between more or less eventful occurrences. A plebiscitarian can assert, for example, that, ceteris paribus, a politician's press conference is more eventful than a rally, a debate more eventful than a series of paid advertisements, and a prime minister's appearance at question time more eventful than the prime minister's professional press secretary fielding questions in the prime minister's absence. What explains these assertions—which ought to be reflective, after all, of widely held intuitions—is that, in each instance, the leader in the former case is under less control of his or her publicity than in the latter and that, accordingly, the capacity to generate unexpected, significant, and new occurrences, with unpredictable results for those involved, is also much greater in the former case. Second, a plebiscitarian affirms that eventfulness is an intrinsic democratic good: that it serves the interests of the otherwise interestless spectator consigned to watch rather than decide most political events.[30] In upholding eventfulness as a moral value, a theory of plebiscitary democracy appeals to the relation between spectatorship and morality that Kant first identified, but from the reverse direction. Whereas Kant deduced from the event—in his case the French Revolution and the sympathy it generated from passive onlookers—evidence of a universal moral judgment among detached spectators, the plebiscitarian theory I defend begins with the need for a political morality for spectators and, from this, deduces the value of the event.[31] This should not be taken to mean that candor calls for revolutionary events, but rather events that go on within a well-established constitutional system of rights and liberties.

An elitist will respond: "People to whom nothing has ever happened cannot understand the unimportance of events."[32] But it is precisely to such people that a theory of plebiscitary democracy is devoted.

1.5 The Egalitarian Value of the Ocular Model: Machiavellianism for the People

The principle of candor not only affects the nature of events in mass democracy but also places leaders under conditions of intense risk and pressure. Certain leaders, it is true, might thrive in such circumstances, but history suggests that even the most charismatic politicians have sought to maximize control over their public appearances. Indeed, anyone who doubts the great degree to which candor imposes constraints and stresses upon leaders need only reflect upon the paucity of candid occurrences in contemporary political life. The almost universal carefulness with which politicians seek to avoid institutional conditions of candor is itself evidence of the critical, transformative potential of the ideal. A leader who appears without full control of his or her image is subject to the risk of error and misstep, confrontation, inadvertent revelations, and simple shame. Above all, candor brings uncertainty, which is itself destabilizing to the maintenance of power.

It is because candor imposes such extra burdens on public figures—burdens unlikely to be experienced by ordinary citizens in their private lives—that it reflects a kind of egalitarianism. To be sure, this egalitarianism is not of the usual type, since it does not look to place all citizens on an equal plane, bestowing equal opportunities for political action, but rather has its eye on having political elites compensate the public for their disproportionate, never fully legitimate power. A theory of plebiscitary democracy is grounded on the condition of inequality between political leaders and everyday citizens. The egalitarianism it seeks, therefore, is of a corrective, remedial, and above all *negative* type: one that imposes special, ocular burdens on the select few whose voices have been specially empowered to represent others, to deliberate with fellow elites, and to engage in the actual decision making that will determine a polity's fate.

It is this insistence on placing special burdens on leaders as a form of compensation for their never fully legitimate authority that is likely to be considered the most controversial aspect of my defense of a theory of plebiscitary democracy. After all, it might seem that in calling for this negative form of political equalization—which seeks to bring down the high rather than uplift the low—candor is an inherently *pessimistic* political value, intended to help alleviate the strain of a fallen political universe rather than point the way toward new achievement and unprecedented progress.

Further, it might seem that this pessimism is not limited to the issue of
negative egalitarianism, but also is implicated in other aspects of plebiscitary democracy, including its acceptance that everyday citizenship is characterized by spectatorship rather than action and its desire to transcend
rather than improve the troubled rubric of representation. And, indeed,
I admit that these charges are true: that a politics of candor is in fact im-
bued with a spirit of pessimism—or, as it is often called, a spirit of *realism*
and, in particular, a willingness to lower political purposes out of respect
for obstacles and difficulties that are deemed unnavigable. But I object to
the insinuation that such pessimism is somehow an automatic indictment
of a politics of candor. After all, at the level of statecraft, there is a well-
established tradition of pessimism: without much exaggeration it can be
said that the advent of pessimism is concomitant with the dawn of a modern theory of politics free from the classical and Christian legacy.[33] With
Machiavelli, for example, who is often treated as the most pivotal theorist
of this modern, pessimistic political awakening, it is explicitly argued that
governments and the leaders who run them must forgo the grandeur of
traditional moral teachings and aim, instead, for lower and more realistic
political goals. Such Machiavellianism has three key components. First, it
means that the purpose of politics ought not be what is high, metaphysical, and difficult to verify, but, rather, what is near at hand, attainable, and
most basic; in Machiavelli's case this meant security, order, and stability of
rule. Second, in pursuing these objectives, Machiavellianism dictates that
one is to proceed, *not* as if from a zero point where neither good nor evil has
been established, but rather from within an embedded context in which
one always already finds oneself surrounded by threats, disappointments,
enemies, and dangers.[34] That is to say, political morality, according to this
pessimistic Machiavellian logic, is a morality for minimizing a preexisting
set of evils; it has little to do with attaining some positive good. This leads,
third, to a political morality that is clearly at odds with traditional ethical
norms, well established on the *personal* level, such as prohibitions against
cruelty, deceit, conspiracy, and violence. One saves the city through means
that are different from, and sometimes opposed to, the way one saves one's
soul.

If these three elements define what is at the root of the familiar, modern, Machiavellian conception of *raison d'état*, equally important is the fact
that neither Machiavelli nor realists who followed him have been prepared
to extend this pessimism to the political morality shaping the ethics and
behavior of everyday citizens. In its dominant form, Machiavellianism applies only to the few who possess great power, not to the many destined
to live ordinary political lives on the sidelines of statecraft. As Machiavelli
himself elaborates in the *Discourses on Livy*, everyday citizens are to continue to be examined and evaluated under a premodern ethical horizon. If

a good prince needs to learn how not to be good, a good citizen for Machiavelli is still someone who realizes traditional (and, indeed, profoundly non-Machiavellian) traits such as honesty, piety, self-sacrifice, faithfulness, and sincerity.[35]

Why, I ask, if leaders and states are permitted to find direction in the cold sagacity of a distinctly modern political education, must ethical discourses pertaining to the everyday citizen continue to require a fusty sentimentality? Why must political modernism be an achievement restricted to the few, leaving the many behind in an Athenian *ekklesia*? The plebiscitarianism I defend argues that Machiavellianism ought not be limited to the governing elite and the conduct of statecraft—that the redefinition of political ethics can and ought to be extended to the ethics of the everyday citizen. Accordingly, a politics of candor is best understood as part of a *reverse Machiavellianism*—or, more precisely, a *Machiavellianism for the People*. In defining the everyday citizen's interest in terms of the candor of leaders, the same three elements that I have identified as foundational to a Machiavellian theory of leadership are redeployed on the level of civic ethics. Thus, first, in elevating the candor of leaders as the primary democratic goal, the plebiscitarian defines the citizen's interest in terms of what is achievable and clearly able to be secured. The point is not simply that candor is a value that does not require a wholesale transformation of political society, as would Marxism or certain versions of participatory democracy, but, on the contrary, is eminently suitable to politics as we know it: a politics dominated by television, personality, low turnout, and spectatorship. What is even more significant is that, especially when defined institutionally as the norm that leaders not be in control of the conditions of their publicity, candor is relatively easy to gauge and measure. In this regard it compares favorably to grander, more traditional ideals—such as representation and autonomy, not to mention deliberation, participation, and transparency—which are notoriously difficult to assess in a particular situation and whose precise meanings are also highly contested. Insofar as candor overlaps with some of these traditional ideals, as I have argued it does, then the prioritization of a concrete and clearly discernible goal like candor would make it an effective method of achieving loftier aspirations.

But, of course, it is also my claim that candor is something different and distinct—so that it cannot be seen simply as a surrogate for these traditional democratic values. Acknowledging this leads to the second way that the plebiscitarian elevation of candor reflects a kind of Machiavellianism for the People: namely, that rather than aim for the attainment of some positive good, the insistence on candor draws its moral impetus from the reaction and resistance to a prior evil. The evil in question is the profoundly unegalitarian situation of contemporary mass democracy, which, as I shall more fully discuss in chapter 2, makes the political experience of the everyday citizen characterized by a subordinate relation to the select few who do get to make legislative and other political decisions. The divide separating political elite and everyday citizen is a familiar issue in political science, but the usual tendency is to neutralize it, either by affirming that it is overstated (that elections and public opinion to a large extent control the decision making of leadership), or by seeking reforms (such as redistricting, compulsory voting, or economic justice) that would effectively restore to the People a more equal share of political decision making. In either case, although by very different means, the inequality between leader and ordinary citizen is denied as an essential feature of the way democratic life is encountered by everyday citizens. For the plebiscitarian, however, guided by the spirit of Machiavellianism, the point is not to cancel political inequality, but to design a political ethics suitable to it. Candor realizes such an ethics because its rationale is not to return decision-making power to the People, but to ensure that those who do have massively disproportionate authority and power in a democracy in some sense be compelled to *recompense* the public for this privilege. As the norm that leaders not be in control of the conditions of their publicity—and that they in fact be subject to public investigations, contestations, and other struggles unimaginable as requirements for ordinary private citizens—candor demands that the power of the decision maker be compensated by a vastly heightened level of surveillance over his or her person.

To defend the importance of a negative egalitarianism does not mean that plebiscitarianism espouses a wholesale ethic of resentment meant to govern private relations, work, or other aspects of society. This leads to the third point of parallel with the Machiavellian tradition. Just as Machiavelli aims to defend a distinctly *political* morality that in numerous ways contradicts—but does not altogether replace—traditional moral norms operable on the individual level of personal ethics, so too is the negative egalitarianism of candor restricted to the specific dimension of political life. What is politically necessary is not always what is morally right. But the ultimate consequences of this pessimistic teaching are neither clear nor fixed. Whether in a particular instance one should choose politics or morals—save one's city or one's soul—is not something about which the plebiscitarian takes a stand. What the plebiscitarian does insist upon, however, is that this existential dilemma not be considered an elite prerogative, a sublime burden to be enjoyed by the few, but rather that it be extended to include the political ethics of everyday citizens. Ordinary citizens are entitled to their own pessimism. And a plebiscitarian politics of candor, with its explicit objective of exposing leaders to public instances of stress and uncertainty, is one way to provide them with their own Machiavellianism.

1.6 The Solidarity Value of the Ocular Model: The Recovery of the Concept of the People

One final value to the plebiscitarian approach of seeking popular empowerment through ocular means (the control of the means of publicity) rather than vocal ones (the control of the means of lawmaking) is a solidaristic one: namely, that plebiscitarianism promises to restore the notion of the People as a meaningful concept of collective identity within contemporary political life.

It might seem that the existence of the People is obvious, but it is in fact the case, for two different sets of reasons, that the People remains a remarkably unpopular figure within contemporary political life. On the one hand, the leading normative approaches to the study of democracy have managed to do without a rigorous notion of the People. Pluralists reject the notion of a single People, dissolving the concept into a collection of discrete minority groups that must both cooperate and compete for power. Likewise, theorists of deliberative democracy, the dominant normative paradigm for the study of citizenship and political legitimacy, focus on the communication between individuals engaged in sovereign decision making and are therefore uninterested in the mass electorate as such. And while the aggregationist model makes use of the People—as the author of majority decisions produced by a democratic voting processes—it understands this aggregation as reducible to the individual wills of the citizens who form it. Thus, it too discards any rigorous conception of the People in its collective capacity. On the other hand, among political philosophers the tendency has been to deny the conceptual integrity of the People and to find it as a constructed notion that lacks an underlying basis in reality.[36] It is noteworthy in this regard that Lyotard's famous account of postmodernism as a suspicion of grand narratives is inseparable, as is less often realized, from a parallel suspicion of grand subjects, such as the People, who might be considered the protagonists of such narratives.[37] Indeed, even radical democrats are fond of taking up Hobbes's argument that the People is merely an aftereffect of power—and thus something wholly unsuited to be the agent or subject of a radically emancipatory form of politics.[38] The suspicion of the People as a collective entity stems no doubt from a recognition of the totalitarian abuses to which the concept has been subject. It is definitive of the totalitarian party (or leader) that it claim to speak for the People in a direct and unmediated way, so that it can claim absolute legitimacy for its projects and acknowledge no limits to its power.[39] Although, as I will discuss in chapter 7, some like Habermas have tried to redefine the People without appeal to a subjective will, and thereby undermine any totalitarian manipulation of the concept, there has been a much more powerful trend to analyze democracy without explicit attention to the People.[40]

Plebiscitary democracy, with its ocular model of popular power, coun-teracts this trend of either forgetting or marginalizing the concept of the People. It does this, first and foremost, by defining the People neither as a mere philosophical abstraction nor as an unrealistic, potentially dangerous legislator with a single will, but as the mass spectator of political elites. To refer to the People in its collective capacity as a mass spectator is not to say that all political spectators watch the same political events (although there are certain events that approximate this circumstance), but rather that those whose experience of politics is shaped by spectatorship rather than action have a *collective interest* as a result of this fact.[41] Candor, which defines this interest, designates a critical ideal that not only empowers or-dinary citizens, but, if pursued continuously and explicitly, would provide them with a sense of solidarity with other ordinary citizens also consigned to experience politics passively in a spectating capacity. In this way, it would be possible to bring the People back as a real and important subject within both political theory and democratic practice. Conceived in ocular terms, this revitalized People would have numerous advantages vis-à-vis its vocal predecessor. It would have a constant presence rather than an epi-sodic one, since political image making, unlike elections, is ongoing in con-temporary mass democracy. No unscrupulous demagogue could claim its support, since, as an ocular entity, it would be silent about specific policies and decisions. This would mean, further, that the People could function as a true source of unity, transcending partisan struggles and the outcomes of particular contests.

None of this is to dissuade ordinary citizens from taking up a more active brand of politics and supporting particular candidates, organiza-tions, ideological platforms, or other policies. However, my claim will be that we need to understand such activism as what specific individuals and groups do, not what the People—the mass of ordinary, non-office-holding citizens taken in their collective capacity—does. As I have already argued and will explain more extensively in chapter 7, the concept of the Peo-ple ought to be reserved for what is more truly collective: not the exceed-ingly rare achievement of being heard and having one's voice determine the conduct of a particular political matter, nor even the vote, which is itself quite exceptional (and in any case divisive insofar as it produces a winning majority and a losing minority), but the all-too-common *passive* experience of being silent and deferring to the decision making of a select cadre of political elites. Activists seek victory for themselves, and well-meaning ones seek it for the good of others who are not active. But there are very few substantive causes that are truly collective. Most help some and injure others. Rather than enlist the People as an alleged supporter of policies that are truthfully not supported by, or in the interest of, all citizens, the plebiscitarian perspective I defend breaks from any will-based conception of the People, choosing instead to locate the People in the ocular processes of spectatorship rather than the vocal processes of activism and decision making. Activists can and must participate if a republic is to survive, but this acknowledgment is itself sufficient respect for their public service. Given the pluralism and intense debate that shape the formulation of most political issues, it seems unnecessary—and in fact inaccurate and illusory—to interpret any particular solution to today's political issues as what the People wants, needs, or otherwise supports. Citizens and groups win and lose as they compete for power, but the People, precisely because it is a collective notion, must be beyond victory and defeat. The People only watches; it does not win.

1.7 Plan of the Book

The following chapters aim to justify and develop the underlying perspective and principles I have presented in an initial way here. Chapter 2 is devoted to the elaboration of the moral impetus behind this project, addressing the rationale for wanting to move beyond standard perspectives within democratic theory and pursue a novel plebiscitary model. I defend the claim that there is a need for a political theory whose ideals are consistent with the fact of political spectatorship. Further, I demonstrate that the figure of the citizen-spectator, though fundamental and emblematic of political life as it lived by most people most of the time, has been systematically avoided, denied, or otherwise marginalized by dominant perspectives within contemporary democratic theory.

Chapter 3 defends a claim I have made repeatedly in this opening chapter, without sufficient substantiation: namely, that there is such a thing as traditional democratic theory. To this end, I argue that the vocal model of popular power, which considers the People as a decisional entity that expresses opinions, values, and interests, has defined democratic orthodoxy from the rebirth of democracy at the end of the eighteenth century down to the present day. I demonstrate the pervasiveness of the vocal model among classical theorists of democracy: Rousseau, Publius, Bentham and James Mill, J. S. Mill, Tocqueville, and others. I show that notwithstanding that twentieth-century political science began to challenge the underpinnings of the vocal model, this model perversely continued to exert its dominance even among those most aware of its shortcomings. I also draw attention to the central weaknesses of the vocal model: specifically, its lack of realism (its overstated estimation of the capacity for voice on the mass scale), its inaccuracy (since it is only majorities or well-organized minorities that speak in mass democracy, not the collective People itself), and its hegemonic function (the vocal model conceals the exclusion from government that is fundamental to the phenomenology of everyday political life).

Having exposed the difficulties of the vocal model, chapter 4 seeks a fresh alternative. It revisits the overly maligned concept of plebiscitary democracy, reviewing its historical development, and arguing for its relevance as a present-day ethical paradigm. Through an initial discussion of Weber and other plebiscitary theorists and a close reading of two of Shakespeare's Roman plays, I argue, against the usual tendency to understand plebiscitary processes in an altogether pejorative light, that there is in fact an undertheorized ethical component to plebiscitary democracy: namely, the ocular model of popular empowerment, with its fundamental principle of candor, which I have introduced here.

Chapter 5 seeks a further elaboration of the plebiscitary paradigm, providing a detailed exposition of the original and most significant plebiscitarian: Max Weber. My aim is simultaneously to demonstrate that Weber's model of plebiscitary democracy ought to be appreciated for resituating popular empowerment on ocular, rather than vocal, grounds *and* to make clear why Weber's fundamental reinvention of popular power did not succeed in taking hold within twentieth-century political science. In this latter regard, I turn to Weber's two most influential intellectual successors—Carl Schmitt and Joseph Schumpeter—and show how these two heirs to the Weberian legacy did not develop their own plebiscitarian accounts in a manner fully consonant with the ocular paradigm implicit in Weber's novel democratic theory.

Part of the process of recovering a vibrant and relevant plebiscitarian model of democracy is demonstrating how a plebiscitarian would encounter issues of democratization in a distinct and original way. In chapter 6, I take up this task and examine the practical consequences of applying a plebiscitarian approach, centered on the ideal of candor, to contemporary mass politics. In particular, I argue for the distinctiveness of a plebiscitarian brand of democratic progressivism, describing how a plebiscitarian defines and pursues democratization in a way different from deliberative democrats, participationists, and those committed to transparency. By reviewing three practical applications—presidential debates, public inquiries, and press conferences—I show how the pursuit of a plebiscitary politics of candor would lead a progressive democrat to structure reform differently from these more familiar schools of democratic thought.

Chapter 7 concludes by addressing the important question of how plebiscitarianism ought to be reconciled with traditional norms of participatory citizenship. Because the plebiscitarian principle of candor regulates leaders instead of everyday citizens—and because it refers to how leaders ought to appear rather than how they are to decide the most pressing issues of the day—certain readers will object that plebiscitarianism is irresponsible or, in any case, of limited significance to citizens committed to using whatever influence they possess to serve and improve the common good. In response to these concerns, I explain how the plebiscitarian ethics I defend plays three different roles for three distinct types of citizens. It *supplies* an ethical perspective to the passive spectator, *supplements* the ethical perspective of the active partisan, and *supplants* the ethical perspective of the democrat committed to popular sovereignty (redefining popular sovereignty in terms of candor rather than self-legislation). One's reception of plebiscitarianism depends, then, on a certain degree of self-knowledge about the type of citizen that one is.

2

The Citizen as Spectator

Be secret and exult,
Because of all things known,
That is most difficult.
　　　　　　　—W. B. Yeats

2.1 Seeing the Spectator

Contemporary mass democracy is both a continuation of the democratic
tradition that began 2,500 years ago in Athens and a departure from that
tradition. While we tend to be quite aware about what is distinctive about
mass representative systems on the *constitutional* level (the institutional
structures that define contemporary representative democracy, such as
elections, competitive parties, and separation of powers), when it comes
to appreciating what is distinctive about the *citizen* who lives within such
a regime, much less has been written or understood. The question of the
nature and interests specific to the citizen in a mass representative democracy
has not been adequately addressed. For the most part this citizen has been
treated either as identical to the participatory citizen constitutive of direct
democracy, or as a depoliticized economic agent without any sustained
interest in political life. Both accounts deny that there is a distinctive form
of citizenship that arises within the modern mass democracies of today:
either democratic citizenship is what it has always been—action and speech
before a body of coparticipants—or it is not political at all.

Against the reduction of citizenship to these two models, my claim
is that mass representative democracy engenders and normalizes a type
of citizen that, as a matter of law and abstract principle, has full political rights but, as a matter of practice, experiences politics primarily as a
spectator. This type of citizen, which I shall refer to as the *citizen-spectator*
(and also, following Aristotle, as the *citizen-being-ruled*), occupies an
intermediate position between two much more well-known figures within
democratic theory. On the one hand, there is the figure of the *citizen-
governor*, or participating citizen, who discusses, acts, joins, protests, takes
a stand, legislates, and above all *decides*—the figure at the center of the most
eloquent testimonials to the modern democratic tradition as it has been

presented by Rousseau, Jefferson, J. S. Mill, Tocqueville, Dewey, down to the contemporary deliberative theorists of today. On the other hand, there is the *apolitical citizen*, who is a citizen only in the juridical sense of being an individual with legal rights and social entitlements guaranteed by the state. The apolitical citizen takes little interest in public affairs, lacks knowledge about government, has no sense of being an efficacious political actor, and either does not vote or votes without a clear sense of what is being selected. This is the figure that early exponents of representative democracy, such as Sieyès and Constant, predicted would predominate in commercial republics in which the primary concern for production and exchange consumed most political energies.[1] And this is the figure that, until the twentieth century, was purposefully cultivated by voting restrictions based on property, gender, and race. It is the figure, moreover, that postwar studies on civic behavior appeared to uncover, albeit with substantial debate as to the meaning of this apoliticism: whether it marked the failure of democracy or a necessary relaxant on the system, and whether it signaled mass incompetence on the part of the electorate or, instead, a rational response to the conditions of mass politics that still managed to salvage something in the way of a successful representation of underlying interests.[2]

What both the citizen–governor and the apolitical citizen exclude is an intermediate position of citizenship in which there is meaningful psychological involvement with politics, but which nevertheless does not lead to active participation in political life. What is missing, in other words, is an appreciation for the citizen for whom a knowledge and interest about politics (even if low) far exceed the degree of active engagement. The citizen who occupies this middle space—whom I shall designate both as a *citizen-spectator* (because spectatorship defines this citizen's political experience) and as a *citizen-being-ruled* (because being-ruled reflects the power dynamics of spectatorship)—can be seen as a mixture of aspects from both the citizen–governor and the apolitical citizen. The citizen-being-ruled does have a political experience, but it is mainly a vicarious one. The citizen-being-ruled has an interest and personal involvement in government, yet is inactive. The citizen-being-ruled watches and observes and follows politics, but is neither a politician, nor an advocate, nor a leader, nor even an active member of a political organization. As far as preferences, the citizen-being-ruled might have them, or might not, or might have a generalized preference that matters be handled well without specifying what in fact this means, but in the context of each specific political issue, the citizen-being-ruled understands his or her own preferences are not determinative of the outcome. As a spectator rather than a participant, the citizen-being-ruled is not a political animal but a frequent attendee at the political zoo. As a spectator, moreover, the citizen-being-ruled understands a clear distinction between his or her own political life and the site of political decision.

Here, in chapter 2, my aim is to defend the claim that being-ruled—
that is, the spectatorial engagement with politics characterized by *involvement without participation*—is a form of citizenship that is extremely prevalent
within twenty-first-century conditions, yet nonetheless something that
has been neglected by the major discourses constituting the contemporary
study of democracy. In sections 2.2 through 2.4 I discuss Aristotle's theory
of being-ruled (which is roughly similar to the usage of being-ruled I employ)
and argue that whereas Aristotle might have had good reason for giving
the citizen-being-ruled only slight attention within his democratic theory,
modern institutions and moral commitments ought to elevate the figure
of the citizen-being-ruled to a position of primacy. Yet the relevance of
being-ruled has not been appreciated by modern democratic theorists. In
sections 2.5 through 2.8, I review the most influential perspectives within contemporary democratic theory—including civic behavior research,
pluralism, and deliberative democracy—and demonstrate the *systematic*
neglect of the citizen-spectator. In the final section, 2.9, I address what it
would mean to develop a democratic theory oriented around the experience of being-ruled and how the plebiscitary model I shall defend in the
subsequent chapters affords respect to the citizen-spectator.

2.2 Aristotle's Theory of Being-Ruled and Its Marginalization within His Theory of Politics

While contemporary democratic theory tends to deny or marginalize the
citizen-spectator, the concept of an intermediate position of citizenship—
between participation and apoliticism—can be found at the very beginning of the discourse on citizenship, in the political theory of Aristotle. Yet
Aristotle is himself not altogether committed to the study of being-ruled,
as the concept receives very little attention, especially compared with his
much more extensive treatment of ruling. Thus, Aristotle is important
not simply because he acknowledges this second experience of citizenship,
being-ruled, but because he also sets the stage for its subsumption under a
primary discourse on ruling.

According to Aristotle, the citizen in a democracy had to have two distinct virtues: the virtue of ruling and the virtue of being-ruled.[3] The first
refers to the citizen in his capacity as a governor and a legislator: someone
who decides, deliberates, holds office, makes judgments, occupies positions
of leadership and responsibility. The second refers to the everyday experience of citizenship: those who do not possess office or prominent positions of decision-making authority, but who nonetheless remain involved
in political life as the recipients of political decisions and passive observers of political events.[4] Aristotle thought that both virtues were necessary

for the same citizen—since the ancient democratic practice of rotation in office meant each citizen ideally would alternate between these two different roles—but ruling and being-ruled were still conceptually distinct on Aristotle's account.

Aristotle's theory of being-ruled, which stands at the very beginning of the Western discourse on citizenship, is remarkable in at least three ways that are still deeply relevant to the democratic politics of today. First, Aristotle's theory is a reminder that citizenship is not a uniform phenomenon, but essentially diverse and pluralistic in the practices and commitments it requires. Second, in highlighting the figure of the citizen-being-ruled, Aristotle draws attention to a crucial, if often neglected, experience within democratic life. Being-ruled refers to political experience that is distinguishable both from possession of office and decision-making power and, at the same time, from outright exclusion from the political community. The citizen who is being-ruled is not a leader or magistrate, but neither is he apolitical or antipolitical. Between governor and outsider, the citizen-being-ruled indicates the everyday character of citizenship as it is experienced by ordinary people—people who are full members of the political community, but lack office or any other position of particular prominence.

Lastly, what is perhaps most remarkable is that Aristotle understands being-ruled as possessing its own distinct virtue. Being-ruled is not simply something that must be accepted by imperfectly egalitarian regimes. Rather, it is a foundational aspect of even the most perfect democratic state. Hence, the figure of the citizen-being-ruled is presented within Aristotle's most idealized account of democratic life.[5] Specifically, Aristotle defines the virtue of being-ruled as the excellence of a certain kind of obeying, which he likens to the way a wife obeys a husband, or the way the passions obey the intellect. In all three cases, the nature of the rule is grounded on persuasion and is therefore constitutional rather than despotic and violent. It involves obeying an equal, rather than a natural superior as in the slave's obeying of a master or the body's obeying of the soul. Whereas the virtue of ruling is *phronesis*—the capacity to deliberate in the active search for the means by which to realize the common good—the virtue of being-ruled is "right opinion" [*doxa alethes*], or the passive acceptance of decisions that *others* have correctly thought through and made.[6] Further, the two virtues of ruling and being-ruled correspond to the two components of a conversation: speaking and listening. The virtue of ruling consists in the making of speeches and persuasive arguments before the Assembly, while the virtue of being-ruled lies in the careful attention and reception to the arguments that are made.[7]

That Aristotle conceived of a second dimension of civic life—distinct from active political processes of speaking, legislating, and governing—is more important to students of contemporary mass democracy than the particular way he defined the ethical implications for those occupying this dimension. Indeed, Aristotle's own understanding of being-ruled was developed to refer to the particular political realities of ancient direct democracy. What is crucial, however, is that Aristotle announces a second set of civic ethics whose practitioners are not the governors but the governed, and for which the *site* of civic virtue is not the collectively binding decision but the passive interaction with those who are active participants.

Still, even though Aristotle introduces this second dimension of civic life into the vernacular of democratic theory, his theory also presages the marginalization of the concept within contemporary democratic thought. Despite his formal distinction between ruling and being-ruled, Aristotle does not develop an autonomous theory of being-ruled. The notion of being-ruled receives very little attention. And when it comes to explaining the value of being-ruled, the concept is totally subsumed and subordinated beneath the primary value of ruling: that is, of holding office and giving judgments as an active and participating member of a political community. The value of being-ruled, according to Aristotle, is that it prepares one who is not yet a ruler for a future time when he will in fact hold office and participate as a leader on the public stage. In order to be a good ruler—to be well skilled in *phronesis* and the other civic virtues—one must first undergo the political education afforded by being-ruled. The constitutional ruler, who rules over equals, "must learn by obeying, as he would learn the duties of a general of cavalry by being under the orders of a general of cavalry, or the duties of a general of infantry by being under the orders of a general of infantry, and by having had the command of a regiment and of a company. It has been well said that he who has never learned to obey cannot be a good commander."[8] A citizen learns to obey and accept the good intentions of those in charge so that he may himself become a leader, or so that when he does occupy positions of authority he uses them well. Thus, Aristotle at once separates the two virtues of ruling and being-ruled, only to then collapse them within the single axiological dimension of ruling.

As I will now discuss in the next two sections, Aristotle's reluctance to theorize being-ruled as an autonomous dimension of political experience was enabled, on the one hand, by specific institutional and demographic aspects of the polity in which he lived—aspects that blurred the distinction between ruling and being-ruled—and, on the other hand, by a moral philosophy that elevated active participation in politics as the telos of the well-functioning human being. But when we look at the institutions, practices, and moral commitments that comprise contemporary representative democracy, the situation is different. For present-day theorists of democracy, inattention to the citizen being ruled—that is, to the citizen who is a spectator rather than a participant, politically aware but not politically active, interested in politics but without a clear and well-developed sense of political interests—becomes far less justified. In section 2.3 I discuss institutional aspects of modern mass democracy that make the figure of the citizen-being-ruled especially relevant. And in section 2.4 I address how certain modern moral commitments—equality and the dignity of the ordinary—similarly render the citizen-being-ruled extremely pertinent to the present-day theorization of democratic politics.

2.3 The Relevance of the Citizen-Being-Ruled Today: Sociological Factors

The institutional conditions of ancient Athenian democracy explain, even if they do not fully justify, Aristotle's marginalization of the concept of being-ruled as something preparatory for the central practice of ruling. There were two components to these institutional factors. First and most important, the rotation of offices, combined with the small size of the ancient city-state, made it likely that each citizen would serve on the Council once in his lifetime or at least hold one of a plethora of other offices.[9] Thus, it was understandable to treat being-ruled as a preparation for ruling, since by the fifth and fourth centuries B.C. there really was a meaningful exchange of roles within the polis. To be sure, rotation was an ideal that was never fully carried out in practice. The most important positions in finance and the military were not subject to lot, property requirements kept many out of contention for office, and recent studies have emphasized the oligarchic dimensions of Athenian political life and, hence, the existence of a permanent subordinate class within the Assembly that, while in possession of full civic rights, nonetheless did not take part in active civic practices such as speech making and office holding.[10] Still, the relative inclusiveness of Athenian politics explains why Aristotle could treat being-ruled as a preparatory experience for ruling and, thus, why he could marginalize the concept of being-ruled within his political theory.

Second, it was not simply the rotation of offices that led Aristotle to marginalize the concept of being-ruled; what also mattered was that the structure of Athenian politics was such that it was difficult to make a clean separation between the two roles of ruling and being-ruled. For Aristotle, being-ruled was still spatially, temporally, and ideologically linked to active governing, even if it was also defined in terms of exclusion from the offices and practices that constituted this governing. What is definitive about the experience of being-ruled is that it is an involvement with politics that does not realize itself in terms of active participation. But the distinction between involvement and participation was difficult to maintain within the Athenian context where the site of active participation—the

Assembly—was simultaneously the location of being-ruled. The citizen who sat passively and silently within the Assembly, watching and listening to the political speeches of magistrates and other distinguished leaders, was still a member of a legislative body and, thus, could always be considered a colegislator. Within the Assembly, he had the right to speak and come forward and say whatever was on his mind before his political equals. He could be heard. Membership in the Assembly also meant that he was the direct addressee of those who made political speeches. The citizen-being-ruled could question, or more likely shout down, magistrates and other leaders who spoke before him.[11] Obviously, to the extent that the Assembly allowed everyday citizens the chance to participate in important legislative decisions, it contributed to the blurring of the distinction between ruling and being-ruled. But even if we assume a skeptical attitude toward the egalitarian aspects of ancient Athenian democracy and agree with many scholars who have stressed the strong likelihood that only a small minority of citizens made use of the right to speak before the Assembly, the passive spectator who sat in the Assembly was still the direct addressee of the speeches that were made and still had the opportunity to respond, if not with articulate speech, at least through some immediate acclamatory or disruptive interruption of the leader who spoke. An analogous situation existed in the Roman *contio*, which lacked formal legal power but still brought citizens-being-ruled to the site of the participation of citizen-governors and offered a similar chance for collectively applauding or shouting them down.[12]

These two institutional factors—the rotation of offices and the overlapping of the sites of participation and mere involvement—made it understandable, if not fully justifiable, for Aristotle to privilege ruling within his study of citizenship and provide being-ruled with no more than an occasional and subordinate analysis. But in modern conditions, by way of comparison, there is far less reason for devaluing or ignoring the figure of the citizen-being-ruled.

First, whereas the rotation of offices made it likely that a citizen-being-ruled in ancient Athens would someday occupy a position of rule, the modern context is such that the experience of being-ruled takes on a certain permanence. While not absolute, this permanence is nonetheless strongly supported by a variety of sociological and historical factors. Modern democracies are representative systems in which the nonparticipation of most citizens in governmental office holding and decision making is built in to the very constitutional design of the state. The demographic explosion that accompanied the industrial revolution begun in the eighteenth and nineteenth centuries has produced democratic polities of enormous scale and has thus greatly intensified the nonparticipatory consequences of representative government. Today, the so-called large

American republic about which Madison theorized, which in 1790 had 4 million inhabitants, of which three-quarters were excluded from full citizenship, is smaller than many small cities within large democratic states.[13] Indeed, even local politics in mass democracy (especially urban local politics) is often conducted on such an enormous demographic scale that it resembles, much more than it differs from, politics at the national level. As populations have grown, so too has the extent of government involvement in the everyday life of ordinary individuals. The self-rule offered by nineteenth-century republicanism was as much a consequence of the government's exclusion from the private sphere—leaving a still largely rural and agrarian community free to operate within an unregulated economy— as it was a function of the capacity to use public lawmaking as a device to actively manage and shape the conditions of everyday life. Since the twentieth century, however, the state's role in regulating commerce, managing economic growth, overseeing education, ensuring social welfare, and shaping the direction of science, technology, and health care has become the norm. This means that the nonparticipating citizen, who occupies no special position of authority or responsibility within government, cannot help but be affected in meaningful ways by the governmental decisions in which he or she has no direct share. Furthermore, since the appearance of the first daily newspaper in 1702, London's *Daily Courant*, the steady development of mass communication technologies—telegraph, radio, film, television, internet—has only magnified the exposure to government of the governed by delocalizing the political spectator from the site of actual political decision making. Finally, the extreme nature of the security risks in contemporary geopolitics, and the clandestine politics that manage these risks, render the ordinary citizen utterly dependent on the goodwill and intelligence of a few select leaders to ward off disaster. Even a radical democrat like Bachrach committed to the ideals of mass participation observed a generation ago, in the aftermath of the Cuban missile crisis: "The exigencies of life in the industrial and nuclear age necessitate that key and crucial political decisions in a democracy, as in totalitarian societies, be made by a handful of men."[14] The collection of these factors—the representative system, the rise of mass society, the activist welfare state, the conduct of politics via the mass media, and the nuclear bomb—ought to render the citizen-being-ruled the most familiar and well-theorized figure within contemporary democratic life.

Second, it is not just the semipermanence of the citizen-being-ruled that distinguishes contemporary from ancient democracy, but the spatial, temporal, and ideological separation of ruling from being-ruled. The experience of involvement without participation, which was difficult to maintain in the ancient context, becomes fully recognizable within contemporary conditions. The reciprocal (if not equal) experience of being the addressee of political speech and thereby having the capacity to respond is absent in the modern context of mass representative democracy. As C. Wright Mills observed, one of the definitive features of mass society is that "the communications that prevail are so organized that it is difficult or impossible for the individual to answer back immediately or with any effect."[15] It is not just that far fewer speak politically than listen to political speeches (for this was likely the condition of ancient democracy too), but that the conduct of politics via the mass media means that the recipient of political information and observer of political deeds need not be present at the site of governance, and that political events can be experienced well after they have actually occurred. Today, it is normal for the citizen-being-ruled to be both spatially and temporally removed from the setting of political activity. This separation makes possible apathetic indifference to politics, but it also sets the stage for a vicarious engagement whereby the citizen-being-ruled follows politics from afar. Moreover, it is not simply that the transaction of politics through the mass media facilitates specta-torship, but that it enforces it. Any effort at meaningful response must itself be mediated. Without the amplification of organization and tech-nology, the citizen-being-ruled's political voice is virtually negated.

This situation enables an involvement with politics fully separated from active engagement. It enables a form of citizenship that can take place in solitude, in silence, and in a seated position. It also marks a transforma-tion in the principal organs of citizenship. In the ancient context epito-mized by Athenian democracy, being-ruled was never entirely severed from the use of *voice*: the shouting down of leaders before the Assembly, the response to a leader with a question, or, following Aristotle, the pos-session of "right opinion" (even if one did not achieve this opinion through one's own deliberative efforts). However, because political involvement in the modern context is vicarious and mediated by communication technolo-gies, because one is asked hardly anything except for whom to vote, the ethic that Aristotle assigns to the citizen-being-ruled—right opinion—has little application today.[16] Rather, it is *sight* and *hearing*, the passive organs of sense, that typify the modern experience of being-ruled. Indeed, what is most radical about the modern form of being-ruled is not that the opinions of the citizen-being-ruled go unheeded, but that the need for opinions is no longer a precondition of political experience. Only in rare moments does being-ruled express itself vocally, whether in the unstructured rupture of protest and riot or the institutionalized vote—but the normal position is one of reception, in which one listens and watches but does not speak. An ordinary citizen does not hold office, does not give judgments, and does not necessarily or usually have an underlying preference for the policies that emanate from the government. Yet the ordinary citizen *is* involved in politics, in the sense of possessing some knowledge and interest in major political events and in being continually exposed to politics through the mass media.

Aristotle could marginalize being-ruled, subsuming the concept beneath a primary discourse on ruling, because sociological conditions made it understandable to treat being-ruled as a preparation for ruling—or, at least, made being-ruled an experience that never strayed too far from the activities of those that did rule. The institutional and historical developments I have discussed here make the case that these sociological conditions are not exportable to present-day representative democracy.

2.4 The Relevance of the Citizen-Being-Ruled Today: Moral Factors

Aristotle also had a moral reason for subsuming the citizen-being-ruled under a primary discourse on ruling: a moral philosophy that presented the participating citizen, giving judgment and holding office, as the telos of the well-developed human being. Even if being-ruled was necessary to this process, since some would have to be passive while others took up active political life, it was nonetheless clear that ruling occupied the final stage of the process of civic development and constituted the most perfect form of human behavior within society. Aristotle's decision to privilege ruling over being-ruled stemmed in part, then, from a moral philosophy that dignified the human being as a self-ruler, capable of directing and shaping the conditions of communal life.

A moral and political philosophy grounded on the ideal of self-rule remains a key fixture within contemporary democratic thought—indeed this ideal has a virtual monopoly on normative considerations of democracy today. Various models of democracy—deliberative democracy, pluralism, aggregation, participatory democracy—continue to subscribe to this ideal and uphold the promise of a polity in which the addressees of the law might also understand themselves as the law's authors.[17] Yet, unlike Aristotle, contemporary democratic theorists must also operate in accordance with an additional moral ideal: the ideal of human equality. The norm of equality means not only that democracy must be theorized as something that is fundamentally opposed to the naturalization of inequality in such institutions as slavery and the subordination of women, but that one of the definitive features of present-day democracy (and contemporary political philosophies grounded on the democratic ideal) is a concern for the political lives of everyday individuals. Democracy means different things to different people, and there is probably no single assertion within democratic theory that some democratic theorist has not refuted or would not refute. But few would object to the simple and general claim that democracy, as a system of state uniquely committed to political equality, affords dignity and a place of prominence to the political lives of ordinary people—people with everyday amounts of wealth, influence, education, fame, intelligence, strength, wit, charm, and moral sensibility.

The question becomes, then: How ought democracy dignify the lives of everyday individuals? The normal response to this question is either to posit the citizen as a depoliticized economic agent who can maximize self-interest in the absence of a political life or to remain solidly within the Aristotelian tradition—overlooking Aristotle's claims about natural inequality—and hold that there can be no dignity for the democratic citizen other than as a citizen-governor: that is, as a citizen who deliberates, takes a stand, negotiates, protests, administrates, and decides. That the citizen-being-ruled might have its own kind of dignity is not usually considered. This is regrettable but not surprising. After all, the condition of being-ruled necessitates a hierarchical division between the select few with the power to effect collectively binding decisions and the vast majority who take no active role in political life. The category of being-ruled would appear to be a direct violation of human equality and the commitment to democracy as a uniquely egalitarian regime. This is not to say that democratic theorists are blind to the hierarchical dimensions of political life within contemporary representative democracy. Yet when it comes to articulating democratic ideals that dignify the political lives of ordinary people, the conventional wisdom is that this idealization must proceed by defining the ordinary citizen as a citizen-governor, empowered to make significant decisions about the collective life of the polity.

Before demonstrating the prevalence of the citizen-governor and absence of the citizen-being-ruled within various discourses of contemporary democratic thought, something should be said about the general principles these discourses rely upon to privilege ruling over being-ruled in the study of citizenship. Clearly, the modern elevation of the citizen-governor is not grounded on an Aristotelian teleology. Rather, the dignification of the everyday democratic citizen as a citizen-governor rests on at least three well-known sources. First, the juridical equality that all citizens share as a consequence of formal membership in a state provides universal accessibility to government. In a well-functioning representative system, no one is legally prevented from taking an active part in government. Anyone who would like to can run for office, file a petition, organize a protest, assemble a meeting, join or form an association within civil society, suggest laws and policies, and vote in elections. Second, the fitness of the ordinary citizen to engage in politics is, today, a basic postulate that informs virtually every articulation of democracy as a moral ideal. Either this fitness is asserted as a self-evident fact, as in Thomas Paine's appeal to the common sense of the everyday citizen and its capacity to replace the absolute rule of hereditary monarchs.[18] Or, this fitness is asserted as a fitness of all individuals to learn and benefit from the necessary arts of citizenship and self-government. With Mill and Tocqueville, for example, the promise of political equality does not mean that all individuals already possess the essential traits for a free and responsible collective life, but that each individual is deserving of being able to participate in the collective enterprise so as to undergo the psychological, intellectual, and moral growth afforded by a civic education. And third, the everyday citizen can be treated as a citizen-governor because the system of representation ensures that citizens' preferences and interests do matter: they will be reflected in the policies and decisions of the select few who do actually decide. Democratic theorists may disagree about how everyday citizens achieve representation—whether it comes through voting and the polling done by representatives who must face reelection, or by the groups and voluntary associations that share power in a polyarchic order, or by deliberative processes that produce results which have a presumption of rationality and fairness—but all these models afford dignity to the ordinary citizen by affirming that the legislative output of a representative system be considered as something with which the represented can identify as a coauthor and colegislator.

These three principles—universal accessibility, fitness to govern, and the representation of the interests and preferences of the citizenry—explain the moral impetus to make the citizen-governor the key figure within contemporary democratic thought.[19] They specify the ideal conditions and aspirations that can serve as regulative principles for the pursuit of a free and equal democratic polity. But how do they relate to the everyday? How well do they succeed in dignifying the political lives of everyday citizens? Insofar as the distinguishing mark of political everydayness is the lack of office, the lack of opportunity for legislative decision making, the lack of any special position of influence, power, wealth, or knowledge, it must be said that these principles deny or ignore the everyday experience of politics. The three principles, while they possess undeniable appeal as regulative ideals, nonetheless obscure the way politics is experienced by ordinary individuals. Behind each of these principles is an everyday political reality that remains undignified so long as the citizen-governor is taken as the central protagonist of democratic thought.

To see this, first consider the principle of formal or legal equality. This ideal is a real and meaningful feature of contemporary democratic states, but just as real is the de facto hierarchy that characterizes the everyday experience of government. The theoretical potentiality that anyone can run for office, occupy a position of leadership, or form a political organization does not alter the real fact that the vast majority will never do any of this, but instead will live in democratic polities in which citizens other than themselves are empowered to make the binding decisions that

govern the collective life of the political community. Whether this absten-
tion from active political life is a free choice, a necessary consequence of
the organizational logic of collective action, or a contingent and revisable
feature of current sociological conditions, the fact remains that the vast
majority of democratic citizens are engaged with politics in a way that takes
it for granted that others besides themselves have the power, influence,
responsibility, prominence, and prosperity of political leadership and government office.[20]

Next, consider the conventional idealization of the everyday citizen as
someone fit to govern. While this commitment is a well-established tenet
of contemporary political psychology, we are still left with the reality that
it is precisely the absence of formal political decision making that is a basic
feature of democratic citizenship in its everydayness. That any citizen is
theoretically fit to govern does not cancel the fact that it is just the experiences of decision making, deliberation, negotiation, and politicking that
are unavailable to the everyday citizen. For most citizens, the only political
decision they will make is the casting of the vote in occasional elections.[21]
While it is true that some elections have clear import for the overall direction of the polity, we overburden the meaning of the vote if it is uncritically
linked to governing itself. Unlike voting, the decision making performed
by persons in possession of political power tends to be regular (not occasional), generative (not reactive), articulate (not confined to a binary yes-
no choice), and legislative (not about the selection of leaders). Even if it
is true, as some studies suggest, that everyday citizens vote according to
policy and ideological preferences, this means only that policy preferences
affect the way people vote, not that voting is itself a selection of policies.
Moreover, the true meaning of decision making is not the ideological push
for a certain predetermined goal. When the goal is clear, there is nothing
to decide other than how to win. True decision making is the situation
in which a person is asked to make a judgment or determination about a
question for which there is no preexisting bias or position. A select few
are empowered to make such decisions. Economic crises, security threats,
overtures and challenges from foreign governments, developments in science and technology that require an immediate government policy—all are
examples of the unpredictable flow of events that require decisions. The
everyday experience of citizenship has nothing to do with these decisions.

Finally, whereas the model of the citizen-governor affirms the citizen
as a colegislator, since representation transmits the preferences of the electorate to the output of the government, the everyday experience of citizenship is such that there is not an underlying preference for each and every
output of law and policy. Note that this is not the standard critique of
representative government that representatives are sufficiently insulated
from the electorate that they have leeway to enact policies of their own

choosing, *against the underlying preferences of their constituents*. Nor is it the claim that representatives manipulate the preferences of the elector- ate by framing issues in ways that are self-serving. Rather, it is the claim, grounded on a growing body of empirical research, that the everyday citi- zen is irreducible to a warehouse of preexisting opinions and preferences on the basis of which governmental output might be held accountable.

It is well known, for example, that respondents to survey questions manifest profound instability in their answering of certain questions—they pronounce views that conflict with each other, or, even more vexingly, they waver about opinions on the same issue.[22] In a famous 1964 study that ana- lyzed response instability from surveys pertaining to the election of 1956 as well as other elections that seemed to invite interpretation as a mandate, Converse concluded that the primary cause of response instability was a lack of strong feelings about most political issues: "Large portions of an electorate simply do not have meaningful beliefs, even on issues that have formed the basis for intense political controversy among elites for sub- stantial periods of time."[23] This finding of "nonattitudes" contradicts the conventional wisdom about democracy that citizens do have underlying preferences that are stable and thus capable of representation. It disturbs the standard democratic faith that each government output correlates, or ought to correlate, to a parallel input from the electorate.

Initially, Converse's study and similar findings were strongly criticized. The usual challenge has been to interpret response instability as a conse- quence of measurement error caused by the difficulty of wording questions in ways that capture respondents' true preferences and, thus, not as some- thing indicative of nonattitudes.[24] Given the size of the alleged measurement error, however, and given that few have been able to explain precisely how it occurs, there is a growing tendency within political science to rethink the central assumption of citizens as possessing preexisting policy preferences on most issues.[25] Studies in the psychology of survey response have begun to abandon the model of fixed opinions, rejecting the file drawer paradigm of opinion and arguing, instead, that everyday citizens have a conflicted database from which a reported attitude is a "temporary construction."[26] Research has suggested that reported opinion not be conceived as some- thing prior to and independent of the survey question, but, rather, that it be understood as dependent to a certain degree on the question itself and the way it is asked. In many cases, respondents do not report a pre-held opin- ion so much as construct an answer to a given question.[27] The dependence of survey response on the question being asked makes the formulation of survey questions especially important.[28] Further, acceptance of nonat- titudes as a genuine political phenomenon has been aided by a growing appreciation for "issueless politics"—political experiences irreducible to legislative agendas, but oriented around personality or intangible factors.[29]

One of the most important efforts to rethink citizens' preferences has been John Zaller's book *The Nature and Origins of Mass Opinion*. Zaller makes the case that the well-known effects of question ordering and question framing on public opinion ought not be conceived as methodological artifacts, but "they should be seen, rather, as revealing a fundamental property of mass political preferences—a tendency for people to be ambivalent (even though perhaps unconsciously so) and to deal with this ambivalence by making decisions on the basis of the ideas that are most immediately salient."[30] Zaller explains: "If different frames or question orders produce different results, it is not because one or the other has distorted the public's true feelings; it is, rather, because the public, having no fixed true opinion, implicitly relies on the particular question it has been asked to determine what exactly the issue is and what considerations are relevant to settling it." On the one hand, Zaller's thesis diverges from the conventional wisdom that assumes everyday citizens have clear and preexisting opinions on the questions that are asked. Instead, Zaller argues that "individuals do not typically possess 'true attitudes' on issues, as conventional theorizing assumes, but a series of partially independent and often inconsistent ones." On the other hand, Zaller's findings also differ from those of Converse, since whereas Converse stressed the nonattitudes of everyday citizens, Zaller instead focuses on the ambivalence and indeterminacy of everyday attitudes. That is, Zaller does not question that everyday citizens have reactions to politics—"that the public has hopes, fears, values, and concerns that are, to a large extent, independent of elite discourse." What Zaller does reject is that this opinion is crystallized into clear policy preferences capable of being represented by elected leaders. Zaller's claim is that "the public's feelings are, in their unobserved state, unfocused and frequently contradictory."[31]

Why do ordinary citizens' reactions to issues tend to be characterized by such high levels of ambivalence? The reason, Zaller suggests, is not due to any failure in basic competence on the part of ordinary citizens, but rather stems from the hierarchical conditions of everyday political experience and the fact that most citizens will never be called upon to make a political decision, outside of voting: "Most people really aren't sure what their opinions are on most political matters, including even such completely personal matters as their level of interest in politics. They're not sure because there are few occasions, outside of a standard interview situation, in which they are called upon to formulate and express political opinions."[32] While the select few who are highly engaged with particular issues may possess the kind of clear and stable preferences that conventional opinion research takes to be the norm, "for the majority of persons on the majority of issues, inconsistencies in their considerations concerning different aspects of a given issue remain unresolved and probably unrecognized."[33]

This reinterpretation of public opinion as something nonindependent of the question-asking process and as something often characterized by nonattitudes and ambivalence undermines the conception of the everyday citizen as a citizen-governor with preferences that are represented in the output of governmental policy and legislation. Achen, an early critic of Converse's finding of nonattitudes, worried that if such a finding were true, "Democratic theory loses its starting point."[34] This disruption of starting points is precisely what is implied by the new public opinion research—and, indeed, it indicates an alternate starting point for democratic theory: the citizen-being-ruled.

Against the three principles of juridical equality, fitness, and representation, these three alternate aspects of the everyday experience of citizenship—hierarchy, nondecision, and nonpreference—suggest that the dignification of everyday citizenship not be centered around the familiar figure of the citizen-governor. When the citizen-governor is taken as the central protagonist of the discourse on democracy, the everyday citizen is the object of democratic theory, but not its subject. Contemporary democratic theory sets out to make all citizens into rulers, either by describing citizens as already being rulers or by outlining the ideal conditions under which they might attain this status. What is not pursued is the acceptance of the citizen-being-ruled as the key figure within contemporary democracy and the discovery of ways to dignify this citizen in the very condition of being-ruled. This is regrettable. Because democracy affords a special respect and prominence to citizens in their everyday capacity, it is appropriate and indeed necessary to think through the nature of this everyday position, treating it on its own terms, in order to fulfill the promise of an egalitarian democratic philosophy in an unegalitarian political world.

To call for the dignification of the citizen-being-ruled is not to suggest that it is better to be ruled than to rule or that the passive spectatorship of politics ought to be validated as something preferable to active forms of civic engagement. What justifies taking seriously the citizen-being-ruled is its *actuality* (i.e., its prevalence, if not predominance, within modern mass democracy), not its intrinsic superiority. Whereas other forms of political philosophy can have their teachings confined to the few, the theorization of democratic citizenship cannot remain unconcerned by the nature of political experience common to ordinary individuals. While this does not mean that democratic theory is prohibited from transacting in civic *ideals* (which by their very nature exceed the common practice of citizenship and, thus, constitute standards of civic excellence), it does mean that there is a limit to how detached from ordinary life such ideals can be. Especially when institutional conditions restrict the actual applicability of a particular civic ideal to a minority of citizens, there is a danger of overly ambitious civic ideals unintentionally disrespecting the ordinary citizen in real-world democracy.

Ultimately, the question of how democratic citizens are to be dignified is a question about who ought to be the subject, or *protagonist*, of democratic theory—in other words, who is the figure in reference to whom democratic thinkers ought to construct ideals and seek understanding? Should they select a figure, such as the citizen-governor, who represents the ideal promise of what the experience of democracy ought to be? Or, in a very different fashion, should democratic theorists select the citizen-being-ruled who, while lacking the obvious exaltation of the citizen-governor, refers to a political experience that is far more widespread and common? In other branches of philosophy, the frequency of an experience indicates little in the way of its value: quantity is distinguished sharply from quality. But, as I have suggested, in political philosophy of a democratic stamp, numerical considerations are not at all irrelevant. Democratic theorists, insofar as they are committed to the political lives of ordinary people, are not free to choose their protagonists, but must be guided in their selection by the nature of political experience available to everyday citizens. Accordingly, my argument has been that being-ruled, even if it is not to be treated at the exclusion of the citizen-governor, is too prevalent and permanent a form of citizenship in modern mass democracy for it to go unheeded within the dominant paradigms of democratic theory.

And yet, as I will now demonstrate, the citizen-being-ruled has been systematically neglected. In the remainder of this chapter, my aim is to detail some of the primary ways in which contemporary democratic theory tends to deny or ignore the figure of the citizen-being-ruled.

2.5 The Recognition, Yet Subordination, of Being-Ruled within the Empirical Research of Civic Behavior

The intermediate position of the citizen-being-ruled—specifically a psychological involvement in politics that is not joined together with active participation in political life—is in fact something that the literature on civic behavior has recognized. The National Election Studies (NES), for example, which provide the single largest data set for research in American political behavior, contain various measures, such as political interest and knowledge about politics, that are distinct from active political engagement. These measures capture an aspect of political experience that is irreducible to participatory forms of engagement such as campaigning, writing petitions, giving money to candidates, running for office, and serving in government. Moreover, it is also normal for studies of civic behavior to make use of a measure of nonparticipatory political involvement.

This measure is calculated in different ways and goes by different names, for example, political interest and involvement, cognitive ability, political sophistication, political expertise, ideological sophistication, and political awareness.[35] Although occasionally these measures of involvement do include some aspect of participatory forms of engagement, most often they are kept distinct from active political participation.[36]

While there is no single definition of political involvement, generally speaking it can be defined as "awareness of politics, interest in politics, information, attention to the media, and so forth."[37] It is political experience that takes the form of political knowledge, interest, and the spectatorship of politics. Participation, on the other hand, refers to the more rigorous and rare kinds of political engagement, such as campaign work, public advocacy, and the holding of public office. Voting can be seen as a liminal behavior. It is an active form of engagement, but if it is the sole form of participation, it is not enough to render one a participant in the manner of a candidate, judge, public opinion leader, ideological activist, or lobbyist.[38]

Moreover, not only is political involvement a distinct variable in most analyses of civic behavior, but it is a well-established fact of contemporary democratic life that political involvement is much more common than political participation. While estimates about this differential vary somewhat from study to study, it is common to assign a participatory role to no more than 5 to 10 percent of the population, as compared with the 60 to 70 percent that is at least minimally politically involved.[39] The remaining segment of the populace, approximately 20 to 30 percent, is described as completely apathetic and thus neither active nor involved in political life.[40] This divergence between involvement and participation is not surprising. For reasons already discussed and quite evident to any political observer, the conditions of mass representative democracy do not afford active political lives to any but a small segment of the population. Yet the same conditions, especially the mass media, also make it likely that citizens will be exposed to politics in the sense of having at least a minimal awareness and interest in government.

Nonetheless, in spite of the existence of a variety of technical terms to measure political involvement as something distinct from participation, and in spite of the fact that this measure captures the everyday political experience of the vast majority, there has been a curious lack of focused investigation of this important category of democratic citizenship. When involvement is studied, as it often is, it is done so as a *predictor* or *correlate* of participation. What is overlooked, then, is not involvement as such, but involvement that is detached from participation: that is, the condition of being-ruled.

Even studies that have done the most to stress the numerical and hierarchical differential between the majority who are involved and the select

few who are active have tended to simultaneously subsume political
involvement within a primary analysis of active citizenship. Milbrath's
influential study *Political Participation* (1965) reveals this quite clearly.
Milbrath distinguishes three levels of political engagement: the apathetic
who "in most cases ... are unaware, literally, of the political part of the
world around them"; the spectators who are involved but do not participate (or, as Milbrath says, "they watch, they cheer, they vote, but they do
not do battle"); and "gladiators" who hold office, participate in campaigns,
solicit political funds, attend caucuses and strategy meetings, and also
engage in *borderline* activities such as attending political meetings or rallies,
contributing money to a party or candidate, or contacting a public official
or political leader. Milbrath found that roughly 60 percent of Americans
were spectators, 30 percent apathetic, and 10 percent gladiators. (Only 2
to 3 percent were pure gladiator, with an additional 5 to 7 percent if borderline activities are included.) Yet, even though spectatorship is by far
the most common form of political behavior and even though the activities
of the gladiator are the least common, Milbrath orients the entire study
around the characteristics of the small minority of highly active democratic citizens. Most of the research is devoted to showing the types of
behaviors that are predictive of active participation: for example, that one
kind of participation makes another more likely (i.e., that the forms of participation tend to be mutually correlated with each other) and how socioeconomic status is linked to participation.[41] When political involvement is
analyzed, it is likewise treated as a predictor of active participation: "The
more political stimuli received by a person, the more likely he is to be active in politics."[42] Milbrath is interested in showing how there is a gravi-
tational pull moving up the scale of political engagement—from apathy to
involvement to participation. This may be true, but it leads one to overlook
the sheer existence of the majority of spectators, who are involved but not
active.[43]

This understanding of political involvement as a form of political
experience conceptually distinct from active engagement—yet something
that is nevertheless a predictor of participation—is extremely common and
is repeated in many other studies of political behavior that reduce political
involvement to a positive correlate of active forms of political life.[44] The
predictive quality of involvement is by no means wrongly identified—
indeed, Neuman has found that for every 1 percent increase in involvement,
there is a 0.6 percent increase in participation—but when involvement is
interpreted solely in this fashion, the great remainder of citizens who are
involved but nonparticipatory is disregarded.[45]

The spectatorial condition of being-ruled—involvement without
participation—is also overlooked by studies that emphasize that both involvement and participation are extremely low as compared with classical

norms of democratic citizenship. Since the development of modern survey techniques in the 1920s and 1930s, studies have repeatedly demonstrated that citizens possess an embarrassingly low amount of political knowledge, information, and interest in political life. Large numbers—usually around 50 percent—cannot name their elected representatives, coherently present a political opinion, locate themselves on an ideological continuum, or reflect awareness of the major issues of the day.[46] What is forgotten is that these measures, while low, are still vastly greater than the percentage of citizens who take an active role in political life. Thus, Neuman, who presents what is likely the most detailed and rigorous account of political involvement (what he terms "political sophistication"), is so impressed by the low amount of political involvement in absolute terms that he neglects its *relative* frequency as compared with active political engagement.[47] The differential between involvement and participation, which is constitutive of the citizen-being-ruled, is neglected by any wholesale treatment of the decline or insufficiency of civic behavior.

2.6 Four Basic Reasons for Inattention to the Citizen-Being-Ruled

Inattention to the citizen-being-ruled, and the parallel elevation of the citizen-governor as the key figure of democratic theory, have many sources. Sometimes the denial of the citizen-being-ruled involves a factual denial. Celebrants of Western representative democracy, for example, tend to present contemporary representative systems as realizing something approximating popular-self-rule—in other words, as a regime that transforms everyday citizens into active political agents who collectively legislate the conditions of their coexistence and determine their fate. The lionization of democracy in such a fashion leaves no conceptual space for the citizen-being-ruled who experiences only a partial and passive involvement with government.[48]

From the other side, critics who worry that existing levels of democratization are incomplete usually concern themselves with a form of political exclusion much less subtle than the mild exclusion of citizens-being-ruled, which, as has been said, presupposes formal membership within the polity and full liberal rights and protections. When most democratic theorists think about exclusion, they have in mind individuals or groups denied formal political rights and opportunities—such as immigrants, ethnic and racial minorities, women, and fundamentalist religious sects. In the case of the United States, the fact that full voting rights were not institutionalized until 1965 means that only recently has the relative impotence of the vote as a form of political participation been appreciated. When some are systematically excluded from voting, there can be little worry about the limitations of voting and its difference from more active forms of political engagement. The factual condition of being-ruled only appears as such within polities that are neither blinded by the self-adulation of occupying the end of history nor burdened by the legalized exclusion of targeted groups from political life.

The denial of the citizen-being-ruled also stems from the theorization of representative democracy as a convenient division of labor. From as early as Sieyès, the representative system has been defended as an institutional structure suited to the fact that in a modern commercial republic, oriented primarily around economic trade and production, most citizens have neither time nor interest for the kind of active political participation characteristic of the classical polis and medieval city-state. Sieyès defended representative government as a division of labor that would render government a specialized profession, leaving the rest of the citizenry free to engage in economic and professional activities.[49] On the basis of such reasoning, the power differential between the citizen-being-ruled and the citizen-governor is covered over by an alleged unwillingness on the part of the former to take up the position of the latter. Such arguments continue to be made today. Indeed, what Oscar Wilde said in critique of socialism—that it would be a good idea, if not for the fact it took too many evenings—has often been cited as a reason that participatory democracy, in addition to the technical impossibilities of realizing mass participation, simply does not make sense in the modern context.

Clearly, politics takes time, commitment, and energy, all of which are precious commodities that must compete against the demands of career, family, money, and leisure. That not everyone would want to engage in an active political life is obvious. But to presume that everyone who does want to participate in politics is able to do so—to suggest that nonparticipants have not been acculturated to their role as a matter of necessity—is no less outlandish than the expectation of universal civic engagement. Indeed, if representative democracy has been defended on the basis of the scarcity of evenings available for political discussion and decision making, it must also be recognized that a distinctive feature of everyday political experience within contemporary democratic regimes is the *superabundance of evenings*: that is to say, the oversupply of political energies for which there is no demand.

Recent events have reminded us of the fact of the oversupply of evenings and the scarcity of opportunity for meaningful political engagement. Less than one week after the terrorist destruction of the World Trade Center, the mayor of New York held a nationally televised press conference in which he advised concerned citizens from across the United States about the best way they could contribute. "To people from all over the country who want to help, I have a great way of helping: come here and spend money. Go to a restaurant, see a show. The life of the city goes on." A few days later the president echoed this sentiment, urging citizens interested in contributing to the recovery process that they could benefit the nation's welfare by traveling as tourists throughout the country, visiting destinations like Disneyland.

We misconceive the import of these comments, uttered in the context of a world-historical moment that will be remembered for centuries, if they are interpreted as the elevation of the private life over the public or as a sign that the classical concern for the common good has been reduced to the exigencies of economic growth. Who is the addressee of these remarks? It is not the citizen-governor empowered to pursue the common good—who deliberates, legislates, decides, acts, and participates as an equal partner in definitive historical moments. The mayor and the president announce that this citizen can play no function in the current crisis—and that the health of the state is more dependent on citizens in their private capacities as consumers and economic agents than as political actors devoted to the common good. And yet it would be just as wrong to see the addressee of these remarks as the very private, commercial, economic agents the mayor and president would hope to see activated. Rather, these memorable exhortations are addressed to citizens who would like to play a greater role, but for whom no meaningful position is available. The suggestion to go shopping and return to the private sphere is directed not to those already in the private sphere, nor to those occupying positions on the public stage, but to those in the intermediate position of the political spectator, or the citizen-being-ruled.

Even if Sieyès was essentially correct, then, in his classification of the modern citizen as someone whose private and commercial interests would greatly predominate over political energies, it is misleading to interpret the representative system that enables this kind of citizenship as a division of labor. The problem is not simply that a division of labor suggests only specialization, whereas the relation between power holder and private citizen suggests hierarchy. What is also inaccurate is that a division of labor presupposes an actual separation of tasks, whereas the private citizen is not entirely separated from the work of the government leader or official, but must watch, listen to, or read about such people on a daily basis. When one group is the audience of another, and when the latter make decisions that affect the lives of the former without a reciprocal countereffect, the result is not a neutral division of labor but a power-laden division between ruling and being-ruled.

Finally, the reality and prevalence of being-ruled—that is, of political spectatorship characterized by psychological involvement but not participation—is overlooked insofar as political scientists *deflect* attention from the citizen-being-ruled to other forms of political experience that might plausibly be said to recover something in the way of self-legislation. One important example of this tendency is the emphasis on local politics, where the citizen allegedly *is* able to be something like a citizen-governor. Another is civil society theory, which, among other things, notes the tendency of the voluntary associations constituting civil society to take up political positions and become, in effect, quasi-advocacy groups.[50] To be sure, it would be wrong to underestimate the significance of both local politics and associational life to contemporary democratic politics. Both provide alternate contexts, besides the national one, in which citizens can more easily take up the position of the citizen-governor (i.e., someone who decides, deliberates, politicks, stands up for a cause)—although in the case of civil society, membership does not always (and perhaps does not *usually*) produce experiences analogous to those of the citizen-governor.[51] And, in the case of local government, given the tremendous size of many localities under conditions of mass society, one might legitimately question how inclusive this type of politics actually is. It is also possible, therefore, to exaggerate the significance of local government and civil society. While they might deflect attention from the citizen-being-ruled (who exists primarily on the national level), they do not thereby cancel the experience of being-ruled: that is, the experience of having a passive, spectating relationship to government characterized by the expectation that others besides oneself will make the most important decisions about the fate of the polity. While one certainly can find political contexts less characterized by being-ruled than the national politics of contemporary mass democracies, such disengagement from the problem of being-ruled is no argument against those who choose to confront it.

2.7 The Denial of Being-Ruled via the Denial of Ruling and Sovereignty: Pluralism

Being-ruled necessarily involves the experience of a relative powerlessness vis-à-vis politicians, officials, and leaders of public opinion. Being-ruled means being outside a polity's government and administration. It means acknowledging that however many preferences and opinions one may have, this number far exceeds, almost infinitely so, the occasions on which these are requested. Being-ruled is a condition of political spectatorship in which others besides oneself are empowered to make binding decisions, whether through legislation, judicial decision making, executive action, or the construction of public opinion from important positions of leadership in the press or other organs of society. Being-ruled means being outside of the history-making processes that these political actors undertake. It means that one is not famous, not powerful, not important—yet still at least minimally attentive to those who are.

One of the ways to deny the figure of the citizen-being-ruled has been to deny the existence of the entity to which it is opposed: the sovereign, power-holding citizen who makes authoritative decisions determining the conditions of collective life. If no one has the power from which the citizen-being-ruled is excluded, the very category of being-ruled would appear to be drained of its meaning, with its challenge to leading discourses of democratic theory thereby eliminated.

The denial of sovereignty—and, with it, the denial of being-ruled— is well illustrated by theorists of pluralist democracy, who recognize the diverse and pluralistic essence of political power. Denying that the state has a power center that some occupy and from which others are excluded, pluralists recognize that the groups that are the principal actors within a pluralist democracy—government bureaucracies, political parties, ethnic and religious groups, occupational associations, corporations, public interest organizations, the great diversity of voluntary associations in civil society—share and barter power by forming diverse coalitions depending on the particular issue at stake.[52] Although there have been recent pluralists who have acknowledged the persistence of power hierarchies within a pluralist regime, the basic thrust of pluralist theory has been to quell, rather than accentuate, concerns about the relative disempowerment of the vast majority of everyday citizens.

The pluralists' denial of a single and unified sovereign power, their insistence on the multicenteredness of power in modern representative democracies, is especially valuable as a corrective to two other viewpoints in political theory. On the one hand, pluralism exposes the fear of majoritarian tyranny, so common among nineteenth-century democratic theorists like Tocqueville and J. S. Mill, as an exaggeration.[53] Pluralists hold that most policy decisions are decided, not by the majority, but by a minority that either exercises power unimpeded within its own limited sphere (e.g., a local police department) or has been able to bargain with other groups to form a temporary coalition (e.g., the farm lobby that routinely secures agricultural subsidies). Different issues have different issue publics by whom and for whom specific questions are decided.[54] On the other hand, in stressing the multiplicity of groups sharing power and the constant competition and negotiation between groups, pluralists reject the notion of a ruling elite—a monolithic governing class hypothesized by certain elite theorists such as C. Wright Mills—as an oversimplified and unnecessarily bleak account of power in modern representative systems.

Pluralism's effectiveness as a critique both of the tyranny of the majority and of a unified elite does not make it effective in assuaging concerns about the condition of being-ruled. The multiplicity of power centers is not the same thing as a sharing of power. The lack of a monolithic elite class does not imply a lack of nonelite citizens. In truth, there is inequality between groups: sizable differences in groups' access to resources and, as a result, differing degrees of influence to effect law and policy.[55] Further, there are hierarchies embedded in the very formation of groups. The ordinary citizen does not occupy a position of leadership within a group and, even if he or she is a member, must play the role of foot soldier while others take positions of leadership within the organization. The question of decision does not arrive for this citizen—either the decision has already been made (the group has already predetermined what it wants) or, in the event of strategizing and negotiation, it is a matter for the group's leadership to decide. The formal equality to start one's own association is a true and meaningful aspect of a free society, but it does not translate into an actual equality of decision making, let alone any equality in the subjective feeling of empowerment. Finally, the existence of multiple issue publics does not mean that each citizen is a member of different issue publics. On the contrary, research has shown that most citizens do not have specialized, issue-based concerns that orient their attention and engagement.[56] The diversity of issue publics helps us understand the nature of elite power, not the everyday citizen in the condition of being-ruled.

By defining modern representative democracy as a political system where "minorities rule"—as opposed to both the rule of the majority and the rule of a single minority—pluralism could be seen as lending theoretical support to the claim that on most issues, most citizens play no determinative role and, thus, take up the spectatorial position of a citizen-being-ruled.[57] Yet pluralists have not taken this path. Instead, the denial of a single power center has usually been linked to the parallel denial of the exclusion of citizens from power. Pluralism is most commonly a theory of representation that explains and justifies the equilibrium that allegedly characterizes contemporary representative democracies. Pluralists are inclined to believe that even though most people do not participate in political decision making, the net result of group competition and the constant reformulation of coalitions produces public policy that is generally in the best interests of the collective citizenry.[58] Moreover, pluralists have thought that there is a limit to what any coalition can achieve—that active political participants are constrained by a preexisting consensus in the populace that reflects strong underlying preferences regarding procedural rules and permissible policy alternatives.[59] This consensus, combined with regular, competitive elections, means that individual political leaders do not have as much leeway as might be thought, despite the nonexistence of an articulated majority preference.[60] And the liberalizing function of multiple groups bargaining and competing for power has been interpreted as satisfying a minimal definition of representativeness, in the sense that highly valued individual liberties are protected. Thus, rather than evidence for the exclusion of most citizens from positions of government and leadership, pluralism is most often expounded as a theory of democratic representation that keeps elites accountable to the underlying interests of the electorate.

To be sure, more recent pluralists have attended to the hierarchical aspects of pluralistic society. Dahl's later work pays special attention to the unegalitarian structure of economic organizations, and so-called neopluralists recognize the inequality of influence and resources that typifies group competition in a pluralist system.[61] But the basic structure of the pluralist paradigm, which insists on the localized, fragmented, and partial nature of political power, is fundamentally ill equipped to consider the citizen-being-ruled, defined by a position of nonpower that is in fact *general* and *nondifferentiated*. As Held recognizes, even when pluralists acknowledge the hierarchical aspects of democratic life that persist within the pluralist system, it is exceedingly difficult for pluralist theory to adequately pursue the implications of these inequalities: "For the central premises of this position—the existence of multiple power centers, diverse and fragmented interests, the marked propensity of one group to offset the power of another, a 'transcendent' consensus which binds state and society, the state as judge and arbitrator between factions—cannot begin to explain a world in which there may be systematic imbalances in the distribution of power, influence, and resources."[62]

When pluralists do look at the individual citizen in the condition of his or her everydayness, what is usually emphasized is the multiplicity of civic ties and loyalties. Truman stressed the "protean complex" of modern civic relationships, arguing that "tolerably normal" people have diverse memberships.[63] By normalizing the multiplicity of civic ties, pluralism overlooks what is also normal: that in relation to most government decisions and politics in general, most citizens remain, at best, only tenuously connected to the processes by which collectively binding decisions are negotiated and agreed upon. Moreover, one of the distinguishing characteristics of everyday political experience is a profound lack of well-articulated policy preferences, such that might be adequately reflected in the outcomes of elite decision making.

This normalcy—the citizen-being-ruled—not only is overlooked by the pluralistic model, but also challenges the extent to which we can find meaningful the pluralist critique of a central, unified sovereign power. There is, after all, a unified set of prohibitions and policies backed by the force of governmental power. There is, after all, law. And even if a variety of groups contribute to its formulation, for the everyday, passive, unorganized citizen, who must obey the law rather than make it, the law can in fact be experienced as a unified phenomenon. It might not make sense to speak

of a centralized legislator or sovereign power, but this does not remove
the relevance of the nonsovereign majority, silent and passive, for whom
political experience primarily consists of spectatorship.

2.8 The False Universalization of the Citizen–Governor: Deliberative Democracy

The theory of deliberative democracy, which turns to deliberation as a
device for transforming preferences and arriving at collective decisions
that emerge out of rational discourse, marginalizes the experience of
being-ruled in a variety of ways. To be sure, when deliberation is taken to
be an elite practice, intended only for representatives within a parliament
or for other select leaders within a similarly distinguished setting, the division between elite and everyday citizenship is presupposed, if not developed and elaborated. However, even though this elitist version has deep
roots within political theory and is the original form in which deliberation
has been theorized (as, for example, by Aristotle, Burke, and J. S. Mill),
and even though some contemporary theorists subscribe to this version or
see it as an unavoidable aspect of a deliberative schema for politics, today
it is much more often the case that deliberation is linked to a broadly egalitarian and participatory politics. Today, as a theory of institutional design,
the theory of deliberative democracy is self-consciously presented as the
set of procedural conditions that would need to apply in order for citizens
to understand themselves as authors of the norms and values shaping the
collective life of the political community.[64] This focus means that while the
condition of being-ruled might be recognized as a presently existing fact,
it is not perceived as having a permanent place within a well-functioning
democratic polity. On the contrary, deliberative procedures stand for the
promise of erasing the category of being-ruled by achieving a politics in
which the law's addressees might also understand themselves as the law's
authors. In its most metaphysically ambitious form, deliberation is conceived as producing decisions that, though fallible, have the presumption
of being what all citizens *would themselves have decided* had they been party to the discussion.[65] So conceived, deliberation injects rationality into
political life, replacing the competition of wills with the rule of reason. The
rationalist promise of deliberation makes the question of who participates
secondary, if not irrelevant. So long as the active participants are able to
represent most identifiable interests within a polity, what matters is that
decisions fulfill the rationalist promise of an ideal speech situation, not
who specifically gets to engage in the actual conversation and who, on the
other hand, must remain in a position of spectatorship. The very concept
of being-ruled collapses in the face of a rational politics.

While it is clear that the philosophical underpinnings of deliberative democracy reject the enduring relevance of the citizen-being-ruled to democratic theory, we miss out on the most significant way in which deliberative democracy denies the category of being-ruled if we reduce that theory to its most ambitious and controversial metaphysical claims. The most important and pervasive method by which deliberative democracy overlooks the figure of the citizen-being-ruled involves, not epistemological assertions about the rationality of deliberatively derived legislation, but practical guidance in the form of a civic ethics of public reason. As a theory of ethics, deliberative democracy extracts from the normative preconditions of an ideal speech situation the ethical constraints a deliberator must adopt in the collective process of reaching a mutual understanding. This ethics outlines the citizen's responsibilities and duties with reference to the central practice of deliberation over the common good. While there is much argument as to the meaning of these ethics—whether they apply only to debate about constitutional essentials or also to statutory law, whether they should be limited to establishing consensus or also shape and moderate conflict, whether they require speech be limited to reasonable views forswearing the whole truth or also enable the expression of comprehensive doctrines—at the most basic level deliberative ethics can be defined as the behavioral practices and social commitments that ensure that political discourses reflect the ideals of reciprocity, mutual respect, and equality.[66]

How do these civic ethics relate to the marginalization of the citizen-being-ruled? While deliberative ethics have undeniable relevance to those who do in fact engage in processes of collective decision making, they are much less germane to the great majority for whom political life involves no decision but the occasional vote. Might there not be a different set of ethics for citizens in their everyday function as passive spectators? The problem is not simply that deliberative democrats do not pursue this question, preferring to analyze the conduct of decision makers rather than everyday citizens, but that they deny the very legitimacy of this question by presupposing, or in fact explicitly arguing, that deliberative ethics are universally applicable to *all* citizens within a well-functioning democratic polity. Even though deliberation is necessarily an activity for those in power—that is, for those in a setting of decision making—it is nonetheless conceived as a model for all citizenship.

Consider, for example, Rawls. The strictures of public reason include, Rawls says, a duty of civility, a willingness to listen, and fair-mindedness when making decisions.[67] Rawls understands these strictures not simply as pragmatic or ethical guidelines for political power holders, but "as an ideal conception of citizenship for a constitutional democratic regime" and one that "presents how things might be, taking people as a just and well-ordered society would encourage them to be."[68] Rawls's sketch of public reason makes explicit appeal to "the ideal of citizens governing themselves in ways that each thinks the others might reasonably be expected to accept."[69] The universalization of the legislating class—and the parallel flattening of the distinction between everyday citizen and official power holders—leads to the valorization of public reason as an ethics applicable to all democratic citizens. To be sure, Rawls does not totally ignore potential differences between the political function of elites and everyday citizens. Thus it is the Supreme Court—which depends on discussion of basic constitutional principles by a few select jurists—that emerges for Rawls as the exemplary institution of public reason. Rawls also says that the strictures of public reason hold most basically "for citizens when they engage in political advocacy in the public forum, and thus for members of political parties and for candidates in their campaigns and for other groups who support them."[70] Yet, despite the difference between citizens who do engage in politics and those who only watch from the sidelines, the overall effect of Rawls's theory is to link both the elite and the everyday within a single, overarching ethical horizon: "Public reason sees the office of the citizen with its duty of civility as analogous to that of judgeship with its duty of deciding cases. Just as judges are to decide cases by legal grounds of precedent and recognized canons of statutory interpretation and other relevant grounds, so citizens are to reason by public reason and to be guided by the criterion of reciprocity, whenever constitutional essentials and matters of basic justice are at stake."[71] Rawls defines citizenship as a singular and universalizable practice. He conceives the "fundamental political relation of citizenship" as "a relation of free and equal citizens who exercise ultimate political power as a collective body."[72] By basing the ethics of the good citizen on the deliberative ethics of a reasonable decision maker, Rawls takes for granted the opportunity of efficacious and readily available political action as a basic premise. The context of exercising political power is thus an underlying assumption.

Some deliberative theorists are more attuned to the condition of being-ruled. In their influential statement of deliberative theory, for example, Gutmann and Thompson admit: "The disadvantage [of representative democracy] is that most citizens become mere spectators; they participate in the deliberation only vicariously. Moreover, and perhaps most critically, representative democracy places a very high premium on citizens' holding their representatives accountable. To the extent that they fail to do so, or are prevented from doing so, their representatives may fail to act responsibly, or even honestly."[73] Yet, as for Rawls, the acknowledgment that there are different levels of political engagement does not lead to the development of a distinct normative theory for citizens not actually participating in deliberative decision making. While Gutmann and Thompson do explore the conditions under which protest may be necessary—when the deliberations of power holders are not sufficiently responsive or accountable to their constituents—this nondeliberative ethic is organized around the exceptional malfunction of the representative system, rather than in reference to the normal, everyday condition of being-ruled.[74] The normal condition for Gutmann and Thompson is one in which both the representative and the represented partake of the same deliberative ethics. Thus they can define all citizens as "active," asserting, as a matter of general statement, that "citizens are active subjects who can accept or reject the reasons for mutually binding laws and policies, either directly, in a public forum, or indirectly, through their accountable representatives."[75]

It would be wrong to deny any applicability of public reason to the everyday citizen. Clearly, insofar as the citizen engages in discussion with others, the idea of public reason has a palpable relevance. But the reality is that the average citizen is distinguished precisely by the lack of frequent or meaningful opportunities for the exercise of public judgment. Yet it is characteristic of deliberative democracy to elide just this difference between representative and represented—to overlook the very institutional factors that make the universalization of deliberative practices impossible. Thus, deliberative theorists deny or avoid the fact that there is a structural difference between the decision about legislation and the decision about whom to vote for. Indeed, they import a logic of legislation to apply to the latter. For example, Ackerman and Fishkin's recent book, *Deliberation Day*, applies deliberative ethics to voting.[76] As a result, they blur the distinction between legislative decisions about binding norms and policies (which, as has been said, are regular, generative, and articulate) and mere electoral decisions about leadership (which usually are occasional, reactive, and confined by binariness). Further, Ackerman and Fishkin select the rare and exceptional instance of decision making within citizens' political experience as the basis for their ethical reflection on citizenship generally, thus ignoring or denying that the everyday experience of politics is the passive spectatorship of the select few who are engaged in public decision making.

In sum, the citizen who is excluded from decision-making procedures, who is not invited to deliberate over issues of fundamental importance, and whose opinion lacks any obvious connection to the legislative output of the state is largely forgotten by the discourse on deliberative ethics. The problem that launches the deliberative democrat's reflection on civic ethics—the question of how members of a polity ought to talk with each other in conditions of conflict and diversity—*presupposes* the context of sovereign decision making and thus presupposes precisely what is lacking in the condition of being-ruled. This tendency, if not universal, is at least extremely prevalent. The ethics of the deliberative citizen is the ethics of the citizen empowered with a capacity for legislative and administrative decision making.

2.9 What Would It Mean to Dignify the Citizen-Being-Ruled?

The *citizen-being-ruled*—or *citizen-spectator*—challenges the applicability of the leading theoretical accounts by which democratic life has been presented as ethically rich and fundamentally progressive. It challenges the paradigm of deliberative ethics because the citizen-being-ruled is not engaged in political discussion and debate, as the deliberative democrats presuppose, but rather watches politics as a spectator, looking neither to convince nor to be convinced by political arguments. Likewise, the citizen-being-ruled disturbs the pluralist paradigm of democracy. Whereas pluralists, encouraged by the absence of a single power center, are usually led to deny the exclusion of citizens from power, the citizen-being-ruled refers precisely to a passive relation vis-à-vis government where it is understood that *others besides oneself* will make the most important decisions determining the fate of the polity. Finally, whereas the literature on civic behavior finds in political involvement only a correlate or predictor of active participation, the citizen-being-ruled is defined by the divergence between involvement and participation—by involvement without participation—and thus insists upon the consideration of *mere involvement* as a permanent, and indeed predominant, form of political experience in modern mass democracy. Thus, despite their manifest differences, these various theories and standpoints within contemporary democratic theory—deliberative democracy, pluralist theory, and civic behavior research—share the same tendency to overlook the existence and importance of the citizen-being-ruled.

In contrast to these leading paradigms and perspectives, the plebiscitary tradition I aim to revive and defend in this book does respect the citizen-being-ruled. It does so, first of all, by respecting the *reality* or sheer existence of the citizen-being-ruled. Whereas dominant approaches within contemporary democratic thought have the effect of ignoring or marginalizing the difference between political elites and everyday citizens—so that the very notion of a citizen-being-ruled is itself overlooked—a plebiscitarian approach to democracy is grounded precisely on this difference. The plebiscitarian ethics I develop in the ensuing chapters is based on an understanding of the political world in terms of a basic division between the many without an active, legislative, vocal political life and the few who do possess substantial decision-making authority. Second, a key effect of a plebiscitary account of democracy is to provide the citizen-being-ruled with a larger group to which he or she can belong: namely, *the People*—defined as the mass of everyday citizens understood in their collective capacity. Under the pleb-iscitary model, the People designates a political entity that might be termed the *organization of the unorganized*: political spectators linked together in their shared experience of nondecision, nonpreference, and relative sub-ordination to political elites. Whereas the normal tendency in democratic theory is to dissolve or marginalize the concept of the People, a plebiscitary account of democracy rehabilitates the notion, in order that it might provide otherwise isolated citizens-being-ruled with a collective group to inhabit. Finally, when considering what might be the interest of this group—what it might mean for the People conceived as a mass spectator to rule—a theory of plebiscitary democracy respects the citizen-being-ruled by developing an account of democratic progressivism that is consistent with, rather than antagonistic to, spectatorship. Unlike the standard emphasis on autonomy, the plebiscitarian principle of candor, with its insistence that leaders not be in control of the conditions of their publicity, is a critical norm specifically intended to refine the spectator's experience of political life.

Chapters 4 through 7 are devoted to elaborating and defending the plebiscitary model. In the next chapter, however, I continue my critical overview of democratic thought by defending a key claim: that there is such a thing as "traditional" or "normal" democratic theory and that, specifically, such democratic theory is defined by a *vocal model of popular empowerment*.

3

Overcoming the Vocal Model
of Popular Power

Old things need not be therefore true,
O brother men, nor yet the new;
Ah! still awhile the old thought retain,
And yet consider it again!
—Arthur Hugh Clough

3.1 The Dominance of the Vocal Model

Given that spectatorship is endemic to the way mass democracy is experienced today, why has it been neglected? Why does our understanding of democracy continue to be guided by the central figure of the citizen-governor when in fact most of us most of the time have political lives typified by spectatorship rather than action? Why in spite of all the obstacles in the way of meaningful political decision making for so many of today's citizens do democratic thinkers tend to look past the phenomenon of spectatorship and assume either that ordinary citizens already are decision makers or could take on greater decision-making roles without too much difficulty or structural reform?

The answer to these questions, something to which I have already alluded in the first two chapters, is what I will now further elucidate and substantiate here: namely, that democratic theory has not adequately addressed the spectator because it has been incapable of conceiving of popular power other than as a vocal force. That is to say, democratic theory, despite the diversity of approaches that have shaped its trajectory from its rebirth at the end of the eighteenth century down to the present day, has been confined by a threefold inability: an inability to treat the *object* of popular power as anything other than the laws, norms, and policies that might give shape to a popular voice; an inability to treat the *organ* of popular power as anything other than the decisions that express this voice; and an inability to treat the *critical ideal* of popular empowerment as anything other than autonomy (the ideal that the People might use its voice to engage in authorship of the terms and conditions of public life). I call this orthodoxy regarding the ontology of popular power—that is, this assumption that the People's force consists, at the most basic level, in an expressive and decisional *voice* (or voices)—the vocal model of popular power.

The vocal model of popular power makes it impossible to treat spectatorship as anything but tangential or corrosive to the realization of democracy. This is because the vocal model assumes that popular empowerment must involve self-legislation—a process from which the spectator, as such, is necessarily excluded. To be sure, the People in a representative democracy does not actually make law as members of a legislative assembly—for this possibility is obviously foreclosed by representative institutions. But at the core of the vocal model of popular power is a rich and expansive account of the one instance where the People does engage in formal decision making: the vote. From the standpoint of the vocal model of popular power, the vote has a significance that goes beyond its literal function as a selection of leadership. The electorate does not only choose leaders but effectively determines, with varying amounts of specificity, the content of the policies leaders will implement. The electorate can approximate such a legislative function not only because the moment of voting is conceived precisely as an expressive legislative act—candidates are understood to run on the basis of programmatic platforms, and voters are understood to elect into power candidates with preferred platforms—but also because of a variety of indirect mechanisms that enable instances of formal electoral decision making, which are in themselves quite rare, nonetheless to exert a *perpetual* regulative influence on the policy decisions of elected officials. Of these mechanisms the three most fundamental are the desire of elected representatives to win reelection, which creates a strong incentive for the politician to make decisions that are in accordance with those of the public at large; strong competition from minority parties and new office seekers, which makes the risks of not following the popular will costly; and the existence of sources for gauging public opinion, such as polling, which provide politicians committed to legislating in the public interest a means of recognizing what the public demands. On the basis of these mechanisms, the vote, which might otherwise appear to be an act of quite limited expressivity—one confined to leadership selection, not policy selection, and one hampered by its rarity, reactivity, and tendency toward binariness—is rendered a highly articulate and subtle device capable of communicating the underlying opinions, values, interests, and preferences of the electorate and bringing them to bear upon the actual output of governmental policy. It is a matter of course, therefore, that the function of popular power, when conceived according to this vocal model, is to supply a substantive substrate for the norms and policies that govern public life. Representative institutions are of course insulated from this power—there is no legal obligation to obey it—but this does nothing to invalidate the modeling of popular power in terms of a real or latent legislative will. By conceiving of popular power in this legislative fashion—by understanding it as an expressive force that defines the potential *content* of norms, statutes, and policies—the vocal model crowds out any concern for the silent, nonlegislating, non-decision-making spectator.

While the rest of this book is about articulating a nonvocal, ocular model of popular power that does take seriously the phenomenon of spectatorship, this chapter is devoted to defending the claim that there is such a thing as a vocal model of popular power that has dominated democratic theory over the last 250 years. For without further elaboration, the assertion that democratic theory has been guided by an assumption about the vocal nature of popular power is bound to face two kinds of objections. First, it is common for contemporary democratic theorists to be so impressed by the variety of perspectives within the tradition of modern democratic thought that they deny the existence of any central ideology linking such diverse approaches. Second, the concept of the People—and by extension the ontology of popular power—is one of the most complex and difficult topics within democratic theory and, for this reason, seemingly unlikely to generate consensus on the nature of its being. Filmer's observation from the seventeenth century—"What the word people means is not agreed upon"—is certainly no less relevant today.[1]

Against these challenges, I shall argue that there is in fact an orthodox and still dominant conceptualization of popular power as a vocal, legislative force. Whatever the diversity of democratic theory in other respects, it is simply the case that the vocal model has shaped the way representative democracy has been theorized from the eighteenth century to the present. To demonstrate this fact, I trace the way the first theorists of representative democracy in the eighteenth and nineteenth centuries understood the nature of popular power within the new representative system. I begin in section 3.2 by reviewing three dominant models for conceptualizing popular power prior to the birth of representative democracy in the eighteenth century: the People as *legislature* (the dominant model within premodern democratic thought and practice), the People as *multitude*, and the People as *constituent power*. I argue that while none of these prior models was exportable to the specific conditions of modern mass representative democracy, this circumstance was not appreciated by the canonical theorists of representative democracy. On the contrary, as I demonstrate in section 3.3, democratic theorists in the eighteenth and nineteenth centuries continued to conceive of the People as if it were a legislature, even as representative institutions ought to have made this impossible. Among otherwise diverse democratic thinkers (such as Rousseau, Publius, Bentham, James Mill, J. S. Mill, and Tocqueville), there is a systematic tendency to understand popular power in representative democracy as a legislative force: that is, as a *decisional* and *expressive* power that realizes itself in the *content* of the laws, norms, and policies enacted by government. In section 3.4, I turn to more recent trends in democratic theory. While the vocal, legislative model of popular power continues to define the commonsense interpretation of representative democracy, numerous political scientists have in fact recognized serious problems in understanding the People as a legislative force in contemporary mass democracy. Yet, unable to imagine the People in any other way than as a vocal, expressive being, these same theorists have been led, not to a new alternative, but rather, paradoxically, to a reconfirmation of the vocal model. This hegemonic tendency—whereby the vocal model is ultimately endorsed even by political scientists most familiar with its shortcomings—is but the most recent example of the degree to which the vocal ontology of popular power dominates democratic theory.

With respect to the inherent difficulty surrounding the concept of the People, I must make two points. First, in drawing attention to this vocal ontology of popular power—to the systematic tendency to imagine the People as if it were a parliament and popular power as a force that realizes itself ultimately in laws and policies—I do not mean to get caught up in familiar debates about whether the People's voice should be treated as a corporate entity with a single will or as an aggregation of numerous wills.[2] Rather, my aim is to document and emphasize that, regardless of the number of wills believed to constitute the People, the fundamental assumption has been that the *essence*, or *substance*, of popular power is an expressive, intentional, willful, legislative *voice*. Thus, I do not deny that the concept of the People has enjoyed a diversity of interpretations with regard to its number: I claim only a common ideology about its ontological substance. Second, it needs to be appreciated that any concern that the People is not a rigorous concept and thus ought to be jettisoned is itself the ultimate legacy of the vocal model of popular power. As I discussed in chapter 1 (section 1.6), unable to conceive of the People as something other than a legislative force, yet aware of the various problems and dangers associated with this approach, recent philosophers of democracy have been led to abandon the very concept of the People—that is, the concept of everyday citizens understood in their collective capacity. This unhappy result of a democratic theory without any notion of a demos is a disservice not only to the etymology of democracy, but to a political theory capable of speaking to ordinary citizens. It is through the People that everyday citizens can have a political theory and a political life that respect and respond to their everyday condition of spectatorship. Democratic theory's abandonment of the People is an abandonment of the only collective body that might serve as the organization of the unorganized and that, as such, might be capable of addressing everyday citizens in the condition of their everydayness.

Rather than abandon the concept of the People, the People must be restored as a meaningful entity within democratic theory and practice. This chapter revives the People by way of critique, identifying the widespread, but deeply suspect, assumption that the People must be considered via a metaphorics of voice. My aim is both to document and to explain the *scandal* of modern democratic thought: that despite the People's official and obvious exclusion from government, popular empowerment has been imagined, almost without exception, as a vocal, legislative force— as serving the function that a legislature serves, that is, as *authoring* the underlying norms, policies, and statutes that are to shape the polity's fate. Among the many problems besetting the vocal model, the most urgent are that it is *unrealistic* (it exaggerates the potential of the popular voice in mass representative democracy), *inexact* (any voice that is heard in a modern democracy is not that of a genuinely collective People, but only of a majority—or, what is just as likely, a well-organized minority), and *hegemonic* (when the People is theorized as a vocal, legislative being, its exclusion from government is concealed and considered nonexistent). This last point is especially important. Exclusion and the spectatorship it engenders are fundamental to the contemporary experience of democracy. But when the People is conceived as a legislative force, popular power becomes understood only in relation to what the People—or, more accurately, a majority—occasionally might say and not in relation to what the People always *sees*: namely, individual leaders, with vast and disproportionate power, who continually appear on a public stage only a few can occupy. Given these difficulties with the vocal model, whose existence and dominance I shall attend to here, the following chapters further develop an alternative, *ocular* account of popular empowerment as the centerpiece of a rehabilitated theory of plebiscitary democracy.

3.2 The Conundrum of Popular Power at the Birth of Representative Democracy: The Unavailability of Three Traditional Models

The conviction that popular power must be of a vocal nature, that its ultimate function must reside in its contribution to the legislative output of the state, is an assumption that owes a great deal to the historical lineage out of which representative democracy arose. The history of democratic practice prior to the birth of representative democracy was so dominated by the institutionalization of the People as an actual legislative assembly that it was difficult for philosophers of the new representative system to imagine the People playing any other role, even if the very structure of representative government ought to have inaugurated precisely such a rethinking.

Before the rise of representative democracy in the late eighteenth century, it was a basic axiom of democratic and republican thought that the People manifested its power through lawmaking. While there was important variety within this model—differences, for example, pertaining to whether the People would deliberate or only vote, or whether the People enjoyed an exclusive right to lawmaking or shared this right with other nondemocratic bodies—the basic conception of popular power in terms of the power of a legislative assembly to enact the general terms of collective existence was nonetheless the predominant way popular power was understood and institutionalized. Four different permutations of the equation of popular power with the power of a legislative assembly can be identified. First, this equation is most readily observable in direct democracies, such as ancient Athens, Swiss cantons, and New England townships, where the People was virtually identified with the legislative organ of the polity. In Athens, for example, as Hansen has demonstrated, the demos was equated with the polis, and in particular with the lawmaking *ekklesia*.[3] Second, it is not just direct democracy that reveals the dominant tendency to equate popular power with the power of a legislative assembly: within the republican tradition, the ideal of the mixed regime—which combines monarchical, aristocratic, and popular elements—was usually understood as realizing the popular component through the empowerment of an assembly, open to all full citizens, capable of enacting binding legislation on the entire polity. In Rome, for example, the power of the People was identified with the power of legislative assemblies, especially the *comitia centuriata*, *comitia tributa*, and *concilium plebis*—each of which in its own way could impose (and sometimes also propose) collectively binding laws, albeit in conjunction with the Senate and the consular power. In Sparta, too, the People was identified with the collective body of citizens as institutionalized in a legislative assembly that, though it could not initiate legislation, still voted on substantive proposals in up-down votes. In more recent times, the Venetian republic similarly conceived of its popular component in the Great Council, which along with the Senate was the main legislative chamber of the state, albeit one that only an extremely small minority of Venetian inhabitants had the right to attend. Indeed, the exclusivity of the Venetian citizen body points to a third source of the traditional equation of People with legislature. It was not just that republics that employed the power of the citizenry in its collective capacity located this power in legislative assemblies, but that, from the other side, even in states that made no such use of the collective citizenry, political elites in legislative assemblies very often conceived of themselves, not as representatives of the People, but as the People itself. Nowhere is this more clearly seen than in the English parliamentary tradition of the seventeenth century, in which the equation of Parliament and People was commonplace, at least so long as there was a king against which both People and Parliament could define themselves.[4] Finally, the equation of People with legislature revealed itself in the initial expectations of democratic revolutionaries from the late eighteenth century. For example, as Wood describes, it was common for American revolutionaries to understand the promise of the Revolution in terms of delivering to the People a direct possession of the legislative power of the colonies. At first, in keeping with Whig doctrine, they assumed that overthrowing monarchy would empower the state legislatures, which they took to be synonymous with the People itself. When the actual implementation of this program proved problematic—that is, when in the aftermath of the Revolution it became clear to the radicals that the state legislatures most definitely were not to be equated with the People-at-large—the radicals nonetheless remained committed to conceptualizing popular power in terms of a legislative power: now insisting that this power could be realized by the People overriding the state legislatures through extraparliamentary assemblies, conventions, petitions, and written instructions. The radicals assumed, in other words, that what popular government meant was nothing other than the People taking up the role of the legislature, if not permanently at least at its own discretion.[5]

If the equation of the People with an *actual legislative assembly* in premodern democracies and republics made the legislative model of popular power to a certain extent irresistible, the emergence of representative democracy in the eighteenth and nineteenth centuries ought to have challenged the conceptualization of the People as a legislative force. After all, it is precisely against this conception of the People as possessors of the formal legislative power of the state that representative democracy is theorized. According to Madison's classic statement about the meaning of representative government, what made it different from direct democracy was the *"total exclusion of the people in their collective capacity* from any share of [Government]."[6] And yet, it is essential to remember that just as much as representative democracy rejects the empowerment of the People as a legislature, so too does it stand for the empowerment of the People relative to the People's position in almost all other types of regime. Even if the People would not be an organ of government, it would still continue, as in direct democracy, to possess substantial, if not supreme, power. Thus, the same Madison who made it clear that representative democracy would exclude the People from any share in government still insisted that the new system at the same time would preserve "the spirit and the form of popular government."[7] This norm that representative government would empower the People is of course only more well established today. If early theorists of representative government—especially French thinkers like Sieyès, Constant, and Guizot—always treated representation as much as a check upon popular power as a device for extending it, in the following generations of the nineteenth century and beyond, when formal aristocracy had altogether receded from social life and voting rights became gradually universalized, representative government was widely interpreted as a fully democratic institution that served, rather than restricted, the power of the People.

From the perspective of political philosophy, the challenge posed by representative democracy was the theoretical challenge of how to reconcile the empowerment of the People with its exclusion from its traditional institutionalization in a legislative assembly.[8] What type of power does the People possess if not the power to sit in assembly, make proposals, deliberate, and ratify laws? What would popular government mean if not the People's establishment within the government?

To be sure, political theory prior to the emergence of representative democracy was no stranger to the problem of how to model popular power in a way that took for granted the People's exclusion from government. Besides the model of the People as legislature, dominant within republican and democratic thought, there were two other alternative models of popular power—the People as *multitude* and the People as *constituent power*. Yet not only were neither of these fully exportable to the specific normative and institutional conditions of modern democracy, but even when they have been employed in a democratic direction, their usage has been colonized by the very legislative model they would appear to rival.

First, since Roman times, antidemocratic authors have understood the power of the People as a *multitude*—that is, as a chaotic, disordered, violent force. When conceived as a multitude, popular power is both dangerous and impotent—something to fear, yet something limited by its inability to have more than a destructive function. The metaphorical language used to depict this conception of popular power is especially rich in describing a kind of power that lacks autonomy and is incapable of revealing itself within the fixed boundaries of territory and laws. One common metaphor, for example, especially prominent in the Renaissance, was the *many-headed monster*.[9] Another metaphor, frequent in ancient Rome, was to liken the power of the People to that of an *ocean*: a force outside the body politic, but which in rare moments of crisis imposes an unstoppable destructive energy.[10] In both cases, the People lacks the capacity for stable and autonomous decision making and is thus ripe for manipulation by demagogues. On the one hand, when conceived as a multitude, popular power is understood as a wholly unpolitical force that lacks any of the qualities necessary for political agency.[11] On the other hand, those who have developed the idea of the People as multitude in a democratic direction have done so by finding in the multitude's ever-present threat of imposing chaos upon the polity an indirect yet highly effective means of securing laws, policies, and governmental conduct that is in accordance with the interests of the majority. One of the earliest instances of this argument comes from Spinoza, who suggests that the very disorder of the mass—the potential violence it always threatens—serves in fact to realize the furthering of the majority's aims and interests—or at least the governors' estimation of what these might be.[12]

That popular power in a representative democracy is irreducible to the power of a multitude ought to be clear. The People in a representative democracy is organized into a mass electorate that votes in a regular if infrequent manner. Even if any usage of this electoral right dissolves the unity of the People (between voters and nonvoters and between opposing preferences and partisan attachments), the organized inclusion of the People within the constitutional structure of the state means that popular power is not disordered, but orderly—not a threat to the foundation of the state, but a necessary part of it. The People in a representative democracy is outside of the government but still part of the constitutional system. Moreover, even if we accept Spinoza's democratic rendering of the power of the multitude—according to which the ever-present risk of violent unrest guarantees a continual respect for the interests of the majority—this guarantee is not particular to representative democracy, but something that would be present in *any* type of regime.[13] Thus, the concept of the multitude helps nothing at all in the way of trying to grasp the type of popular empowerment specific to representative democracy.

Second, conceived as a *constituent power*, the People is an entity that authorizes the government, emerging, if at all, only in rare moments of crisis to settle a dispute between ruling powers or to impose some new constitutional norm, but which most of the time lies dormant, deferring to the leadership and political organization of political elites. There are various ways of conceiving of the People as a constituent power, with more or less democratic overtones. The least democratic versions include the *imperial* (the People authorize the sovereign in a purely formal and fictitious manner, as in the "election" of Roman emperors by the Senate and popular assemblies) and the *medieval* (the People resist and rebel against unjust monarchs as a last resort, yet without challenging the system of monarchy).[14] With Locke, this notion of the People as a constituent power begins to be interpreted in a republican way. Although he sometimes makes reference to the typical Whig notion of popular power, which equates the People with Parliament, Locke's most systematic use of the People is as a prepolitical society that consents to be governed by a certain form of government, yet reserves the right to change the government and constitution if the authorities do not rule in the People's interests. For Locke, the People as constituent power is not itself a governor, but enters in moments of conflict between Parliament and executive—or itself can be involved in a conflict with either of these branches.[15] While it might seem that modeling the People as a power that appears in highly exceptional moments of revolutionary crisis would exclude from the People any legislative power, recent democratic theorists have developed the constituent power model in such a fashion so as to restore to the People a legislative function—albeit of a distinct and special type. Ackerman is the key theorist in this regard. According to Ackerman, most of the time the People is dormant, living under statutory laws and administrative decrees that it has not directly shaped. Yet, in rare "constitutional moments," characterized by mass mobilization, the People becomes activated and helps author or amend a polity's fundamental or constitutional law. Thus, in Ackerman's account of the American experience, monumental occasions of higher lawmaking, such as the Founding, the Civil War amendments, and the New Deal, are conceived as being authored by the People.[16] Wolin, too, with his notion of "fugitive democracy," according to which the People exercises autonomy in effervescent moments of heightened activism, can also be seen as restoring a legislative function to the People as constituent power.[17]

Even if one were to accept that the model of the People as a constituent power is relevant to understanding the kind of power the People exercises in modern mass representative democracy—since there are, after all, extremely rare moments of crisis when everyday citizens undergo a heightened sense of political participation and autonomy and act with a much deeper degree of unity than normally prevails—the model of the People as constituent power is insufficient to answer the question at hand: how to conceptualize popular power within the *everyday* functioning of a mass democratic regime. In America, for example, the People—or, more accurately, a strong majority—might have acted as a constituent power in revolution against the British, and also a decade later in ratifying the new constitution in extragovernmental assemblies, but this is not at all the People about which Madison theorizes, excluded from government yet at the same time empowered within the normal, routine functioning of the state. In mass representative democracy, the People is something *more than* a constituent power that arises once in a generation, if that often, and because of this fact, there is a need for an additional classification of the ontology of popular power.

Given the inapplicability of these three well-established models of popular power—the People as legislature, the People as multitude, and the People as constituent power—to the specific normative and institutional conditions of modern mass representative democracy, it is not too much to say that modern mass representative democracy brought with it a unique type of People with its own distinct form of popular power. And yet, it is characteristic of democratic thought of the eighteenth, nineteenth, and even twentieth and twenty-first centuries to resist confrontation with the newness of the People in representative democracy and, instead, to fall back on a vocal paradigm, according to which the People is understood

as a legislature and popular power as a legislative force. While there have
been exceptions to this trend, it is nonetheless the case that the dominant
paradigm for conceptualizing the nature of popular power in representative democracy has been a vocal model that defines popular power as
the power to shape norms, laws, and policies.[18] According to this vocal
model, the People might not make the actual decisions about legislation
in a formal way, but its power is precisely an expressive power, dictat-
ing the *content* of government policy. When conceived as a vocal, legislative force, the People defines potential answers to what must be done,
and it is the job of representatives either to enforce these prescriptions,
transform them through deliberation, or ignore them in the name of a
superior wisdom. According to the vocal model, then, representative
democracy does not require that popular power always be obeyed, but only
that what obeying the People means is *heeding the People's voice* regarding legislation and other policies. So conceived, the People is not the government, but the government-behind-the-government: its role is to have
views on the decisions governors make. In effect, the vocal model of popular power seeks to solve the conundrum of popular power in representative democracy—how to reconcile representative democracy's exclusion of
the People from any share in government with its empowerment of the
People relative to other regimes—by minimizing the differences between
direct democracy and representative democracy. The People continues to
have a legislative function, albeit an indirect one.

3.3 The Vocal Model in the Eighteenth
and Nineteenth Centuries

To claim that classical authors most closely linked to the modern rebirth
of democracy in the eighteenth and nineteenth centuries shared a common
understanding of the nature of the People as a legislature and of popular power as a vocal, legislative force runs up against a pervasive tenet of
contemporary democratic historiography: that there is too much diversity even among the most canonical of these authors (Rousseau, Publius,
Bentham, the two Mills, Tocqueville, and others) to warrant any comprehensive claims about the kind of democracy they all endorsed.[19] But this
resistance to the very notion of traditional democratic ideology is vulnerable on three counts. First, while it is true that there is indeed substantial
debate among the classical authors—especially over the question about
whether democracy would have an educative and developmental effect on
citizens—when the very idea of a unifying theoretical concept encompass-
ing the most seminal pieces of democratic thought from the eighteenth and
nineteenth centuries is deemed prima facie an absurdity, the critics run

the risk of overstating their objections. The decision to see commonality or difference among a set of theoretical works is not a purely rational one, but depends on how wide or narrow one sets the basis of the comparison. Thinkers who are helpfully grouped together as committed to the same general philosophical project—such as James Mill and Bentham, Marx and Engels, or Habermas and Rawls—could just as legitimately be distinguished from each other in order to expose more subtle tensions and conflicts that persist beneath a unified surface. Both approaches have clear value. The one permits a comprehensive understanding of general principles and overall commitments, while the other allows a more finely calibrated appreciation for diverse alternatives and the unique attributes of any individual thinker. Given the virtues of *both* unification and distinction, it seems unjustified to reject, a priori, any possibility for a comprehensive treatment of classical democratic texts that appeared with the rebirth of democracy in the eighteenth and nineteenth centuries.

Second, the prima facie rejection of the very concept of traditional democratic theory not only invalidates the perfectly legitimate goal of striving for a comprehensive understanding of eighteenth- and nineteenth-century democratic thought, but is especially detrimental to the ambitions of a theory of plebiscitary democracy that, as I have indicated, aims to articulate a *new* conception of democracy commensurate with the conditions of contemporary mass society. By making it impossible to grasp the past in any comprehensive way, the assumption that there is no traditional democratic theory obstructs the effort to move beyond the past and articulate distinct lessons from political experience of the last century.

Of course, defending the possibility of an orthodox democratic theory is not at all the same as articulating just what this orthodoxy might entail. This leads to the third and most important justification for overcoming the bias against the very idea of a traditional democratic theory: that the canonical authors—including Rousseau, Publius, Bentham, James Mill, John Stuart Mill, and Tocqueville—assume the same understanding of popular power as a *decisional* and *expressive* power that realizes itself in the *content* of the laws, norms, and policies enacted by government. My argument, in other words, is that a vocal, legislative ontology of popular power is in fact a shared theoretical commitment that links otherwise divergent approaches to democratic theory in the eighteenth and nineteenth centuries, and indeed beyond.

The Importance of Rousseau

Given Rousseau's well-known hostility to representative government, it might seem inappropriate to invoke Rousseau as a master theorist of the vocal, legislative model of popular power in modern representative democracy. In response, it should be said, first of all, as a matter of scholarship, that Rousseau's opposition to representation is very much a controversial point. Rousseau appears to have changed his mind more than once on the matter, raising the possibility that his political theory might be more conducive to representative democracy than readers of the *Social Contract* would be led to think.[20] But outside of this issue, it needs to be realized that despite the *Social Contract*'s polemical opposition to representation, the sketch of democratic politics that is undertaken in that work shares important similarities with representative government. Most of all, as in representative democracy, within Rousseau's theory of democracy the People is considered the sovereign power, yet is separated from the government. Thus, Rousseau can even argue that popular sovereignty is consistent with governments of an aristocratic or monarchical nature.[21] What made Rousseau different from theorists of representative democracy was that Rousseau's popular sovereign, although not permanently engaged in the everyday activities of governance, was still supposed to assemble and interject its will. The People was to be outside of the government, yet constantly capable of reentering the site of governance. For representative democracy, on the other hand, the People, with the possible exception of rare moments of constitution making, is never assembled, and its formal participation is limited to voting for representatives. Yet despite this difference, the point remains that Rousseau, because he separated the People from government, had to answer the same question facing the theorists of representative democracy: namely, if not the power to govern, what is the nature of popular power in modern democracy?

In answering this question, Rousseau made three key innovations vis-à-vis the way in which earlier social contract theorists, such as Hobbes and Locke, made sense of the nature of popular power. First, unlike Hobbes, the People for Rousseau is conceived as prior to government. Whereas Hobbes had claimed there would be only "tumults" and "multitudes" without a state power to impose order—so that the People as a collective and organized entity was essentially an aftereffect of power—Rousseau, like Locke, began with a notion of the People as a prepolitical society that precedes the formation of government. Second, also like Locke and unlike Hobbes, Rousseau defined the People, not the government, as the sovereign. The job of the government is to serve the preexisting entity of the People: "If it is to be legitimate, the government must not be united with the sovereign, but must serve it as its ministry."[22]

But, third, and most important, Rousseau departed from both Hobbes and Locke when he argued that the *essence*, or *medium*, of popular power was not contract—a willing consent to live under a system of government—but *law*: substantive determinations about what should be a democratic polity's binding norms. Or as Rousseau put it: "The sovereign, having no other force than the legislative power, acts only through the laws, and since the laws are nothing other than authentic acts of the general will, the sovereign can only act when the people is assembled."[23]

When popular power is understood as a legislative force, the People becomes an expressive entity that defines what is to be done within the polity. Popular power becomes a normal, instead of an extraordinary, force. Rather than merely respond to preexisting events and problems, the People, so conceived as a legislative power, becomes capable of *initiating* the terms and conditions of public life. And with law as its medium, the People becomes articulate, now able to communicate with a high degree of subtlety and exactness. Indeed, in identifying the exercise of sovereignty with lawmaking, it is clear that Rousseau did not simply limit popular lawmaking to rare constitutional questions, but expected the People to enact statutory laws, such as those relating to civil law and punishment, and in general all ordinances that cohered with the key constraint of universality.[24] To be sure, in making the distinction between sovereign and government, Rousseau expected that the latter would itself be engaged not just in particular applications of the law, but also in administrative decrees that resembled lawmaking. But the government would be overridden whenever the sovereign People assembled.[25]

In defining popular power as legislative power, Rousseau not only understood the People to possess a much more vocal and expressive power than it had been given by earlier social contract theorists, but also instilled lawmaking with a newfound position of prominence within the state. The state's very life, Rousseau claimed, was its legislative power.[26] Law was to be conceived, no longer only as a relatively fixed and stable body of basic rules, but as a dynamic vehicle for the popular will, a device by which a historically distinct People would express its unique nature, injecting an immanent rationality into an otherwise contingent trajectory of social evolution.[27] Or as Rousseau put it: "We can no longer ask *who* is to make laws, because laws are acts of the general will; no longer ask if the prince is above the law, because he is part of the state; no longer ask if the law can be unjust, because no one is unjust to himself; and no longer ask how we can be free and subject to the laws, for the laws are but registers of what we ourselves desire."[28]

Rousseau, then, at once separated the People from government, yet made the People into the expressive entity that provided the *source of the underlying content* for the laws that the government was supposed to execute and administer. Within the *Social Contract*, the People is presented not as the government, as in traditional models of direct democracy, but as the government-behind-the-government. That is to say, although Rousseau distinguished the People from government, he modeled the People as a government, conceiving of it as nothing other than a legislative assembly empowered to make binding decisions on the fate of the polity. If Rousseau intended this image literally, fully expecting the sovereign People to interject its will into politics and supervene, instruct, or fundamentally alter government through the enactment of general laws, for the representative model of democracy that spread throughout the West in the century after Rousseau, the People served this legislative function without actually becoming assembled.

Thus, even if not a clear supporter of representation, Rousseau is nonetheless foundational to the philosophy of representative democracy insofar as its subsequent theorists rely on the essentially Rousseauian notion of the People as a government-behind-the-government.

The Federalist Papers

Whereas Rousseau and revolutionary radicals upheld the possibility that the People could enter the terrain of government and inject its own rulings above and beyond those of formal representatives and officials, early theorists of representative democracy, such as Publius, advocated a dramatic reduction, if not elimination, of the occasions for direct political agency by the People-at-large. The authors of *The Federalist Papers* expected that, but for voting or rare constitutional crises, the People would not make any direct political decisions. Thus, to repeat it again, Madison could assert: "The true distinction between these [direct democracies] and the American Governments lies *in the total exclusion of the people in their collective capacity* from any share in the *latter*."[29]

However, this exclusion of the People from formal governance did not come at the expense of conceiving of the People in a vocal and legislative fashion as a government-behind-the-government. The People might not make laws in an official and formal way, but the nature of popular power was still conceived as a legislative force: as the collection of interests, preferences, opinions, and values that might determine the content of government policy. Even if the elected representatives deliberating in representative institutions were to make their decisions insulated from the People, the People was still defined as a power that had legislative ambitions and that, but for its detachment from government, would realize itself in binding norms and policies. Thus, the doctrine of "the exclusion of the People" was interpreted by Publius only in terms of *position* (the decisions of the Government are not necessarily the decisions of the People-at-large) and not also in terms of *ontological differentiation* (according to which the People would no longer be seen as a power that realizes itself in the governmental medium of law).

The Federalist Papers' reliance on a vocal ontology of popular power—
one that expected that the ultimate object of popular power would be
law—can be seen in each of its three component authors. First of all, there
is Madison's defense of representative institutions as a *refracting device* that
takes the underlying views of the electorate and produces decisions that
are more consonant with the true interests of the People. In "Federalist
No. 10," Madison claims that one of the advantages of the delegation of
the government to a small number of citizens elected by the rest is that the
effect of such an arrangement will be "to refine and enlarge the public
views, by passing them through the medium of a chosen body of citizens,
whose wisdom may best discern the true interests of their country, and
whose patriotism and love of justice, will be least likely to sacrifice it to
temporary or partial considerations." The metaphors of "refinement" and
"enlargement" indicate a conception of representative government that
takes a preexisting popular will (or wills) and makes it better: more rational, peaceful, effective, beneficial. The representatives who have power are
conceived as vehicles for realizing preexisting, if often poorly articulated,
legislative aims. What is questionable about such a rationale for representative democracy's superiority vis-à-vis direct democracy is not the very
plausible suggestion that the decisions reached by careful deliberation of
the few might be superior to the nondiscursive aggregation of the many—
or, as Madison put it, that "it may well happen that the public voice, pronounced by the representatives of the people, will be more consonant to
the public good than if pronounced by the people themselves convened for
the purpose"—but the uncritical assumption that popular power would
continue to be of such a nature that it would be satisfied and realized in the
legislative output of the state. Madison's willingness to rethink the institutions of democracy was not paralleled by a willingness to reimagine the
nature of popular power. On the contrary, the People's power remains for
Madison just as it was in direct democracy: the power to have its opinions,
preferences, and values—now aided by the refinement and enlargement of
representative bodies—determine the polity's collectively binding laws.[30]

To be sure, a repeated metaphor in *The Federalist Papers* is to liken
the decisions of representative institutions to *reason*, and the unmediated
forays of the People into direct governance as *passion*.[31] This distinction
does point to important differences in the way Publius conceives of the
People as opposed to the government. The decisions of the former are
characterized by fluctuation, "violent movements," and "temporary errors
and delusions."[32] The decisions of the government, on the other hand,
are stable, deliberately wrought, and conducive to the long-term health of
the republic. But beneath this difference lies the fundamental similarity
that both the People and government are defined by an *intentional will* that
realizes itself in *decision*. Because of this ontological identity, the People

can be conceived as the government-behind-the-government, and popular empowerment can be understood as taking legislative form.

Hamilton, too, presented representative government as a refracting device and thus also conceived the People in legislative terms as an underlying substrate of intentional desire. In his discussion of representation in "Federalist No. 35," Hamilton begins by rejecting any mimetic hope that the representative bodies will mirror the social and professional makeup of the People-at-large. He is especially critical of proposals for occupational representation by which all different occupations would have representatives in the government. On the one hand, Hamilton is refreshingly frank about the exclusionary elements of the new regime. Insisting that the "idea of an actual representation of all classes of the people is altogether visionary," Hamilton admits that there would be only three occupational groups likely to hold office in the new republic: merchants, members of the learned professions, and large landowners.[33] In making this admission, Hamilton acknowledges that representative government was not only inherently exclusionary (since unlike direct democracy most people would play passive roles), but that this exclusion would be accentuated by a powerful class dimension in which ordinary citizens—freemen, journeymen, mechanics, small-scale farmers—would find no occupational representation. Yet, when in this same essay Hamilton elaborates how the representative system would actually function in practice, the exclusionary element drops out from his analysis and we are left, instead, with a republic that pursues with the highest fidelity the underlying interests of the citizens not actually seated in positions of power. Like earlier theorists of virtual representation, Hamilton makes appeal to the logic of economic interests that links representative and represented in shared views about what kind of decisions are necessary and advantageous. It turns out, for example, that not only is any particular merchant elected to power likely to exercise power in a way satisfactory to any other merchant, but that what is good for merchants is also good for mechanics, manufacturers, and certain other excluded occupations. The merchant is "the natural patron and friend" of the mechanic and manufacturer—so much so, Hamilton argues, that the merchant represents these occupational classes better than they would represent themselves.[34] Likewise, all landowners could expect to have their own interests—such as low property taxes—defended by the few wealthy landowners that actually held office.[35] The learned professions would be pure forces of reason, representing no economic interest, and thereby acting as ideal moderators between the merchants and landowners. Yet, the logic of interest is not altogether effective. Elections would also be necessary to ensure that the natural bonds of interest remain intact. Elections would mean that the representative will "inform himself [of his fellow citizens'] dispositions and inclinations and should be willing to allow them their proper degree of influence upon his conduct." Elections would enable the representative to familiarize himself with the "general genius, habits and modes of thinking of the people at large." These two factors— the doctrine of interests and the role of elections—ensure all that can be expected of representation. "In any other sense the proposition has either no meaning, or an absurd one."[36]

By conceiving of government as a tool in the pursuit of underlying economic interests, Hamilton's theory of representation clearly can be accused of overlooking the way in which each representative, qua representative, is irreducible to a landowner, merchant, or member of the learned professions—but is in fact a *politician* with substantial power, authority, prestige, and influence. There is no acknowledgment that the governing elite have their own set of interests and concerns. But leaving this criticism aside, what should be emphasized is how Hamilton's theory of representation presupposes that the People embody a quasi-legislative power. It is only because the excluded mass of everyday citizens are understood to be bearers of well-defined economic interests with clear agendas for the output of governmental legislation that Hamilton is able to present an idealized account of representation as something that manages to serve the People-at-large without giving it any share in government.

The conceptualization of popular power as a quasi-legislative force can also be found in Jay, who relies on anthropomorphic imagery to describe the People as an expressive being that realizes a power of self-determination. Indeed, Jay's optimism about the future success of the Constitution was aided by his parallel optimism about the American People: specifically, "that Providence has been pleased to give this one connected country, to one united people, a people descended from the same ancestors, speaking the same language, professing the same religion, attached to the same principles of government, very similar in their manners and customs, and who, by their joint counsels, arms, and efforts, fighting side by side through a long and bloody war, have nobly established their general Liberty and Independence."[37]

The People's role in ratifying the new Constitution did point, it is true, to an alternate, Lockean conception of the People—one in which the People would be dormant and silent most of the time, being activated only to settle constitutional questions. Yet even here, as a maker, ratifier, or amender of the Constitution, the People was still defined as a lawmaker: only now it was not statutory law but the nation's fundamental law that would be legislated.

In sum it can be said that Publius treats the People as a collection of interests, values, and preferences that are exogenous to government and fully translatable into laws, norms, and policies enacted by the formal governing powers.

Bentham, James Mill, and the Conception
of the People as a Tribunal

Whereas Rousseau favored democracy but not representation, and constitutional founders in the United States and France for the most part favored representative government but not democracy, the Philosophical Radicals of the succeeding generation were among the first to present, endorse, and theorize the now familiar amalgam: representative democracy.[38] When one examines the two crucial theorists of this school, Jeremy Bentham and James Mill, one finds the same general tendency of conceptualizing popular power in legislative terms—that is, as an expressive force that realizes itself in the *content*, whether actual or potential, of the laws, norms, and policies shaping the polity.

In making this claim, I do not mean to reduce Bentham's and Mill's contributions to a mere reiteration of eighteenth-century theories, or to deny substantial differences between their model of democracy and the more participationist accounts emanating from Rousseau and, later, John Stuart Mill. Unlike the participationists, Bentham and Mill did not conceive of political life as educational or character transforming, but rather only as a set of practical institutions that secured the enjoyment of individual liberties to own property, realize the fruits of one's labor, and, especially in Bentham's case, maximize social welfare. Bentham and Mill clearly did not conceive of the People as a creative agent that, in Rousseauian fashion, turns to lawmaking to realize a unique historical identity. Moreover, where Rousseau spoke of the general *will* of the People, Bentham and Mill spoke primarily in terms of collective *interests*—although it would be a mistake to make too much of this distinction because neither Bentham nor Mill thought that the maximization of interests would be self-regulating, but rather still needed political will in order to be defended against the so-called "sinister interests" of governing elites. Finally, relative to other democratic idealists from the nineteenth century, Bentham and Mill emphasized the People's exclusion from government, especially from the state's executive and administrative apparatus. As a result, they were unique in the extent to which they worried that the government, detached and distinct as it was from the People, posed a constant threat of misrule and abuse.

Yet, despite these important differences, Bentham and Mill ended up positing a vocal, legislative conception of the People very similar to that of their contemporaries and philosophical rivals. However much they appreciated the difference between the People and the government, they could conceive of democratic progress in no other terms than as that which would work toward the ultimate elimination of this difference. And if their worry about government's tendency toward misrule seemed to contemplate a more minimal kind of popular power—one limited to resisting the abuse of the government rather than realizing the People's self-legislation—in fact, for both thinkers popular power would reveal itself not just in protection against arbitrary leadership, but, ideally, in wide-ranging legislation uniquely reflective of the universal interest of the political community. As a result, any appreciation for the People's ocular relation to the government—to the spectatorship that would necessarily accompany the People's exclusion from a government it could not fully control—was entirely overshadowed by the familiar vocal wish that through indirectly controlling the government's legislative output, the People could in effect overcome its exclusion and see its own will reflected in the state's decision making.

In the case of Bentham, the vocal, legislative model of popular power is especially evident in the choice of metaphor Bentham came to adopt when conceptualizing the People and the nature of its power in representative democracy: the power of a *tribunal*. From as early as 1790, Bentham turned to this image of the People, arguing that "the public compose a tribunal, which is more powerful than all the other tribunals together."[39] Despite the judicial rather than legislative connotations of a tribunal—and even though he emphasized that a key responsibility of the People-as-tribunal would be its judgments about the character and potential misdeeds of individual leaders—Bentham made it clear that the ultimate function of the People-as-tribunal was nothing less than the articulation and enforcement of the People's substantive judgments about legislation and policies. The People who constitute the tribune are to be understood as "judges, by whom every person and everything are to be judged."[40] As a result, the power of the People-as-tribunal "may be considered as a system of law, emanating from the body of the People."[41] In addition to other responsibilities, the People-as-tribunal would provide what Bentham called a "melioration-suggestive function," putting forward suggestions on virtually any public matter, and doing so on a continual basis.[42] Through its power as a tribunal, the People would enable government "to know the real wishes of the governed"—and also, to a large extent, have these wishes enforced vis-à-vis officials and other formal officeholders.[43]

What is remarkable about Bentham's conception of the People-as-tribunal is not simply that it describes how the People, though officially excluded from lawmaking, would still engage in decision making about substantive statutes and policies, but how in doing so it would tend to define the *universal interest* of the state. This argument is especially apparent in Bentham's *Plan for Parliamentary Reform*, in which he links democratic institutions, such as universal male suffrage, the secret ballot, and annual parliaments, to the promotion of the universal interest of the entire political community. By the "universal interest," Bentham contemplated not merely security concerns, although these were given a place of prominence, but additionally three other fundamental areas: subsistence, abundance, and equality.[44] As Postema has suggested, Bentham's concept of the universal interest anticipated the more modern notion of public goods, such as public health, economic development, and infrastructural services like roads and bridges.[45] Good government, then, was not to be altogether minimal. It would be engaged in policies and lawmaking that promoted general social welfare. And to the extent popular power was equated with the universal interest, it too was to be realized in the legislative output of the state. As Rosenblum summarizes: "Popular sovereignty expresses itself in two ways, Bentham thought—in resistance to rulers, or self-defense; and, where political society is organized to give it full expression, in law."[46]

On what basis could the People be considered as the bearers of a legislatively manifested universal interest? How precisely would representative democracy serve the universal interest? Such questions are complicated by the fact that Bentham relied on two different standards for the determination of the universal interest. On the one hand, there was the classical utilitarian response that the People represent the universal interest because they are more numerous: their interests make up a much greater portion of the common interest than aristocrats and monarchs, and thus their interests should serve as a proxy for the universal interest. In his early work, to be sure, Bentham explains the universal interest precisely in this aggregative manner.[47] But in Bentham's later writings—which coincide with his most explicit endorsements of representative democracy—the universal interest is increasingly defined as those interests that all individuals have in common. Now it is not aggregation, but a common core of overlapping interests, that defines the universal interest.[48] If the older, aggregative model of formulating the common good could potentially bypass democratic institutions (relying instead on the judicious usage of the felicific calculus), the later version was much more intimately tied to the practice of democracy.[49]

Although Bentham is not altogether consistent in separating these two different methods of determining the common good, in general it can be said that Bentham tended to interpret the People's electoral power as contributing to the later notion of the common good (an overlapping set of interests), while he understood the informal power of public opinion as articulating the common good in the older, aggregative sense. In the case of democratic elections, Bentham argued that while all individuals would prefer to pursue their own individual interests, the electoral mechanism placed obstacles in the way of doing so. The average elector would find no candidate willing to pursue his (i.e., the elector's) own interest at the expense of all others. Thus, for this ordinary elector the best decision would be to vote for the candidate who most supported the universal interest.

The secret ballot would only further motivate this tendency for electors to pursue the universal interest over their private ones when voting.[50]

The People's function as a legislative tribunal was not confined to its electoral function, but also included its role as the bearer of public opinion. Indeed, Bentham applied the metaphor of the tribunal most often in regard to the People's informal power of having its opinions impact the official decision making of elected officeholders. Making repeated reference to the notion of a "public opinion tribunal," Bentham found in public opinion an approximation of the universal interest; and he believed that in an enlightened political society this approximation would only become increasingly capable of defining the common good:

> To the pernicious exercise of the power of government it is the only check; to the beneficial, an indispensable supplement. Able rulers lead it; prudent rulers lead or follow it; foolish rulers disregard it. Even at the present stage in the career of civilization, its dictates coincide, on most points, with those of the *greatest happiness principle*; on some, however, it still deviates from them: but, as its deviations have all along been less and less numerous, and less wide, sooner or later they will cease to be discernible; aberration will vanish, coincidence will be complete.[51]

Representative democracy would foster a legislatively manifested universal interest, then, not simply by electing individuals who were more likely to pursue it, but by guiding the decision making of representatives toward the universal interest once they were in office. This was, of course, an indirect process. Bentham shared the prevalent view that representative democracy would not subject officeholders to binding mandates from the People and that popular elections would be limited to leadership selection, not referenda about policies. But if representatives were left to make their own decisions, Bentham thought that given annual elections they would nonetheless be inclined to base these decisions on their estimation of the People's view and that this process would in fact tend toward the universal interest.

To be sure, as much as Bentham is a paradigmatic example of nineteenth-century idealism, his examination of the informal power of public opinion led him in certain respects to anticipate more recent skepticism regarding the role of mass opinion in a democracy. Not only did Bentham sometimes acknowledge that public opinion was rarely a product of a single public, more often emerging from smaller subpublics, but he admitted that the very concept of public opinion was a theoretical construction, designating it with such phrases as "unofficial," "imaginary," and "a purely fictitious and verbal entity."[52] And yet these theoretical difficulties did not lead Bentham to question the existence or the potency of public opinion. The public opinion tribunal's "existence will be apt to be suspected of being no other than figurative and merely nominal. On the other hand the name of it is not more perfectly familiar than the existence of its power is universally recognized."[53]

As a result of these two mechanisms—the selection of representatives dedicated to the universal interest and the indirect guidance of leaders about wherein the universal interest consisted—Bentham understood popular power as a device that realized itself not just in the formal vote for leadership, but in the actual, if indirect, legislation of norms and policies. For Bentham, as for Rousseau and the authors of *The Federalist Papers*, popular power functions not simply as a selector of leaders or as a check on a ruling elite—not simply as a collective power that guarantees liberal rights and a minimally invasive state—but as a key articulator of what is in the interest of the entire political community. Popular power, though more muted and less creative than in Rousseau's account, nonetheless has the same essential quality of determining what types of laws and policies a democratic government ought to be enacting. Indeed, it was precisely because Bentham understood popular power to have this legislative component that he could idealize representative democracy both in the abstract and in America, where in the early nineteenth century it was most fully practiced. Thus, Bentham could write of representative democracy that it was "a form of government in which the interest of the people is the only interest that is looked to—in which neither a single man, with a separate and adverse interest of his own, nor a group of men with a separate and adverse interest of their own, are to be found—where no interest is kept up at the expense, to the loss, by the sacrifice, of the universal interest to it."[54]

It is not necessary to detail at any length the democratic theory of Bentham's intellectual compatriot James Mill because Mill ended up espousing the same notion of popular power as a quasi-legislative force. True, Mill, more than Bentham, identified the overriding end of good government as the provision of security. And Mill was especially concerned that the executive power of the state—which Mill calls "Government"—that was to provide this security would itself tyrannize and abuse the People. Further, Mill espoused little hope that the actions of the Government might be determined or authored by the People itself. Rather, the People's function was to disrupt the Government, in the sense of preventing it from attaining the oppressive domination to which it would otherwise naturally tend.[55] However, the relationship between People and Government was not the only relation in Mill's political theory. There was a third group— the representative assembly elected by the People (or at least by those qualified to vote on the basis of Mill's rather strict standards of age [forty and above], property [richest two-thirds], and gender [males only])—whose job it was to check the Government and protect the People from the power that protects it. Mill called this organ a "checking body," and, importantly, its chief function was lawmaking.[56] About this body Mill wrote: "All the power, therefore, which the one or the few, or which the one and the few combined, can apply to insure the accomplishment of their sinister ends, the checking body must have the power to overcome, otherwise its check will be unavailing."[57] To avoid an infinite regress—in which the checking body itself needs to be checked—Mill asserted that People's relationship to the checking body was different from the People's relationship to the executive power of the state. If popular power only has a protective function vis-à-vis Government, the People takes on a vocal, expressive power in relation to the representative assembly. The assembly "must have a degree of power sufficient for the business of checking. It must also have an identity of interest with the community; otherwise it will make a mischievous use of its power."[58] Why could the People expect only to avoid domination from Government yet expect to have an identity of interests with the representative assembly? Like Bentham, Mill found the electoral process to be capable of communicating the People's interests and of having these interests enforced against the representatives' natural tendency to pursue private, "sinister" aims: "Frequent elections and limitations of voting to those with independence are the means whereby identity of interest between electoral body and representatives and electoral body and community are secured." Especially when held frequently, elections could have this legislative meaning, Mill thought, because electors would make their selections on a legislative basis—or, as Mill put it, "because those who choose will, according to the principle of human nature, make choice of such persons as will act according to their wishes."[59] Such an argument not only places great faith in the capacity of electoral institutions to transmit and enforce the electorate's policy preferences, but it presupposes that the People are to be defined from the start as an interest-bearing, wish-having entity that relies on representatives to legislate its designs.[60]

For both Bentham and Mill, then, popular power is conceptualized on the basis of a vocal ontology that takes the object, or final manifestation, of popular power to be law. Even if critics like Pateman are correct when they argue that Bentham and Mill's democratic theory "does not imply that, on most issues, the electorate have an opinion as to which policies are in their, and the universal, interest, and hence an opinion on which policies their delegate should vote for," it is still the case that for both Bentham and Mill the ultimate index of popular power was to be measured in the legislative output of the state.[61] Within such a paradigm, leadership selection is marginalized, treated only as a device in the service of legislation, rather than the very site on which the ultimate meaning of popular power plays out. It is not just that Bentham and Mill, like all exponents of the vocal model of popular power, conceive of popular power as a decisional power that realizes itself in moments of choice (e.g., elections), but that electoral choice is interpreted, *not* in terms of what it most obviously is (i.e., the selection of a leader), but rather in terms of the very legislative power that representative democracy denies everyday citizens. Thus, Bentham could define an elector's electoral choice as "the choice of a person, by whom, in the representative assembly, his interest shall be advocated, be possessed and exercised."[62]

John Stuart Mill

J. S. Mill is another canonical theorist of representative democracy. Like the other figures discussed so far—Rousseau, Publius, Bentham, and James Mill—it would be inaccurate not to acknowledge distinctive features of Mill's contribution to democratic theory. Mill elaborates an educational theory of democratic engagement that is altogether lacking in the Philosophical Radicals and much more fully developed than Rousseau's suggestions in this regard. Moreover, some of Mill's particular proposals—such as proportional representation, the open ballot, and, especially, the provision of additional votes to the more competent and better educated—distinguish him from other canonical democratic theorists and lend his own theory an idiosyncratic flair. Most of all, Mill's presentation of representative government as a highly inclusive type of regime that was nonetheless likely to defer to the deliberate judgment of educated and talented political elites—a regime that, as Thompson helpfully describes it, would combine a principle of participation with a principle of competence—makes Mill's democratic theory especially committed to the ideal of rational discourse as well as unusually balanced between popular and elitist elements.[63]

Yet, notwithstanding these distinctive aspects, if one examines Mill's theorization of representative democracy—and in particular his *Considerations on Representative Government* (1861), which must be considered the most comprehensive and influential work on the topic from the mid-nineteenth century—one finds the same assumption about the vocal ontology of popular power that not only was typical of the other canonical democratic theorists I have examined, but, after the opening decades of the nineteenth century, was part of the commonsense understanding of representative democracy. In presenting Mill, then, my aim is twofold: to show how his account of democracy took for granted a vocal ontology of popular power—one that assumed popular power was an expressive, vocal force that realized itself in substantive norms and policies—and to show how Mill's particular reasons for affirming this ontology were not at all anomalous, but fully consonant with widespread assumptions of nineteenth-century political thought.

On Mill's account, service in juries, participation in parish offices, and the occasional advocacy of a particular issue were the likely forms of active participation for most citizens in a representative democracy. Mill is ambivalent about how much these practices would enable everyday citizens to realize popular self-rule. In some cases, he makes it seem as if these activities made possible a popular capacity to self-legislate, while in others he is quite clear that they are too paltry in terms of the power they embody to be valuable other than for their educative function.[64]

But even if he wavered about how much these modest forms of civic engagement afforded everyday citizens with a mechanism for self-legislation, Mill still conceived of representative democracy as a regime in which the People—the mass of everyday citizens not formally engaged in regular governance—was a quasi-legislative force: a government-behind-the-government that realized its power through the medium of governmental decision making. As Mill states:

> The meaning of representative government is, that the whole people, or some numerous portion of them, exercises through deputies periodically elected by themselves, the ultimate controlling power, which, in every constitution, must reside somewhere. This ultimate power they possess in all its completeness. They must be masters, whenever they please, of all the operations of government.[65]

Here, as throughout *Considerations on Representative Government*, Mill elides, rather than accentuates, the difference between the power of the People and the power of the elected representative assembly. The assembly is considered as the very organ of popular power in the state. When Mill claims that in the British Constitution, it is the "popular power" that is "the strongest power" and has "substantial supremacy over every department of the government," his meaning is not so much that the People, disconnected from its representatives has such a power, but rather that it belongs to the elected body of legislators who represent the People in Parliament.[66] Of course it is just this distinction between People and Parliament that Mill's analysis constantly destabilizes. It is not surprising, therefore, that in a restatement of the passage just quoted, a few pages later Mill can replace the power of the People with the power of the representatives:

> It is essential to representative democracy that the practical supremacy in the state should reside in the representatives of the people. . . . Great varieties in this respect are compatible with the essence of representative government, provided the functions are such as secure to the representative body the control of everything in the last resort.[67]

There is something here of the old Whig identification of Parliament with the People. But if the basis for this old view was the doctrine of virtual representation—and also the uncritical assumption that a nonmonarchical power would be ipso facto a popular power—for Mill it is the electoral process and freedom of debate both inside and outside the legislative chamber that enable popular power to be so easily identified with the proceedings and enactments of the legislative assembly. In Mill's most idealized treatment of representative government, the legislative assembly is the site of the collective opinion of the polity. It is "an arena in which not only the general opinion of the nation, but that of every section of it, and as far as possible of every eminent individual whom it contains, can produce itself in full light and challenge discussion; where every person in the country may count upon finding somebody who speaks his mind, as well or better than he could speak it himself."[68] Thus Mill can write of the representative assembly that it is supposed to be "a fair sample of every grade of intellect among the people." Such a view assumes, of course, that the People is, in its essence, the opinions and economic interests to be considered and deliberated over by the elected representatives—and that, accordingly, the representative assembly is "an organ for popular demands."[69]

To be sure, Mill did not expect the popular will to be identical to the decisions that emerged from the deliberation of elected representatives. In his earlier work he explicitly called for a detachment of elected leaders from public opinion, and in his later work, even if he moderated this stance and affirmed the necessity of leaders taking account of the popular view, he still expected deliberative processes to alter and inform the People's own considerations on political matters. The point, then, is not that Mill thought the People would engage in direct self-legislation, with elected representatives as no more than mouthpieces, but that popular power was conceived in terms of a vocal ontology and that, whether the People was obeyed or not, what it meant to obey the People was to realize its substantive opinions, preferences, and values pertaining to what a government should or should not be doing. Mill could elide the difference between popular power and the power of the representative assembly because of the ontological assumption that popular power was of such a nature that it realized itself in legislative content.[70]

For Mill the vocal, legislative ontology of popular power is as much a tacit assumption as it is an explicit argument. Yet it can be seen with special clarity in three sets of concerns that orient Mill's treatment of representative government. First, Mill's conception of *voting* in representative democracy articulated a vision in which the People would indirectly determine legislative content through the selection of leaders. Second, Mill's idealized notion of *public opinion*—as a force mostly prior to the political elites it affected—was another major avenue whereby he understood the

People as realizing a power that was fundamentally expressive and legislative in nature. And third, Mill's most pronounced worry about the regime he delineated and defended—*the tyranny of the majority*—assumed from the start that the nascent institutions of representative democracy would empower the People—or majority—in such a fashion that its literal decision, the selection of leadership, would become in practice a decision about underlying norms, laws, and polices. What is more, in each of these three respects, Mill was not unique but was only reiterating, albeit with uncommon eloquence and care, widespread conceptions about popular power typical of the political philosophy of his age—and, indeed, hardly unfamiliar to our own.

The Fetish of the Vote

Mill's elision of the difference between electoral and legislative decision making is perhaps the clearest evidence of his subscription to the vocal model, according to which popular power in representative democracy is conceived as a legislative force that realizes itself in the content of government decision making. Mill, who favored a wide suffrage tempered by literacy and minimal property restrictions, took it for granted that exclusion from voting was exclusion from the management of political society and that, likewise, inclusion in the electorate meant the possession of a quasi-legislative power: "Whoever, in an otherwise popular government, has no vote, and no prospect of obtaining it, will either be a permanent malcontent, or will feel as one whom the general affairs of the society do not concern; for whom they are to be managed by others; who 'has no business with the laws except to obey them,' nor with the public interests and concerns except as a looker-on."[71] Mill thus provides a very good example of the standard nineteenth-century paradox that the very limitation on voting rights engendered a hyperbolic estimation of the vote's potency. The more the vote was restricted, the easier it was to think that voting was not what it literally was—the selection of leadership—but first and foremost a quasi-legislative act.

Mill's overestimation of the vote—his assumption that voting was most fundamentally a device by which the People decided issues—was evident in his rationale for restricting the vote to those who satisfied literacy and property requirements. It was only because the vote was so potent—that is, so capable of being translated into legislation—that it needed to be carefully restricted. As Mill wrote, "No one but those in whom an *a priori* theory has silenced common sense will maintain that power over others, over the whole community, should be imparted to people who have not acquired the commonest and most essential requisites for taking care of themselves; for pursuing intelligently their own interests, and those of the

persons most nearly allied to them." The literacy requirement was justified, Mill thought, because it would exclude only those citizens whose
deficient education precluded them from the capacity of having "any real
political opinion"—an argument which makes it quite clear that those who
did possess the vote were supposed to somehow communicate substantive
opinions through the occasional and often binary selection of leadership.
Likewise, Mill's proposed property requirement for voting, which would
prevent those on parish relief from inclusion in the electorate, was explained on the basis that only the economically independent could "claim
the exclusive management of ... common concerns"—again, indicating
that the vote was conceived as a form of governance and not merely as a
selection of those who would govern.[72]

For Mill, the right of suffrage had to be curtailed and closely monitored precisely because it was so powerful. Citizens with the vote enjoy,
Mill thought, not simply the indirect benefits of liberal protections that
come with full formal membership in a political community, but an authorial vehicle to express and enforce substantive norms for the governance
of society. When electors become free to vote, "they are no longer passive
instruments of other men's will—mere organs for putting power into the
hands of a controlling oligarchy. The electors themselves are becoming the
oligarchy."[73] How exactly could the electorate translate its limited formal
power of leadership selection into such a comprehensive legislative power?
Mill's account was remarkably naïve in its belief that the People would
always be able to legislate if it wanted:

> For let the system of representation be what it may, it will be con-
> verted into one of mere delegation if the electors so choose. As long as
> they are free not to vote, and free to vote as they like, they cannot be
> prevented from making their vote depend on any condition they think
> fit to annex to it. By refusing to elect anyone who will not pledge him-
> self to all their opinions, and even, if they please, to consult with them
> before voting on any important subject not foreseen, they can reduce
> their representative to their mere mouthpiece, or compel him in hon-
> our, when no longer willing to act in that capacity, to resign his seat.[74]

Such an argument neglects, of course, the fact that electors must limit their
decision to a particular set of choices—one that already circumscribes the
issues up for debate and the consequences of one side's victory over the
other—and that each elector, empowered with but a single voice in a polity
of millions, can expect little in the way of a meaningful authorial power.

One of the best examples of Mill's affirmation of a vocal, legislative ontology of popular power occurs when he examines the question of
whether electors ought to vote directly for representatives or, instead, for

an intermediate body of electors that itself selects the actual representatives. Mill argues firmly against the latter proposal. Even though the electors in both instances would not be making actual legislative decisions but only voting—more or less directly—for the representatives who would be empowered to make such decisions, Mill thought there was a substantial difference between the two proposals.[75] Mill was not wrong, of course, to see the election of electors as more tangentially related to legislation than a direct vote for leadership. But it is significant that whereas Mill acknowledges that placing electors two steps from governance would drain their vote of any legislative function, he recognizes no such restrictions of the expressivity of the vote when it is only one step removed. Rather, Mill took it for granted that the elector voting directly for leadership "cannot be expected not to make conformity to his own sentiments the primary requisite." While Mill remained concerned about this tendency, hoping that various devices such as proportional voting, the deliberative character of the assembly, and personal restraint on the electors to leave leadership alone would temper it, he also thought that any check upon the legislative ambitions of the electorate could only be partial: "Even supposing the most tried ability and acknowledged eminence of character in the representative, the private opinions of the electors are not to be placed entirely in abeyance." Mill thus assumed that electors would vote on their own opinions, and that the electoral power would successfully transmit these opinions, bringing them to bear upon the decision making of the deliberating representatives.[76]

If some of Mill's particular proposals for voting were eccentric, his strong tendency to conflate electoral and legislative decision making was highly typical of the nineteenth century. So long as the vote was restricted, yet continually becoming less so, there was an excitement—and also a fear—about the vote's capacity to empower the People as a legislative force within the polity. As Weibe describes it, "Rather than the 18th century act of giving one's vote to someone else, of ratifying superior-inferior relations through support, balloting became a form of self-expression, an assertion of one's place alongside innumerable others in the collective act of self-government."[77] So long as the franchise was not extended to all citizens, the inclination to see the electorate as a government-behind-the-government was almost irresistible.

This proneness of a political culture without universal suffrage to overestimate the meaning of voting—to resist the literal function of voting as a selection of leadership and, instead, to define the electorate as *governors* capable of initiating, formulating, and ratifying the specific norms and conditions determining social life—can be seen in a variety of ways. It can be found, for example, in the rhetoric of those who opposed restrictions on voting and looked forward to a future of universal suffrage. Thus John

M. Broomall, congressman and delegate to the Pennsylvania constitutional convention of 1872–1873, could optimistically predict: "This thing is coming. It is only a question of time. The progress is onward. For thirty years I have been an advocate of universal self-government, and during that time I have marked the progress of it steadily onward."[78] The women's movement also tended to see electoral power, legally denied to women, as an expressive power to determine the content of government policies. Thus the suffragist Sears could say in 1874: "Our political system is based on the doctrine that the right of self-government is inherent in the people.... Women are a portion of the people, and possess all the inherent rights which belong to humanity. They, therefore, have the right to participate in the government."[79] The important difference between voting for governors and participating in government was thus elided within a context of exclusion. The very iniquity of denying women the vote instilled an inflated confidence over what the vote would bring. Certainly Stanton was later proved wrong when she, as had many other suffragists, predicted: "When our mothers, wives, and sisters vote with us, we will have purer legislation, and better execution of the laws, fewer tippling shops, gambling halls, and brothels."[80] It was only after voting rights were extended to women that it gradually became apparent how limited the vote actually was as a legislative mechanism—no doubt essential for equalizing gender relations at home and in civil society, but highly restricted as a device for legislating governmental policies in a "feminized" fashion.[81]

On the other hand, those who, like Mill, advocated certain voting restrictions did so on the basis that it would be dangerous to extend a *legislative* power to all members of society, especially to women and those without sufficient property or social standing. Whereas the old eighteenth-century argument against universal suffrage was that the propertyless lacked will and, thus, if given the vote, would be manipulated by demagogues, the typical concern of the nineteenth century was that the newly enfranchised would be all too willful and pursue class legislation that would overturn property rights.[82] Typical was Charles Francis Adams Jr., who claimed universal suffrage would mean "the government of ignorance and vice" and the victory of the proletariat.[83] Moreover, beginning in the last quarter of the nineteenth century, there was a backlash against the extension of voting rights and a new call for competent electors—a call that was informed by the assumption that voting involved far more than a selection of leaders but was essentially a quasi-legislative force within the state.[84] As late as 1928, the Harvard political scientist William Munro wrote "Intelligence Test for Voters," a tract that argued that while universal suffrage had become a permanent and basic principle of modern representative democracy, the electorate could still be regulated at the margins. Munro argued that "about twenty percent of those who get on the voters' list have no business to be there. Taking the country as a whole, the total number of these interlopers must run into the millions. There are enough of them to swing an election. Can rational men be fairly expected to place unwavering faith in a system of suffrage which commits the destinies of a great nation into such hands as these?"[85] This is an elitist view, yet one committed to the possibility that the People, though excluded from governance, could still control the destiny of the nation simply through voting.

To be sure, it would be a gross mistake to underestimate the importance of voting. The gradual realization of universal voting rights in the nineteenth and twentieth centuries was a historic achievement that meaningfully altered the social standing and dignity of previously excluded groups. Moreover, the inclusion of millions of citizens in the electorate altered the practice of politics, helping to facilitate the rise of mass parties competing for electoral support. But what has become increasingly obvious to contemporary observers of mass democracy—the structural difference between voting for leadership and legislating policies—was underappreciated in an era when voting rights were not yet fully extended. So long as the vote was restricted, it was easy to think that if only everyone had it, then the People would rule over itself. Thus, it is hardly coincidental that the major challenges to the meaningfulness of the vote—whether social choice theory's skepticism regarding the possibility of rationally aggregating individual preferences into a collective preference or the revival of participatory democracy and its objection to mere voting—are recent phenomena that have only come *after* the removal of the last vestiges of de jure discrimination in voting laws.[86]

The Idealization of Public Opinion

Mill's overestimation of the vote—his tendency to collapse the distinction between the voter's electoral decision and the representative's decision about laws and policies—was not the only aspect of his subscription to a vocal, legislative ontology of popular power. Besides the formal power of voting, the People's capacity to legislate the norms and conditions of public life also derived from the informal power of public opinion. Although not nearly as elaborated as his views on voting, Mill's understanding of public opinion reflects a key aspect of the vocal ontology of popular power that pervades his democratic theory.

In his magisterial study on public opinion from 1961, the political scientist V. O. Key wrote of the nineteenth century: "In an earlier day public opinion seemed to be pictured as a mysterious vapor that emanated from the undifferentiated citizenry and in some way or another enveloped the apparatus of government to bring it into conformity with the public will."[87] Indeed, it was highly typical of democratic theorists from the nineteenth century to conceive of public opinion as an autonomous force that was prior to and independent of the government that it regulated. Thus, for example, the jurist Frederick Grimke could state that public opinion was a democratic government's "moving force."[88] When so conceived, public opinion was a direct way by which the People, otherwise excluded from government, could nevertheless control the decisions that government officials reached. Stephen Douglas was not simply engaging in empty rhetoric, but espousing a general tenet of nineteenth-century democratic thought, when he asserted that if "the people demand a measure, they will never be satisfied till their wishes shall have been respected and their will obeyed."[89] It was a matter of course to democratic idealists that public opinion existed independently of government, that it could be identified with the will of the People, and that it would be translated by a well-functioning representative democracy into governmentally enacted law and policies. Politicians thus could claim that their decisions were those of their constituents. This is colorfully illustrated by the Whig politician Justin Butterfield, who, when asked whether he would support the Mexican War, exclaimed that he was but a mouthpiece of the popular will, and that if the People wanted it, "I am for *War, Pestilence and Famine*."[90]

On the one hand, Mill resisted the naïveté of such reasoning because for him public opinion was not a fixed and prior entity, but something that emerged out of dynamic processes of communication. Even if Mill occasionally fell back on the idea of public opinion as a mechanism by which the People controlled government from the outside,[91] he nonetheless made it clear that a representative democracy, aided by the rise of new communication and transportation technologies, simply would not transmit the People's opinion to elected leaders, but constitute a deliberative arena where opinion might be rationalized and perfected through constant debate.

And yet, Mill too was guilty of a certain naïveté when he imagined that publicity alone would be sufficient to overcome the exclusion of the People from government and produce a political system in which the People could be considered, as in direct democracy, as co-deliberators who engaged in a virtual process of legislative decision making. It was not simply that elected representatives would have their decision making closely monitored by an attentive public with its own set of opinions about what ought to be done—a situation, as Mill described it, "where unbounded publicity, and an ever present newspaper press, give the representative assurance that his every act will be immediately known, discussed, and judged by his constituents, and that he is always either gaining or losing ground in their estimation."[92] Rather, what was most hyperidealistic about Mill's account was his claim that the modern technologies of public opinion formation were sufficient to return to the People the very legislative power that representative government—with its division between active and passive citizens—otherwise appeared to have sacrificed. Thus Mill could claim what no sensible contemporary observer of mass democracy would posit today: "The newspapers and the railroads are solving the problem of bringing the democracy of England to vote, like that of Athens, simultaneously in one *agora*."[93] In asserting this doctrine of one agora, Mill did not think merely that leaders would be beholden to the opinion of their constituents, but that the constituents would be members of a nationwide deliberative body that effectively canceled the division of the polity between citizens with and without a formal legislative power.[94]

Mill's hope that the power of public opinion, and the communication technologies on which it rested, might undo the exclusion of the People from governance is evidence not only of the high idealism with which Mill, like most other democratic theorists from the nineteenth century, treated representative democracy, but of the vocal, legislative ontology of popular power that was definitive of the way democratic authors made sense of the new regime. On Mill's account, all citizens, both everyday ones and select leaders, would be linked in a common communicative network in which issues would be debated, errors exposed, and decisions reached. It was a matter of course that the People in such a scenario would continue to realize its power through the medium of decision making about what laws and policies ought to shape public life.

Majoritarian Tyranny: Mill and Tocqueville

The prevalence of a vocal, legislative model of popular power can also be seen in the most distinctive *fear* that galvanized Mill: the tyranny of the majority and, especially, the specter of class legislation. This notion of the "tyranny of the majority," which runs throughout Mill's political philosophy, followed necessarily from the other elements that underlay Mill's assumption that popular power would reveal itself through the determination of substantive laws and policies.[95] If elections were ultimately about issues and not leaders, and if public opinion was an autonomous ruling force in a democratic polity, then it seemed to follow that a majority would hold full sway in representative democracy.

In recognizing the potential for majoritarian tyranny, Mill conceived of himself as part of a new generation of democratic theorists who, unlike the previous generation that included such figures as his father and Bentham, had a more realistic and critical understanding of what was at stake in the practice of representative democracy. In *On Liberty*, Mill argued that democratic revolutionaries from the late eighteenth century and Philosophical Radicals from the early nineteenth century were so swept away by the promise of the new institutions of representative democracy, and their obvious moral superiority vis-à-vis monarchy and aristocratic

privilege, that they failed to recognize the possibility that democracy might
produce its own kind of tyranny in the form of illiberal and oppressive
treatment of minorities.[96] For Mill, what was most characteristic of the earlier generation of democratic theorists was their tendency to imagine that
representative government would empower the *entire* People understood
as a single, comprehensive entity. He described their reasoning thus:

> What was now wanted was, that the rulers should be identified with
> the people; that their interest and will should be the interest and will
> of the nation. The nation did not need to be protected against its own
> will. There was no fear of its tyrannizing over itself. Let the rulers be
> effectually responsible to it, promptly removable by it, and it could
> afford to trust them with power of which it could itself dictate the use
> to be made. Their power was but the nation's own power, concen-
> trated, and in a form convenient for exercise. This mode of thought,
> or rather perhaps of feeling, was common among the last generation
> of European liberalism, in the Continental section of which it still
> apparently predominates.[97]

Mill thought that this naïve account of the People as a unified entity with
a single corporate will was typical more of democratic theorizing in the
abstract than of the understanding of democracy that grew out of experience with the actual practice of representative government. And what
entitled Mill to a superior comprehension of the matter, he felt, was
precisely that he had lived in an age that had more hands-on familiarity
with representative democracy than had his father's generation—an age
when "a democratic republic came to occupy a large portion of the earth's
surface." Paradoxically, the expansion of democracy was a lesson in the
potential limits of democracy—or, as Mill put it: "Success discloses faults
and infirmities which failure might have concealed from observation."[98]

The key fault and infirmity of the earlier generation's understanding
of democracy was its failure to appreciate the distinction between the rule
of the People and the rule of the majority. What was just beginning to be
realized, Mill claimed, was that "the 'people' who exercise the power are
not always the same people with those over whom it is exercised; and the
'self-government' spoken of is not the government of each by himself, but
of each by all the rest. The will of the people, moreover, practically means
the will of the most numerous or the most active *part* of the people." Thus,
if the first generation of democratic idealists tended to overlook the problem of liberal protection—on the assumption that "the nation did not need
to be protected against its own will"—Mill's account of representative
democracy remains concerned throughout with the important question of
how minorities and individuals might have their rights protected against

a majority unfairly presenting itself in the guise of the People in its entirety.[99] It is noteworthy in this regard that Mill reinterprets the notion of "sinister interests" that figured prominently in Bentham and James Mill's democratic theory. If for them the sinister interest referred to the interest of individual leaders and oligarchic minorities that threatened to rule against the universal interest, for J. S. Mill the term applies to *democratic majorities* insofar as they tyrannize over individual rights.[100]

What needs to be realized is that Mill's effort to inject realism into his understanding of democracy contained its own kind of utopianism: namely, that the power of elections and public opinion would be sufficient to empower the majority, otherwise excluded from any share in governance, with the capability of enforcing its own set of preferences, opinions, and values through the vehicle of lawmaking and public administration. In other words, if Mill rejected the notion that the People (considered as a single, all-inclusive entity) self-legislated in representative democracy, he still assumed that the People (considered as the majority) would have this power. The fear of majoritarian tyranny was inseparable from a vocal, legislative ontology of popular power—that is, inseparable from the notion that a majority of citizens, bereft of any official power to make law, would still be able to determine the content of the norms and policies governing public life. As Mill explained, "In a representative body actually deliberating, the minority must of course be overruled; and in an equal democracy (since the opinions of the constituents, when they insist on them, determine those of the representative body) the majority of the people, through their representatives, will outvote and prevail over the minority and their representatives."[101] On such an account, it was easy to see the People (understood as the majority) as threatening the same tyrannical power that in earlier times had been embodied in monarchs. In the United States, where according to Mill "the numerical majority have long been in full possession of collective despotism [and where] they would probably be as unwilling to part with it as a single despot or an aristocracy," it was particularly suitable to conceive of the People as a tyrant.[102] "The Demos . . . being in America the one source of power, all the selfish ambition of the country gravitates towards it, as it does in despotic countries towards the monarch: the people, like the despot, is pursued with adulation and sycophancy, and the corrupting effects of power fully keep pace with its improving and ennobling influences."[103]

While Mill understood himself to be expounding a second wave of democratic theory—which unlike the first wave recognized that it was the majority of the People, not the People in its entirety, that was in ultimate possession of state power—he overlooked the possibility of a *third stage*, increasingly common in the twentieth century, in which governmental decision making is considered not as necessarily grounded in a preexisting substratum of the electorate, but rather as something that begins from the initiative of organized political elites in possession of political power. It is true that in chapter 7 of *Considerations on Representative Government*, Mill briefly contemplates the possibility that the rise of mass parties would empower organized minorities—or what Mill aptly calls "the majority of the majority"—and thus invalidate the traditional understanding of representative democracy in terms of majoritarian rule. Yet, however much this conjecture anticipated future developments in political science—including elite theory and social choice theory—Mill did not pursue it, arguing instead that the power of organized minorities was not an urgent problem (at least not in England) and, to the extent it existed at all, it could be eradicated by his proposals for proportional representation.[104] And, besides, as I have tried to demonstrate, Mill's democratic theory was not organized around the threat of the disempowerment of the People, but, on the contrary, was shaped by the opposite concern that the People, understood as a majority, would have too much sway in a representative regime that was not simultaneously moderated by liberal protections, extra voting power for the highly competent, and other devices for quelling majoritarian tyranny. This fear of unadulterated popular power presupposed that the basic institutions of representative government—elections and public opinion—were enough to bestow upon the People a quasi-legislative power.

The concern about majoritarian tyranny—and the vocal, legislative ontology of popular power that this concern presupposed—was not at all particular to Mill, but was a basic feature of the discourse on democracy that emerged in the nineteenth century. It receives perhaps its most classic formulation from Tocqueville, Mill's contemporary and intellectual compatriot, in *Democracy in America*. Like Mill, and indeed like all other exponents of the vocal model, Tocqueville believed that the majority, even though it lacked formal empowerment as a legislative body, would nonetheless possess a massive legislative power within the state. For Tocqueville, the key institutional development of nineteenth-century democracy—the widening of the suffrage through the continual reduction or elimination of property requirements—was interpreted in such monumental terms that the power to elect was seen as virtually synonymous with the power to legislate.[105] Thus Tocqueville could write, "The majority, being in absolute command both of lawmaking and of the execution of the laws, and equally controlling both rulers and ruled, regards public functionaries as its passive agents and is glad to leave them the trouble of carrying out its plans.... it treats them as a master might treat his servants if, always seeing them act under his eyes, he could direct and correct them at any moment." Tocqueville recognized the sovereignty of the People not simply as an abstract dogma, but as a vital principle that determined the everyday reality of political experience within the United States and other nascent democratic systems: "In America, the sovereignty of the people is neither hidden nor sterile as with some other nations; mores recognize it, and the laws proclaim it; it spreads with freedom and attains unimpeded its ultimate consequences."[106]

Tocqueville's argument about the quasi-legislative power of the majority, and the tyranny it threatened, receives its most explicit treatment in a chapter from *Democracy in America* entitled "The Omnipotence of the Majority in the United States and Its Effects." Here Tocqueville insists that in America, the power of the majority is "not only predominant but irresistible." And he makes the bold declaration: "The absolute sovereignty of the will of the majority is the essence of democratic government, for in democracies there is nothing outside the majority capable of resisting it." The power of the majority means that elected officials are "obliged to submit not only to the general views but also to the passing passions of their constituents." All organs of government are understood to be controlled closely and directly by the majority: "In matters of government the majority of a people has the right to do everything." Likewise, Tocqueville claims that "the majority is the only power whom it is important to please." And it was not only the government that would be determined by the majority, but everyday life outside of politics. Thus Tocqueville concludes: "The majority in the United States has immense actual power and a power of opinion which is almost as great."[107]

Tocqueville's observations and interpretations reveal how the fear of majoritarian tyranny served to minimize, rather than emphasize, the difference between direct democracy and representative democracy. Thus, Tocqueville could be led to say: "Sometimes the body of the people makes the laws, as at Athens; sometimes deputies, elected by universal suffrage, represent it and act in its name under its almost immediate supervision." The representative system, far from excluding the People from taking a role in lawmaking, was considered in fact as a device in the service of this legislative function:

> The people take part in the making of the laws by choosing the lawgivers, and they share in their application by electing the agents of the executive power; one might say that they govern themselves, so feeble and restricted is the part left to the administration, so vividly is that administration aware of its popular origin, and so obedient is it to the fount of power. The people reign over the American political world as God rules over the universe. It is the cause and end of all things; everything rises out of it and is absorbed back into it.[108]

Today we are more inclined to see Tocqueville's equation of popular power and divine power in an altogether different, *secular* light: the People's sovereign power is just like divine power in the sense that both are absent—so that any assertion to the contrary runs the risk of masking the actual power of those who in fact occupy the seats of government. Even if one resists such Götterdämmerung, it is nonetheless clear that developments in politics and political science in the century and a half since Mill and Tocqueville have had the effect of making fears of majoritarian tyranny appear somewhat hyperbolic, if not paranoid. There is greater sensitivity today both to the pluralistic nature of political power and also to the way mass politics elevates organized minorities and single individuals into positions of great power. But regardless of whether Mill and Tocqueville were wrong to see the majority as omnipotent, the point is that their fear of majoritarian tyranny was premised on a vocal model of popular power according to which the People would act as a government-behind-the-government and thereby reveal itself in the substantive laws and policies governing public life.

3.4 The Continuation of the Vocal Model in the Twentieth and Twenty-first Centuries

In one sense, the vocal model of popular power—according to which the People is defined as an intentional voice that articulates a set of preferences about what kind of policies government ought to be legislating—has continued unimpeded in the twentieth and twenty-first centuries. There is a wide consensus, both in political theory and in empirical research, that popular sovereignty in contemporary representative democracy (and hence popular power) means precisely that governmental decision makers be responsive to the underlying preferences of the People.[109] Either this responsiveness is asserted as something that is already to a large extent achieved by existing democratic institutions—as in the median voter theory popularized by Downs or the theory of retrospective voting that I shall presently discuss—or it is something that wise democratic reform is thought capable of obtaining, as in most proposals coming from theorists of deliberative democracy or participatory democracy.[110] The vocal model of popular power is also reflected in the commonsense understanding of democracy, typical of journalism, which likes to refer to the People as a willful being that supports or disapproves of particular policies, individuals, or political ideologies and that uses elections, which would appear to refer only to who should hold power, as a means of voicing a larger set of legislative intentions for the polity.

Yet in truth the vocal model's continuation from the nineteenth century to the twentieth and twenty-first centuries has hardly been smooth or unhindered. The central building blocks on the basis of which the vocal model was originally articulated—elections and public opinion—

have been examined with a level of thoroughness and skepticism unseen in the nineteenth century. As far as elections, recent observers have been much more attuned to the way electoral decisions are not automatically policy decisions: how they are reactive, occasional, often binary, and of course nonbinding in any legislative sense. With respect to public opinion, there is hardly anyone today who asserts a simple and straightforward connection between public opinion and governmental decision making. Contemporary students of politics are highly aware of problems largely unknown to nineteenth-century observers: the nonexistence of genuine public opinion on many issues, the dependence of public opinion on the very political elites who are supposed to be regulated by it, public opinion's tendency toward vagueness and irrationality, and, most of all, the difficulty of making any solid assertions about the power of public opinion in a democracy. Even the most confident defenders of public opinion today recognize that this power is partial, meaningfully affecting policy as little as one-third of the time.[111] Moreover, whatever the absolute measure of government responsiveness to public opinion, recent literature suggests that the direction is negative: that responsiveness is on the decline, as politicians increasingly track public opinion not to make policy, but rather to determine how to craft their public presentations.[112]

On the one hand, if it should be the case that government does not faithfully reflect the underlying preferences, values, and opinions of the citizenry—or does so to a too minimal extent—this does not by itself negate the vocal model of popular power. The vocal model does not say that the People are always obeyed, but only that what obeying the People means is carrying out its substantive wishes for legislation and other policies. The vocal model is thus able to contemplate situations in which the People's preferences remain unheeded. On the other hand, however, when the People's voice is routinely ignored, when it often does not exist, when its existence is shaped by the very government it is supposed to control, when there is no established criterion for measuring the degree of this control, when the devices for its self-expression are crude and thereby severely limit its articulacy, and when it is always more accurate to speak of the voice of some segment of the People that manages to be heard rather than the People itself, one would expect that students of democracy might begin to rethink the vocal model and explore alternatives. At the very least, the imperfect, limited, occasional power of vocal processes on the mass scale ought to lead to an understanding of the People as something irreducible to its voice—as something whose phenomenology includes, not just a voice which instructs government, but also an ocular, spectatorial dimension: the *eyes* of the People that must watch government insofar as the popular voice is nonexistent, nondeterminative, or otherwise inactive. And when one considers that any voice successfully transmitted from below is never truly that of the People but only a subset of the electorate, there is further reason to be skeptical of the notion of the People's voice and to conceive of the People, instead, in terms of the more genuinely collective experience of spectatorship.

However, with the major exception of the underappreciated plebiscitary tradition I aim to recover, this rethinking has hardly occurred. The vocal model has remained triumphant. There have been three main reasons for this fact. First of all, there has been a lack of theoretical imagination: it has been wrongly assumed that democratization can only be pursued via the enrichment and empowerment of the People's voice, so that other potential avenues of democratic progressivism—like ocular processes centered on the People's eyes—have been altogether ignored. Second, the endurance of the vocal model in spite of a growing recognition of its problems stems undoubtedly from a well-entrenched theoretical bias against transacting in anything but perfect ideals. Without citing Kant directly, much contemporary democratic theory nonetheless is informed by a strong Kantian spirit: specifically, by a deeply felt theoretical obligation not to let the divergence between theory and practice lead to any attenuation of the commitment to the perfect ideal of equal political autonomy for all.[113] Because in a perfect world citizens would be equal decision makers rather than spectators, a Kantian-inspired democratic philosophy insists upon theorizing about politics in a way that treats all citizens as potential decision makers with an equal capacity to shape the laws and conditions of public life. Although admirable and extremely prevalent, such an approach leads to democratic theory that sidesteps the unpleasant but acute reality that for most citizens mass democracies today are defined by spectatorship, not active decision making.

A mixture of these first two hindrances in the way of getting beyond the vocal model has produced a third. The most perplexing reason for the stability of the vocal model in the face of increasing problems with it—and the one I will focus on here—is what can be referred to as the *hegemonic status* of the vocal model. By this I mean that those who have done the most to expose the weakness of the People's voice—its rarity, its limited articulacy, its questionable capacity to render government responsive to its alleged legislative preferences, and its failure to embody genuine collectivity—have not argued against conceiving of the People as voice, but, on the contrary, have been some of the most influential supporters arguing on behalf of this identification. Indeed, what is most noteworthy about democratic theory of the last century, at least from the perspective of the ontology of popular power, is the schizophrenia by which the recognition of the inarticulacy, weakness, and nonexistence of the People's voice has tended not to disturb the ontological conception of the People in terms of voice but only to reinforce it.

It is this hegemonic circumstance, by which those who have challenged the People's capacity as a vocal, legislative entity functioning as a government-behind-the-government have still not been able to get beyond the vocal model but have only found themselves reasserting it, that I examine here. It can be seen in at least four different contexts: the theory of retrospective voting, the all-too-easy assumption that the binariness of electoral decisions reflects an ideological binariness among the electorate, Bernard Manin's concept of audience democracy, and the irrational optimism that governs the way the various complexities besetting public opinion most commonly have been treated. In each case, one witnesses the same basic trend: political scientists whose work has most upset any easy acceptance of the vocal model are still deeply confined by this model. Their revisions, even when sizable, have not led to the acknowledgment of the People as spectator, but have for the most part inspired a renewed theorization of the People as a legislative being, and a fairly effective one at that.

Retrospective Voting

This hegemonic function of the vocal model can be seen most clearly in the account of the People that occurs in the influential theory of retrospective voting. Initially developed by V. O. Key—but also relied upon by numerous other theorists—the theory understands the People's electoral function primarily as a retrospective judgment of the past rather than a prospective set of instructions for the future.[114] Although there is some variety within this model, the basic idea is that the People votes up or down on the incumbent administration on the general issue of whether the country is better off than it was from the last election. Even those who emphasize that this judgment can have a prospective element, like Fiorina, still understand the electoral choice to be an occasional determination of which party will perform better in general, rather than any specific set of instructions about what precisely should be done. Whereas democratic idealists of the nineteenth century did not distinguish sharply between the election of leaders and the choice of policies—finding the former a straightforward and direct way of transmitting the latter—the theory of retrospective voting would appear to appreciate the constraints on the articulacy of the People's voice: namely, that the People does not really legislate, but is confined to making infrequent verdicts on the past performance of elected officials.

On its surface, this theory has the virtue of being a more accurate description of what literally happens in mass elections (where the choice of administration is direct and real, and any result for policies indirect and debatable) and, accordingly, of acknowledging the People's spectatorial role in contemporary politics. After all, if the People does not supply the underlying preferences and opinions that government is to realize, then it is not legislating, but only reacting to the legislation of its governors. Likewise, if the People—or electorate—is limited by infrequent up-down votes, then it is hardly articulate, but confined to long periods of silence punctuated by rare moments of simplistic grunts. Insofar as retrospective decisions are reactive, binary, and infrequent, then, the theory of retrospective voting seems to admit that most of the time the People must stand back and watch political events unfold and that, as a result, government will pursue a variety of activities that the People could not have predicted, that it did not choose, and that perhaps it did not want. In these respects, retrospective voting is a theory that, while acknowledging the reality of the electoral decision, minimizes the function of this decision far below what nineteenth-century idealists had anticipated and, consequently, would appear to recognize a feature of the People's political experience hardly noticed or addressed by these idealists: that of exclusion and the spectatorship that exclusion engenders.

And yet, this is not at all how the theory of retrospective voting has been interpreted. Even though this model recognizes a clearly diminished articulacy of the People's voice, its purveyors reduce the consequences of this diminishment to the point of nonexistence. In the hands of its central expositors, it turns out that retrospective voting leads to the same kind of results predicted by the nineteenth-century theorists. Key, it is true, did acknowledge some of the unideal consequences, arguing that it would be "a mischievous error to assume, because a candidate wins, that a majority of the electorate shares his views on public questions, approves his past actions, or has specific expectations about his future conduct."[115] But this insistence on the diminished expressivity of the People's voice—its limited articulacy and the difficulty of connecting governmental output to an underlying popular will—has been remarkably absent in later iterations of the theory. On the one hand, it is argued that because elections are repeated and competitive, candidates will ultimately try to anticipate what they think the electorate wants and, thus, over time come to approximate the popular will.[116] Such a view appears overly sunny when one considers the infrequency of elections, candidates' skill at concealing policy aims behind "crafted talk," the difficulty of gauging the extent of actual responsiveness, and, finally, the problem that there may not be an underlying popular will for many issues in the first place.[117]

On the other hand, the limited expressivity of popular voice has been apologized for through the argument that the People does not really want specific policies anyway, but just generalized performance. Thus Fiorina can argue, "I feel safe in claiming that large majorities prefer peace to war, low unemployment and stable prices to high unemployment and inflation, social harmony to social tension, energy self-sufficiency to dependence on imported oil, and so forth."[118] Fiorina thereby makes the case that in general politicians need not worry about which policies the electorate wants, only which policies will produce the best general outcomes. But this distinction between policies and performance is overdrawn and oversimplified. In many cases, like abortion, the policy cannot be separated from the result. Moreover, even if it is true that nearly everyone wants peace, wealth, and low unemployment as general goals, what matters in actual political contests is how these goals are defined and how they are balanced with each other. While it is certainly satisfying to think that politicians who lose an election lose because they did not perform their jobs adequately—or because their rivals performed their jobs too well—the truth is that there is no clear standard of what performance means. In fact, it is always the case that those who win define good performance differently from those who lose. In politics the ends are not set, as they are in a track meet, but are themselves up for constant debate and redefinition.

None of this is to suggest that theorists of retrospective voting are wrong to interpret elections as retrospective judgments on past performance. What is objectionable is the ease with which this limited, occasional, binary, reactive kind of decision making (which after all only voices a preference of the majority, not the People itself) is translated into a much more expressive and authoritative kind of vocal power. That the very theorists who have emphasized the retrospective nature of the popular voice have tended not to confront the inherent limitations connected to retrospection, but on the contrary have been by and large fully content with the expressivity afforded by it, is an exemplary indication of what I mean by the hegemonic function exerted by the vocal model of popular power today.

The Problem of Binariness

As the theory of retrospective voting evinces, recent political science, unlike democratic idealism from the nineteenth century, appreciates the fact that popular decision making tends to be binary. In two-party systems, this binariness seems almost natural. But even in parliamentary states organized around proportional representation, developments have tended toward binariness as various parties increasingly ally themselves into two opposing camps at election time.[119] It would seem that this yes-no binary structure would be a serious limitation on popular expressivity. Max Weber, for example, whose plebiscitarian theory will be analyzed in subsequent chapters, argued that it was precisely the binary aspect of the popular voice that made it so ineffective as a legislator.[120]

But this conclusion has not been the normal one. Instead, the difficulties posed by binariness have been sidestepped in various ways. One of these, as I have just shown, is the theory of retrospective voting. Another is the widespread belief that binary competition over time will organize itself around genuine cleavages in the electorate and thus approximate the underlying preferences of the mass citizenry. But underlying both of these is the view that political issues themselves are of a fundamentally binary nature. This claim, which is especially widespread in America, finds its clearest articulation in the view that most issues can be mapped on a single liberal–conservative continuum. Indeed, political scientists who are most confident about the People's ability to have its preferences, opinions, and values channeled into government policy also tend to rely on this ideological continuum.[121] So, for example, as the usual story goes, when a "conservative" wins office, the People have selected a whole nexus of issues, including gun rights, defense spending, law and order, traditional family values, fiscal responsibility, and opposition to abortion. By voting for a "liberal" candidate, the People likewise is in effect voting for gun control, abortion, welfare, minority rights, and a more pacifistic foreign policy. Thus, the People is not seen as simply giving an up–down verdict on past performance but defining the general ideological direction the polity should be tending toward. According to this reasoning, because most policy choices are connected on a common ideological scale, the People need make only one choice, and this will successfully implement a host of others. Candidates are not who they literally are—particular individuals who either hold or seek office—but rather to some meaningful extent ideologues who will work to implement a logically connected set of views. Thus, not only is an electoral decision actually a legislative decision, but it is a remarkably efficient legislative decision: through an infrequent, binary choice about leadership, the People is actually able to indicate a much more subtle determination of policy preferences.

On the basis of such reasoning, then, the diminished expressivity of the People's voice which would seem to be necessitated by the binary structure of most elections is ameliorated by the good fortune that most major issues are themselves binary. Because all issues are reducible to one big question—liberal or conservative, Democrat or Republican, party of tradition or party of hope—then the binary nature of voting is not at all restrictive of the People's voice, but contains the DNA, so to speak, that will shape the way a variety of more particular policy preferences will be effected. Such reasoning also serves to soften the blow of the vote's infrequency. Because there is really only one choice worth making—should the country go conservative or liberal—it would actually be counterproductive to make this choice too often. There needs to be time, after all, for the legislative consequences of the decision to manifest themselves.

There are clearly many problems with this all-too-easy solution to the binary, infrequent character of voting. First of all, the great assumption underlying this approach—that most issues are logically connected—is very much suspect. The ideological alignment of issues owes at least as

much to the contingencies by which rival parties distinguish themselves
from each other as to logical relations between the issues themselves. In
America, for example, there is no logical reason to link support for the
death penalty with opposition to abortion as kindred conservative causes.
This linkage results from the vagaries of party alignment, not from rational,
natural, or otherwise necessary features of what it means to be a conservative. Moreover, in two-party states, it is especially difficult to reduce party
identifications to ideological ones, since there may be considerable ideological diversity within a party.[122] Second, any appeal to an ideological
continuum has to face the problem that only a small fraction of citizens
exhibit the *slightest* ideological attachment and that, even among those who
do identify themselves in this way, there is great confusion about what
such designations actually mean.[123] In other words, clear policy mandates
do not necessarily follow even from ideology-based voting.[124] Third, how
to measure the liberal–conservative continuum is itself in dispute, making
it all the clearer that the very notion of such a dichotomy is oversimplified.[125] Finally, it needs to be remembered that in contemporary mass
democracy there are many decisions that are not ideological, but rather
arise out of the unpredictable trajectory of history itself. How leaders react
to unforeseen crises and events, such as issues of foreign relations in need
of immediate response, depends on the independent judgment of the select
few empowered to make such decisions and cannot be deduced from an
ideological algorithm.

   The belief in the natural ideological tendency of issues assumes that
the mute grunt of electoral decision contains within it a finely calibrated
mandate for policies. It finds in the election of an individual person the
election of a conservative or liberal and, from this, the selection of conservative or liberal policies. It is the conceit of ideological thinking that
most decisions can be grouped in a way so as not to be out of the control of
those rare and binary moments of popular expression. In other words, such
reasoning denies—or at least allows one to overlook—the fundamental difference between those who do and those who do not get to engage in actual
decision making.

The So-Called Theory of Audience Democracy

One of the best examples of the hegemonic status of the vocal model—that
is, the way in which political scientists' very efforts to expose problems
with the vocal model paradoxically have led to the defense and reasser-
tion of this paradigm—is the theory of audience democracy developed by
Bernard Manin. More than most other approaches within democratic theory, Manin's model of audience democracy would appear to be reflective
of the fact that the collective citizenry in contemporary mass democracy

has come to take on characteristics of a spectating audience. Manin understands audience democracy as the third and latest phase of representative
government, following a parliamentary phase characterized by the rule of
notables in a deliberative setting and a party phase in which ideological
parties simultaneously compete and cooperate for control of the state. If
the party phase had given voters a fairly clear sense of the kind of policies
their electoral choices supported, within audience democracy it becomes
much less clear how electoral decisions are linked to the state's legislative output. Manin argues that by the end of the twentieth century it "is
impossible to have the impression" that there is "an identity (real or
imagined) between governing elites and those they govern." He notes that,
from the 1970s onward, election results have been much less correlated
with the socioeconomic and cultural composition of the electorate. This
means, for example, a decline in class-based voting from which a relatively
clear set of policy preferences might be inferred. Instead, political cleavages are subject to perpetual redefinition, constantly being challenged and
reshaped, usually from the top down by organized political elites. With the
main issues of political life no longer stable or certain, politics in audience
democracy becomes acutely concerned with the individual personalities of
politicians—a trend that only further facilitates the rise of issueless politics and, with it, the replacement of a discursive political culture with an
imagistic one. Under audience democracy, it therefore comes to be expected
that elected officials will bring their own creative agenda into politics, that
they will deal with unforeseen historical crises and opportunities on the
basis of their own judgment, and that, consequently, the collective citizenry will tend to watch political events unfold as a spectator rather than as
a collection of autonomous decision makers. As Manin acknowledges, such
developments are not neutral phenomena, but challenge the core ideal of
popular self-legislation:

> The social and cultural gap between an elite and the mass of people is
> a difficult thing to gauge, but there is no reason to think that present
> political and media elites are closer to voters than the party bureau-
> crats were. Nor is there any sign that those elites are in a position to
> inspire feelings of identification on the part of voters. More than the
> substitution of one elite for another, it is the persistence, possibly
> even the aggravation, of the gap between the governed and the gov-
> erning elite that has provoked a sense of crisis.[126]

And yet Manin's appeal to a "sense of crisis" is more rhetorical than real.
Rather than understand audience democracy as destabilizing the integrity or influence of the People's voice and expanding the chasm between
ordinary citizens and political elites, Manin actually presents audience

democracy as being capable of both forming an authentic popular voice and having this voice meaningfully determine the legislative decision making of the governing politicians. Espousing a version of the theory of retrospective voting, Manin argues that even though the People cannot voice itself in a way that makes clear determinations about the future, it can still issue a verdict about the past. And even if the choice posed to the People on any particular election might be largely determined from above, the fact that elections are repeated means that politicians in the long run will be constrained to present the People with choices that reflect genuine cleavages in the electorate: "Since . . . the politically most effective cleavages are those which correspond to the preoccupations of the electorate, the process tends to bring about a *convergence* between the terms of electoral choice and the divisions in the public." Manin invokes this convergence both as something that already occurs in audience democracy and as something that can be further maximized. To the ordinary citizen living within an audience democracy, Manin therefore advises: "In a representative system, if citizens wish to influence the course of public decisions, they *should* vote on the basis of retrospective considerations." Thus, if audience democracy seemed to threaten the People's traditional status as a vocal self-legislator, Manin's development of the theory leads to the opposite result: "Through their retrospective judgment, the people enjoy genuinely sovereign power."[127]

What is objectionable is not simply that retrospective voting cannot fully compensate for the limited, binary, and occasional nature of electoral decision making, nor that Manin's endorsement of it conflicts with his own doubts about the existence of a popular will.[128] What is most problematic, at least from a political-philosophical perspective, is that Manin chooses to present this account of popular expressivity under the banner of *audience* democracy. Manin's description of the People as an audience ought to signify that the People does not engage in effective decision making in contemporary mass democracy—that its voice is effectively silenced, bypassed, or rendered vague and inarticulate. An audience as such does not decide. Instead, Manin's ultimate move is to drain audience democracy of its potential critical, polemical, and novel elements by assimilating the concept of the People-as-audience to the traditional, familiar, *opposite* figure of the self-legislating People. Consequently, the People in Manin's audience democracy does precisely what it did in the earlier democratic regimes: it supplies the underlying substrate of preferences, opinions, and values that will guide the enactment of substantive legal norms. As a description of the problem of spectatorship, Manin's theory is insightful and rightfully influential; but as a solution to this problem, Manin's account suffers from the weakness that it can address the problem of spectatorship only by avoiding it: that is, by redescribing the spectating audience as if it were a sovereign judge.

A genuine theory of audience democracy—such as the ocular model of plebiscitary democracy I am defending in this book—would seek norms of empowerment consistent with spectatorship. And since it is precisely nonparticipation that defines spectatorship, such a theory would not involve the spectating public overcoming its spectatorship and becoming active decision makers. This is not to say that audiences can never make decisions, but only that if one wants a theory of democracy true to the experience of spectatorship, it cannot rely on decision making as its central feature. The plebiscitary model can be considered a more authentic form of audience democracy because it relies on the People's gaze, rather than its voice, and because its core principle of candor is intended to regulate and reform the experience of spectatorship rather than cancel it. In any case, the point to be stressed here is that Manin's theory of audience democracy is perhaps the paradigm case of the hegemonic status of the vocal model: even as Manin labels the People an audience, he seeks its empowerment as an active, autonomous, decision-making force.

The Morass of Public Opinion

One of the sharpest differences between democratic idealists of the nineteenth century and students of democracy from the last century concerns the analysis of public opinion. With few exceptions, democratic theorists in the nineteenth century understood public opinion as a simple and straightforward entity: public opinion, it was widely believed, existed in easily identifiable ways on most major issues, was generally independent of the governmental elites it sought to regulate, and could communicate preferences with a high level of precision. The most influential interpreters of nineteenth-century democracy, including Bentham, J. S. Mill, Tocqueville, Bryce, and Acton—concluded that public opinion was an extraordinarily effective and potent force. Bryce's study of America, for example, could claim: "Towering over Presidents and State governors, over Congress and State legislatures, over conventions and the vast machinery of party, public opinion stands out, in the United States, as the great source of power, the master of servants who tremble before it."[129] Given its simplicity and its potency, it was easy to conclude that public opinion was the voice of the People—the prime mechanism by which everyday citizens in their collective capacity, otherwise excluded from government, could communicate and often dictate their will to political elites. It was a matter of course, in other words, that whatever public opinion turned out to be could be interpreted as what the People wanted government to do and that, accordingly, if public opinion were ignored, so too were the People.

Over the course of the last century, however, both the simplicity and the effectiveness of public opinion have been called into question. This is especially true with regard to simplicity as there is virtually unanimous agreement among political scientists working on public opinion today that the nature of its functioning is complex and still quite uncertain. The uncertainty stems, first of all, from the fact that government's responsiveness to public opinion, the bedrock assumption of the nineteenth-century view, is now a subject of much debate—a debate that has only widened and intensified over the last two decades.[130] It stems also from the lack of confidence attached to specific empirical findings. Researchers on both sides of the responsiveness question usually emphasize the need for more study.[131] Part of what obstructs a clear understanding of the nature and power of public opinion is the fact that to whatever extent public opinion operates in a democracy, it does so in a manner much more circuitous than nineteenth-century theorists had contemplated. Accounts that vindicate the power of public opinion rely on complex models that stress the interrelation between the public, political elites, and the media, making any simple assertion about the public's control of government policy seem naïve and reductive.[132] Although many hold out the promise that future political scientists will unlock the secrets of public opinion's true functioning, it is fair to ask whether the ambiguity and uncertainty surrounding existing knowledge of public opinion are intrinsic to the very concept of public opinion itself, which, as the diffuse set of preferences not formally expressed in governmental institutions, must always suffer from a high degree of equivocality. Key's warning from a half century ago—that "to speak with precision about public opinion is a task not unlike coming to grips with the Holy Ghost"—seems no less applicable today.[133]

It is not just the simplicity of public opinion that has been called into question in the twentieth century, but its potency and overall effectiveness. While the debate over responsiveness continues, numerous recent studies have suggested that, whatever the absolute amount of correspondence between public opinion and governmental policies, the direction of this correspondence is negative: that government is moving away from, rather than toward, a greater responsiveness to the public. Increasingly, it appears that politicians elect to pursue their own policy goals in spite of public opinion or, even more disturbingly, have relied on manipulative public appeals to pursue their own aims while falsely appearing to satisfy public opinion. The capacity of special interest groups to override centrist public opinion has also been emphasized—although this too remains, characteristically, controversial.[134] Beyond these concerns of elite indifference and manipulation, there has also arisen over the course of the last half-century a greater appreciation for the intrinsic limitations hampering the overall expressivity of public opinion. For example, there is a growing awareness that public opinion's impact is confined to a few salient issues and that whatever is outside of these issues remains relatively immune from public sanction.[135] Given political elites' role in defining the agenda, there is thus a real methodological and moral difficulty of distinguishing genuine responsiveness from top-down construction of public opinion. Further, public opinion also seems to reveal itself in what Almond called "formless and plastic moods," rather than in precise articulations; and if recent work has tried to rescue the rationality of these moods, they are still far less communicative than the public opinion contemplated by nineteenth-century idealists.[136]

That public opinion is anything but simple and that its effectiveness as a regulator of governmental policy is beset by many doubts and concerns make it reasonable to call into question the traditional identification of the People with public opinion. Given the empirical difficulties of defining what public opinion is on a given matter, measuring the responsiveness of government to public opinion, and understanding the complex interrelations by which public opinion is formed—and given the centuries-old moral dilemma in representative democracy about whether public opinion even ought to be obeyed by government—there is a real danger that any equation of the People with public opinion runs the risk of making popular power provisional, always capable of being suspended, and hence permanently uncertain. This is not to say that public opinion is not important—that political scientists ought not continue to work to understand it or even find ways of making its impact more pronounced within contemporary democracy—but only that it may be wiser to reserve the concept of the People, the collective interest that defines what everyday citizens share by virtue of their everydayness, for a political ambition less prone to manipulation, confusion, and effective neutralization than the ambition that public opinion regulate governmental output. This at least is the path I take in defending and developing the plebiscitarian account of a nonvocal, ocular paradigm of popular power.

But before returning to the ocular model of plebiscitary democracy, it is important to stress here that political scientists have altogether resisted the disidentification of the People with public opinion. While this might be expected from those still committed to traditional accounts of public opinion, what is interesting—and, again, indicative of the hegemonic function of the vocal model—is that political scientists most skeptical of the role of public opinion in contemporary mass democracy have still labored under the assumption that the collective interest of the People must be defined in terms of public opinion. That is to say, those who have done the most to upset the traditional understanding of public opinion as a straightforward and highly effective device of popular empowerment have continued nonetheless to treat public opinion as the central way the People are empowered in a democracy.

This paradoxical tendency can be seen most clearly in what is still probably the most important study on public opinion to date, V. O. Key's seminal text, *Public Opinion and American Democracy*. Key recognizes all the major reasons for doubting public opinion's role as an "initiating entity" of the popular will: its dependence on leadership, its limitation to the small segments of the population that actually have opinions, its tendency to be reactive, binary, and inarticulate.[137] As a result of these factors, Key argues against "simplistic conceptions, such as the notion that in some way public opinion exudes from the mass of men and produces guidelines for governmental action." He likewise admits the substantial and ineliminable discretion enjoyed by political elites: "The generality of public preference, the low intensity of the opinions of many people, the low level of political animosities of substantial sectors of the public, the tortuousness of the process of translation of disapproval of specific policies into electoral reprisal, and many other factors point to the existence of a wide latitude for the exercise of creative leadership."[138]

And yet, when it comes to evaluating the moral meaning of democracy, Key can only fall back on the familiar wish that government respond to the popular will as manifested in public opinion and—most paradoxically of all—conclude that this wish is generally fulfilled in mass democracies like the United States. Key asserts that "governmental operations" are "in the main in accord with [citizens'] preferences."[139] A great deal of Key's confidence in this regard comes from his concept of latent opinion—that is, the opinions that exist passively in the minds of citizens but are not activated politically. Politicians are both constrained by latent opinion (they know that there is a "permissive consensus" beyond which they do not dare cross) and take latent opinion into account when they anticipate how their chosen policies will sit with the populace. This line of reasoning allows Key to find in the very silence of the People a kind of tacit consent for government policies.[140] Yet even here Key is also aware of the fundamental limitations of latent opinion: specifically the sizable leeway it gives leaders for carrying out specific decisions and policies. Most latent opinion is never aroused, is of low intensity, and thus is unlikely to have consequences for politicians. And even to the extent such opinion is brought to bear on politicians, there is still a large amount of discretion for officeholders as to "what action they will take and which sector of the attentive public they will heed."[141]

In fact, it turns out that Key's appeal to the ultimate responsiveness of government to public opinion is as much a faith and a wish informing his analysis as it is a conclusion emanating from it. Key concludes his study by arguing that even if public opinion often is vague or nonexistent, democracy depends on the belief that public opinion matters: "Fundamental is a regard for public opinion, a belief that in some way or another it should prevail....The belief must be widespread that public opinion, at least in the long run, affects the course of public action."[142] Most surprisingly, Key is forced to argue that what in the final analysis underwrites the power of public opinion in mass democracy is leaders' own honesty and willingness to be guided by it. Ethical leaders must possess "fidelity in the attempt to give definition to vague popular aspirations and in the search for technical means for their effectuation" and must avoid "calculating manipulation of opinion."[143] The integrity of popular self-rule thus depends on the leaders, not the People: "This legitimization of the view that the preferences of the governed shall be accorded weight by the governors constitutes the moral basis of popular government, an ethical imperative that in mature democracies is converted into consistent habits and patterns of action among those in places of authority and leadership."[144]

To define the People's control of politicians in terms of politicians' willingness to be controlled is certainly an unsatisfying normative conclusion. What explains this tortured moral reasoning is Key's inability to break out of the vocal model: his assumption that "the preferences of the governed shall be accorded weight by the governors constitutes the moral basis of popular government."[145] Rather than reconstruct and redefine the moral meaning of democratic government in a manner consistent with the many difficulties besetting public opinion, Key in the end can only return to a traditional conception of democratic power that understands public opinion, however inappropriately, as an independent, self-directing, and potent force in mass democracy.

The basic structure of Key's moral stance—specifically, the way his revelation of the many difficulties undermining the rationality, priority, existence, and expressivity of public opinion in no way upsets his assumption that the People is to be equated with public opinion and democracy is to be defined as a system in which public opinion to a meaningful extent rules—repeats itself in a variety of more recent contexts. First of all, it can be found among purveyors of the so-called *miracle of aggregation* who readily admit that *individual* opinions are plagued by instability, nonattitudes, and other problems, but argue that when opinion is aggregated at the collective level its results are stable and rational and, hence, can rightfully be equated with the will of the People on a variety of major policy issues.[146] Leaving aside the ways in which the claim to rationality has been debated and the fact that the successful aggregation of opinion does nothing to make it more potent, there is still the problem that this approach defines the People in a way that is explicitly alien from the political experiences that tend to characterize the everyday citizens who constitute it. That is to say, the admission that everyday citizens do not have meaningful opinions on most issues ought to suggest the moral value of redefining the People as something other than opinion. Yet, for expositors of the miracle of aggregation such a circumstance only motivates the search for a way to recover the conceptualization of the People in terms of substantive, legislative preferences. Insofar as one accepts the principle that the People ought to define the collective interest of everyday citizens in their every-dayness, such a recovery must be seen as falling substantially short of the miraculous.

Second, this tendency for the critique of public opinion not to disturb the definition of both the People and democracy in terms of public opinion can be found among deliberative theorists. These theorists are some of the most forceful opponents of public opinion as it usually functions in mass democracy: the opinion generated from opinion polls and the poll-ster democracy that such opinion generates. Yet, while they oppose exist-ing public opinion as superficial, uninformed, and prone to manipulation, these theorists argue that *deliberative opinion*—the opinion that is formed through face-to-face deliberative exchanges between citizens—could legitimately function as a proxy of the People's voice. Deliberative polling, which polls citizens' opinions only after they have been afforded a chance to deliberate on the issue at hand, may produce results that are more rational than normal public opinion (although this is a matter of ongoing debate), but linking the People to the results of such polls seems unwise both because of its exclusionary aspect (deliberative contexts are highly exclusive ones) and, more pressingly, because deliberative polling, like the earlier excitement over the discovery of scientific polling in the 1930s, has a strongly utopian aspect to it.[147] In the interval between the past, when it was believed that scientific polling satisfactorily revealed public opinion, and the future, when deliberative polling will succeed in doing so, lies the present moment in which no dependable mechanism of formulating the People's genuine voice has yet taken root and found significant institu-tionalization. By holding out the promise of a more deliberative future, the deliberative critics recognize but do not face the dysfunctions besetting the People's voice and the popular *silence* that effectively results from them. This silence needs to be heard.

Finally, the tendency to at once critique yet embrace the effectiveness of public opinion in democracy—and to continue to equate popular power with the power of public opinion despite doubts about its independence, existence, and rationality—can be located in the remarkably low standard that has come to be accepted for measuring whether governmental policies are responsive to public opinion. Whereas nineteenth-century observers believed public opinion to be the supreme force in the emergent democra-cies they analyzed, today the most optimistic examinations of the power of public opinion usually find its significance limited to a minority of issues. Burstein, for example, concludes that while public opinion may influence three-quarters of public issues, it meaningfully affects how is-sues are decided in only one-third of the cases—and yet this result is taken to be supportive of the general effectiveness and potency of public opinion in American democracy.[148] One could easily imagine an alternate interpretation of these findings that emphasized the disempowerment of public opinion in contemporary democracy and, accordingly, the disempowerment of the People conceived as voice.

To be clear, the point is not to deny that public opinion plays a meaningful role in contemporary mass democracy: that leaders are acutely aware of it, that they are compelled to respond to it in various ways, that it sometimes helps determine policies, and that it therefore marks an important means by which those inside government must take into consideration the preferences of those on the outside. Rather, the key question I have tried to raise is whether it makes sense to equate public opinion with the People and to assume that if public opinion is empowered in a democracy then so too is the People. Given the various difficulties surrounding the measurement, existence, rationality, independence, and potency of public opinion in mass democracy, any linkage of the People with public opinion threatens to make popular power too uncertain, too complex, and too susceptible to circumvention. Moreover, when one considers that public opinion is never entirely public, but only reflective of a fraction of those whom it measures, it likewise seems reasonable to reserve the collective concept of the People for an experience like spectatorship, which is more genuinely collective.

Interestingly, such a disidentification of the People with public opinion can be located, albeit in a pretheoretical and almost subconscious way, in the widespread distaste in contemporary mass democracy for politicians who obviously and slavishly seek to follow and obey public opinion. On the surface, this seems odd—especially in light of traditional democratic ideology that seeks the empowerment of the People precisely through public opinion's capacity to control elected leaders. Why would the People worry about politicians who listen too closely to public opinion? The usual interpretation for this phenomenon is a remarkably undemocratic one: namely, that there is a public preference for strong leaders who will take personal responsibility for the direction of the polity and not buckle to temporary fluctuations in public mood. What seems equally likely, however, is the explanation that the public's hesitance about public opinion represents a flash of awareness, however faint, that traditional democratic ideology does not hold: that the People is misidentified ontologically as voice and that, accordingly, democracy is itself misunderstood if its only critical aspiration is to have government respect and respond to whatever voices emerge from below.

3.5 An Alternate Ontology of Popular Power

Over the course of this chapter I have sought both to establish that there has been a dominant approach toward understanding the nature of the People and its power in mass democracy—namely, the vocal model—and to expose the limitations, contradictions, and ever-growing doubts about the adequacy of this paradigm. Whereas political scientists are increasingly aware of these difficulties, few have allowed themselves to look elsewhere than the vocal model for a conceptualization of popular empowerment. A great deal of this reluctance stems, to be sure, from the assumption that there simply is no alternative to the vocal model: that popular power *must* be interpreted as an expressive force realizing itself in the substance of norms, laws, and policies. The aim of the following chapters will be to overcome any sense that the vocal paradigm, however flawed, is an inescapable or inevitable assumption of any responsible democratic theory and to show that it is possible—and indeed preferable—to think about the power of the People in *ocular* terms.

4

The Concept of Plebiscitary
Democracy: Past, Present,
and Future

Live with your century, but do not be its creature.
—Friedrich Schiller

4.1 Toward a Theory of Plebiscitary Democracy

It is indicative of the curious mixture of suspicion and inattention that characterizes prevailing attitudes toward mass democracy that the leading theoretical construct by which mass democracy has been examined to date—plebiscitary democracy—is almost universally considered a profanity by democratic theorists committed to an ethical understanding of political life. For such theorists, the concept of the plebiscitary serves as a shorthand for a sham form of democracy that is nondeliberative and nonparticipatory and mired in manipulation by conniving elites.[1] In this shorthand usage, *plebiscitary* often connotes totalitarian or proto-totalitarian tendencies.[2] When so conceived, plebiscitary democracy is considered not as a full-fledged theory, but as a historical condition that, like a black hole, threatens to devour "real," vibrant forms of democratic existence. That one might refer to oneself as a *plebiscitarian*—akin to a pluralist or deliberative democrat—appears to most democratic theorists as absurd. Accordingly, to date there has been no master theoretician of plebiscitary democracy, analogous to a Dahl for pluralism or a Rawls or Habermas for deliberative democracy, whose work encapsulates the meaning and promise of a plebiscitary regime. One looks in vain for book-length works about plebiscitary democracy, although this deficit has now begun to be somewhat remedied.[3]

Indeed, plebiscitary democracy is a nascent theory that has yet to mature. It exists more in hints and suggestions than in formal theorizing. Its current state can be likened to that of deliberative democracy a half century ago—a time well after the foundational contributions of Aristotle,

Burke, and Mill, yet prior to the formal theorization of public reason in Rawls, Habermas, and the many other deliberative theorists of today. Or, it can be compared to the state of the pluralist account of democracy circa 1900, when the seminal analyses of polyarchic structures had already been undertaken by constitutional framers like Madison and Guizot, but had not yet been condensed and consolidated into political scientific concepts by Laski, Truman, and above all Dahl. Another way of putting this is that plebiscitary democracy, in its current condition, has its theorists but is not yet a theory. We know that Max Weber, with his highly unusual account of *plebiscitary leader democracy*, was the first formal theorist of plebiscitary democracy and that his successors, Carl Schmitt and Joseph Schumpeter, can also be described as plebiscitarians. And we know, further, that the history of political thought prior to the twentieth century contains proto-plebiscitary contributions, most notably Shakespeare's Roman plays, which were of special interest to Weber. But these and other sources of plebiscitarian thought remain unusually disordered and disunified. This has had the result that while we know what a deliberative democrat or a pluralist is, we do not yet know what it would mean to describe oneself as a *plebiscitarian*—what commitments, struggles, likes, and dislikes are implicit in such an appellation. But that there is such a thing as a plebiscitarian democrat—that plebiscitary democracy can rightfully be considered a full-fledged theory of democracy, with its own unique set of institutional possibilities and moral values, and that it is an especially compelling model under contemporary conditions of mass democracy—is precisely the claim I wish to defend and elaborate here.

This chapter is organized as follows. In section 4.2, I review the standard, purely pejorative interpretation of plebiscitary democracy that has arisen among contemporary political scientists: the understanding of plebiscitarianism as a politics of diremption. Against this reductive and negative interpretation of the meaning of plebiscitarianism, in section 4.3 I return to the theoretical origins of plebiscitarianism and recover a forgotten, highly innovative, ethical component of plebiscitary democracy: namely, an *ocular model* of popular power whose basic features I introduced in chapter 1. In the final section, 4.4, I turn to two of Shakespeare's Roman plays, *Coriolanus* and *Julius Caesar*, as concrete examples that illustrate the ocular model in action and that demonstrate the moral logic for wishing to revive a plebiscitarian alternative within contemporary democratic thought. Chapter 5 continues the reclamation of plebiscitary democracy as a viable school of democratic thought, defending the relevance of Weber's theory of plebiscitary leader democracy as well as analyzing the reception of this theory in the work of Schmitt and Schumpeter.

4.2 The Usual Understanding of Plebiscitary Democracy: A Politics of Diremption

That of all the concepts of the political lexicon *plebiscitary* should come to denote a politics of diremption is not without a certain irony. After all, the word's most literal meaning refers to the plebiscite, which itself literally means the "decision of the People." This etymology would seem to link the concept of the plebiscitary to a politics of popular activism in which the People plays a direct and meaningful role in political decision making. Yet, while this literal rendering still persists in some quarters, so that plebiscitary democracy is occasionally treated as a synonym for direct democracy, it is nonetheless the case that, in a peculiar reversal of this original definition, the concept of the plebiscitary has increasingly come to have a virtually opposite meaning: not the politics of popular decision making, but rather a sham democracy in which popular decision making has become superficial, merely formal, and illusory.[4] Certainly one important cause of this reversal has to do with a sobering reassessment of the democratic potential of the plebiscite itself, whether because it has been too closely linked with totalitarian abuse or because even in a liberal society it is highly susceptible to irrationality and manipulation.[5] Yet, the counterliteral rendering of the plebiscitary—so that it refers to a fallen democracy bereft of genuine popular decision making—extends well beyond any reevaluation of the plebiscite. It is as if the disappointment over the democratic potential of the referendum has been generalized, so that the plebiscitary has come to indicate a disappointing kind of democracy: a democracy that is more fictive than real and fails to provide the autonomy, equality, and inclusion promised by classical democratic theorists. This polemical usage is certainly the one employed by democratic theorists of a participatory or deliberative stamp, who use the concept to denote the paltriness of a democracy of mere voting and public opinion polls—a "fig leaf," pollster democracy insufficiently grounded in rational discourse and active engagement from the citizenry.[6] The diremptive, counterliteral rendering of the plebiscitary is also evinced by presidential scholars, who use *plebiscitary* to refer to the distinctive tools and resources available to contemporary politicians in modern mass democracies and to a description of the nature of the leadership embodied by such politicians. Thus there has arisen the concept of the "plebiscitary president"—which designates a kind of president who, far from being chosen by the People and having his or her policies dictated from below, is unprecedentedly free from popular decision making, whether because of a bold assertion of executive independence or because public opinion is aggressively manipulated and managed from above.[7]

What unites these counterliteral, negative usages of the plebiscitary is not only that they point to various ways by which ostensible democratic practice might bypass genuine and rigorous standards of popular decision making, but that they all intend to describe a political reality definitive of the *contemporary* world. Indeed, one final usage of the plebiscitary—and one that encompasses these other, polemical variants—occurs when the concept is used to define *the most current stage* of representative government and to distinguish it from earlier stages.[8] While there are, of course, some differences in the way *plebiscitary* has been defined, those who treat it as the latest stage of representative government tend to emphasize the same five general characteristics.

First, plebiscitary politics are *conducted through the mass media*—such as newspapers, radio, television, and internet—and not in the immediate context of face-to-face contact. Plebiscitary politics are thus especially reliant upon appearance and the cultivation of images.[9] The now familiar picture of a parliamentary leader making a speech before an empty legislative assembly, but televised to a mass public, is a fecund symbol of the plebiscitary. The mass media also make it possible for leaders and politicians to contact the public directly, independent of party and platform.[10] In parliamentary states, this means that the site of representation shifts from parliament and other governmental institutions to the mass media, for it is here where public images are constructed and popularity won. Under plebiscitary conditions, political support is gained and maintained less through the expansion of party membership than through well-planned media messages that garner public support. This process accelerates the exclusion of everyday citizens from the practice of mass politics, since substantial resources and organization are required to engage in media-based political marketing.[11]

Plebiscitary democracy refers not just to the kinds of resources available to presidents and other politicians, but to the transformation, and indeed elevation, of leadership itself. Thus, the second characteristic of plebiscitary politics is the *personalization of politics*. The personalization of politics is a function of numerous factors, including the capacity of the mass media to enable a seemingly direct connection of the leader with the mass of ordinary citizens. As Manin has pointed out, "Television confers particular salience and vividness to the individuality of the candidates. In a sense, it resurrects the face-to-face character of the representative link that marked the first form of representative government"—with the important difference, of course, that everyday political experience is only *virtually* face-to-face and, in fact, is marked by the spatial and temporal separation of the emitter and receiver of political messages.[12] The personalization of politics also stems from the unprecedented complexity of government and the heightened degree to which decision-making contexts arise quickly and unpredictably. This has the result that it becomes rational that the "personal *trust* that the candidate inspires is a more adequate basis of selection than the evaluation of plans for future actions."[13] Accordingly, elections in plebiscitary democracy depend increasingly on intangible personality and character issues and less on specific platforms.[14] This means that the party is more and more a machine at the service of the politicians who make individual appeals in order to win and maintain power. Moreover, the personalization of politics can be found in what has been termed the *presidentialization of leadership*—the fact that, within government, the single individual of the prime minister or president is the most powerful institution within the state.[15] This can be seen, for example, in the fact that the cabinet, which in most European countries had been subordinate to the parliament, is increasingly responsible to the chief executive.[16]

Third, plebiscitary politics refers to the growth of a *discretionary power* among leaders within contemporary representative systems. To be sure, there has always been a substantial discretionary power within modern representative states. Locke's notion of prerogative assigned to the executive the right to determine all specific questions that could not be determined by general laws. And later theorists of representative government rarely made appeal to naïve notions that the representatives would constitute a mirror image of the represented or that they would be constrained by binding mandates. Yet the discretionary power embodied in plebiscitary politics exceeds the kind contemplated by these earlier models. For one thing, within plebiscitary politics, it is no longer just a formal, constitutional kind of executive prerogative that is at stake. Rather, it is increasingly expected, if not accepted, that leaders have their own wills, not just to respond to particulars that cannot be deduced from general laws, but also to take an active role in framing policy, defining the agenda, and making broad, often irreversible decisions such as those pertaining to war and foreign policy.[17] Przeworski, Stokes, and Manin, for example, explain that it is definitive of plebiscitary politics that leaders have their own goals, interests, and values and that they make use of their time in office to undertake their own endeavors.[18] The discretionary power of leaders is also augmented by certain sociohistorical trends. For instance, since the 1970s various empirical studies have demonstrated that it is increasingly difficult to explain election results as a function of the socioeconomic and cultural makeup of the electorate.[19] Relatedly, issue-based voting seems unable to explain electoral behavior under plebiscitary conditions.[20] This means that what are considered the main issues in political life are themselves in flux, and the leader has leeway to determine what sorts of cleavages to emphasize and exploit and, thus, can shape the agenda. Further, the discretionary power is augmented by the heightened sense in contemporary politics that the issues a leader will face while in office will tend to be new and unpredictable—and that this rapid pace of historical change enables greater freedom from the electorate.[21]

Fourth, it is not just that leaders under plebiscitary conditions enjoy discretion to pursue their own aims. What is also intended by the designation *plebiscitary* is a kind of politics in which leaders shape and even manufacture the public opinion and majoritarian will that allegedly hold them accountable. While the leader's initiative in this regard is not total, it is still extremely important. As Kösösényi describes it, what is distinctive about "leader democracy" (which should be seen as a synonym for plebiscitary democracy) is that "rival politicians attempt to obtain greater support not by accommodating the political preferences of the electorate but by trying to manipulate and produce electoral preferences themselves. The active players of politics are not the constituents but the politicians. Constituents are *re*active. This is because in the model of leader democracy political action is based neither on truth nor on interests but on opinion and resolve."[22] Politicians set out to produce—or, more cynically, manipulate—public support for themselves and their policies. The plebiscitary model thus stands opposed to the economic theory of democracy, which, from Bentham to Downs, has presupposed the electorate to embody a set of preexisting and well-established preferences and opinions waiting to be translated into policy.[23] For an incumbent, this means making decisions and implementing policies and, *only afterward*, defending them before the public.

Finally, these four aspects of plebiscitary politics—the mediatization of political communication, the personalization of political power, the discretion of leadership, and the creative power of the leader vis-à-vis public opinion and the popular will—suggest a fifth feature that to a large extent summarizes the entire meaning of plebiscitary democracy, at least as it is usually understood in its pejorative sense. This is that the People's *voice*— whether in its official manifestation as the majority's electoral choice or its informal function as public opinion—is rendered superficial and to a large degree fictive.[24] The People's capacity to voice itself and thereby autonomously express its values, preferences, and opinions is seriously undermined under plebiscitary conditions. It is this feature more than any other that explains why democratic theorists are so resistant to understanding plebiscitary democracy as anything other than a profanity in political theory and why, accordingly, the concept of plebiscitarianism receives so little attention among democratic theorists committed to an ethical understanding of political life. As an account of how the voice of the People comes to be effectively silenced in contemporary mass democracy, plebiscitarianism would appear to have little to say about the political experiences of everyday citizens—the *great many* on behalf of whom democracy, as its very etymology attests, is supposed to find its deepest and most fundamental purpose.

Yet it is a mistake, I argue, to jettison the concept of plebiscitary democracy. For one thing, the five aspects I have just outlined have an undeniable descriptive importance. Like it or not, plebiscitarian conditions are the distinctive conditions of *our* politics. While it is always tempting and to a certain extent unavoidable to transact in democratic ideals derived from a classical past, as an age with more hands-on experience with democracy than any other, it is incumbent on today's democrats to confront democracy in terms reflective of the unique circumstances that have shaped its modern rebirth. And this means overcoming the fetishization of fifth-century B.C. Athens or eighteenth-century Philadelphia and confronting democracy in a way that gives center stage to the utterly exceptional, if admittedly fraught, demographic, technological, and social circumstances that have guided democratic practice since the twentieth century. In an ideal world, plebiscitary conditions would not exist. But because they do, they justify working out a democratic theory that can operate in light of them.

Of course, if all plebiscitary democracy had to offer was a better description of contemporary political reality, there would be little to recommend it. Mere description, without any delineation of political *ideals*, is blind to the reality that part of what democracy signifies is precisely a regime widely understood to be morally superior to its rivals and something that injects moral ideals into political life. However, the key argument I want to defend is that embedded within the tradition of plebiscitary democracy—buried in the literary and theoretical origins of plebiscitarianism—is an ethical component. This ethical component does not deny the five features I have outlined, but it does offer some way of structuring democratic progressivism within them. At the most general level, the ethical contribution consists in grounding democracy on the *eyes of the People*, as opposed to the extremely widespread assumption that democracy must refer ultimately to the People's voice. Properly understood, plebiscitary democracy is not just a negative critique of the voice of the People, but a positive theory that translates popular power from a vocal to an ocular register. This means that plebiscitary democracy is misconceived merely as a sociological account of how contemporary politics effectively cancels the People's voice. It is also a political philosophy constitutive of a nonvocal, *ocular* kind of democracy.

4.3 Plebiscitary Democracy's Ocular Model of Popular Power

In order to discover and elaborate this ethical dimension of plebiscitarianism, it is necessary to get beyond the reductive, purely pejorative understanding of plebiscitary democracy employed by contemporary political scientists and return to the origins of the concept. This means revisiting the original and still the most important theorist of plebiscitary democracy, Max Weber, as well as the contributions of his successors Carl Schmitt and Joseph Schumpeter. It also means examining certain key works from prior to the twentieth century that anticipate present-day plebiscitarianism, most of all Shakespeare's Roman plays (which influenced Weber) and Benjamin Constant's theory of public inquiry. These various figures and fragments can be designated as contributions to a theory of plebiscitary democracy in the sense that they reflect much of what has been said about plebiscitarianism in regard to the derogatory, diremptive connotation just described. They are highly skeptical about the meaning and scope of popular decision making in mass democracy. They challenge the extent to which elections and public opinion serve to make leaders responsive or accountable to the popular will. Accordingly, they recognize leadership—in the sense of a select group of political elites with immense, creative decisionmaking discretion—as an inescapable feature of modern democratic life. However, as is less often appreciated, they also point the way toward the development of an ocular approach to democracy. In this and the remaining chapters of the book, I aim to reclaim for the contemporary study of democracy the overlooked insights of these important though often much maligned democratic thinkers. And yet this reclamation project is not without limits. It must be admitted that although Weber and the others must be seen as key sources of instruction and inspiration for a revitalized account of plebiscitary democracy, the incompleteness, imprecision, and occasional misdirection of their democratic theory mean that the recovery of an ethical conception of plebiscitary democracy cannot consist in a simple presentation of their thought, but must ultimately rely on their analyses as building blocks for a more comprehensive and theoretically precise normative contribution.

On the basis of this methodology, which simultaneously relies on the philosophical and literary originators of plebiscitary democracy, yet looks to go beyond them, it can be said that plebiscitary democracy contains an ethical component insofar as it presents a novel account of the nature of popular power within modern mass representative democracy. Plebiscitary democracy can be understood as a radical alternative to the traditional and still dominant vocal model of popular power that I analyzed in the last chapter and which has three sub-elements: that the object of popular power is *law*; that the organ of popular power is the People's *decision*; and that the critical ideal of popular empowerment is *autonomy*. Plebiscitary democracy's ocular model can be seen in contrast to each of these three elements.

First, with regard to the *object* of popular power, whereas the traditional, vocal paradigm understands the ultimate manifestation of popular power to be the set of substantive regulations defining the conditions of social existence, the ocular paradigm recognizes *the leaders who are watched* as the ultimate medium wherein popular empowerment makes its impact felt. That is to say, according to the plebiscitary model, popular power takes as its object not so much the content of decisions as the public life of the decision makers. With Schumpeter, for example, who defines democracy in terms of a "competitive struggle" among elites for power, the introduction of the People into a polity's political system impacts not the laws but the experience of those in power: that they must be regularly subjected to the risk, uncertainty, and vulnerability to attack that are inherent in democratic electoral processes.[25] Likewise, for Weber, who understands the People in mass democracy less as an electorate than as a charismatic community (i.e., as the public whose attention and recognition are a necessary concomitant to any individual's claim of charismatic authority), the ultimate register of the People's effectuality inheres, not in the substance of legislation, but in the personality and comportment of the leader: specifically, in the degree to which the leader takes on charismatic traits. Building on both Schumpeter's and Weber's insights, a theory of plebiscitary democracy develops this idea of the personal terminus of popular power under the plebiscitary model. A modern–day plebiscitarian, I argue, judges the degree of democratization, not by the extent to which governmental decisions reflect the input of the electorate, but rather by the degree to which politicians and other decision makers have the personal conditions of their public life (i.e., the nature of their publicity) disciplined and in a certain sense controlled by the People.

That popular power takes as its object the leaders who are watched rather than the laws that are written points toward the *second* dimension of contrast between the vocal and ocular models of popular power. Normally, as conceived according to a vocal paradigm, the organ of popular empowerment is the People's *decision*: whether in the form of *choosing* whom to elect, *expressing* the preferences, opinions, and values toward which leaders ought to be responsive, or *making judgments* in elections and in public opinion that hold leaders accountable for their actions. The traditional view, in other words, is that the People are empowered insofar as its voice is empowered—and its voice is empowered through the act of decision. Under the ocular model, it is not the People's voice but its sight that serves as the site of popular empowerment. Accordingly, whereas the decision represents an empowered form of voice, the People's *gaze* represents an empowered form of vision. If the decision indicates that form of voice that is binding, explicit, imperative, clear, and authoritative, the gaze indicates that type of sight that partakes of supervision, inspection, examination, and scrutiny. Although the People experiences various forms of visualization, it only engages in the empowered form of sight that is the gaze when it can both observe the few without being observed in turn by them and when what it gets to see is not preprogrammed or rehearsed but constitutive of a genuine type of surveillance. The ocular manifestation of power is something political science and the study of democracy have not sufficiently studied or acknowledged. But this is precisely the virtue of such contributions as Shakespeare's Roman plays, which, as I shall explain in section 4.4, explore the difference between empowered and disempowered forms of popular spectatorship. And it is likewise the virtue of Weber's highly innovative theory of democracy, plebiscitary leader democracy, which is probably the first, if admittedly incomplete, theoretical treatment of the People in terms of its gaze. As I will make clear in the next chapter, both in Weber's analysis of the ancient charismatic community before which the biblical prophets appeared and in his application of this ancient model to his theory of modern mass democracy, the People, despite various deprivations and abuses, is the beneficiary of an empowered form of looking in which it gets to survey otherwise powerful leaders under special conditions of heightened public risk. Together, both Shakespeare and Weber (as well as other plebiscitarians who follow them) explode any understanding of spectatorship as an undifferentiated experience about which the political scientist might make a simple, comprehensive moral evaluation. There are different forms of spectatorship: some represent the empowerment of the viewer, while others do not. This recognition, though remarkably simple and straightforward, has not penetrated into democratic theory. Democratic theory lacks precisely such a notion of an empowered form of looking, or *gaze*. A plebiscitarian account of democracy seeks to remedy this deficit.

These first two features of the ocular model—that it locates the object of popular power in the leader rather than the law, and that it empowers the People's vision rather than its voice—points to a third line of difference: that pertaining to the critical ideal at stake in a plebiscitary account of democracy. Whereas within the vocal model of popular power this principle is the People's control of the means of lawmaking, or *autonomy*—that is, the People's participation in the authorship of the substantive norms and conditions shaping public life—under the ocular model this ideal is defined, at the most general level, as the People's *control of the means of publicity*. In other words, the ideal that gives shape to democratic reform pursued from a plebiscitarian perspective, that specifies both what popular empowerment causes and what causes popular empowerment, is the ideal that the People, not its leadership, controls the conditions under which leaders appear on the public stage. The People's control of the means of publicity requires that leaders not hide from public view, but rather that they be compelled to come before the People in frequent and regular public appearances. But it is not enough that the leader merely appear. What is also required is that the People can be said to control the conditions of the leader's appearance. As we know, most of the time leaders are themselves in control of the conditions of their publicity. They decide the timing, location, and duration of their appearance. And they control the outcome of the event insofar as it is scripted, rehearsed, or otherwise carefully orchestrated. What the People's possession of the means of publicity entails is a breaking down of leaders' control of their own public image making. We find something like the popular control of the means of publicity in those rare yet vital institutional practices that have arisen with mass democracy: the press conference, the leadership debate, the public inquiry, and the British practice of question time.

However, as these very examples make clear, the People's control of the means of publicity is a *negative* ideal: it is realized not in the People's actual direction of the precise conditions under which leaders appear (which would be impossible because the People lacks both a unified insight about what format any particular public appearance ought to take and the effective means of ensuring compliance), but rather in leaders not controlling these conditions. I call this negative ideal the principle of *candor*— by which I mean not primarily the psychological norm of sincerity, but first and foremost the institutional norm that a leader not be in control of the conditions of his or her publicity. As any observer of contemporary mass politics can attest, candor is a scarce commodity. But the fact that candor is the exception rather than the norm in no way disqualifies its status as a critical ideal—as an articulation of the direction democratic reform should take and as the goal toward which progressive energies ought to be devoted.

The ideal of candor is the great unelaborated ethical commitment of plebiscitary democracy. Although Weber does not directly thematize it, within his theory it is nonetheless a necessary condition of any attempt by a leader to generate charismatic authority.[26] Certainly, the modern political figures who inspired Weber's theory, Gladstone in Britain and perhaps also Andrew Johnson in the United States, were innovators precisely insofar as they subjected themselves to unprecedented forms of candor. Schumpeter's noneconomic notion of competition (the existential competition leaders regularly undergo as a result of electoral challenge), which he unfortunately did not fully develop, could be read as the norm that democracy requires those in power to be forced into conditions of candor. And candor is a commitment that likewise informs pre-twentieth-century anticipations of plebiscitarianism, whether Constant's proposal for widely expanded public inquiries that would bring political leaders before the public under inherently unpredictable conditions of heightened risk, or Shakespeare's Roman plays, which as I shall presently examine, define what distinguishes the republican *candid-acy* of Coriolanus from the imperial one of Caesar.

These, then, are the three main shifts at stake in plebiscitary democracy. They inform the reclamation of plebiscitary democracy as a legitimate paradigm of democratic thought. And they shape both what is recovered from the various figures to which I turn and what is criticized and resisted in their thought. Before confronting the formal theorists of plebiscitary democracy in the next chapter, it is appropriate to begin with Shakespeare. A comparison of two of his Roman plays, *Coriolanus* and *Julius Caesar*, not only documents these three aspects of ocular democracy with uncommon insight and clarity, but also provides an excellent, if preliminary, indication of the moral commitments justifying the shift from a vocal to an ocular model of popular empowerment.

4.4 Shakespeare and the Candid Candidate: Coriolanus versus Caesar

The selection of Shakespeare's plays is by no means arbitrary. If plebiscitary democracy (as a regime distinct from both direct and conventional representative democracy) begins to find explicit *theorization* only in the twentieth century—and here only partially and without full elaboration—the *dramatization* of plebiscitary conditions, and especially of a plebiscitary conception of popular power, is much older. Shakespeare's Roman plays are perhaps the most suggestive documentations of plebiscitary politics prior to the twentieth century. *Coriolanus* in particular is remarkable in that it presents a nontraditional account of democracy—that is, one not grounded on the value of popular self-legislation. Weber knew *Coriolanus* well.[27] This is not surprising, since the play illustrates the central meaning of plebiscitary democracy: the reinterpretation of popular power so that it no longer relates primarily to the People's vocal capacity to enunciate, express, and determine the laws and norms governing public life, but rather involves the empowerment of the People in its capacity as a spectator. If one accepts that literature is not simply fictional, but often capable of presenting reality, both physical and moral, with a superior clarity and directness, then Shakespeare offers what is probably the best introduction to the ethical component of plebiscitary democracy.

For these reasons it is worth considering two of Shakespeare's Roman plays, *Julius Caesar* and *Coriolanus*. As many commentators have observed, the two plays taken together are a study in the political corruption of the Roman people, tracing their fall from a relatively noncorrupt condition in the fifth century B.C. (the setting of *Coriolanus*) into the virtual total corruption in which they appear in *Julius Caesar*.[28] This judgment is surely correct, and it mirrors the interpretation of historians of Roman politics, from Sallust to Machiavelli, who have made similar judgments about Rome's moral decline. However, what is less often recognized is that this story of political corruption, as Shakespeare tells it, takes place under the horizon of an ocular, rather than vocal, understanding of popular power. After all, in *both* plays, the People has little *decisional* power to determine laws, let alone to enunciate substantive opinions about norms and policies. Thus in both plays we see a clear devaluation, if not denigration, of the People's voice. A metaphor running repeatedly through both works is the People's *bad breath*, an affliction that symbolizes a malfunction of the People's oral capacity to speak in a coherent and autonomous fashion.[29] In *Julius Caesar*, the People is presented as idle (I.i.32–55), inarticulate, and "tongue-tied" (I.i.62), confined to expressing itself through unstructured shouts rather than through the subtle and articulate speech of legislation, and, most of all, fickle and hopelessly susceptible to the reckless manipulation of demagogues (III.iii.4–38). But this is just as much the case in *Coriolanus*, where the People is inherently unreliable and variable—described as "the many-headed multitude" (II.iii.16–17)—so that Coriolanus can castigate it, exclaiming: "With every minute you do change a mind" (I.i.181). Unable to direct itself, it is prone to apathy and indecision. Hence Coriolanus accuses the People of liking neither peace nor war (I.i.166–170). In both plays, then, we witness a situation in which the People's actual decisions are few and superficial. Indeed, it is difficult to assign any genuine choice to the People. Shakespeare deconstructs the intentionality of the People, so it is really impossible to say whether, in *Julius Caesar*, for example, it does or does not favor elevating Caesar to emperor or, following Caesar's death, whether its interests lie more with Brutus or Antony. And, in *Coriolanus*, the question of whether the People really decides to elevate Coriolanus to consul—and, later, whether it genuinely elects to strip him of his powers—is equally opaque. The existence of a popular will that autonomously expresses interests or insights is compromised both because the People wavers violently from one position to the other and because the motivation underlying such wavering results not from any internal determination or deliberation among the People itself, but rather stems from outward suggestions by statesmen and conniving demagogues.[30] Shakespeare suggests that any effort to locate the true opinion of the People is misguided from the start, since it is grounded on an ontological mistake about the nature of the People's being. The People does not take the form of substantive opinions, values, and interests waiting to realize themselves in law and policies; rather, it is through the faculty of vision—and the potential critical requirements that a visual field might place on those who appear within it—that the People most clearly reveals and experiences its power.

And it is likewise vis-à-vis this ocular dimension that the story of the Roman People's fall into political corruption plays itself out. In *Coriolanus*, a play that presents the People in its prelapsarian state, we find remarkable documentation of a well-functioning and critical ocular brand of politics. At the dramatic core of the play is Coriolanus's reluctant and profoundly uncomfortable decision to appear before a public whom he despises and, as a result, to subject himself to its probing, observation, and abuse. Coriolanus comes before the People on two occasions: first, as part of the process by which he becomes elected consul and, then, soon after, as part of the crisis by which he loses this office and becomes an exile. Coriolanus's strong dislike for these appearances reflects not only an aristocratic disdain toward canvassing the People's support, but the way in which the People in its capacity as a mass spectator does constitute a disciplinary, ocular force with real and potentially critical effects on those compelled to appear before it. Indeed, each of the three aspects of the ocular model of popular power that I outlined as fundamental to a theory of plebiscitary democracy can be seen in dramatic form in *Coriolanus*.

First, if one asks what is the *object* of popular power in *Coriolanus*, it is clear that it is not the law (the statutes, decisions, and policies that are to govern the Roman polity), but the figure of the leader—in this case Coriolanus himself. When Coriolanus's mother, anxious that her son win and retain the title of consul, sends him to face the amassed People with the words "Go, and be rul'd" (III.ii.90), she recognizes a conception of popular rule that has nothing to do with a decisional and expressive capacity to author laws, but rather realizes itself via the surveillance of individual personalities. The behavioral constraints placed upon Coriolanus—his felt compulsion to make himself public and the exposure he must endure as a consequence—are the mark and measure of democracy in the play. The site of democracy has relocated to Coriolanus's own person.

Second, the *organ* by which popular empowerment proceeds relates not to the empowerment of the People's voice in the manner of a decision, but to the empowerment of the People's sight in the manner of a *gaze*. When Coriolanus approaches the masses, it is as someone who is already chosen as consul. There is nothing really for the People to decide. But if the content of the decision about who will be consul is beyond the People's control, there is still the norm that as a condition of such promotion Coriolanus must *appear before the People*. Even if the People is inherently confused or ineffectual regarding what it wants, all of its members are of a like mind about the requirement that Coriolanus should come before them, "all agreeing/in earnestness to see him" (II.i.210–211). Specifically, Coriolanus must "appear i'th'market-place . . . [and] on him put/The napless vesture of humility" (II.i.230–233). As is alluded to in this line, it is significant that Coriolanus enters his public appearance wearing the "gown of humility" (II.iii.41)—what in Latin is known as the *candidatus*, a white robe signifying Coriolanus's dedication to openness, honesty, and frankness. The *candidatus*, referred to as his "humble weeds" (II.iii.153, 219),

is repeatedly invoked by characters in the play as a key feature of Coriolanus's publicity. Coriolanus's *candidacy* for office, then, is linked less to
the canvassing for votes than to his exposure before the public—a public
that Shakespeare brilliantly labels "worshipful mutiners" (I.i.249). Within
the moral landscape of the play, what the People receives by virtue of its
membership in a republic is not so much a special capacity to be heard and
make decisions, but a special opportunity to supervise, inspect, and otherwise survey its leadership. While it is true that the former is the condition
of the latter—since without the formality of election Coriolanus would not
need to appear—the clear message of the play is that the effectual power
of the voting mechanism is not the decision it expresses but the publicity
it demands.

Third, as both the etymology and the symbolism of the *candidatus*
attest, the *critical ideal* of popular government in *Coriolanus* is not the ideal
of popular autonomy or popular self-rule, but the ideal of candor. This candor has numerous elements. It involves, first of all, that Coriolanus humble
himself before the People—that his public appearances neither contain the
pomp of royalty nor be an occasion for Coriolanus to lord over everyday
citizens. As one ordinary citizen says, the condition of Coriolanus's ascension to consul is that he "ask it kindly" (II.iii.75). Further, Coriolanus's
candor involves his being probed and questioned in public. There is also
a requirement that he display his wounds—which has a literal meaning
(that he expose his battle scars) as well as a figurative one (that Coriolanus expose himself and render himself vulnerable before the public). This
requirement is precisely the one Coriolanus most resists, but to which he
eventually relents. What all of this means is that Coriolanus is not at all in
control of his public appearances. If the citizens who watch Coriolanus do
not actively direct his publicity, they at least know that they are observing a
man who himself is not managing his public displays. Coriolanus's candor
thus involves unpredictability and drama. It is unclear what will happen in
the public encounter—what will be asked and demanded of Coriolanus and
how he will respond—which is partially why it works so well as theater.

By contrast, in *Julius Caesar*, a play about a corrupt republic on the
verge of collapse in the face of "the spirit of Caesar," the ocular dimension
of popular power is itself on the brink of being neutralized. Although a
condition of Caesar's power is his willingness to appear constantly before
the public, such appearances are managed and controlled by Caesar and
his party. They have taken on a vapid, carnivalistic character.[31] To be sure,
we are presented with one striking symbol of the plebiscitarian theory of
popular power: in the description of Caesar's appearance at the Lupercal
festival, Shakespeare reinterprets the historical Caesar's epilepsy, giving
it a political-philosophical meaning. It is not epilepsy but the People's
own "stinking breath" (I.ii.245) and "bad air" (I.ii.248) that are said to

be the culprit for Caesar fainting on the public stage. Thus, the elevation of the leader's political power is tied to the leader's humiliation—a connection drawn by Weber in his analysis of charismatic rule. Caesar only accentuates this linkage between the ascension to decision-making power and undignified fall before the public gaze when, before his fainting, he opens up his doublet and offers his throat to be cut should he be deemed desirous of ending the republic and becoming emperor.[32] So even as the People's capacity to make laws and substantive decisions is denigrated (by its vacillation, suggestibility, and obvious subordination to a few oligarchs), there is a suggestion that the People does exert a kind of regulative function upon the person of the leader him- or herself. And yet, this suggestion remains much more of a latent hypothesis than a practical reality, since Caesar retains near-complete control over the conditions of his publicity.

The comparison between Coriolanus and Caesar also helps to specify more precisely the logic of privileging institutional candor over the psychological variant. If candor were a matter of the psychological issue of which leader was more honest, sincere, and forthright, it would be difficult to assess which of the two was the more candid. With Coriolanus, the problem is not simply that the matter of his inner state during his public appearances—what he meant, whether he was genuine in his supplication before the People—is beyond full verification, but that there are in fact real signs that Coriolanus intended to be deceptive and dishonest in his public self-presentation. After all, one is told that Coriolanus wears his *candidatus* "with a proud heart" (II.iii.152) and "contempt" (II.iii.219); moreover, Coriolanus reveals in private that he will dissemble in his public appearances and "will counterfeit the bewitchment of some popular man" (II.iii.100–101).[33] Caesar, on the other hand, really does seem to humble himself when he exposes his throat to a dagger and when he collapses in public. Furthermore, there is no sense in the play that Caesar does not believe anything he says to the People or that his love for it is in any way disingenuous.

If candor is measured strictly in terms of psychological standards of sincerity and honesty, it is possible to make the judgment that it is Caesar, not Coriolanus, who is more candid and, hence, more sufficiently democratic from a plebiscitarian perspective. This unwelcome result is avoided if candor is defined institutionally. No matter what he may have intended or revealed about himself, it is undeniable that Coriolanus had to appear under conditions much more outside of his control than did Caesar. With Caesar, the gestures of humility—including the dagger to the throat—are entirely self-imposed. Caesar faces no questioning, no probing, no submission to someone else's direction of his publicity. Coriolanus's great aversion to public appearances as compared to Caesar's fondness for them ought not be explained entirely in terms of personal disposition, but follows from the fact that Coriolanus's moments of publicity are characterized by interactive exchanges that are hostile and challenging. Although Coriolanus's inability to demonstrate sufficient mildness and contrition during his public appearances points to an aristocratic disdain for the People, it also indicates the disciplinary power of the public gaze—its ability to jar Coriolanus out of any politic attempt to fool the People with a pretended modesty.[34] Coriolanus complains that his coming before the People amounts to being *grinded* (III.ii.103). What all this suggests is that even if we cannot be assured that Coriolanus is himself more candid than Caesar, we can be confident that Coriolanus's *appearances* are.

In addition to illustrating the central features of plebiscitarianism's ocular model of popular power—its identification of the *object* of popular power as the leader, the *organ* of popular power as the popular gaze, and the *critical ideal* of popular power as candor—Shakespeare's *Coriolanus* also indicates the particular political goods secured by the ocular paradigm. To be sure, some of these goods are familiar values that overlap with those of the vocal paradigm. Up to a point, candor works to promote traditional goals like deliberation and transparency. And to the extent electoral politics in mass democracy is oriented around the selection of leaders with certain personalities, candor is a value that promises to make electoral processes more likely to test and reveal candidates' characters. It is as a result of his candid appearances, after all, that Coriolanus's disdain for the masses is revealed and he is removed from office. However, *Coriolanus* is not ultimately about such familiar, voice-based democratic processes— processes whereby the People achieves meaningful representation from the governors who rule over it. On the contrary, as I have argued, all notions of political representation are undermined in the play because the very notion of a popular will that might be the subject of such representation is altogether deconstructed: it is too variable, too subject to elite control, and, in many respects, simply nonexistent. What makes *Coriolanus* invaluable as a contribution to a theory of plebiscitary democracy is that it dramatizes how candor is a value that can function independent of any appeal to political representation. Candor does not require that citizens have preferences about what government should be doing. Nor does it depend, as the ideal of representation does, on complex and contested criteria about when it is in fact being realized. Candor is simple, straightforward, and eminently measurable. For citizens without a clear sense of what they want from government, or who are skeptical about government's capacity to take heed of voices from below, or who are simply unable to decipher what political representation requires in any particular instance, candor provides an alternate metric by which to evaluate the democratic progressivism of government.

Coriolanus illustrates not only this theoretical feature of plebiscitarianism—that its central ideal of candor is outside the rubric of representation—but, in addition, three more tangible political goods. First among these is the good of eventfulness. It is not by chance that Coriolanus's candid public appearances are the dramatic centerpiece of the play, since they are meant to portray the spontaneous and unscripted appeal of a historical individual under conditions of pressure and intensity. Caesar's noncandid public addresses, by contrast, are of much less interest: they are merely described rather than portrayed. These dramatological features indicate a political one: namely, that candor injects eventfulness into political life. The separation of speech from deed, constitutive of pseudo-events, is counteracted through candid appearances. Coriolanus's attempts at propaganda, empty flattery, and posturing are effectively overcome by the norm that he not be in control of his public appearances. And one of the consequences of Coriolanus's subjection to candor and the eventfulness this generates is that Coriolanus is compelled to engage in a much higher degree of self-revelation than Caesar. Indeed, even though plebiscitary democracy grounds itself on institutional candor (putting leaders in public situations that they do not control) rather than psychological candor (the genuineness of the leader), this privileging ought not be conceived as an indifference to generating genuine moments of self-disclosure from political leaders. That is to say, even if psychological candor needs to be subordinated to the much more reliable and discernible standard of institutional candor, it is still legitimate to hope that the provision of the latter will yield the former. In a sense Coriolanus is after all much more genuine than Caesar: his very failure to play the part of a faithful servant of the People is revealed as a result of his public appearance, and as a consequence, his aristocratic hostility to the People shines through.[35] Caesar, on the other hand, remains famously elusive and enigmatic, the only one of Shakespeare's title characters to die by the third act. A politics of candor links acts and words and thereby promotes the revelation of characters who perform them.

Second, a darker but no less significant aspect of plebiscitary democracy is that otherwise powerful leaders are placed under uncommon conditions of risk where they might be probed, exposed, and potentially humbled. The moral logic of plebiscitary democracy is that while hierarchical power cannot be eradicated from political life as traditional democratic ideology assumes, it is nonetheless possible that those in positions of massive and disproportionate political authority *pay* for this never fully legitimate imbalance by enduring the consequences of a critical form of publicity. Within the republican world of Shakespeare's *Coriolanus*, the presence of hierarchy is undeniable. The power of the political elite is in no way canceled or rationalized by the popular assemblies. The decision about who should be consul and, much more vitally, the decisions about what should be done—whether to fight the Volscians or seek peace, how to address the grain shortage, and so on—remain out of the hands of the People itself. However, what is no less clearly presented in the play is the moral principle that the select few who do possess such decision-making authority must recompense the public by being "grinded" before it. Thus, the long-standing democratic wish that arbitrary power be neutralized—either through popular self-legislation (because the People allegedly cannot behave tyrannically toward itself) or, as in more recent theory, through deliberative processes that in their most ambitious form look to transform *will* into *reason*—is not utterly forgotten in plebiscitary politics but only interpreted differently. The plebiscitarian accepts that there will be individuals in possession of great discretionary capacity to make monumental decisions as well as creatively define the substance of the public agenda, but it is precisely these individuals that the plebiscitarian seeks to see subjected to the rigors of an intense, dramatically expanded surveillance. For the plebiscitarian, then, arbitrary power is neutralized not by eliminating it altogether from the world—as the more perfect ideals of autonomy and deliberative reason contemplate—but by imposing upon power holders new public burdens that, among other things, serve as a source of compensation for their disproportionate and never fully legitimate authority.

Finally, another benefit of plebiscitary democracy is that it recovers and revitalizes an entity that has become increasingly controversial and marginalized within democratic theory: the People. However much the People might be disempowered as a decision-making entity in *Coriolanus*, its existence is beyond question. It is a key actor in the play. Indeed, its relative lack of power only makes its existence all the more apparent. This is due to the paradox that the same plebiscitary conditions that undermine popular participation in government throw the existence of the People—that is, the mass of ordinary citizens that occupies no office and plays no direct role in the management of public life—into especially stark relief. Because plebiscitary democracy emphasizes the initiative, discretion, and raw power of political elites, it also acknowledges the great remainder of nonleaders—that is, the People—as a collective entity.

I have already discussed in chapter 1 the tendency in democratic theory to avoid any direct or rigorous usage of the concept of the People—a topic to which I shall return in chapter 7. It is a serious weakness of contemporary democratic thought that it cannot speak about the People. The People is a uniquely vital and emancipatory notion that offers the promise of conceptualizing what is in the interest of everyday citizens by virtue of their everydayness. What is remarkable about *Coriolanus*, and about plebiscitary democracy in general, is that it not only insists upon the existence of the People, but that its ocular understanding of the People in terms of sight rather than voice provides a way to bring back the People without falling into the usual intellectual and moral difficulties that inhibit its usage. Understood as an ocular rather than a vocal force, the People realizes itself in the conditions under which leaders appear before the public: specifically, in the degree to which leaders' appearances are not staged or planned by the leaders themselves but are characterized by moments of spontaneity such that they provide the spectating public with the sense that its spectatorship is also surveillance. Further, when the People is conceived in this fashion—as the mass of *nongovernors* in their collective capacity—the People is drained of any totalitarian application, since what is designated is precisely the silence and nondecision of the People relative to the select few elevated into positions of formal decision-making authority. At the same time, because an ocular understanding of the People relates not to the exceptional moment of election but to the public appearances of leaders typical of everyday politics, plebiscitary democracy carries with it the promise of making popular empowerment something that is experienced and realized by ordinary citizens within their ordinary, daily lives. For these reasons the collectivist concept of the People is rehabilitated by a plebiscitarian approach in a manner that renders it meaningful, safe, critical, and inclusive. In a plebiscitarian world in which leaders were regulated by the constraint of candor—in which the People were invoked as a justification for placing leaders under conditions of publicity they do not control—the People would have a sense of its reality that is much sharper than that enjoyed today. Whereas currently membership in the People is insignificant—pluralists go so far as to deny it altogether—an ordinary citizen in a well-ordered plebiscitary regime could identify with the People and consider him- or herself a member of the People. This membership would mean at least as much as—and likely much more than—membership in one of the countless organizations within civil society with which political scientists are so familiar today.

Coriolanus documents these four benefits of the ocular paradigm— its independence from complex and contested norms of representation, eventfulness, the burdening of leaders as a form of recompense for their never fully legitimate authority, and the reintroduction of the People as a meaningful political concept—and, consequently, demonstrates that it is after all possible to differentiate political image making from the democratic point of view. Rather than exhibit hostility to political spectacles as such, plebiscitarianism provides a principle of candor on the basis of which political images might be evaluated and reformed.

5

Max Weber's Reinvention of Popular Power and Its Uneasy Legacy

> The hygiene of the optical, the health of the visible
> is slowly filtering through.
> —László Moholy-Nagy

5.1 The Distinctiveness of Mass Democracy

Although there can be no doubt that contemporary democracies differ from earlier democratic regimes by virtue of the enormity of their populations, the vastness of their territory, the complexity of their administrative bureaucracies, and, perhaps most important, the indirect, vicarious, and passive form of political experience enabled by mass communication technologies, the meaning of the difference between small-scale and mass democracy for the study of democratic *ideals* has not been adequately addressed. On the one hand, the conventional wisdom still subscribes to the Madisonian view that the possibilities for self-government are not seriously altered by a democracy's size and that, if anything, large-scale democracy only solidifies and strengthens the popular self-rule realized by small-scale democracy. On the other hand, the most important attempts to undercut this conventional wisdom and to insist upon distinct characteristics of mass democracy have tended to present mass democracy either as a normative failure, unable to realize the popular self-rule of small-scale democracy, or, in purely descriptive terms, as a regime without ideals or moral aspirations, and thus wholly unsuited to guide or motivate processes of democratic development.[1] Against both of these trends, Max Weber's theory of *plebiscitary leader democracy* and to a lesser extent the contributions of this theory's two most important inheritors, Carl Schmitt and Joseph Schumpeter, argue for the consideration of mass democracy as a distinct regime that contains its own set of possibilities for citizenship, popular power, and critical standards of democratization.

As the original theorist of plebiscitary democracy, Weber provides the most fruitful path to the rediscovery of plebiscitarianism as a fresh normative landscape within which to comprehend contemporary mass democracy—and, specifically, a politics inundated by the problem of spectatorship. Weber's account of democracy is often seen as unappealing for the *goal* Weber attached to it: the generation of charismatic leadership. What is not often realized, however, is that Weber's plebiscitarianism was innovative also for the role that the People would play in this process of leadership cultivation. Specifically, on Weber's account, the People contributes to the generation of charisma not so much via the mechanism of *voice* (e.g., choosing or acclaiming the charismatic leader in the manner of an election) as through the disciplinary force of the People's *gaze*—an ocular requirement that would-be leaders appear in public, perform in ways likely to maintain the People's attention, and, ideally, undergo the risk and unpredictability of extemporaneous forms of publicity.

My aim in this chapter is to elaborate the ocular model of popular power implicit in Weber's neglected and overly maligned account of democracy. Sections 5.2 to 5.5 reconstruct Weber's democratic theory. I demonstrate that underlying Weber's concern for charismatic leadership lies an ocular understanding of popular power and, with it, the threefold shift I have repeatedly invoked to characterize the plebiscitary model of popular power: the shift in the object of popular power (from law to leader), in the organ of popular power (from decision to gaze), and in the critical ideal of popular power (from autonomy to candor). Having rehabilitated Weber's novel contribution to the study of democracy, the final two sections, 5.6 and 5.7, discuss why this contribution went largely unrecognized throughout the remainder of the twentieth century. While there are numerous causes for this, I argue that the plebiscitary theories of Weber's two most influential successors—Schmitt and Schumpeter—lent the nascent plebiscitary tradition, unnecessarily, an air of unpalatability.

5.2 Why Weber's Theory of Plebiscitary Leader Democracy Is Not Addressed and Why It Ought to Be

Although almost a century has passed since his death, Max Weber's contribution to political science continues to exert a profound, and indeed discipline-shaping, influence. Weber's definition of the state as the monopoly of legitimate violence, his distinction between three forms of legitimate domination (traditional, legal-rational, and charismatic), his analysis of the vocational politician in terms of the distinction between an ethic of conviction and an ethic of responsibility, and his diagnosis of modernity as a process of disenchantment grounded in the unchecked spread of bureaucracy and instrumental reason are just some of the most notable examples of Weberian concepts that continue to inform and stimulate ongoing research in contemporary political science.

Yet, if Weber's global relevance to present-day political science is certain, what is less clear is the specific relevance of Weber's contribution to the contemporary study and pursuit of democracy. The problem is not simply that, as many scholars have noted, Weber's writings on democracy lack the clarity and systematic structure one would expect to find from a proper democratic theory.[2] Rather, what is most preventative of the serious treatment of Weber as a democratic theorist is that the account of democracy he did in fact sketch in both his sociological and his partisan writings—*plebiscitary leader democracy*—has not generally been treated as a genuine democratic theory at all, but on the contrary has been seen as hostile to the very spirit of democracy as a regime uniquely committed to the empowerment of the People.

By "leader democracy" (*Führerdemokratie*), Weber meant a form of democracy whose rationale was not its ability to realize traditional democratic values such as inclusiveness, equality, popular self-legislation, or the cultivation of the intellectual and moral capacities of the citizenry, but rather its capacity to produce *charismatic* leaders capable of providing strong, independent, and creative direction to the modern, industrial nation-state. Charisma is a technical sociological term for Weber. It designates one of three grounds upon which hierarchical power relations (*Herrschaft*) might be found legitimate. Unlike the other two grounds, traditional and legal-rational authority, charismatic authority is based on the enigmatic power of individual personalities to instill trust and confidence, usually in the service of some higher purpose or mission. In its pure form, charisma is an entirely individual quality that, rare and extraordinary, fades from the world as soon as its bearer dies or loses his or her special powers. It is, as Weber says, "a certain quality of an individual personality by virtue of which he is considered extraordinary and treated as endowed with supernatural, superhuman, or at least specifically exceptional powers or qualities. These are such as are not accessible to the ordinary person, but are regarded as of divine origin or as exemplary, and on the basis of them the individual concerned is treated as a 'leader.'"[3] Weber found in Jesus' "Although it is written, I say unto you ..." and Luther's "Here I stand, I can do no other" classic statements of pure charisma, illustrating both the individual grounds of charismatic authority and its revolutionary function as a creator of new norms and values. Importantly, the charismatic leadership Weber expected to see cultivated by democratic institutions was not of this pure type. Whereas pure bearers of charisma—such as founders of religion like Moses, Jesus, and Mohammed, the biblical prophets, magicians offering healing through occult powers, and political geniuses like Pericles, Caesar, or Napoleon—appeared only rarely in world history, and were unlikely to reappear within the highly rationalized, secularized, and disenchanted conditions of modern mass society, Weber believed that twentieth-century mass democracy offered a way to manufacture a kind of leadership that, while not purely charismatic, nonetheless took on charismatic traits and could be regularized into a routine feature of the modern political landscape.

How precisely would democratization engender quasi-charismatic leaders? For one thing, the highest offices of mass democracies, such as the prime minister in parliamentary states, the Reich president in the Weimar Republic, and the president in the United States, were themselves invested with a certain aura—what Weber called "office charisma"—that meant whoever filled them would be treated with a special authority that exceeded the office's legal function. In addition, mass elections would re-create the acclamatory moment typical of ancient forms of pure charisma, in which the mass following of the charismatic leader affirmed his or her special merit. But neither of these fully explains how democratization would facilitate the rise of quasi-charismatic leaders. The charisma of democratic leaders would not be altogether depersonalized so that anyone who held the highest offices would be ipso facto charismatic. Rather, it was Weber's expectation that democratic institutions, like universal suffrage, mass parties, and frequent elections, would *train* and *cultivate* charismatic qualities among those who sought popular support. Specifically, democratization would empower *politicians* capable of winning a mass following— as opposed to bureaucrats with technical expertise, plutocrats with great wealth, or aristocrats or monarchs with a claim to blood lineage. And it was distinctive of successful politicians in mass democracy, Weber thought, that they would tend to have three qualities that approximated those of the pure charismatic leader.

First, they would be experts in *struggle*: their power would depend on their own capacity to beat out rivals in competition, rather than on any claim to expert knowledge or right of inheritance. Like the bearer of pure charisma, the modern, democratic politician would possess an authority stemming from his or her own manifest strength, proved in continual contest with rivals and enemies.[4] Second, the democratically elected leader would have, in the support of the People, an independent ground of authority from which to articulate and defend *new values and direction* for the polity— especially in the sense of national purposes and aspirations beyond those of mere technical efficiency—and would thereby resemble the pure bearer of charisma who, as Weber explains, "demands *new* obligations."[5] Third, democratically elected leaders would be *personally responsible* for their decisions. Whereas the bureaucrat could disclaim responsibility—pointing either to the dictate of a superior or to the impersonal requirements of a specialized expertise—the successful politician in mass democracy would make decisions that were not only public, but inseparable from his or her own personal judgment. Such a situation would resemble that of ancient

magicians, prophets, and warlords—pure bearers of charisma whose fates
were inextricably tied to the success of the enterprises they led.[6]

If the expectation for quasi-charismatic politicians defined the
"leader" aspect of plebiscitary leader democracy, by "plebiscitary" Weber
meant, first of all, a democratic politics in which leaders would be selected
directly by popular election, rather than indirectly by a parliament or from
party lists. Thus, for example, it is commonplace among Weber scholars
to speak of a shift in Weber's thinking from a parliamentary phase (when
he expected leaders to be generated from the competition of rival members
within parliament) to a plebiscitary phase (when he considered mass elections to be the most effective means of generating charismatic leadership).
Yet it would be a mistake to limit the meaning of plebiscitarianism simply
to direct elections for leadership. Weber also intended an additional meaning: namely, that plebiscitary politics would be those in which popular
decision making took on a superficial, formal, and hence fictive character.[7]
If the most drastic example of plebiscitary politics was the referendum by
which an uncontested single ruler legitimated his or her rule or reforms—
such as the plebiscites used by both Napoleons—Weber did not think the
superficial character of popular decision making was necessarily obviated
by the introduction of a few additional choices. For one thing, to the extent
electoral contests in mass democracy were fought, *not* over substantive
issues, but rather over emotional and intangible appeals, then the results
could not be said to indicate a clear meaning for how the polity should be
governed.[8] For another, the plebiscitary character of mass democracy also
inhered in the fact that electoral victory for Weber usually indicated, not
the revelation of the popular will in a certain direction, but the superior
initiative of the successful politician and his or her party machine. Under
plebiscitary conditions, "it is not the politically passive 'mass' which
gives birth to the leader; rather the political leader recruits his following
and wins over the mass by 'demagogy.' That is the case even in the most
democratic form of state."[9] Here it is important to point out that Weber
defended his proposal for plebiscitary leader democracy via appeal to the
highly ambiguous terminology of the "self-elected leader of the masses"
(*selbstgewählten Vertrauensmann der Massen*)—a term that could mean
either the People's right to elect their own leaders or, what is more clearly
in keeping with Weber's account of plebiscitary democracy, that the leader
would be someone who was self-elected: in the sense of being someone
who, unlike the bureaucrat or aristocrat, would achieve office by virtue
of his or her own machinations, initiative, effort, and capacity to lead and
direct a political machine.[10]

So defined, the Weberian notion of the plebiscitary has little in
common with conventional representative democracy (which sees the
People as exercising an indirect but powerful control over the substantive

decisions shaping public life), or with Roman plebiscitary democracy (which engaged the People directly in legislation through frequent plebiscites).[11] Weber's rendering of *plebiscitary* does closely resemble, however, that of subsequent democratic theorists, for whom the term is shorthand for a sham or fictive democracy in which the propaganda and spectacles of mass leaders and their political machines undermine deliberation and genuinely participatory contributions from the wider citizenry.[12] Indeed, a consequence of plebiscitary politics (in the Weberian sense) is that leaders are free of constraints upon their actions from their constituents—or at least much more free than democratic idealists from the nineteenth century had contemplated. A plebiscitary leader pursues a substantive agenda that is his or her own, not that of the People, and thus possesses an extraordinary degree of independent decision-making authority. The plebiscitary leader "feels that he is answerable only to himself and that, as long as he can successfully claim [the People's] confidence, he will act according to his own judgment and therefore will not act like an elected official, i.e., in conformity to the expressed or supposed will of the electors, who are the elected official's master."[13] Although Weber did not think the democratic leader would be entirely unaccountable, the People was not a source of this constraint.[14] Against the dominant trend in democratic theory to see elections, along with public opinion, as key devices whereby the People, with varying degrees of exactness, controls and directs the representatives who actually hold office, within Weber's plebiscitary model both public opinion and elections are seen as the effect of successful leadership, rather than its cause and justification.

Taking both the "leader" and "plebiscitary" elements together, then, Weber's concept of plebiscitary leader democracy is a theory of democracy oriented around the cultivation of charismatic leaders who fulfill their political tasks with only ostensible attention to the values, concerns, and opinions of the mass populace that formally elects them.[15] It is hardly surprising that this theory, so conceived, has received scant attention from contemporary democratic theorists and has been almost universally criticized by Weber scholars. If the most virulent form of criticism—that Weber's theory of democracy is proto-totalitarian and actually facilitative of the emergence of National Socialism in Germany[16]—is excessive and unfair for a variety of reasons, much more understandable is the very common complaint that plebiscitary leader democracy, while not necessarily fascist or illiberal, is not really a democratic theory at all. One finds repeated from numerous commentators the objection that Weber's political theory lacks any positive account of popular power: specifically, that it presents democracy in such a fashion that there is no capacity for the People to participate in the articulation and ratification of the norms, laws, and policies governing the conduct of public life.[17] Beetham, whose study of Weber is still one of the most authoritative, sums up the conventional wisdom when he writes: "What is distinctive about this account of democracy ... is that it makes no reference to democratic *values*, much less regards them as worth striving for." Despite Weber's support of basic democratic institutions like an independent parliament and direct election for leadership, his theory of government "cannot be called a *democratic* theory, since it did not seek to justify such government in terms of recognizably democratic values, such as increasing the influence of the people on policies pursued by those who governed." Accordingly, Beetham can say of Weber: "His strong leader was legitimated by a conception of democracy that was anything but democratic."[18]

Against this prevailing and dismissive view, my argument is that we need to understand Weber's plebiscitary leader democracy as a democratic theory that stands, not for the abandonment of popular power, but for its *reinvention*. The prevailing interpretation that plebiscitary leader democracy has no positive account of popular power only makes sense so long as one operates within a familiar *vocal paradigm of popular power*: one which assumes that popular power must refer to an authorial capacity to self-legislate the norms and conditions of public life, or at least to express substantive opinions, values, and preferences about what kinds of decisions political leaders ought to be making. If popular power is conceived according to this vocal, legislative model, then Weber's plebiscitary leader democracy will surely appear disqualified as a genuine democratic theory, since it obviously undermines the People's capacity to express opinions, legislate norms, and, in short, engage in substantive decision making about the fate of the polity.

But there are three reasons for considering plebiscitary leader democracy as challenging this vocal paradigm and pointing, instead, to a reconceived conception of popular power specific to the conditions of modern, mass representative democracy. First, Weber drew explicit attention to the moral distinctiveness of twentieth-century mass democracy relative to earlier forms of smaller-scale democracy, arguing that the former "have different obligations and therefore other cultural possibilities."[19] Although Weber obviously thought that part of these new obligations and possibilities would relate to the figure of the leader and the generation of a powerful nation-state capable of world-historical action on the global stage, his description of his proposals for plebiscitary leader democracy in such *popular* terms as the "the palladium of genuine democracy" and as "the *magna carta* of democracy" suggest that the People would also be party to the reformulated political ethics Weber contemplated.[20] Second, even if Weber supported democratization as but a means to select leaders with charismatic qualities, the very instrumentality of popular power implied in such a gesture points to a real, if unelaborated and unorthodox, conception of the People. That is to say, if the People were an entirely ineffectual actor, there would be no reason for Weber to have supported the very institutions that brought the masses, at least formally, into political life.[21] What is needed is an understanding of the nature of popular power in plebiscitary leader democracy, not an insistence that such power does not exist simply because it violates expectations of what it should be.

Finally, and indeed most importantly, it is a mistake to interpret the goal Weber linked to plebiscitary leader democracy—the generation of *charismatic* leadership—as something altogether antithetical to popular power. Critics of Weber's relevance as a democratic theorist have failed to recognize that the charisma around which Weber oriented his consideration of democracy is not a strictly individual or personal quality as is often thought, but in fact is a *relational* concept that refers to a mode of interaction between the charismatic leader and the *charismatic community* before which the leader must appear and through which the charisma is both tested and generated.[22] Unlike other forms of authority, charismatic authority depends on the attainment and maintenance of a mass following that, at the very least, beholds and receives the charismatic individual. The possibility of a charismatic individual without a mass following is rejected by Weber as sociologically meaningless. Hence, whenever Weber considers the charisma of an individual, the capacity to achieve popular recognition is a key criterion: "[A leader's] charismatic claim breaks down if his mission is not recognized by those to whom he feels he has been sent. If they recognize him, he is their master—so long as he knows how to maintain recognition through 'proving' himself."[23] This requirement about charismatic authority—that is, that it depends on the *recognition* by the People (or charismatic community) of the leader—indicates that there is after all a norm of popular power implicit in the concept of charisma. Of course any effort to specify just what kind of power this is must face the immediate objection that Weber always insists on the purely formal or fictive nature of popular support for charismatic leaders—a fact that would appear to strip the norm of popular recognition of its critical bite. After all, as has already been said, the People does not *choose* the charismatic leader so much as acknowledge him or her. In the case of the pure charisma of religious founders and biblical prophets, this is because the phenomenology of charisma is such that it strikes the mass of everyday onlookers as something wondrous and magical—hence something already deserving of their attention. Thus Weber can write of the pure bearer of charisma that "he does not derive his right from [the charismatic community's] will, in the manner of an election. Rather, the reverse holds: it is the *duty* of those to whom he addresses his mission to recognize him as their charismatically qualified leader."[24] In the case of the manufactured charisma of the modern democratic leader in plebiscitary leader

democracy, the People's recognition, even though now constitutive and
not just reflective of the leader's charismatic authority, is likewise not an
autonomous choice—not because popular support of the leader is a duty,
but because the plebiscitary conditions by which this support is extracted
mean precisely that the leader's electoral success is not grounded in any
genuine popular judgment and, instead, stems from propaganda and the
effective working of a political machine.[25]

But the recognition that the charismatic community bestows upon the
charismatic leader does not only (or primarily) take this active form of an
actual display of support. Weber distinguishes between active and passive
forms of recognition, the latter characterized, *not* by a vocal expression of
a certain choice or decision, but by a passive receptivity in the manner of
an audience.[26] It turns out that it is this passive form of recognition—the
attention an audience pays to an individual appearing on the public stage—
that is most constitutive of the charismatic authority of the leader and, also,
the key dynamic by which the People (or charismatic community) exerts a
real power over the leader. The requirement of popular recognition is not
a requirement that charismatic leaders listen to and obey the popular *voice*;
rather, it is a requirement that they attain, undergo, and endure the public
gaze. As Weber makes clear in his analysis of both the pure charisma of
the biblical prophets and the manufactured charisma of democratic leaders
in plebiscitary leader democracy, and as I will detail in the remainder of
this chapter, the charismatic status of the individual leader depends on an
ability to *sustain an audience*: understood in the threefold sense of having
the audience prosper under the leader's direction; doing what is necessary
to win and maintain the audience's attention; and, most critically, enduring the surveillance of the public gaze through making candid appearances
that are unscripted and unrehearsed. If the first of these suggests a familiar, vocal, legislative ontology of popular power (the People conceived as
the possessor of substantive needs that leaders try to fulfill in the legislative
output of governmental policies), the other two point to a novel conception
of popular power as an *ocular* force that realizes itself, *not* in the achievement of certain legal or policy outcomes, but rather in the control of the
conditions according to which leaders with immense power appear before
the eyes of the People.

Taken together, these points—that Weber occasionally presented
mass democracy in highly idealized terms, that he did after all support
political institutions that would bring the People into politics, and that his
notion of charisma indicates a novel conceptualization of popular power
modeled on the *ocular* power of the charismatic community—suggest that
plebiscitary leader democracy needs to be understood, not as violating *any*
acceptable notion of popular power, but rather as transgressing a *particular*, traditional norm of popular power (the vocal, legislative one) in the

name of a novel account of popular power modeled on the way that the charismatic community is empowered vis-à-vis the charismatic leader. I shall argue, in other words, that Weber's democratic theory is an invitation to rethink the nature of popular power under the conditions of mass democracy.

In making this claim—that is, in interpreting Weber as a theorist who reinvents the meaning of popular power—I do not mean to deny that Weber's primary interest in democracy was leadership as opposed to the People. What I do suggest, however, is that latent within Weber's novel conceptualization of democracy as a charisma-generating regime is an equally novel theory of popular empowerment which, even if it remained underdeveloped in Weber's writings, nonetheless is a worthwhile and fecund feature of his thought that has the promise of making Weber relevant for progressive democratic reformers today. What follows here, therefore, is as much my own development of an ethical promise largely concealed within the Weberian corpus as it is a presentation of Weber's transparent arguments about the meaning of mass democracy.

In order to appreciate the innovative conceptualization of popular power embedded in Weber's theory of plebiscitary leader democracy, I shall discuss this theory not simply in its own terms, but in comparison with the traditional and still dominant vocal model I discussed in chapter 3. Plebiscitary leader democracy is best understood in terms of three *shifts* vis-à-vis this model—shifts relating to the *object*, *organ*, and *critical ideal* of popular empowerment in a democracy.

5.3 The Shift in the *Object* of Popular Power: From Law to Leader

Whereas the customary approach in democratic theory, as I detailed in chapter 3, is to see the election of leaders (the one formal moment of decision making enjoyed by everyday citizens in their collective capacity) as translatable into a determination about the content of governmental laws and policies, Weber denied that universal suffrage, mass elections, or public opinion would bestow upon the People a sovereign power to determine, even indirectly, the norms and conditions of public life. Yet, if Weber's objection to the People's capacity to meaningfully influence substantive laws and policies made him similar to the so-called elite theorists—Pareto, Mosca, and Michels—who denied the possibility of the unelected many to control the decision making of political elites, Weber differed from the elite theorists by insisting that popular power would nonetheless play a meaningul role in mass democracy: that it would determine the *character* of the very elites empowered to make political decisions, even if it could not determine the content of their decisions. Popular power would have its object in the leader, not the law.

For Weber, the People's incapacity to seriously influence the content of a polity's laws, policies, and overall direction was an inescapable sociological fact of mass democracy. For one thing, as a student of bureaucratization Weber was intensely aware of the degree to which the complexities of the modern, industrial, administrative state meant that many norms would be determined by specialized bureaucrats with expert training and not by democratic processes of opinion and will formation.[27] Further, Weber argued that in the modern context of fast-paced changes and developments—of sudden economic crises, unpredicted wars and conflicts, internal instabilities requiring immediate response, the rise of new technologies requiring regulation—political decision making would always have to confront a large number of issues that were new and unexpected, for which there would not be a prior popular will. And in any case, Weber thought that, by themselves, elections were too rare and too limited in the choices they offered to link the decision making of the elected to the underlying values, preferences, and opinions of the electors in anything but a highly superficial sense.[28] More ambitious devices for accountability were too rarely used (as in the case of recall) or too prone to manipulation and irrationality (as in the case of referenda) to bestow upon the populace genuine mechanisms of self-legislation.[29] Moreover, on Weber's account most everyday citizens were passive, without clear political commitments, and thus highly receptive to the way political elites defined the agenda and framed issues.[30] The rise of mass parties only accentuated the disconnectedness of the People from legislative decision making, since parties placed even most political activists into situations in which their first priority was to serve the machine for which they worked rather than to engage in free and independent decision making.[31]

For these reasons, Weber did not share the dominant perspective in democratic theory, according to which elections, along with public opinion, are key devices whereby the People controls and directs the representatives who actually hold office. On Weber's model the People does not have a legislative power over the candidates.[32] Given such views and analyses, it is tempting to see Weber as an elite theorist, equivalent to Pareto, Mosca, or Michels, who understood all political regimes as divided between an organized elite minority with decision-making power and an unorganized mass without any real political power. But whereas for the elite theorists, the necessity of this division led to two assertions—that democracy was more fictive than real,[33] and that the People was destined to obtain no form of empowerment from political life[34]—for Weber, the subtlety of his political sociology as well as the democratic progressivism of his proposals for Weimar led him to resist such conclusions.

Weber distinguished between three fundamentally different kinds of elites—aristocrats, bureaucrats, and politicians—and was concerned to find a workable balance between them within the conditions of modern society. Although an admirer of vibrant aristocracies, such as those in England and Germany prior to the nineteenth century, Weber thought the possibilities for genuine aristocracy had exhausted themselves by the twentieth century, especially in Germany, where leaders who owed their authority to tradition had behaved irresponsibly and ineptly during World War I. And although Weber recognized that bureaucracy was a potent administrative device and an essential and permanent feature of modern politics, he believed that it had leapt beyond its proper bounds and imposed its own hegemony within the modern state. Thus Weber turned to the *politician* as the one kind of elite that could take effective responsibility and tame the overgrown bureaucratic apparatus. Under well-functioning political leadership, the bureaucracy would be put to use in pursuit of national projects, noneconomic substantive values, and higher goals.

This diagnosis not only prevented Weber from employing a simplistic dichotomy between elite and mass, but led him to assert an enduringly relevant, if unorthodox, notion of popular power within mass democracy.[35] Weber liked to say that governmental forms mattered little to him and that he would support whichever set of political institutions produced the *politicians* he hoped to see cultivated.[36] But the fact remains that Weber never contemplated any other method for generating the charismatic leadership of politicians besides the institutions of democracy. The introduction of the wider populace into political life—through elections, universal voting rights, and mass parties—was uniquely capable of empowering and cultivating politicians who could inject a charismatic element into modern mass society.

Thus whereas the elite theorists considered the People disempowered because it had no legislative power, Weber recognized an instrumental (yet indispensable) power in the People to generate the charismatic leadership of democratic politicians. This meant that Weber could affirm popular power as a real force in mass democracy—only now its locus had shifted: it no longer realized itself in the domain of law, as traditional democratic ideology assumed, but rather took as its object the character of the elites empowered to govern. A democratic regime produces one kind of leader—a quasi-charismatic one—whereas other types of regime produce other variants. Weber's important suggestion, in other words, was that the People in mass democracy is something that primarily disciplines and determines the personal traits of those who hold power, rather than voices and specifies which interests, opinions, and values ought to be represented in the output of governmental decision making.

5.4 The Shift in the *Organ* of Popular Power:
From Decision to Gaze

The relocation of the object of popular power in the leader rather than the law is unusual, but not altogether unprecedented in political theory. There is an important tradition of republican thought, running through Aristotle, Machiavelli, Guicciardini, Harrington, and Montesquieu, that emphasizes the People's special capacity for judgment—especially the judgment regarding the merit of individuals as potential leaders.[37] Within this tradition, one of the alleged benefits of including the People in a polity is that more capable and deserving leaders tend to be selected. Moreover, with Montesquieu, whose affirmation of popular judgment regarding leadership was paralleled by disparagement of the People's competence for legislation, we find something that roughly resembles Weber's understanding of popular power as a force that disciplines leadership rather than determines laws.[38] Yet the weakness of this historical linkage needs to be recognized. Most of all, there is a key difference regarding the mechanism by which the People generates exemplary leadership. For the republican theorists, it was the collective *judgment* of the People—the popular *voice* that expressed itself in an autonomous *choice* about who should lead—that effected leadership selection. According to this tradition, the People, in its collective capacity, possessed an *insight* about the merit of leaders. As Machiavelli put it: "To know well the nature of peoples one needs to be a prince, and to know well the nature of princes one needs to be of the people."[39]

By contrast, Weber's analysis of mass democracy continually undermines any conception of popular power in terms of the mechanism of *voice* (or in terms of such parallel concepts as deliberate judgment, choice, expressivity, or insight). Weber challenged the traditional democratic tenet of the articulacy of the People: that is, that the People could use elections, public opinion, and other devices to communicate a coherent and clear view about particular political decisions. Against this traditional view, Weber did not simply doubt the capacity of the People's preferences, opinions, and values to determine the decision making of government leaders, but also called into question any understanding of the People as something that took the form of articulate views. That is to say, Weber objected to the age-old maxim—*vox populi, vox dei*—not simply because he recognized that in mass democracy the power of the People was anything but divine (but deferred in most respects to the political decision making of political elites and the organizations they controlled), but additionally because he challenged the propriety of the vocal ontology of popular power, which defined popular power, to whatever extent it might exist, as an expressive force realizing itself in substantive decisions about what should be done or who should rule. We have already seen that the one decision the electorate regularly does make in modern, mass representative democracy—leadership selection—was something that Weber deconstructed in such a way to deny it of initiative, autonomy, and true choice. This was but the most provocative feature of a more general rejection of modeling popular power in terms of *will*: that is, in terms of an expressive voice calling for a particular course of action to be undertaken in reference to specific issues and questions.[40] It was not simply that the electorate too rarely engaged in formal decision making for popular power to be interpreted in decisional terms, but that those decisions the electorate did in fact make were usually highly limited in their expressivity. Both the binary structure that tended to restrict the devices of mass decision making and the fact that the terms and conditions of such decisions were usually shaped from above meant, for Weber, that it was a mistake to see in the occasional manifestations of popular decision making a true indication of the People's voice as an expressive and autonomous agent.[41] Difficulties such as these led Weber to posit as a general paradox that the very devices whereby the People supposedly expressed its decisions—recall, elections, referenda—proceeded in such a fashion that they only solidified the influence of organized political groups (such as interest groups and mass parties) vis-à-vis everyday citizens in their condition as a mass electorate. Or, as Weber put it: "All attempts at subordinating the representative to the will of the voters have in the long run only one effect: They reinforce the ascendancy of the party organization over him, which alone can mobilize the people. Both the pragmatic interest in the flexibility of the parliamentary apparatus and the power interest of the representatives and the party functionaries converge on one point: They tend to treat the representative not as the servant but as the chosen 'master' of his voters."[42]

Weber's rejection of a vocal ontology of popular power raises a fundamental question about the mechanism of popular power in plebiscitary leader democracy. If the People is essential to the generation of charismatic leaders, but does not contribute to this process through an expressive electoral decision, wherein does the instrumental power of the People to generate charismatic leadership lie? If not through its choice as electors on election day, what was it about the introduction of the People into mass politics that made it such an indispensable source for the generation of charismatic leadership?

The answer that emerges from a close examination of Weber's theory of democratically manufactured charisma is that the People contributes to the production of charismatic authority primarily through the disciplinary power of the *public gaze*, rather than through the expressive, decisional, command-based power of the public voice. In invoking the disciplinary power of the public gaze, I mean something roughly similar to Foucault's notion of disciplinary power as an ocular force whose chief function is to *train and form individuals* rather than to make decisions or levy taxes or lead armies. According to Foucault, disciplinary power is effected by the "compulsory visibility" of the subject. Through such devices as hierarchical observation (in which the observers are hidden from the subjects of surveillance) and the examination (in which subjects are probed and experimented on while under observation), the disciplinary gaze does not compel so much as it molds a particular kind of personality—in Foucault's case, the docile and productive laborer of modern industrial society. And it achieves such character formation not through verbal dictates, but *ocular* requirements and impositions: "The exercise of discipline presupposes a mechanism that coerces by means of observation; an apparatus in which the techniques that make it possible to see induce effects of power, and in which, conversely, the means of coercion make those on whom they are applied clearly visible."[43]

Although the two are not identical, the function of popular power within Weber's model of plebiscitary leader democracy resembles this Foucauldian concept of disciplinary power in a number of respects.[44] Weber repeatedly stressed that democratization generates charismatic authority above all through the *training* of leadership—the actual formation and cultivation of individual characteristics—as opposed to selecting an already deserving candidate or setting up an office (such as the presidency) whose aura would automatically bestow charismatic status upon the person who occupied it.[45] Moreover, if one considers once more the three specific charismatic characteristics Weber expected to see realized by the politician in mass democracy—constant proof of merit through struggle, the creative articulation of new norms and values, and personal responsibility—one finds that the People contributes to the generation of these qualities, not via vocal processes of decision making, but precisely in its capacity as a mass audience that watches and listens to political candidates appearing on the public stage.

First, as has been said, the plebiscitary democratic leader is someone who is constantly proving him- or herself in struggle. But how does the People contribute to this education in struggle? Of course, as the possessor of the vote—the prize to be won in electoral contests—the People is the enabling condition of the competition for power in mass democracy. Yet it would be a mistake to understand the distinctive contribution of the People in terms of the vote. After all, it was also characteristic of the parliamentary system Weber initially favored but then came to reject—in which the competition of parliamentarians for positions of primacy *within parliament* would be the training ground for charismatic leadership—that would-be leaders would have to struggle for votes and other vocal affirmations of support. By the last years of his life, Weber turned against this parliamentary system, claiming that it did not sufficiently test and train would-be leaders, and he instead put forward his proposals for plebiscitary leader democracy in which politicians would compete directly for the support of a mass electorate. What made the competition for popular support more truly a struggle, and hence more educative for leadership than the competition for parliamentary support, was not the ultimate object of the competition (as in both cases the goal for would-be leaders was the same: win the most votes), but that the drive to win popular support would have to be accompanied by a massive campaign effort. This was not a difference just in scale (as the number of votes required by successful leaders in plebiscitary democracy dwarfed the few hundred needed within parliamentary democracy) but in kind. In order to mobilize the electorate on election day, the political leader and the machine he or she led first needed to win and sustain popular attention. The great majority of political activity in plebiscitary campaigns—canvassing, propaganda, rallies—is an effort to secure the passive recognition of the People's attention without which the active recognition of the electorate's explicit support is impossible. Within parliament, the attention of the members to an impending election is a matter of course. Hence, electoral struggle—and also compromise and bargaining— can proceed in accordance with fairly rational and transparent interests. But when it is the support of a mass electorate that is in question, there must also be a struggle for the People's passive attention. It is indicative of Weber's ocular, disciplinary conception of popular power that he did not see election day—the one formal moment when voice and decision occur on a mass scale in modern democracy—as the key event of the electoral process. Indeed, the reprioritization of the campaign over the election is one of the central developments of Weber's late political thinking. The formal support of the electorate in the form of actual election results was merely the premise of the political contest, which was itself the real generator of charisma. It was not the actual election but the *campaign* for popular attention and support prior to election day and the active maintenance of these things following victory that most contributed to the formation and validation of the leader's charismatic authority. It needs to be stressed that during the campaign process, the People contributes, *not* by exercising its voice, but rather by remaining a silent and passive audience of political events, appeals, debates, and so forth.

Second, the charismatic leader in mass democracy would be someone who articulated and defended higher goals, beyond the mere administration of things, such as those connected to a world-historical mission, the defense of culture, and substantive forms of justice. The charismatic leader would inject a passionate element into politics, yet at the same time would have this passion tamed by both inner balance and a pragmatic desire to see the mission realized.[46] Both elements—the passion and the restraint—would be fostered by the norm that successful politicians would need to make frequent public appearances. On the one hand, the necessity of attaining and maintaining the People's attention would encourage successful politicians in mass democracy to articulate and pursue national projects that transcended mere administrative efficiency and were thus capable of inspiring a sense of higher purpose—a quality which the first President Bush aptly referred to as "the vision thing." On the other hand, the unpredictability and pressure of mass appearances—the fact that they would not merely be acclamatory celebrations of the leader's triumph but also tests and proving grounds of the leader's merit—meant that only individuals with a modicum of self-control, poise, and perspicacity could possibly be considered for positions of leadership.

Finally, the People would render politicians in mass democracy *responsible*—not by holding their decisions accountable to the People's own preferences and opinions about how issues should be resolved—but by subjecting leaders to an unprecedented level of surveillance such that it would be impossible for the leaders to disclaim their actions and deny complicity in events in which they were involved. To be sure, Weber supported policies that would enable political leaders to be removed, whether by parliament or by recall. But he did not think this would be a common procedure. What would be normalized, however, was the rise of leaders who were responsible because they were constantly being watched. Leaders could not hide like bureaucrats in obscure hierarchies and opaque technical knowledge. Nor could they conceal themselves behind the traditional pomp of monarchs or aristocrats. Unlike these other types, the politician in mass democracy would feel him- or herself as being under intense surveillance. The People's gaze, in effect, creates a stage—and the stage was a device whereby leaders would be both elevated (empowered to speak in the name of the People or at least directly to the People) yet constrained by the very condition of this publicity. Even though Weber expected leaders to make their own decisions—and to direct the government and shape the political agenda from the top down—he nonetheless called for a government's administration to be subjected to rigorous processes of public surveillance (*Verwaltungsöffentlichkeit*) and inspection (*Verwaltungskontrolle*). The People's most distinctive and important role was not to decide, but to engage in a continuous observation (*die ständige Verfolgung*) of the government.[47] Just as Weber expected leaders to lead, in the sense of providing creative and independent direction to the polity, he expected followers to follow, in the sense of ceaselessly trying to throw light on the goings-on of political leaders and high officials. Although the values of popular autonomy and the surveillance of leaders are not mutually exclusive, Weber emphasized the way in which the two were different and, in particular, the way in which mass democracy satisfied the latter much more than the former.

In each of these aspects—expertise in struggle, articulation of new obligations, and responsibility—the People contributes to the education of charismatic leadership by its sight, not by its voice. Yet, even if this is true, how can such processes be considered features of popular empowerment? That Weber considered the eyes of the People as an instrument in generating a certain type of leadership does not by itself establish that the People are empowered by virtue of its spectatorship. However, it was not just any kind of audience experience Weber contemplated by the popular gaze. As I shall presently discuss, Weber thought that democratic politicians would not be in control of the conditions of their publicity. Instead, they would be subjected to conditions of candor. Thus, ordinary citizens in plebiscitary leader democracy would not simply have their spectatorship serve as a tool with which charismatic leadership would be fashioned, but they would be recipients of a privileged form of looking: the literal inspection and examination of leaders as they appeared under difficult and contested conditions on the public stage. In this respect, the popular gaze was no mere instrument, but an organ of popular empowerment.

5.5 The Shift in the *Critical Ideal* of Popular Power: From Autonomy to Candor

Does plebiscitary leader democracy contain any critical standard according to which idealistic democrats, already living in a democracy, might seek the continual moral and political development of the nation? Does Weber leave any place for democratic progressivism once the basic institutional features of liberal democracy, universal suffrage, elections, and mass parties, have been met? What emerges from an analysis of Weber's theory of charisma is that while Weber rejects the traditional answer to these questions—that the People achieves autonomy from democracy and that democratic progressivism within a democracy is therefore defined as an effort to make democratic institutions ever more responsive to the needs, interests, and preferences of the electorate—Weber's actual case studies of charismatic authority suggest a novel critical ideal: the *candor* of leaders (i.e., their lack of control of the means of their publicity) as they appear on the public stage.

It is in his suggestions about candor that Weber makes his most important contribution to a *contemporary* theory of plebiscitary democracy. The relation between charismatic leader and charismatic community can be analyzed from one of two directions. Whereas Weber primarily opted to favor the figure of the leader and examine critical ideals that flowed in and through leadership, it is also possible to flip this privileging and approach charismatic authority from the perspective of the charismatic community, which, as has been said, is no less essential to the generation of charismatic legitimacy than the leader him- or herself. If the leader's goal is the validation of a claim to charisma, Weber suggests that the charismatic community's interest is that any validation process occur through candid appearances on the part of the would-be leader. Thus, what makes candor important is not simply that it is an underexplored yet fundamental feature of the Weberian model of charismatic authority, but that unlike charisma itself, candor has clear applicability as a democratic ideal. That is to say, while the wish for strong and independent leadership confines political ethics to the select few, the insistence that leaders be candid recovers something popular within an otherwise elitist framework.

Before addressing the essential role that candor plays in Weber's analysis of charismatic leadership, it should first be made clear why Weber objected to the modern-day applicability of the traditional democratic ideal of popular *autonomy*—the ideal that the law's addressees might also understand themselves as the law's authors—and with it, the related ideal that democratic institutions might afford everyday citizens with opportunities for political participation that develop their moral and intellectual capacities. Whether autonomy was an ideal achievable even in small, face-to-face, direct democracies is something about which Weber wavered. What is certain, however, is that Weber's analysis of modern mass representative democracy explicitly rejected the relevance of the traditional ideal of authorship. If the dominant trend among theorists of representative democracy is to assert the *fundamental moral continuity* between representative democracy and direct democracy, so that the same basic ideal of an autonomous People can be achieved by both, Weber took the opposite perspective and insisted on the degree to which the authorship available under direct democracy was not exportable to the conditions of mass democracy. Counter to the Madisonian assertion that a nation's size did not threaten its capacity for self-rule—but if anything facilitated this capacity—Weber argued that mass states, especially those heavily engaged in geopolitics, had to forgo the ideal of popular autonomy: "Any numerically 'large' nation organized as a *Machtstaat* finds that, thanks to these very characteristics, it is confronted by tasks of a quite different order from those devolving on other nations such as the Swiss, the Danes, the Dutch or the Norwegians." Weber argued that "the simple, bourgeois virtues (*Bürgertugenden*) of citizenship and true democracy ... have never yet been realized in any great *Machtstaat*."[48] Weber also took aim at the ideal of civic education—the traditional expectation, found throughout democratic and republican thought, that politics might provide ordinary citizens with a means of intellectual and moral development.[49] Against this ideal,

Weber's analysis of mass democracy—characterized by insuperable power hierarchies between the organized few and the unorganized many, political rhetoric directed to the emotions rather than substantive issues, elections that were insufficient to supply more than an occasional and superficial form of popular control, and mass parties that depended on conformity to a preselected platform and ticket rather than engaged debate from the rank and file—led him to assert that mass democracy fostered the "intellectual proletariatization of the masses."[50] Rather than seek popular autonomy and civic education, then, the modern mass democracies, especially those of enormous size, would have, as has already been mentioned, "different obligations and therefore other cultural possibilities."[51]

But what were these different obligations and possibilities? One answer, common among commentators, is to stress Weber's support of the ideal of national power, so that the *Machtstaat* forgoes popular autonomy, but gains a degree of world-historical influence on the global stage. While this ideal of national strength can indeed be located in Weber's writings (and in the very name *Machtstaat*), it is hardly a democratic value. It does not embody a critical standard by which one state might be deemed more or less democratic than another—or by which a state already in possession of democratic institutions might seek further progress in a democratic direction.[52] The question needs to be posed, then: If not autonomy, is there a critical democratic ideal consistent with Weber's understanding of the People as a mass spectator of political elites—a spectator that disciplines these elites by virtue of its gaze rather than through its voice?

Given that political power in plebiscitary leader democracy realizes itself upon (i.e., takes as its object) the individual leader, it follows that any critical ideal will itself refer to the quality of leadership and seek to regulate the way in which leaders make their public appearances before the People. Of course, political theory is not accustomed to investing political spectatorship with any positive power over the actor who appears on the public stage. From Plato's allegory of the cave to Rousseau's critique of the theater to Habermas's opposition to a contemporary politics of the spectacle, there is strong aversion in political theory to understanding the audience as anything but a passive, if not manipulated and dominated, entity. The most important suggestion to come out of Weber's analysis of charismatic authority, however, is that *sight* is not without a critical function: not only because being forced to appear before the People does discipline leaders (training and cultivating charismatic qualities), but also because there is a critical standard implicit in such appearances. This is the standard of *candor*, defined most generally as the norm that the conditions under which a leader appears in public are not entirely under the control of the leader him- or herself.

It is a basic feature of charismatic authority that the charismatic leader appear in public. Unlike the bureaucrat or the aristocrat, the quasi-charismatic politician in mass democracy must come into regular and direct contact with the People—either in crowds or through the mass media. Charismatic power cannot be hidden. But within this basic norm of appearance, it is possible to affirm a critical standard by which to judge the relative quality of such appearances. After all, not all appearances by leaders in mass democracy are morally equivalent. Some have the quality of being more *genuine* or *candid*—not in any unverifiable metaphysical sense, but in the sense of the degree to which the leader is not in control of the conditions under which he or she appears. Specifically, in mass democracy candidates for office and high officials are candid to the extent their public appearances are not entirely self-produced, but on the contrary carry with them a certain amount of risk, such that it is possible, in the course of a given appearance, for the candidate to be contradicted, opposed, and even humbled. Such openness to risk may take the form of unprecedented visual and audio surveillance of the leader on the part of the citizenry. More often it has taken the form of being open to attack. In either case, not controlling the conditions of publicity means being open to a public humbling. Furthermore, it is characteristic of candor—and something that distinguishes it from mere transparency—that it be punctuated by *moments* in which some sort of memorable (because spontaneous and unscripted) occurrence reveals the political leader to the public in a form out of keeping with ordinary modes of political presentation and in a fashion not entirely under the control of the leader him- or herself. In other words, it is consistent with candor that it tends to produce momentary performances from politicians that, precisely because they are not entirely scripted or rehearsed or otherwise controlled, are worthy of being watched.

If one examines the precise dynamics of the relationship between charismatic leader and charismatic community within Weber's analysis of charismatic authority, one finds that candor, in the sense I have described it, is a necessary feature of would-be charismatic leaders' relationship to their mass audience. This can be seen most clearly in Weber's analysis of the pure charisma of the prophet, who is not only Weber's ideal type of charismatic authority but the charismatic figure who receives Weber's most sustained consideration.[53]

First of all, the appearances of the prophets were characterized by a high degree of spontaneity. This was due not simply to the fact that within the ancient world the absence of modern communications technologies necessitated that no public appearance could be entirely controlled or planned. Rather, as Weber repeatedly made clear, the spontaneous element was intrinsic to the very form of prophetic speech. The prophets were *ecstatic* individuals—not under self-control, but beside themselves in agitated frenzy: "The prophet spoke on his own, i.e., under the influence of spontaneous inspiration, to the public in the market place or to the elders at the city gate." Thus Weber could reflect: "Unconfined by priestly or status conventions and quite untempered by any self control, be it ascetic or contemplative, the prophet discharges his glowing passion and experiences all the abysses of the human heart.... There can be no doubt that these very states, originally, were considered important legitimations of prophetic charisma and, hence, were to be expected in milder forms even when not reported."[54] It should be pointed out, moreover, that the connection between ecstasy (and the spontaneity it elicited) and charisma goes beyond the prophets and is illustrated by many other bearers of pure charisma.[55]

What underwrote the prophets' spontaneity, and in general their *candor*, was not just the ecstatic psychological state characteristic of prophecy, but certain structural features of the relationship between charismatic leader and charismatic community. Most of all, candor was ensured by the fact that the prophet did not control the conditions of his or her publicity—at least not entirely. The prophets had to *endure* the very audiences they attracted and sustained. Their public appearances were characterized by probing and testing, such that they were constantly at risk of being humbled:

> The prophet's vehement attack was encountered by an equally vehement reaction of the public.... Always the life and honor of the prophets were in danger and the opposition party lay in wait to destroy them by force, fraud and derision, by counter-magic and especially counter-prophecy.... The prophets were personally attacked and pilloried, and frequently we hear of violent conflicts.... In the open street the opponents of the prophets engaged them, insulted them, and struck them in the face.[56]

As passages like this make clear, the fundamental *instability* of charismatic authority in its pure form arose not simply because charisma depended on rare individuals whose appearances in the world were few and far between, but also because even when charisma was present it struggled for survival against the twin enemies of opposition and indifference. In other words, even when successful, the prophets were challenged and humbled. Indeed, one of the most notable features of charisma that emerges from the example of the prophets is that charisma is not at all the same as being well liked or popular.[57] The attainment of charisma was consistent with subjection to personal abuse, exposure, and embarrassment:

> Misunderstood and hated by the mass of their listeners they never felt themselves to be supported and protected by them as like-minded sympathizers as did the apostles of the early Christian

community.... Indeed, the pathos of solitude overshadows the mood
of the prophets.... Once the pre-exilic prophet stepped forth and
raised his voice to speak to the multitude he regularly had the feeling
of facing people who were tempted by demons to do evil.... In any
case, the prophet felt himself to be standing before deadly enemies, or
to face men whom his God had intended to make suffer terrible mis-
fortunes. His own sib hated him.... He returned to the solitude of his
home viewed with horror and fear, always unloved, often ridiculed,
threatened, spit upon, slapped in the face.... Unlike the possession
of pneuma in the early Christian sources, the prophet's attainment of
a state of ecstasy or his ability to hear Yahwe's voice is nowhere said
to be a perquisite for his audience. Prophetic charisma rather was a
unique burdensome office—often experienced as a torment.[58]

There is, then, this remarkable quality about charismatic authority: that
the leader is at once elevated and challenged vis-à-vis the mass audience
over whom the leader holds sway. In other words, it would be wrong to
see the burdens endured by the prophets as something antithetical, or
counterpoised, to their charismatic status; rather, it was the very endurance of such public risk that helped to constitute the claim to charismatic authority. In the case of Luther, for example, the utterance of the
famous words "Here I stand, I can do no other"—which for Weber is
the quintessence of charisma—occurs in a public trial in which Luther's
very life is at stake. Likewise, Pericles, whom Weber repeatedly invokes
as a bearer of pure charisma, was successful without necessarily being
popular. He had to endure scandal and prosecution of his closest friends
and allies. The exaltation of the charismatic leader not only was distinct
from his or her exultation, but commonly developed in opposition to
such exultation.

     In addition to the constant risk of being probed and even humiliated, it
was also typical of the ancient prophets that they provided certain *moments*
that were exceptional and beyond the everyday. To a certain extent, such
momentousness was ensured by the fact that, as Weber explains, pure charisma only arises in times of great distress—that it appears in response
to crises that are themselves out of the ordinary.[59] But it is also true of
bearers of pure charisma, especially the ancient prophets, that they proved
themselves through *miracles*. We ought to understand the miracle not only
in its religious sense, as the production of supernatural events, but also
literally as a *miraculum*: something worthy of being wondered at or gazed
upon. What made the prophets special was not simply their proximity to
the public gaze, but that their appearances themselves tended to be highly
unusual and wondrous to behold. Indeed, the condition of their receiving and maintaining the attention of the public was their strangeness.

I have already mentioned the ecstatic states typical of the prophets. But the prophets also undertook other forms of "wondrous" behavior:

> The prophets engaged in strange activities thought to be significant as omens. Ezekiel, like a child, built himself out of tile stones and an iron pan a siege play. Jeremiah publicly smashed a jug, buried a belt and dug the putrid belt up again, he went around with a yoke around his neck, other prophets went around with iron horns, or like Isaiah for a long time, naked. Still others, like Zachariah, inflicted wounds upon themselves, still others were inspired to consume filth, like Ezekiel.[60]

These were spectacles, to be sure, and no doubt in certain instances carefully premeditated, but they must be distinguished sharply from the *pomp* characteristic of the feudal monarch's appearance before amassed minions and also typical of the way most democratic theorists today tend to envision plebiscitary politics. For the would-be charismatic prophet, exposure was inseparable from a self-exposure that humbled, rather than celebrated, the leader and that made his or her appearances something worthy of being watched.

Given the foundational importance of candor to pure charisma, what can be said of its significance for the manufactured charisma of democratic politicians in plebiscitary leader democracy? If it is true that the People (or charismatic community) did not so much enforce the candor of the prophets as respond to it, in the modern context of plebiscitary leader democracy one of the key functions of the public gaze is to create situations in which candidates are compelled to be candid. True, Weber thought the politician in mass democracy was supposed to engage in demagoguery—in mass appeals to the People characterized by a manipulative use of emotion and propaganda. But importantly, Weber distinguished between good and bad demagoguery. At the most basic level this distinction referred to whether demagoguery was organized within a constitutional system—in which active individuals and groups would participate through elections rather than violence and parliament and the courts would remain free and independent and capable of checking the demagogue—or whether it took the form of the "politics of the street" with its reliance upon putsches, sham parliaments, intimidation, and the denial of legitimate opposition.[61] Beyond this, however, Weber also distinguished what was specific about the demagoguery of the politician in mass democracy, which he applauded, from the demagoguery that was increasingly being employed by bureaucrats, monarchs, and other high officials. Weber thought that demagogic means were on the rise everywhere and that *all* political figures had begun to engage in conscious public relations activities: "In their own way, modern monarchies, too, have gone down the road to demagogy. They employ speeches, telegrams, all kinds of emotive devices in order to enhance their prestige." During World War I, German naval commanders took public their conflicts over strategy in the hope of enlisting popular displays of support.[62] Although the democratic politician was obviously no stranger to such practices, what made the politician's brand of demagoguery special was that it was *dynamic* in the sense that it involved an interaction between audience and leader rather than unidirectional manipulation. Gladstone— whose home rule campaign in 1885–1886 was Weber's prototype for plebi- scitary leader democracy—marked a break from British political tradition not just in the degree to which his appeals went over the heads of Parlia- ment and spoke to the People directly, but in the extent to which his pub- lic addresses were extemporaneous speeches before popular crowds that often disrupted and heckled him.[63] Likewise, in the United States, what was innovative about Andrew Johnson's tumultuous presidency—often criticized for its demagogic elements and seen as a harbinger of twentieth- century mass democracy—was not only that Johnson made a great number of public speeches (for Lincoln had done this too), but that his speeches were interactive occasions that threatened, rather than cemented, his elevated status.[64] Tulis describes Johnson's brand of demagoguery as "an interplay with hecklers, and the spiritedness and vitality characteristic of effective extemporaneous talk.... Johnson relied more and more upon the novelty produced by audience interaction rather than upon alternative sets of arguments."[65] Significantly, one of the impeachment charges drawn up against Johnson was the charge of improper rhetoric that "brought the high office of the President of the United States into contempt, ridicule, and disgrace, to the great scandal of all good citizens."[66]

When Weber celebrated "the craft of demagoguery" as uniquely capa- ble of disciplining charismatic leaders within mass democracy, it was this kind of dynamic demagoguery that he had in mind.[67] The public appeals of democratic politicians would be distinguished not merely by a struggle for the public attention, but by a struggle *before* the public's attention. Par- liamentary leaders might struggle without publicity (in closed committee meetings within parliament), and monarchs might seek publicity without struggle (in unidirectional and insulated appeals to the People), but only the politician in mass democracy would routinely be engaged in a *public struggle* in the sense of public appearances characterized by risk, uncer- tainty, and potential challenges. As Weber explained, "The *politician* who achieves public power, and especially the party leader, is exposed to the glare of criticism from enemies and rivals in the press, and he can be sure that the motives and means underlying his rise will be ruthlessly exposed in the fight against him."[68] The simultaneous experience of publicity and struggle is what distinguished the demagoguery of the democratic politician and made it so productive of charismatic qualities. Democratic politicians are trained and tried on the very stage that empowers them. And this fact indicates that implicit in the notion of charisma is a popular ideal: that leaders seeking to enjoy the status of charismatic authority—or any form of popular support—ought to be subjected to candid forms of publicity.

Weber, then, did not rely on a single definition of demagoguery. There was a specifically democratic form of demagoguery, which he applauded, that was not only safe and orderly but also characterized by candid public appearances on the part of politicians.[69] It is not surprising, therefore, that included in Weber's proposals for plebiscitary leader democracy was the call for a much expanded capacity of *public inquiry* in which leaders would be brought before the public gaze under conditions of intense investigation. As an architect of the Weimar Constitution, Weber wanted the right of public inquiry not to be limited to parliamentary majorities and proposed, instead, that only one-fifth of the Reichstag be sufficient to undertake investigations. He proposed that the proceedings of such investigations be published in their entirety—the most publicity that could be expected in a time before the full development of radio, let alone television and internet. And he sought to extend the right of inquiry to local governments, which could call for a national investigatory committee if one-fifth of the local parliament made such an appeal, or on the initiative of one-tenth of the local voters.[70] Such proposals sought to dramatically increase the frequency of occasions on which leaders would appear in conditions of candor on the public stage. They reflected Weber's implicit suggestion that popular power in mass democracy was primarily an ocular force, rather than a vocal one.

Weber envisioned plebiscitary democracy as a politics of spectacles, but not in the derogatory sense that this term is often used. While plebiscitary politics certainly would have its share of fabricated and purely manipulative public appearances, it would also have moments of *candor*—of dynamic demagoguery when leaders were forced to appear before the public gaze under conditions of relative spontaneity and contestation. Whereas the pure charisma of the ancient prophets occurred within a preexisting circumstance of distress, it can be said of modern, democratically manufactured charismatic authority that it would induce distress by placing leaders into special situations of public struggle.[71] And if pure charisma tended to arise in response to a situation that was already out of the ordinary—such as war, pestilence, or famine—mass democracy would itself transcend the everyday by producing and broadcasting images of powerful individuals subjected to confrontation, abuse, and even humiliation. This was the "miracle" of democratically manufactured charisma—not the performance of some magical act, but the forced candor of otherwise reticent or manipulative powerful elites.

But this unusual account of democracy has gone unnoticed. The principle of candor and the reinvention of popular power that it signaled have remained on the periphery of political theory, underanalyzed and underappreciated. Plebiscitarianism is not currently considered a viable democratic model among students of democracy. Part of this stems, to be sure, from Weber's failure to fully develop the novel account of popular empowerment implicit in his theory of plebiscitary leader democracy. But part of the blame must be placed, as well, on Weber's two most influential successors: Carl Schmitt and Joseph Schumpeter. Although both thinkers developed accounts of democracy clearly inspired by Weber's seminal insights, neither adequately pursued the ocularity at the heart of the Weberian approach. Schmitt acknowledged many weaknesses impinging upon the viability of a vocal model of popular power. However, on the basis of an alleged homogeneity between leader and led in a well-ordered democracy, Schmitt ended up returning to a vocal understanding of popular power nonetheless—and a dangerous and illiberal one at that. With Schumpeter, on the other hand, a sharp critique of vocal processes led to a theory in which popular power appears to be all but negated: Schumpeter celebrated no alternative critical ideal, like candor, that might take the place of autonomy. Thus, Schmitt resolved Weberian plebiscitarianism into the very vocality it would seem to reject, whereas Schumpeter steered the plebiscitarian tradition in the direction of pure negativity. While there are redeeming features of both theories, their difficulties help explain why the Weberian reinvention of popular power did not take hold among ethically minded democratic theorists of the last century.

5.6 Carl Schmitt's Incomplete Critique of the Popular Voice

Carl Schmitt, like Weber, identified himself as a proponent of plebiscitary democracy. The extent of Weber's intellectual and personal influence on Schmitt, however, is a topic of intense scholarly debate. Given Schmitt's collaboration with the Nazi regime in the 1930s, the debate is hardly a dispassionate academic question, but has led to wholesale judgments about Weber and Schmitt alike.[72] Within the specific dimension of democratic theory, it would seem that the linkage between the two thinkers is complex. Albeit for somewhat different reasons, Schmitt followed Weber in insisting that it made no sense to interpret large-scale, liberal representative democracies of the twentieth century—what Schmitt called the "parliamentary legislative state"—as realizing the voice of the People. Like Weber, Schmitt insisted that the laws that came out of a parliament could not be conceived as the People's will and that, accordingly, popular autonomy was not achieved in the normal functioning of the modern state.

But if, as I have demonstrated, Weber's critique of the popular voice led him to abandon a vocal paradigm of popular power and to redefine the moral promise of democracy in accordance with a nonvocal, ocular ideal of candor, Schmitt's plebiscitarianism remained within the confines of the very vocal model it criticized and aimed, instead, at reviving a popular voice that would now be mediated by an authoritarian leader. Thus, even though Weber and Schmitt shared a common critique of the capacity of liberal mass democratic states to realize popular autonomy, their respective visions for advancing beyond nineteenth-century idealism were distinct and to a large degree opposed.

Schmitt was especially hostile to the notion that the parliamentary legislative state derived its legal norms from reason. He rejected, therefore, any claim that law indirectly satisfied a hypothetical kind of popular sovereignty (what the People as rational actors *would* want). Schmitt took critical aim at the various forms of rationality often attributed to the parliamentary state. To the extent such rationality was supposed to inhere in the deliberative discourse of a parliamentary chamber, which collected together diffuse viewpoints into one deliberative whole, Schmitt exposed the various ways in which modern parliamentarians fell well short of deliberative ideals and instead behaved as mere delegates for economic and special interests. To the extent such rationality was supposed to originate out of rational procedures and formalistic constraints on the nature of law, such as generality and universality, Schmitt argued that these standards were too minimal to produce substantive outcomes and, if anything, only weakened the state against potential enemies who would thereby be included and afforded respect.[73]

If the modern parliament could not represent the People by embodying reason, neither could it represent the People by forming a collective popular will. From his earliest writings, Schmitt objected to the notion that the statutory production of parliament could be said to reflect a coherent legislative will, let alone a coherent popular will.[74] Schmitt was a critic of European-style parliamentary elections, which, by proportionally aggregating votes from party lists, had the double weakness of rendering electoral contests bereft of clear and substantive decisions and of thereby making it impossible for the People's unity to take shape.[75] Moreover, like Weber, Schmitt argued that a similar functionalism afflicted decision making within parliament where competition and negotiation among parties and interest groups prevented unification, genuine leadership, and clear commitment to a cause.[76] That parliament might manufacture a provisional articulation of the popular will was a proposition Schmitt found empty and illogical.

To be sure, Schmitt had his own specific understanding of the obstacles in the way of achieving popular autonomy within the constitutional state.

Unlike Weber, Schmitt argued that constitutionalism itself—specifically representative government, the separation of powers, and liberal rights—stymied the emergence of the popular will.[77] And Schmitt was especially struck by the problem that a legal norm, even one allegedly ratified by the People, would still suffer from intense indeterminacy in its application and thus depend on the discretion of judicial, bureaucratic, and executive authorities. But in the broad contours of Schmitt's diagnosis of the modern liberal state, as well as in many of the specific details, Schmitt shared Weber's view that the People was not a government-behind-the-government: it did not indirectly author the norms and conditions of public life. Consequently, whereas nineteenth-century democratic idealists had argued for, or simply assumed, a basic equation of the People with the legislative organ of the state, for Schmitt, like Weber, it became a key feature of the People's essence that it be dissociated from any formal embodiment in the institutions of government. Defining the People in negative terms, Schmitt could write: "The People in its essence persists as an entity that is unorganized and unformed."[78]

However, whereas Weber's debunking of the liberal parliamentary state's pretension of embodying a popular will led him to be altogether skeptical about the existence of such a will, Schmitt went in the other direction. Schmitt's relentless critique of parliamentary government's capacity to represent the popular will did not lead him to despair that such a will existed or that the People might have its voice reflected in the substantive laws and decrees of a properly organized state.[79] He never doubted that the People, though unorganized and unformed, was defined by a substantive homogeneity (*Artgleichheit*) with regard to some set of ethnic, racial, religious, or other criteria. Indeed, for Schmitt, the homogeneity of the political community—its unity, its self-identity, and, above all, its possession of a coherent intentional *will*—was precisely what democracy meant.[80]

The People as a self-identical, homogeneous, intentional entity was kept out of the everyday functioning of the liberal constitutional state, but this did not mean that such an entity did not exist. On the contrary, Schmitt argued that the People could be considered the author of founding constitutional moments.[81] And he claimed, further, that the People was most perfectly realized in instances of acclamation when the collective populace, or a significant portion of it, assembled in direct and spontaneous support of some person, program, or cause.[82] This appeal to the pure presence of the People, to a People that becomes genuine insofar as it appears in a collective and public acclamation, is distinct to Schmitt. Unlike Weber, Schmitt oriented his theory of democracy around the rediscovery of the popular voice and its reinstallation vis-à-vis all the various counterforces that prevented its appearance. Key to this approach was the doctrine: "There are different degrees and scope of participatory immediacy."[83] Acclamation of the pure type was altogether absent from the parliamentary legislative state and, in any case, unlikely to be a regular part of any modern state.[84] Properly conducted plebiscites, however, would be able to approximate the People's pure acclamatory presence.[85] Specifically, Schmitt contemplated a situation in which an authoritarian leader would pose questions to the People. The referenda Schmitt described and endorsed would be voted upon in public (not in secret), without meaningful contestation from an opposing party, and via a question-asking process that was entirely determined from above.[86]

What is striking about Schmitt's plebiscitary theory—and what differentiates his account from that of other Nazi collaborators who also invoked the legitimizing function of authoritarian plebiscites—is that Schmitt was explicit about the structural limitations of the plebiscite itself. Like Weber, Schmitt acknowledged that any direct appeal to the People via a referendum would be confined by structural limitations on the public voice: its binariness, its rarity, and, above all, its dependence on the question being asked.[87] Indeed, Schmitt went so far as to say that "those who pose the question are in a position to decide the substantive outcome through the manner of posing the question."[88] Accordingly, even in his most totalitarian writings, Schmitt continued to define the People as playing a *nonpolitical role* within the state, validating questions structured and submitted by an authoritarian leader.[89] This differentiated Schmitt from Nazi theorists who interpreted National Socialism simply in terms of popular sovereignty, but it also distinguished him from Weber, for whom the various limitations of the plebiscite made it an irrational legislative device that should only be used as a matter of last resort.[90] Schmitt could resolve this apparent contradiction—that even though he acknowledged the passivity of the People vis-à-vis the leader, he still invoked the plebiscite not only as a genuine expression of the popular will, but as one superior to all other formulations in the modern state—only by reiterating his fundamental assumption about the substantive homogeneity (*Artgleichheit*) of a democratic political community. This homogeneity meant that the leader and the People would share a substantive equality that itself would dictate certain courses of action. Democratic homogeneity, according to Schmitt, required "the identity of the homogenous people that includes both those governing and governed. And it denies the difference present in other state forms between the governing and the governed.... On the whole and in every detail of its political existence, democracy presupposes a people whose members are similar to one another and who have the will to political existence."[91] Such a system placed enormous faith in the integrity of the leader: not only must the leader be at one with the substantive identity of the People, but, additionally, the leader must "pose the correct question in the proper way and not misuse the great power that lies in the posing of the question."[92] Schmitt appears to have thought that a question would represent simultaneously a referendum on an issue and an acclamation of the leader (and his or her authority to ask the question)—a twofold result that the actual Nazi plebiscites were also designed to achieve.[93] But it is clear that Schmitt located the ultimate constraint on leaders, not in any institutional voting processes that would hold them responsive and accountable to the public, but rather in the highly suspect, vague, unrealistic, and altogether unappealing assumption of a substantive homogeneity between leader and led and, more generally, between all members of a democratic political community.[94]

Whether or not Schmitt's theory of plebiscitary democracy is rightly described as National Socialist, it is problematic in many ways. From a logical standpoint there are numerous lingering concerns: for example, why are questions posed to the People by an authoritarian leader considered more authentic and legitimate than those asked by parliament? Further, if a leader is already at one with the People, why ask the questions at all? From a philosophical perspective, however, the great objection to Schmitt is that he obstructed the development of the most promising features of Weber's reinvention of popular power. It is not simply, as numerous commentators have rightly insisted, that Weber intended the plebiscitary dynamics he outlined to occur within a liberal state with an independent parliament and judiciary. More deeply, Weber, as I have argued, located the power dynamics in a plebiscitary regime as occurring *between* People and leader, so that the People realizes its empowerment precisely insofar as the leader is constrained. Under Schmitt's model, by contrast, the leader becomes the unchallenged authority that asks questions and that derives legislative will out of the People. Whereas Weber's plebiscitary theory was paradoxically skeptical about the plebiscite, Schmitt made this institution the centerpiece of his account. Thus, while Weber reinvented popular power by moving beyond the traditional conception of the People in terms of voice, Schmitt returned to this familiar vocal ontology. Even though Schmitt seemed to accept that the popular voice would be more muted and passive than previous democratic theorists had thought, this voice, despite all its limitations and imperfections, was still the key dimension of popular empowerment and, strangely, the sole form of legitimation for the authoritarian state.

In one small way, however, a trace of the Weberian legacy remains in Schmitt's plebiscitarianism. Schmitt envisioned the leader as having to appear continually before the People, posing questions and receiving acclaim. While Schmitt focused only on the vocal aspects of this process—understanding the leader as the midwife of the People's voice—the choreography of a public leader regularly appearing before a mass audience is clearly in keeping with Weber's own theory. What Schmitt failed to observe, however, was that such ocular processes also contained their own normative and critical potential that might form the centerpiece of a novel, safe, responsible plebiscitary alternative within democratic theory.

5.7 Schumpeter's Plebiscitarianism

If Schmitt's account of plebiscitarianism will always be mired by its authoritarianism, a potentially more promising development of plebiscitarian ideas was undertaken by Joseph Schumpeter, the Austrian economist and American émigré, in his work *Capitalism, Socialism, and Democracy* (1942). The democratic theory that Schumpeter expounded in this work is the most widely known of the plebiscitary tradition. Not only was it largely inspired by Weber, but it has inspired more recent plebiscitarian efforts as well.[95] At the heart of Schumpeter's account is a fundamental contrast he draws between two interpretations of what goes on in contemporary mass democracy. On the one hand, there is the classical doctrine, which understands democracy in terms of popular self-rule (the People's self-legislation via elections and public opinion). Schumpeter argued that while close analysis of what actually occurs in democratic states solidly refutes the classical doctrine, the doctrine nonetheless continues to dominate the way democracy is conceptualized both within and outside political science. In order to correct this disjunct between theory and practice, Schumpeter provided his own alternate account, which he called "*competitive leadership*," according to which "the democratic method is that institutional arrangement for arriving at political decisions in which individuals acquire the power to decide by means of a competitive struggle for the people's vote." Democracy as competitive leadership is doubly hostile to the classical doctrine. Not only does it define democracy merely as a method of leadership selection and not also as a moral ideal, but it proceeds without any claims about the People's capacity to author the laws and norms under which it lives. As was the case with Weber, on Schumpeter's account democracy no longer takes law as its object, but rather relates above all to specific conditions impinging on leaders: that they owe their power to a competitive struggle and that they know they must face such a struggle again. This shift in the object of democracy from law to leadership and Schumpeter's critique of the People's capacity for self-legislation within the conditions of contemporary mass democracy are the most direct and significant Weberian lineages of his plebiscitarianism.

   While Schumpeter's model of competitive leadership has proved influential among social scientists as an allegedly value-free definition of democracy to be used in determining which states qualify as democratic ones, as an early progenitor of social choice theory, and, however inappropriately, as an inspiration to economic models of democracy,[96] Schumpeter's theory is almost universally criticized and *dismissed* by democratic theorists committed to an ethical approach to political life. One of the biggest obstacles to a charitable reception of Schumpeter's account is the way he drew the contrast between his own model of competitive leadership and the so-called classical doctrine. Specifically, critics have objected that the classical doctrine is nothing but a myth. They have argued that Schumpeter described the allegedly classical ideal of popular self-rule in an excessively rigorous fashion, so that in effect the classical doctrine is no more than a straw man.[97]

Schumpeter certainly opened himself up to such dismissive interpretations. He defined the classical doctrine as asserting: "The democratic method is that institutional arrangement for arriving at political decisions which realizes the common good by making the people itself decide issues through the election of individuals who are to assemble in order to carry out its will."[98] Although this summary definition might seem defensible, or at least innocuous, Schumpeter elaborated his account of the classical doctrine in such a controversial fashion that it has ignited near-universal rejection from democratic theorists sensitive to the history of political thought. First of all, Schumpeter linked the classical doctrine to an extravagant metaphysical conception of the common good: namely, that the common good be conceived as something independent of and prior to the political process and, also, that the popular will which defines the common good be conceived as a corporate entity with a single, monolithic voice. Critics have persuasively argued both that this notion of the common good was not even held by the exponents of the classical doctrine Schumpeter identifies (Rousseau, Bentham, and the two Mills), and, in any case, such a conception is not essential to an account of democracy committed to the ideal of popular self-rule.[99] Second, the account of human nature that Schumpeter associated with the classical doctrine—that citizens enter politics with fully formed, rational opinions on most political issues facing the polity—has been deemed unrealistic and blind to the long tradition of democratic theorists upholding democracy as a setting for lively debate where opinions are formed and transformed through civic interaction.[100] Finally, Schumpeter has been taken to task for suggesting that the only justification for democracy among "traditional" theorists was its capacity to realize popular self-rule, thus forgetting the important line of theorizing that holds democracy's educative and developmental value for citizens to be an additional, if not preeminent, rationale for democratic institutions and practices.[101]

Schumpeter is, I think, vulnerable to these charges. And to the extent that he is, it needs to be realized that Schumpeter's account of the classical doctrine does a disservice not only to a conscientious history of democratic thought, but to the intelligibility and viability of a theory of plebiscitary democracy. By suggesting that the rival of plebiscitary democracy is, as one critic describes it, "improbable metaphysics [and] unrealistic articles of faith about human nature," Schumpeter gave the false impression that the appeal of plebiscitary democracy is merely the appeal of sobriety and minimalism—that is, the appeal of relieving ourselves of absurd claims.[102] In other words, Schumpeter failed the very theory of plebiscitary democracy he sought to outline to the extent he presented that theory in terms of a more chastened epistemology and not in terms of an alternate set of positive ideals.

But this failure was not total. Although Schumpeter's sketch of the classical doctrine did include highly disputable claims about the metaphysics of the common good, an impossibly demanding theory of human nature, and an unnecessarily limited account of the kinds of reasons for which one might support democratic institutions, there was a *fourth* aspect to Schumpeter's account of the classical doctrine that does point in the direction of elaborating a normative conception of plebiscitary democracy. This aspect has to do with the nature of the People in a representative democracy—specifically with the issue of the *vocal ontology of popular power*.

If one rereads Schumpeter's summary of the classical doctrine—"the democratic method is that institutional arrangement for arriving at political decisions which realizes the common good by making the people itself decide issues through the election of individuals who are to assemble in order to carry out its will"—the core assertion, independent of any of the claims that have earned him rebuke, is that the People itself decides issues through the election of individuals.[103] Rather than understand popular power in terms of its most obvious function as a selector of leadership, the classical doctrine, Schumpeter insisted, conceives of the power of the People as a power to shape the substantive political decisions that are actually proposed, debated, and passed by the select few who do hold government office. We caricature this element of Schumpeter's account of the classical doctrine if it is taken to mean that the People determines every policy or every piece of legislation within a representative democracy—or, if it is taken to mean that in a representative democracy the People is always obeyed. Rather, what Schumpeter is describing here, and what he goes on to criticize, is a vocal model of popular power—according to which popular power, to the extent it exists, is understood as a legislative force: that is, that the fundamental meaning of obeying the People is realizing *legislative output* that coheres with the People's opinions, preferences, and values about how the polity should be governed. Schumpeter's critique of the vocal model of popular power cannot be accused of opposing a straw man. As I demonstrated in chapter 3, the vocal model is precisely what binds together and defines "traditional" or "classical" democratic theory. It is not surprising, therefore, that although this issue of the ontology of

popular power is not commonly addressed by democratic theorists who
criticize Schumpeter's account of the classical doctrine, those who have
recognized the ontological argument have been more receptive to it than to
other aspects of Schumpeter's thought.[104]

What specifically did Schumpeter find objectionable about the vocal
ontology of popular power? One problem, according to Schumpeter, is
that everyday citizens do not tend to have clear preferences and well-
framed views that he thinks would be necessary in order to treat the electorate, not merely as a selector of leadership, but additionally as a legislator
of laws, norms, and values. Schumpeter argued that an important shift
takes place when ordinary citizens move beyond the consideration of private and immediate concerns and contemplate political questions affecting
the general public. Schumpeter described this shift as a "reduced sense
of reality." Part of what this means is the highly controversial claim that
citizens become less competent when they turn to public affairs: that they
approach public matters without the kind of responsibility that typifies the
conduct of their private affairs. But Schumpeter also made it clear that
the reduced sense of reality refers, not simply to diminished competence,
but to "an absence of effective volition." It is not just that citizens are less
careful and less prudent when forming their public, as opposed to private,
opinions; it also happens that everyday citizens' engagement with politics
is much less likely to take the form of clear notions about what courses
of action they affirm and oppose than is their approach to private concerns. As Schumpeter described this reduction of volition: "One has one's
phrases, of course, and one's wishes and daydreams and grumbles; especially, one has one's likes and dislikes. But ordinarily they do not amount
to what we call a will—a psychic counterpart of purposeful responsible
action."[105] Politics approaches the citizen from the outside. Political events
and information are almost always prior to the individual who engages with
them. Schumpeter's theory is grounded on the insight that it is wrong to
impute to ordinary citizens an intentionality vis-à-vis the events and issues
they encounter. Not only are elections wrongly seen as legislating certain
policy courses, but even the selection of leadership—which Schumpeter
understood as the true function of electoral power—is conceived, not as an
intentional and autonomous mechanism whereby the People *chooses* leaders of their liking, but rather as a competitive process between political
elites in which the People functions as the prize to be won rather than as the
sovereign to be obeyed.[106] Thus, Schumpeter's critique of the vocal paradigm of popular power was not limited to challenging the *object* of popular
power according to that model (the view that popular power reveals itself
in law), but extended to calling into question the *organ* by which the People
effects its power (its status as a *decisional* entity that makes its force felt
through acts of choice).[107]

Even though it is not merely an assertion about competence but also a claim about the degree to which intentionality typifies the ordinary citizen's engagement with political phenomena, this argument about everyday citizens' "reduced sense of reality" is still highly controversial and likely to find many objections grounded in recent research on the rationality of civic behavior. Numerous studies have argued that citizens do not need to have clearly formed views in order to make decisions that can plausibly be said to further their interests. They can, for example, rely on cues from trusted political elites and follow gut reactions that more often than not successfully further their aims.[108] Although this counterargument is not entirely responsive to Schumpeter's critique—since he meant to call into question the very presence of an underlying sense of interest and not just the capacity to further it—it is nonetheless important to realize that Schumpeter makes a second, very different criticism of the vocal ontology of popular power. Not only do voters often not approach politics with preconceived opinions about policies, but *even if they did*, the institutions of voting do not afford a proper context for expressing them. Even assuming a hypothetical situation in which ordinary citizens in a representative democracy actually did have well-formed and prior opinions on most issues, the vocal ontology of popular power would not necessarily follow: "Even if the opinions and desires [of individual citizens] were perfectly definite and everyone acted on them with ideal rationality and promptitude, it would not necessarily follow that the political decisions produced by that process from the raw material of those individual volitions would represent anything that could in any convincing sense be called the will of the people."[109] Part of the problem, now readily familiar to the social choice theory Schumpeter helped to inspire, is that there are many political questions—especially those that are neither matters of gradation nor reducible to a binary yes-no solution—for which it is difficult to aggregate individual preferences into a meaningful and nonarbitrary, let alone nonmanipulated, collective outcome. But Schumpeter's argument here also refers to something more basic: namely, that the mass electorate is highly limited in what it can say. There is hardly any scope for average citizens to engage in legislative decision making. Even assuming a perfectly rational procedure for vote aggregation, a periodic election for leadership—which is rare, frequently binary, and often experienced as a choice whose options have been preselected—is greatly restricted in its capacity to transmit underlying legislative preferences to the extent these can be found in the electorate.

Schumpeter saw both of these criticisms of the vocal ontology of popular power—that citizens do not tend to have clear views and that the electoral process is an insufficient organ for expressing views to the extent citizens do have them—as being intimately related. Indeed, it is precisely the limited scope for legislative decision making that in part explains the reduced volition of everyday citizens. As Schumpeter argued, "For the private citizen musing over national affairs there is no scope for such a [legislative] will and no task at which it could develop. He is a member of an unworkable committee, the committee of the whole nation, and this is why he expends less disciplined effort on mastering a political problem than he expends on a game of bridge."[110] Thus, Schumpeter can be read as anticipating more recent work in political opinion, like that of Zaller, which links the absence of clear opinions within large segments of the mass electorate to an absence of a context in which it would be appropriate to possess them.[111]

In putting forward these claims about the diminished volition that characterizes everyday citizens' engagement with politics and the institutional limits upon a mass electorate's capacity to express legislative preferences, Schumpeter made it clear that his critique of the classical doctrine, in addition to its other less defensible features, was also a critique of the People—specifically, a critique of the vocal model of popular power. Schumpeter objected to the claim that the People, the mass of everyday citizens in their collective capacity, is a *decisional* entity that realizes its power through the selection of potential laws, norms, and policies that are to be translated into the output of government. Schumpeter thus refuted the very economic conception of democracy to which he is sometimes linked.[112] Whereas the economic model sees citizens, and more generally the People, as consumers who choose candidates in order to maximize preexisting values, interests, opinions, and preferences, Schumpeter challenged this economic conception by arguing that it is incorrect to see the People as an exogenous source of legislative demands. And in making such a challenge, Schumpeter also made a lasting contribution as a historian of democratic thought. Despite other admitted weaknesses of his theory, Schumpeter was essentially correct in his claim that traditional accounts of democracy understand the People primarily as an expressive and decisional entity, since, as I have argued, there is in fact a deep and widespread tendency in modern democratic theory to understand the People in such terms.

Yet even if Schumpeter was right in his critique, there is still another major objection: that his thought is a dead end. This, it seems, is the genuine weakness of Schumpeter's theory, although not a necessary one. In other words, if Schumpeter was a keen critic of the classical doctrine of democracy, he was much less fruitful in providing a replacement to that doctrine. To be sure, the ideal of *competition* that Schumpeter linked to his own account of democracy potentially could be the basis of a novel theory of democracy and democratization—assuming, that is, that competition is understood, *not* as it usually is as an economic ideal very much in keeping with the traditional value of self-rule (the notion that competition among politicians and political parties best realizes the policy interests of the electorate), but rather as an existential condition: namely, that leaders undergo and endure the risk, uncertainty, and unpredictability of having to face challenge and contestation. According to this latter interpretation, the People's impact in politics would be conceived primarily as a risk-inducing force (so that elections, for example, would be understood as imposing uncertainty and destabilization upon leaders rather than securing their legitimation) and, by implication, the empowerment of the People would mean a maximization of leaders' subjection to public contestation above and beyond election day. But this understanding of competition—and, more generally, of Schumpeter's positive contribution to democracy—has not taken hold. On the one hand, Schumpeter himself stymied such a rendering of his theory when he made the brief but nonetheless influential statement that democracy properly understood was no more than a method of leadership selection—and hence not a moral ideal specifying the conditions whose maximization would constitute popular empowerment.[113] And he stymied it further when he actually argued that the People must not increase the risk imposition placed on leaders, but must limit it to election day.[114] On the other hand, those who have been inspired by Schumpeter to take up the notion of competition and use it as the basis for a progressive democratic politics have tended to rely on the familiar, economic rendering of competition (that competition supplies the People effectively with what it wants)—an interpretation that assumes the People to be a quasi-legislative force and that, thus, is wholly out of keeping with Schumpeter's arguments against conceiving of the People as a source of exogenous demand within mass political society.[115]

Schumpeter, then, is like the mirror image of Schmitt. If Schmitt developed plebiscitarianism in a way that actually invoked the notion of a popular will, Schumpeter's theory suffered from the opposite kind of problem: the emphasis of his theory was so negative—it appeared to insist only on the impossibility of popular self-rule in a legislative, vocal sense—that it is not immediately clear what positive ideals or values might be supported by a Schumpeterian approach. Although something like candor remains a latent thought in Schumpeter's notion of competition, he did not develop it.

To be sure, Schmitt and Schumpeter cannot bear the entire responsibility for the inability of Weber's ocular paradigm to take hold. Part of the blame also must be assigned to Weber himself, who never adequately consolidated his reflections on plebiscitary leader democracy into a coherent whole. Yet even if their contributions are imperfect and only partial, these early theoreticians of plebiscitarianism nonetheless indicate plebiscitary democracy's latent ethical potential: the reinvention of popular power in ocular terms and, with this, a replacement of the traditional democratic ideal of autonomy with the novel ideal of candor. Having recovered this forgotten plebiscitary tradition, my aim in the final two chapters is to develop it further and show how it might be applied to present-day democracies.

6

Putting Candor First: Plebiscitarianism and the Politics of Candor

Be sure of it. Give me the ocular proof.
—William Shakespeare, *Othello*

6.1 The Practical Application of Plebiscitarianism

What is at stake when candor—the principle that leaders not be in control of the conditions of their publicity—serves as the critical standard at the heart of a plebiscitarian approach to democracy? Certain aspects of candor already have been intimated. Candor is a political value that is unusual in the sense that it rests on the People's capacity for sight, not voice. It is, accordingly, a critical ideal responsive to the citizen-being-ruled, who is a spectator of politics rather than a decision maker and who, unlike the more familiar figure of the citizen-governor, is in fact representative of the ordinary political experience of everyday citizens in contemporary mass democracy. However, notwithstanding these general characteristics, there are issues pertaining to the practical application of a politics of candor that still need to be addressed. Most of all, there is the question of how a commitment to candor would produce a democratic politics different from existing modes of democratic progressivism. Specifically, how is candor distinct from three other, traditional democratic values: deliberation, participation, and transparency? Given that supporters of these traditional ideals would likely endorse candor to a point (and find candor at least partially implicit in their own chosen principles), it needs to be asked how *putting candor first*—making candor rather than deliberation, participation, or transparency the primary ideal of democracy—would lead the plebiscitarian to support a conception of democracy irreducible to the versions already endorsed by deliberationists, participationists, and those committed to transparency. In this chapter, I take up this issue and demonstrate how a plebiscitarian commitment to a politics of candor shapes a distinctive approach to reforming democratic institutions. Sections 6.2 through 6.5 explore the consequences of making candor the primary value in democratic reform by analyzing three practices of contemporary mass democracy:

leadership debates, public inquiries of leaders, and press conferences. Section 6.6. concludes by summarizing the logic of putting candor first.

6.2 The Meaning of Candor: Its Irreducibility to Participation, Deliberation, and Transparency

Despite the diversity of approaches within democratic theory, it can be said with confidence that few democratic theorists are in favor of scripted and rehearsed public appearances lacking in spontaneity and genuineness. In other words, most share the intuition that, ceteris paribus, candor is a good thing. This is not to say that this intuition is made explicit by dominant approaches within democratic theory—since, in fact, an appreciation for candor has generally remained preconscious and unobserved—but only that even a cursory consideration of familiar democratic ideals reveals a close connection to the novel ideal of candor. If one examines three such traditional democratic values—deliberation, participation, and transparency—one can see that they link up to candor in obvious ways.

So, for example, in the case of deliberation, on most accounts of deliberative democracy, candor is implied as an important aspect of what differentiates a discourse aimed at mutual understanding from lesser forms of social coordination grounded in shared economic interests or mere strategic manipulation. It is difficult to imagine a genuine dialogue that did not include both the personal norm of sincerity and the institutional norm that participants not be in control of the conditions of the discourse but rather remain out of control to the extent they are forced to listen to the claims of others, have their own statements altered by respondents, and, in general, engage in a process whose outcome is fundamentally unpredictable.[1] This connection between deliberation and candor is seen in the British practice of prohibiting prepared speeches to be read out in Parliament. Though the rationale for this prohibition is usually conceived in terms of maximizing the deliberativeness of parliamentary discussion, such regulations reveal the close, albeit undertheorized, linkage between deliberation and candor.[2]

Likewise, not only is candor implicit in most accounts of deliberation, but it also bears an important connection to the goal of participation. Although participationists are almost by definition opposed to a politics of mere spectatorship, being a spectator is often seen as a step on the road to a more fully participatory civic life.[3] Thus, insofar as candid public appearances are more worthy of being watched—and in fact more likely to be watched—candor can be seen as an important, if rudimentary, step in the pursuit of participatory politics. More deeply, it can be said that candor can actually inspire even the most active forms of civic engagement when it reveals to the public political abuses that would be otherwise concealed. Political history contains numerous instances in which the candid appearances of leaders—especially moments that have exposed their offhand remarks and dealings—have inspired renewed civic activism and participation. The Watergate tapes provide one important instance of this phenomenon. For a more recent example, consider that in 2006 the Hungarian prime minister, Ferenc Gyurcsány, was recorded admitting, while addressing a supposedly closed-door gathering of his party, "Obviously we lied [to the country] throughout the last year and a half, two years"—and, further, that his government lied "morning, evening and night" in order to win reelection. The subsequent broadcast of this tape sparked a revival of civic activism in Hungary, leading tens of thousands of ordinary citizens to demonstrate, protest, and meet together.[4]

Finally, the commitment to transparency shares a great deal with candor. It follows that the more candid the conditions of leaders' publicity, the more likely they are to contribute valuable knowledge and accurate information to the citizenry. One of the main criticisms of a politics of mere spectacle, in which leaders control their own public images, is that it is disturbingly vacant as pertains to useful information about issues.[5] The type of confrontation and dynamic exchange characteristic of institutional candor more often that not would aid—or at least not harm—the effort to render government activities transparent and, hence, more accountable and responsive.

These connections between candor, on the one hand, and deliberation, participation, and transparency, on the other, help explain why it is that there is a general intuition that candor is a good thing. However, just as it is important to understand candor's connection to familiar democratic ideals, it is also necessary to appreciate what is distinctive about candor— why, that is, a commitment to candor is irreducible to these three other traditional aspirations. Before detailing this irreducibility with some practical examples, it should be said at the outset, in broad and general terms, why it is that candor is different.

Candor is not the same as deliberation because candor is not necessarily committed to the search for collective understanding about matters pertaining to the common good. Moreover, although deliberation usually requires an element of candor, candor can take place without deliberation. In contested situations of nondeliberative discourse, there is a back-and-forth in which neither party is in control, yet at the same time in which there is little cooperation, reciprocity, or desire to reach an understanding.[6] Another difference is that candor usually takes place in the context of public spectacles, which are deemed by some deliberationists to be inherently hostile to deliberation. Against this tendency of deliberative democrats to look away from the spectacular politics of the few (the leaders with great, disproportionate power in mass democracy) and to focus instead on the potential for more deliberation among lesser legislators and everyday citizens, the plebiscitarian value of candor is a regulative norm that applies precisely to the most powerful decision makers in a polity as they appear on the public stage.

Likewise, candor is not at all the same thing as participation. Insofar as candor applies to the conditions of leaders' publicity on the public stage, it is removed from the small-scale political activities of less prominent citizens. Participationists who take seriously the power of these activities and aim to see them extended cannot help but remain equivocal at best regarding the very topic of leaders' public appearances. The practical areas of interest to a plebiscitarian—such as the three contexts I analyze in this chapter: leadership debates, public inquiries, and press conferences—no doubt will strike many participatory democrats as marginal to the pursuit of democracy precisely because they do not involve maximizing everyday citizens' political voices and their capacities to pursue active political lives. Yet it is just here, in the alleged margins of democracy, in contexts that have to do with imposing restraints on leaders' control of their publicity rather than on the facilitation of popular authorship of norms and laws, that a plebiscitarian finds the most promising contexts for progressive democratic reform.

If the irreducibility of candor to deliberation and participation ought to be clear, somewhat less obvious is the distinction between candor and transparency. The difference is this: transparency is *impersonal*, referring to facts, information, knowledge—the things about which a decision maker would like to know. If a person is described as "being transparent," it is only in connection with a specific public issue or problem. A political event is not itself something that is transparent. Candor, however, especially when it is defined institutionally, refers to the extent to which the conditions of a leader's public appearance are outside the control of the leader him- or herself. With candor, the personal element is key—since it is precisely the individual's relation to his or her publicity that determines the degree of candor. Thus, whereas transparency seeks truth, candor seeks spontaneity and eventfulness, which are related to the pursuit of truth but still irreducible to it.

In sum, it can be said that candor is an ideal that simultaneously shares a great deal with the more familiar democratic values of deliberation, participation, and transparency, yet cannot be compressed into any of them. Putting candor first, therefore, leads to a distinct vision of democratic progressivism. In order to illustrate this distinctiveness, I now turn to three practical examples—leadership debates, public inquiries of leaders, and press conferences—where it can be shown how putting candor first makes

a substantial difference in the way the quest for democracy is defined and
pursued.

6.3 Leadership Debates

From the perspective of plebiscitarianism and the politics of candor,
televised leadership debates—such as presidential debates in American
politics—are an especially important political institution. The debates are
a site particularly well-suited to the critical ideals at stake in candor. The
debates are an instance in which candidates are not in control of the conditions of their publicity—or at least are much less in control than normal.
Thus, there is an inherent risk element in the debates. As live television
events broadcast to what at times is more than a hundred million viewers,
there is an unusual amount of pressure placed on the participants who know
that a single misstep or error could have dramatic consequences.[7] Part of
what makes the debates risky is that they are by nature conflict ridden, if
not combative. For an incumbent, the debates are likely to constitute the
most forceful attack experienced in four years.[8] Candidates must contend
with the criticism of rivals, as well as the potentially difficult probing of
questioners. Also, part of the meaning of candor is that it is productive of
special occasions that reveal leaders and candidates to the public in some
sort of unusual (because unscripted or unrehearsed) way. Debates have
been known to do precisely this, generating a host of memorable political
moments.[9] As a high-stakes, competitive event before an enormous live
audience, the debates are a remarkable occasion for injecting candor into
contemporary democratic life.

Yet, despite their special status as a potent source of candor in electoral politics, it is also clear that the debates could be much more candid.
A plebiscitarian reformer would note the many ways in which the candidates maintain substantial control over the debates. For one thing, in the
United States there is no legal obligation to debate. Thus, there were no
debates in 1964, 1968, and 1972. And even if it is true that since 1976 the
practice of debates has become quasi-institutionalized, key questions such
as the number of debates and their structure are increasingly in the hands
of the candidates themselves (or the parties they represent) rather than in
a neutral body with independent power and authority. Indeed, what has
most contributed to the blockage of a fuller realization of candor (and possibly to candor's retreat in recent years) is that since 1988 the debates have
been controlled by the bipartisan Commission on Presidential Debates
(CPD), which seeks the interests of the two major candidates.[10] Under
the CPD, nondisclosed memoranda of understanding between the two
parties determine every aspect of the debate, selecting mutually agreeable

moderators and panelists, the precise design and structure of the stage, and, most important, the debate's format.[11] As one commentator has put it, the debates have "all the careful spontaneity of a minuet."[12]

What makes the management of the debates by the candidates problematic is not simply that it violates the abstract principle of candor (that leaders not be in control of the conditions of their publicity), but that the tangible result of this arrangement is that candidates have colluded to limit the candor of the debates themselves. From the plebiscitarian perspective, there is no more candid format than having the candidates debate each other directly, asking one another questions, cross-examining each other, and each one holding the other to account for what is said. This format places candidates under the most pressure. It elicits the most conflict and competition. It generates the most risk. And the results of such a format would be the least predictable and controllable. Yet it is precisely this format that the collusion of the candidates has repeatedly prohibited.[13] In 1960, the candidates resisted network suggestions for cross-examination. In 1976, in the face of a similar refusal of the candidates to engage each other, the three journalists serving as panelists in the final debate plotted to confront the candidates on air and force them, against their will, to question each other, but the panelists failed to carry out this plan due to technical mishap.[14] In the 1980 debates, as a result of intense pressure from their nonpartisan sponsor, the League of Women Voters, the candidates initially agreed to cross-examination, but then eliminated this provision in last-minute negotiations. In 1984, cross-examination was finally permitted, but not required, with the result that it did not occur.[15] From 1984 onward, the format of the debates has been determined by memoranda of understanding between the two parties. These agreements have not only banned candidate-to-candidate questioning, but have tended to prohibit other formats also conducive to candor, such as follow-up questions from panelists and moderators, extended response times, and longer debates. In 2008, to be sure, cross-examination was officially allowed, but neither candidate opted to make use of it. Notwithstanding the democratic benefits of having any kind of debates rather than none, the shortcomings of the existing formats—the deep limitations on candor they enforce—have led numerous critics to take aim at their integrity.[16]

There is, then, this ambiguity about debates. On the one hand, they are among the most candid events of democratic politics. On the other hand, they fall well short of an ideal of candor—in the triple sense that the candidates control the format, they use this control to enforce structural limitations on the degree of candor achieved by the debates, and they hide the fact of this control through the CPD, a bipartisan (rather than nonpartisan) institution devoted to serving the interests of the two candidates (as opposed to the People's interest as an ocular entity).

That a plebiscitarian would push for greater candor in the debates is clear. What needs to be explained is how this position distinguishes the plebiscitarian from other perspectives within democratic theory. After all, the insufficiency of candor in the debates is something that exponents of other, dominant democratic ideals—deliberation, participation, and transparency—are likely to acknowledge and criticize. Thus, participationists would also favor more candid debates insofar as it has been shown that they are better able to generate interest in politics from the wider populace or supply those already interested with the information required for making a well-reasoned electoral decision. Similarly, a deliberative democrat would want to see real discourse between the candidates and, as a result, would likely favor many of the same institutional structures that a plebiscitarian would find conducive to candor. The staging and collusion that the plebiscitarian opposes would likewise be rejected by the deliberative democrat as nonconducive to rational discourse.[17] Finally, democrats interested in transparency would see candid debates as more likely to provide the public with the necessary information required for the People to govern effectively. Current practices—which enable candidates to dodge questions— inhibit the public's capacity to find out the truth and assign responsibility.[18]

As I have argued, a plebiscitarian approach to presidential debates not only calls for more candor, but *places candor first*—that is, *ahead* of these familiar democratic ideals. Placing candor first leads to some practical differences vis-à-vis the privileging of other ideals.

Consider, for example, the debates as understood from the participationist perspective. Although the participationist recognizes that the debates potentially generate interest and engagement in politics among the wider citizenry, two differences distinguish the participationist approach to debates from the plebiscitarian understanding of this institution. One of these is the issue of *emphasis* or *relevance*. From the participationist perspective—and indeed according to most democratic theory—the debates are an inherently limited form of politics, as the ordinary citizen is confined to the position of spectator. According to this dominant vantage point, the debates pale in comparison to election day, which is privileged precisely because the electorate gets to escape its everyday position of spectatorship and express itself through a rare moment of decision. When election day is validated as the democratic event par excellence, it becomes tempting for political scientists to consider the debates as paltry, marginal, and epiphenomenal.[19] For the plebiscitarian, however, the debate is the pinnacle of the electoral process as it is currently organized. Recall that Weber, the founding theorist of plebiscitary democracy, suggested a reprioritization between campaign and election, so that campaigns would no longer be for the sake of elections, but elections would be for the sake of campaigns. The plebiscitarian applies this logic to debates. For the plebiscitarian, debates are not primarily an instrument for achieving a more informed electoral choice. On the contrary, they are seen as having an intrinsic significance. Indeed, from the standpoint of political images, the debates are the rarest and most sublime events of the democratic process.[20] Second, and no doubt most important, the plebiscitarian differs from the participationist in regard to the key question of what should be the privileged *format* of the debates. The participatory approach would favor debate structures that include the People in a direct and vocal way, such as the town hall format in which ordinary citizens can ask questions of the candidates. Given the prevalence of a participatory ethos within the political culture, it is not surprising that the first town hall debate from 1992 was dubbed "the People's debate." From a plebiscitarian perspective, this identification of the People with the town hall audience (i.e., with the question-asking, interest-bearing, issue-focused group of individuals who participate in a town hall format) is suspect not simply because there is reason to doubt the representative character of the audience, but much more vitally because such a vocal modeling of popular power interferes with ocular progressivism and the commitment to candor.[21] As has been said, what would be most satisfying to the plebiscitarian would be a direct exchange between candidates, since this format best achieves the confrontation, spontaneity, and pressure that could wrest control of the debates from the candidates themselves. However, such a format necessarily depends on the *silence* of the audience as well as all other surrogates of the People's voice, such as panelists and moderators. The plebiscitary model equates the People with the abstract requirement that the candidates be forced to engage each other—and in this it differs from the traditional, embodied model of the People as a vocal being that expresses opinions and decisions about substantive issues and policies. Here, then, is an instance where the choice between conceptualizing the People on the basis of a vocal or ocular ontology makes a palpable difference in how democratic reform is considered.

Second, with regard to deliberation, one can point to important differences vis-à-vis the plebiscitarian perspective. For the deliberative democrat, the debates are an opportunity for political rivals to engage in deliberative discourse: to discuss issues in a spirit of cooperation, reciprocity, and sincerity—or at least to *listen* to the opposing perspective of the competitors.[22] Although the plebiscitarian would expect the debates to contribute to rather than detract from communication between the candidates, understanding the debates in terms of deliberative discourse is misguided according to the plebiscitarian perspective. Deliberation most classically takes place among equals committed to decision making, rather than among exceptionally powerful individuals trying to propel themselves to victory. But in a presidential debate, there is virtually no sense that the candidates are working together in conditions of cooperation, reciprocity, and mutual respect. The objective is not to reach understanding about the common good—or even to delineate carefully the nature of differences dividing the polity—but to prevail over the other by whatever measure is deemed most advantageous to secure electoral victory.[23] Now it may be the case that this competition takes place on the level of rational discourse: who has the clearest ideas, the most persuasive policies, the best command of the issues of the day. In this circumstance, it might be said that winning the debate is akin to being a better participant in a deliberative discourse. But there is little reason to think that this standard will in fact guide rivals in a debate or that it has done so in the past. Debaters might instead compete over seeming the most "presidential," or the most relaxed, or the wittiest, or the most aggrieved by the conduct of the other. That is to say, the debate is more a strategic process of image cultivation than it is a deliberative process of coming to agreement about policies and issues. Critics of a deliberative stamp have found fault with the debates precisely for their failure to achieve substantive discussion and for their combative and imagistic aspects. Following the first televised presidential debate in 1960, for example, Henry Steele Commager objected to the broadcasts for privileging "the glib, the evasive, the dogmatic, the melodramatic," over the "the sincere, the judicious, the sober, the honest in political discussion"—a sentiment that has been repeated by more recent critics.[24] The plebiscitarian, however, is concerned more with the competitiveness of the debate than the substance of the competition. What matters is that leaders not be in control of the event, not that they be made to enter into a focused discussion on a particular issue or policy.

Finally, the difference between plebiscitarianism and a commitment to transparency in relation to debates needs to be stressed. Those interested in transparency understand the debates as a means of supplying truthful information about government. On this model, the candidates ideally would inform the electorate about various issues and help clarify what each would set out to do if elected. In a limited way the plebiscitarian expects accuracy of information to be a by-product of the debates, in the sense that viewers likely would be more informed about issues and electoral decisions—rather than deceived and less informed—after watching a debate. Still, it is not truth or accuracy of information, but rather competition and candor, that define the purpose of the debate for the plebiscitarian. In other words, what is being transmitted in the debate is not so much impersonal information about policies, issues, and campaign platforms, but the personal qualities of the candidates themselves. Commentators have differed in their explanation of precisely what kind of personal quality is revealed by the debates, using such concepts as stature, facial expression, sincerity, poise, showmanship, quickness on one's feet, preparedness, or organization.[25] However this test of character is defined, what is essential is that plebiscitarianism understands the debates as revealing persons, not issues. A format that put less pressure on the candidates but led to more information—such as candidates being questioned by informed journalists—might better achieve transparency, but would not be the most candid format.

Overall, it can be said that the plebiscitarian perspective offers two things to the study of presidential debates. On the one hand, a plebiscitarian reformer has a clear sense of the proper format for these debates: leaders' cross examination of each other. On the other hand, the plebiscitarian takes the debates much more seriously than they are often treated. The debates are nonelectoral—they have little to do with the People as a vocal, legislating entity—yet they supply the People, in its very condition as spectator, with something worthwhile and satisfying. The debates' connection to the citizen-spectator is a feature usually seen as a drawback, but it is precisely this aspect that makes them valuable from the plebiscitarian perspective. Indeed, it can be said that debates—as institutional structures in which leaders appear in relative candor before a mass audience—are the prototype for plebiscitary progressivism in general.

6.4 Investigations and Trials

As the institutional value grounding a plebiscitarian brand of progressivism, candor refers to the maximization of situations in which leaders' publicity is out of their full control—situations that are subject to risk and public contestation such as are likely to provide a certain momentousness to political life. Public inquiries—in which leaders are investigated, tried, and possibly punished—are a prime example of a site of candor. As with presidential debates, the public inquiry of leaders and high officials is a practice that few would oppose outright. There is wide consensus that no one is above the law in a well-ordered liberal democracy and that there must be mechanisms for bringing transgressing leaders to justice. The question about public inquiries is not whether they should occur but how they should be arranged and organized.

The plebiscitarian seeks the maximization of public inquiries as part of the more general effort to proliferate instances in which leaders appear before the public gaze under conditions not controlled by the leaders themselves. Max Weber's proposal for the Weimar Constitution, which I discussed in chapter 5, is an example of the kind of policy that would satisfy the plebiscitarian. Weber proposed that only a small minority of parliament, 20 percent, be sufficient to launch a public investigation. And he argued against restricting this power to national legislatures, proposing that it be extended to local parliaments as well as to petitions constituting only 10 percent of local electorates.[26] Such devices, which were not ultimately realized in the Weimar Constitution, would have significantly lowered the bar for investigating leaders. Thus, although Weber was profoundly skeptical about the public's capacity to voice itself and legislate the norms and conditions of public life, he did think it was both possible and desirable to meaningfully expand the public's capacity for sight and oversight.

What Weber proposed, in effect, was a decoupling of the right to voice or legislate, on the one hand, and the right to spectate, on the other. The ordinary tendency in political theory is to equate these two prerogatives, so that the same standard of power applies to each. The normal procedure, in other words, is for a parliamentary majority that has the power to enact and ratify laws also to control when to investigate leaders and impose upon them an exceptional form of publicity full of contestation and risk. In the United States, for example, it is taken for granted that the legislative majority controls all committees and, hence, all investigations.[27] Of course, other liberal democracies have somewhat different rules and some have separated to a certain extent the right to oversee from the right to legislate.[28]

Bruce Ackerman, in a recent work on emergency powers, looks to separate oversight from legislation, proposing that "members of opposition political parties should be guaranteed the majority of seats on the oversight committees.... Minority control means that the oversight committees will not be lapdogs for the executive but watchdogs for society."[29] Ackerman limits this proposal to emergencies such as the aftermath of a terrorist attack. Ackerman's logic is that it is both practical and inevitable for emergency situations to empower executives to go beyond the normal law and, conceivably, to violate civil liberties, but that the very exceptionality and dangerousness of these powers demand a heightened parliamentary oversight of the executive. The plebiscitarian perspective extends the logic of this thinking to everyday democratic politics, generalizing the emergency situation to refer to ordinary political experience. Whereas Ackerman's proposal implies a normal situation in which the political legitimacy of the leader or majority party shields them from heightened oversight, the plebiscitarian, unable to affirm the full legitimacy of the political system (i.e., its grounding in an unambiguous expression of popular will), insists upon empowering minorities to launch investigations even in allegedly normal circumstances, thereby intensifying the level of oversight over leaders and high officials.

Plebiscitarian proposals like Weber's or an extended version of Ackerman's create certain difficulties that need to be addressed. A clear consequence of lowering the threshold for public inquiries is that officials and politicians would constantly get called before the public under the inherently hostile conditions of investigation. This circumstance conflicts with the orthodox view that sees investigations as a means to an end—specifically the end of redressing injustice or offence. The usual assumption, in other words, is that political investigations and trials ought to be confined to the fixed and relatively objective standard of prosecuting criminal wrongdoing. In countries like the United States, with a history of illiberal investigations like the McCarthy trials, there is an especially pronounced reluctance to embrace investigations beyond what is obviously necessary to remediate crimes and injustices. The plebiscitarian call for maximizing investigations, however, would expand them beyond this limited (because practical, judicial, and remedial) scope. That is to say, there likely would be many investigations and public trials in which there was little or highly questionable concrete wrongdoing. The plebiscitarian, then, must explain how the maximization of inquiries can be validated. How can the cultivation of investigations above and beyond what might be required for remedying wrongdoing be defended from the charge that such a proposal imposes unnecessary danger and instability upon the polity?

This general worry about the maximization of investigations and trials beyond the minimum that might be necessary to remediate genuine abuse and offense is something that would likely be reiterated by exponents of the traditional democratic values of deliberation, participation, and transparency. As far as deliberation, not only are the mechanics of public investigations often hostile to the spirit of deliberation—involving combativeness rather than cooperation, strategy and manipulation rather than communicative action, and an individual-based focus rather than an issue-based one—but the proliferation of such trials might take time and attention away from other, more deliberative contexts. Similarly, the participationist is suspicious of trials as being distractions from the People's "real" business—self-legislating the conditions of public life. According to this logic, trials and investigations run the risk of "satisfying and stupefying" the People through an overestimation of the importance of particular individuals and a consequent neglect of the mundane but essential contribution of everyday activism. From the perspective of transparency, although trials might potentially produce relevant information about the conduct of government, they are hardly an efficient means of doing so. Famous trials—such as the impeachment of Warren Hastings, Andrew Johnson, or Bill Clinton—have offered little in the way of actionable information for the citizenry. The investigation and trial of leaders is often much less an information-generating process than it is a disembowelment (metaphorical, to be sure) of leaders on the public stage.

Benjamin Constant, the French liberal theorist of the early nineteenth century, offers a very useful blueprint for how to structure expanded public inquiries as well as a delineation of the principles upon which such inquiries ought to rest. Although Constant had numerous approaches to public inquiries—making his ultimate view on the matter difficult to decipher[30]— his proposals in his seminal work, *Principles of Politics Applicable to All Representative Governments*, provide what can be seen as a proto-plebiscitary theory of public investigations and trials. Constant expressed the basic plebiscitarian insight that the rationale for public inquiries was not simply their protective, remedial function (i.e., bringing offenders to justice), but their capacity to render politics and the conduct of leaders more public and, hence, more amenable to public view. Thus Constant could write that the public investigation of ministers satisfied *two distinct aims*: not just the corrective function "of depriving guilty ministers of their power," but the specifically *political function* of "keeping alive in the nation— through the watchfulness of her representatives, the openness of their debates and the exercise of freedom of the press applied to the analysis of all ministerial actions—a spirit of inquiry, a habitual interest in the maintenance of the constitution of the state, a constant participation in public affairs, in a word a vivid sense of political life."[31]

Constant's relevance is not simply that he recognized that the "spirit of inquiry" and *watchfulness* were goals irreducible to the remediation of wrongdoing—that he understood investigations served democracy in their capacity to satisfy and cultivate the position of the political spectator—but that he thought through the consequences of how inquiries would need to be structured if their purpose was not limited to the punishment of guilt and, instead, also included the aspiration of providing the People with political events worthy of being watched. Constant's most important contribution was his insight that any call for expanded public inquiries needed to be joined by the insistence that such inquiries be structured not on the model of a criminal trial, but as a *distinctly political process*. What the maximization of inquiries required, in other words, was the development of a new kind of investigative format that would be self-consciously different from that of a criminal court. This distinctly political form of public inquiry would be guided by four principles.

First, Constant distinguished sharply between the ordinary citizen and the leader (the politician, minister, or high official), arguing that public inquiries be limited to this latter group. This requirement precluded from the start any kind of McCarthyite terror in which everyday citizens are subjected to excessive and unwarranted state investigations. Ordinary citizens would not be eligible for public investigations, but, as Constant observed, "are subjected to other procedures and judged by other judges"—that is to say, their trials would follow the normal requirements of due process and occur on a public stage far less public than that of the nation.[32] Leaders, however, "have made a different pact with society. They have voluntarily accepted, in the hope of glory, power or fortune, vast and complicated functions, forming a compact and invisible unity."[33] It was for these elite figures that the distinctly political form of public investigations and trials that Constant outlined would apply.

Second, divorcing the political investigation and trial from a criminal model meant eliminating the stipulation, common in ordinary law for everyday citizens, that leaders undergoing investigation or trial only be subject to known, written laws. On the one hand, there was an admittedly remedial feature to eliminating the requirement of prior codification for political trials. It was the nature of the political abuse leaders were likely to commit, Constant argued, that it would not easily be covered by particular laws or isolated into a single guilty action over which the law operates.[34] Leaders were capable of producing "great evil" that the prior law had not yet envisioned; further, leaders' transgressions often did not harm specific individuals who would be motivated to pursue a civil action.[35] For these reasons it would be appropriate to judge the leader in a general way, not bound to any particular statute.[36] On the other hand, unhinging the political trial from the law would serve the plebiscitarian interest of maximizing the number of inquiries. Accusers and prosecutors of leaders would not be confined by having to link their charges to preexisting statutes, but would have a much wider latitude in defining the nature of the alleged offense. Thus, one of the clear results of unhinging the investigative process from a juridical model would be the proliferation of public trials and investigations.

Third, it followed that public inquiries of this special political stamp would likely have an arbitrary aspect about them, especially in comparison to ordinary judicial trials in which accuracy and precision in defining and prosecuting the offense were essential. Constant acknowledged this arbitrary element as an inevitable consequence of giving the parliamentary assembly conducting investigations discretion in defining the offense and how it should be remedied, but he also argued that its potential destructiveness could be contained. One key to taming the arbitrary element of the inquiries, Constant argued, was not to limit the capacity to make accusations, but to enhance it and render it public. "Thoughtless declamations, unfounded accusations, wear themselves out; they discredit themselves and finally cease by the mere effect of that opinion which judges and withers them. They are dangerous only under despotism, or in demagogies with no constitutional counterweight."[37] As a way to moderate the potential abusiveness of the investigative process, Constant also proposed that the body empowered to decide such cases be insulated from public opinion and free to follow the conscience of its members, suggesting the British House of Lords as a potential model. This underlines how the expansion of the

People's ability to see and observe was divorced from a capacity to judge and decide. The investigations would be publicized before all, but conducted by an elite few. The public "participation" that Constant invoked as a chief justification for an expanded right of inquiry was thus of a purely spectatorial nature. It did not involve actual control of the outcome. In any case, on the basis of such proposals, Constant envisioned a situation in which there would be a great disparity between the number of accusations and the number of ultimate convictions: "It follows from these arrangements that ministers will often be denounced, sometimes accused, rarely condemned, and almost never punished."[38] This seems inefficient from the standard perspective of criminal justice, which is upset by an excess of groundless charges. But it makes sense if the point of the investigation is the investigation itself—the act of putting leaders before the public gaze—rather than the ultimate decision or result that is reached regarding culpability.

Finally, Constant realized that if the purpose of the investigations and trials was as much about satisfying the public's right to see as it was about assigning guilt, then they needed to be mild in their consequences for the accused.[39] Constant's particular proposals in this regard included a firm opposition to "disgraceful punishments" such as exile or imprisonment, an encouragement that offenders be pardoned by the Crown or some other power, and a willingness to suspend punishment in the hope that electoral politics would itself remove the offenders.[40] Constant also insisted that leniency from the investigative body ought to be joined by leniency from the informal court of public opinion.[41] Thus, while accusations would be quite frequent, punishments would be rare and often inconsequential. Of course, from the standard juridical model of investigation, such proposals make little sense. Why, after all, go through the difficulty of undertaking investigations if so many of the accusations are false and if those that are in fact validated remain unpunished in any tangible way? Constant recognized this apparent perplexity, but reiterated that the purpose of the investigations went beyond the question of guilt: "The problem is not, as it is in ordinary circumstances, to make sure that innocence should never be threatened and crime never go unpunished....What is essential is that the conduct of ministers be readily subjected to scrupulous investigation."[42] Constant, in effect, reprioritized the relation between investigation and verdict, so that the verdict served the investigation, rather than *vice versa*.[43] Leniency was a clear effect of such reprioritization—both because the ultimate question of guilt was marginalized and because too stringent punishments would make investigative bodies overly hesitant in pursuing inquiries and trials.

The investigation and trial surrounding President Clinton's impeachment provide a useful example by which to clarify what is distinctive about a plebiscitarian approach to public inquiries. The usual perspective is to see the entire episode of the investigation of Clinton as regrettable, either because Clinton committed the offenses for which he was accused (and therefore disgraced the office of the presidency and the country), or because Clinton's transgression did not merit the treatment he received and thus distracted the country unnecessarily from genuine public business. Among this latter group, it is a common criticism to say that the impeachment did not stem from any genuine offense, but was *politically motivated*: that the driving cause of the trial was in fact the animus of Clinton's political enemies more than the harm of Clinton's actual transgressions. Against both of these viewpoints, the plebiscitarian does not see the Clinton trial as unfortunate, but rather as a valuable if flawed instance of plebiscitary democracy in action. After all, the proceedings involved two situations of candor—Clinton's deposition in the sexual harassment case of Paula Jones and his grand jury testimony in the independent counsel's investigation of his conduct—plus a third, semicandid exchange in which Clinton, or more likely his lawyers, responded in writing to eighty-one questions from Congress. This is not to say that the plebiscitarian endorses the Clinton trial unequivocally, since, in fact, there is much to criticize. But whereas the customary criticism is to blame Clinton himself or the political nature of the accusations, the plebiscitarian argues that the problem with the investigation and trial was that they were not political enough—that, pace Constant and his theory of public inquiry, they were wrongly based on the model of a criminal trial. The point is not so much descriptive (that, in fact, the evolution of charges against Clinton, from financial misconduct to sexual harassment to perjury to obstruction of justice, suggests the political rather than criminal nature of Clinton's offense) as prescriptive: that the trial of the president would have been better and more efficiently managed if it had been an unabashedly political trial from the start. As a political trial, a worthy plebiscitarian goal, putting the president into a situation of critical publicity, could have been achieved much more quickly (without six years of investigation) and, so, without the same degree of distraction from other public business. Moreover, the same leniency that was finally secured after so much uncertainty and instability for the country would have been more firmly established at the outset. Finally, and perhaps most important of all, as a political trial, Clinton's responses to his questioners would have been more public (live testimony in a public setting, rather than recorded depositions from a trial) and more liberated from the legalese of a criminal proceeding. To make such proposals is not to suggest they were possible under the circumstances. Although the Office of the Independent Counsel does hold the promise of overseeing political trials in accordance with Constant's recommendation, the tendency thus far has been for the institution to present itself more as a criminal prosecutor than a distinctly political kind of investigator.

In sum, then, a plebiscitary politics of candor would call for maximizing investigations of public leaders both by decoupling the power to legislate from the power to investigate (grounding the latter on a lower threshold of support) and also by opposing the tendency to model such investigations on criminal trials. Such a proliferation of investigations might worry those concerned about governmental efficiency, since it might seem that too many inquiries and trials would disturb the necessary business of governance. In response, three points should be stressed. First, one of the effects of defining the inquiry as a political rather than criminal process is that its consequences would be softened. As Constant understood, the inquiry would itself be a kind of punishment and, besides, would serve an interest independent of remediation: the placement of leaders in conditions of critical publicity for the viewership of citizen-spectators. With the stakes lower, one might expect that inquiries would be less disruptive to governance than they are currently. Second, the political character of inquiries and trials would also make them briefer and more punctuated and, hence, less of a long-term distraction from government business. No longer modeled on a criminal proceeding oriented around guilt and punishment, they could avoid the length, complexity, and procedural gymnastics characteristic of legal processes. Finally, it needs to be admitted that there is already in contemporary politics a great deal of political activity with little actual governmental function—that is, the spectacles that populate mass democracy: such as speechifying, photo opportunities, sound bites, and other ceremonies by which leaders seek to manufacture loyalty and signs of support. It is as a substitute for and improvement of these kinds of political spectacles that the value of public inquiries—as well as presidential debates and press conferences—can most readily be acknowledged. A plebiscitarian is not interested in replacing deliberative, legislative processes with nongovernmental candid ones so much as upgrading a politics already fraught with spectacles on the basis of a critical standard that defines what makes a spectacle more or less democratic. Candor, which serves as such a critical ideal, performs the much needed work of providing democratic theory with a means of evaluating whether a given political image or appearance is or is not democratic.

6.5 Presidential Press Conferences

As in debates and public inquiries, the presidential press conference is, from the plebiscitary point of view, a privileged site for the consideration of democratic progressivism. Press conferences are rare moments of relative candor in which leaders appear before the public under conditions

not entirely under their control. With the advent of radio and especially
television, the candid aspect of press conferences has been intensified to a
large degree. In the United States, excerpts of recorded press conferences
were first put on the radio under Truman, televised and accompanied by
complete transcripts under Eisenhower, and aired live under Kennedy.
With the rise of broadcasted press conferences, earlier restrictions on
this form of publicity—such as limitations on what statements could be
directly cited by reporters, the rewriting of official transcripts in contrast
to what was actually said, and restrictions on who was allowed to witness
the event—were overcome.[44] Most of all, as a result of the live television
press conference, leaders have been forced into a risk-ridden, bidirectional
situation of publicity that they do not fully manage. Nonetheless, despite
their live and inherently unpredictable nature, press conferences continue
to fall short of what might be called for by a plebiscitarian reformer pursuing a politics of candor. Even if the practice of prewritten questions
submitted in advance was officially abandoned by Franklin Roosevelt,
presidents and their press advisers have continued to pursue other tactics
by which to restrain and oppose the event's potential spontaneity. Such
practices as planting question askers and scripting responses, punishing
uncooperative journalists with restricted White House access and other
penalties, and trying to satisfy the press with surprise appearances that
are brief and unbroadcasted are some of the mechanisms by which leaders
maintain control of the press conference.[45] At a more basic level, control is
ensured by the fact that the decision to hold a press conference lies entirely
at the discretion of the president, that the setting, length, and agenda are
likewise determined from above, and that reporters rarely have the chance
to follow up (let alone cross-examine) the leader who stands before them.[46]
Thus, while the press conference is certainly more candid than most other
forms of public appearance by political elites in mass democracy, there are
clear ways in which its level of candor might be improved.

To a certain degree, the reforms called for by a plebiscitarian are repeated from other quarters. Since the 1970s, various studies have routinely
recommended making the conferences more frequent and regularized—
usually once a month—and have also made a point of calling for a format
that expands the types of reporters who have the ability to ask questions.[47]
These are proposals with which a plebiscitarian certainly would agree.
But the plebiscitarian goes further. It is not enough that the press conferences be more frequent and formalized, but also that they be less under
the control of the executive administration of the government. This concern has not tended to inform previous research.[48] This difference points
to another one. Earlier studies typically call for changing the format so
as to reduce the *dramatic* aspect of the press conference—to make it less
about the person or personality of the individual leader.[49] French, for

example, distinguishes between three main purposes a presidential press conference might have: an informational purpose in conveying accurate facts and knowledge to the public, a checks-and-balances role in holding the government responsible and accountable for its actions, and, finally, a "means of assessing the president's personal characteristics" by creating a context in which it is possible to see "how well the president thinks on his feet and maintains his poise." French calls this third aspect, which clearly approximates the conferences' capacity to inject candor, "most spurious," since it has no direct linkage to the resolution of substantive problems and political issues.[50] But it is just this third aspect—placing the leader under conditions that he or she does not control for the purpose of imposing an element of risk and spontaneity—that grounds the plebiscitarian's special interest in presidential press conferences.

In order to see how this commitment to candor leads to a distinct assessment of the presidential press conference, it is useful once again to compare the plebiscitarian approach to the perspective that might be expected from exponents of three traditional democratic values: deliberation, participation, and transparency.

The presidential press conference is a practice not easily theorized under the rubric of deliberation. While it is true that most contemporary deliberative democrats favor the kind of publicity and accountability likely to be produced by frequent presidential press conferences, the press conference is not a cooperative effort at achieving understanding among parties deliberating over the common good.[51] Nor is it a disciplined effort to achieve better recognition and tolerance of disagreements and other obstacles to consensus. The participants in a press conference are not equal, sovereign colegislators, but rather are bifurcated into an adversarial relationship between a power holder with exceptional decision-making authority and relatively powerless question askers. The adversarial aspect—which from the plebiscitarian perspective is precisely what makes the press conferences so compelling (the engine of the events' candor)—is something to be avoided or in any case minimized when the press conferences are seen from the perspective of deliberation.[52]

The participationist questions the relevance of the press conference. Indeed, any sense that the subject of the press conference is too marginal to merit much consideration relies on the participatory premise that "true" democratization means amplifying the People's voice—its control over the laws and norms of public life—and not any widening or intensifying of the public gaze. The plebiscitarian disagrees with this dismissal of the press conference. Although press conferences might mean little within a perfectionist portrait of how democratic politics ought to be conducted, within actually functioning mass democracies of the present day, the presidential press conference possesses special importance both in its capacity to provide political spectators with something worth watching and in its capacity to draw power holders out into an uncommon setting of critical exposure.

Finally, the commitment to transparency clearly promotes an appreciation for press conferences insofar as they are devices that supply the public with accurate and ample information about major issues and government policies. However, while sharing this appreciation for the information-generating quality of press conferences, the plebiscitarian demands something more than mere transparency. What matters from a plebiscitarian perspective is not simply the informational value of press conferences, but the fact that they are candid institutions that place leaders under conditions of publicity that they do not fully control. In other words, whereas the value of transparency focuses only on the information produced by press conferences, a plebiscitarian is keenly attuned to the *personal, individual* experience of a leader undergoing questioning on the public stage.

The consequences of this difference can be seen by considering the figure of the presidential press secretary, a figure who has arisen along with the development of the mass media and the modern presidency.[53] From the perspective of transparency, what matters is simply that whoever is addressing the public—whether president or press secretary—does so with honesty and forthrightness. The conveyance of accurate information is what is most key. Historic moments of great deception, such as occurred during Watergate, are seen as a betrayal of the kind of political communication called for by democracy, but in general, so long as the press secretary remains truthful and forthcoming, then there is nothing problematic—and indeed much to applaud—about the institution. From a plebiscitarian perspective, however, the objection to the press secretary runs deeper than worries about the accuracy of the information provided. Instead, the plebiscitarian considers the very office of the press secretary to be intrinsically objectionable, especially when the press secretary comes to be more frequently visible than the leader whom he or she represents.[54] The press secretary is an institutional embodiment of the leader's resistance to candor—a method of dissociating the office of the leader from the person who occupies it, so that publicity might be achieved without personal exposure. Clearly there are practical reasons for the existence of the press secretary, if only as a liaison between the executive administration and the hundreds of journalists who cover it. But the expanded role of the press secretary beyond these secretarial functions—that is, the emergence of formal press briefings in which the secretary speaks publicly on behalf of the president—offends the spirit of democracy as understood from a plebiscitarian perspective. The plebiscitarian acknowledges and in a certain sense accepts that the everyday citizen will not usually contribute to the substance of governmental decision making or the direction that the polity takes in a given situation; but the plebiscitarian does insist that the ordinary citizen at least be able to *see* those who do decide—and to see them often and in a genuine (i.e., candid) manner. The press secretary enforces a double denial of candor. On the one hand, the press secretary shields the leader from a form of publicity (i.e., receiving questions from a collection of journalists on live television) that would have been outside the full control of the leader him- or herself. It is the press secretary, not the leader, who is subjected to candor. This means that, from the plebiscitarian perspective, the press secretary is a surrogate that falsely satisfies the public's right to see leadership live and under pressure. On the other hand, candor is eroded insofar as the press secretary does not speak on his or her own behalf, but addresses the press as a representative of the views, attitudes, and policies of the leader being represented. Just as the leader is shielded by the press secretary, so is the press secretary protected by the fact that he or she is not the leader. The press secretary is never fully accountable for what is said both because the secretary can always claim not to know the leader's thinking on a particular question and, more generally, because what is said pertains always to the mindset, decisions, and opinions of someone else. By separating the president's public statements from the person of the president, the press secretary precludes both elements (what is said and the person who says it) from the full critical force of candid publicity.

Thus, whereas the commitment to transparency concerns itself only with *what* is said (that it be forthcoming and truthful), the plebiscitarian is always also concerned with *who* is saying it. Moreover, although transparency is a goal that the plebiscitarian can endorse, what is most important to the plebiscitarian in evaluating the level of democratization is not the *content* of political communication, but the *form* in which it is disseminated. From the plebiscitarian standpoint, regardless of the quality or completeness of information generated by the press secretary, the press secretary is demonized insofar as it is an institution that prevents sight and oversight of the leader's own person. The press secretary is a trained professional whose very expertise is the reduction of candor. The plebiscitarian argues that those who hold vast, asymmetrical decision-making power ought not be shielded from the public, which does not have this power. Or, less polemically, it is the site of this shieldedness—whether it is penetrated and weakened or permitted to augment itself—that defines how much democratization has occurred.

In taking aim at the press secretary, then, plebiscitarianism not only suggests certain critical aspirations (the placement of leaders under conditions of candor), but identifies obstacles to democratization that would not ordinarily be conceived as such.

6.6 Debates, Inquiries, and Press Conferences as Exemplars of Plebiscitary Reform in General

In this chapter I have argued that the plebiscitarian commitment to candor is in fact different from participation, deliberation, and transparency. While candor shares something with these three traditional perspectives, I have shown how candor is still distinct and irreducible to them. That candor should dictate a distinct approach to democratic reform is consistent with the fact that candor is a political ideal uniquely suitable for everyday citizens in the condition of their everydayness. That is, candor is an ideal that responds to the fact that citizens are first and foremost spectators rather than decision makers. The other three democratic values, by contrast, presuppose the citizen to be a citizen-governor: someone who above all is a *decider*. They dignify the everyday citizen by supposing this citizen to be autonomous, possessing meaningful power by which to shape the norms and conditions governing public life. Yet, seen differently, these three traditional values also *undermine* a respect for the everyday experience of democracy, since they obstruct the way democracy is actually encountered by ordinary citizens in the course of an ordinary day. At their core, these three values are centered on the citizen's function as an elector: since ordinary citizens have the right to vote, so the thinking goes, they must follow the right decision-making procedure when making their choices (hence deliberation), they must try to expand their political engagement as voters to still other areas (hence participation), and they must act and decide with the best and most appropriate information available (hence transparency). But it must be admitted that voting is the rarest and most exceptional moment of democratic life for everyday citizens. It is hardly definitive of ordinary political experience in mass democracy. Election day may not be the only day that citizens are free, as Rousseau suggested, but it is the only day that most citizens behave in the way presupposed by traditional democratic ideology. On all other days, the everyday political experience of democratic citizens is characterized by silence rather than decision, spectatorship rather than activism, and hierarchy rather than equality.

The plebiscitarian approach to democratic reform is valuable precisely because it deprivileges both the specific act of voting and the general conception of the everyday citizen as a decider. The plebiscitarian is attuned not simply to the minimal power of each citizen's vote, but to the fact that voting is not at all determinative of everyday political experience. Most citizens most of the time are not deciders. Candor is a value that responds to the interests and needs of this undertheorized political class of non-decision makers. Rather than focus like most democratic theorists on elaborating, expanding, or rationally disciplining the vote and the People's alleged capacity to express its *voice*, a plebiscitary politics of candor treats everyday citizens primarily as *viewers* of politics and not as authors or actors. This means that plebiscitarian theorizing does not require the suspension of disbelief characteristic of dominant perspectives within democratic theory: that is, the overdrawn and uncritical assumption that contemporary mass democracy affords ordinary citizens sufficient opportunities for self-legislation.

Presidential debates, public inquiries, and press conferences are not normally considered the prime contexts of democratization. Rather, it is such practices as voting in elections, deliberation both within and without the legislative chamber, protests and demonstrations, and other *vocal* forms of political experience that tend to receive the most treatment by democratic theorists. Part of what it means to come under the sway of a plebiscitarian perspective is to recalibrate one's sense of what is and is not politically significant from the democratic point of view. Processes that place leaders in uncommon situations of candor might seem marginal to a traditional democratic ethos, but they are vital to the plebiscitarian who theorizes democracy from the perspective of the citizen-being-ruled—a figure who first and foremost is a spectator of politics rather than a decision maker. A presidential debate with extemporaneous cross-examination, or a public inquiry of a leading politician or senior official, or a lively press conference that places real pressure on the prime minister or president might not serve the autonomy of the everyday citizen (leading to laws and decisions that the citizen could claim as his or her own), but they certainly do serve the integrity of political images—their "watchability" from a spectator's point of view.

This is not to suggest that the plebiscitarian would be fully satisfied with leadership debates, public inquiries, and press conferences. For one thing, I have tried to show how the existing organization of these practices falls well short of the type of candor a plebiscitarian would ideally like to see realized. Beyond this, though, it also can be said that even if they were perfectly reformed in light of a plebiscitarian critique, these practices would not constitute the completion of a plebiscitary politics but only its beginning. In other words, while the plebiscitarian recognizes the importance of debates, inquiries, and press conferences, there is also an acknowledgment that by themselves such practices are limited and that, therefore, they are best understood as blueprints for plebiscitary reform in general—suggestive of the kinds of political institutions and experiences a plebiscitarian would want to see extended—rather than as the culmination of the plebiscitary project.

7

Popular Power in Sight

The arguments against me are always drawn from a Paris, or a London,
or some other small corner of the world, whereas I try to draw mine
from the world itself.

—Jean-Jacques Rousseau

7.1 In Advance of My Critics

It is an irony of the argument I have put forward in these pages that those
most likely to read it will also be least likely to accept its conclusions. Written for everyday citizens in their everyday capacity as spectators of politics,
this book probably will be read by relatively elite citizens, endowed with
an above-average sense of political efficacy, and in possession of an uncommonly detailed and expansive set of opinions about the policies government
should be legislating. For such readers, the principle of candor that I have
defended as the centerpiece of the plebiscitarian's ocular model of democracy will likely seem significant and valid up to a point, but unworthy of the
singular importance I have bestowed upon it. Such readers will have difficulty conceiving of citizenship in terms other than the vocal and participatory values whose virtually unimpeded dominance in democratic theory
this book has tried to counteract. Is it not true, such readers will ask, that
contemporary democracies offer unrivaled opportunities for everyday citizens to make meaningful decisions about the conduct of political life? How
can one look past vocal political institutions like the right to vote, protest,
campaign, publish, or otherwise speak out? And even if meaningful participation is hard to come by, is it not the case that there are real issues facing
contemporary polities—such as those concerning war and peace, economic
justice, health care, the environment, technology, and religion—whose
solution must be the primary concern of any responsible citizen? How can
a nondecisional ideal like candor, which governs how leaders are to appear
rather than what they ultimately choose to do, enjoy a position of prominence in the face of such urgent problems and concerns? In short, how can
a responsible citizen, committed to making use of whatever participation
is possible under conditions of mass democracy, not treat the plebiscitary
value of candor in anything but an incidental and subsidiary way?

Such questions express legitimate concerns, and what they call for, by way of conclusion, is a clarification of how the plebiscitary ethics I have defended are to be reconciled with traditional norms of participatory citizenship. To perform this reconciliation, however, is a matter of some complexity. It is so because it is a mistake, I believe, to universalize a single type of citizenship as the sole form and to thereby conclude that there is only one kind of ethics applicable to all citizens in all circumstances. Just as voters are situated within a different ethical horizon from the select few who hold high office, so too can one distinguish within the great mass of non-officeholders different types of civic experiences. With this consideration in mind, I think the question of how to apply the plebiscitarian ethic of candor follows three different logics—one of *supply*, one of *supplementation*, and one of *supplantation*—depending on the particular circumstances regarding who the citizen is and what kinds of objectives that citizen possesses.

At the very least it ought to be appreciated that the plebiscitary principle of candor *supplies* an ethical perspective to a context where it previously has been assumed that none exists: namely, the context of spectatorship. To the citizen-spectator, without a high sense of political efficacy, consigned to watch politics rather than participate in it, plebiscitarianism provides an ethical framework that respects, rather than seeks to cancel, civic experience of a spectatorial nature. Spectatorship might be a function of a free choice (the choice not to be actively engaged), it might appear natural after years of habituation, or it might stem from a somber awareness of the fact that one's voice matters little in the resolution of most political questions. Whatever the psychological correlates of the phenomenon of spectatorship, it is hardly a controversial point of political sociology to acknowledge that a spectatorial engagement with politics—an engagement not characterized by the desire to realize a specific opinion, decision, or substantive interest—defines the way most citizens interact with politics most of the time and the way a significant number, perhaps even a majority in some democracies like the United States with low voter turnout, interact with politics all of the time. Plebiscitarianism is therefore especially valuable to those citizens so often overlooked by democratic theory: the nonvoter, the nonideologue, the nonaffiliate of a political party, the nonmember of voluntary organizations of civil society. Such citizens, though nonparticipants, are still at least minimally aware of political goings-on. They still have political lives—lives that ought to be acknowledged and respected by any responsible theory of democracy. The plebiscitarian principle of candor announces a political ideal that is for them. And a large part of the value of plebiscitarianism is precisely that it provides a set of ethics to this forgotten yet enormous constituency.

To the participatory citizen, however, the matter is different. For this citizen—who can be schematized as a *partisan* who has a clear sense of what government ought to be doing on numerous issues, votes regularly, joins advocacy groups, and in general seeks to have his or her voice heard—the plebiscitary model *supplements* traditional vocal and participatory values with an appreciation for the ideal of candor. Candor is not after all a controversial value. As I have argued, candor overlaps to a significant degree with traditional, vocal values like transparency and deliberation, so that one would expect candor to enhance them at least up to a point. As a result, candor might also serve as a helpful proxy for determining when these more familiar concerns have been achieved. It is a hard thing, after all, to measure how much deliberation and transparency (and the *representation* these two often promise) have been realized in a particular instance—and even harder to determine the degree to which one's voice is being heeded by government. One of the advantages of candor, by contrast, is that it is relatively simple to determine how much of it exists in a given instance.

Beyond these ways in which a concern for candor links up with the values often invoked in conjunction with participatory citizenship, candor supplements the ethical perspective of the partisan by reminding that citizen of a wider set of concerns. Politics is not just about getting certain legislation enacted. It is also always at the same time about empowering a set of politicians with a highly disproportionate, never fully legitimate authority. Candor is useful because it seeks to regulate this secondary set of concerns: not the policies that are legislated, but the leaders empowered to legislate. To a certain extent at least, plebiscitarianism would expand the ethical perspective of the partisan to include a newfound appreciation for the leader-led relationship and, specifically, the democratization of leaders' appearances on the public stage.

Of course, this supplementation can only go so far. The partisan will never be able to make candor the primary concern of his or her engagement with democracy. This is not only because, as the last chapter detailed, in certain cases putting candor first will conflict with maximizing deliberation, transparency, and civic engagement, but, more deeply, because the partisan's commitment to specific laws, leaders, platforms, and ideologies always will overshadow plebiscitarianism's nonsubstantive principle that leaders—no matter what they stand for—be subjected to public appearances they do not control. What the partisan wants, above all, is to win: to see a particular cause attended to, a specific law ratified, an admired leader elected, and, in general, a certain set of policies govern the conduct of public life. This is not to deny that the partisan will often consider broader interests beyond his or her own when formulating political goals nor that such goals might be transformed as a result of dialogue and interaction with other partisans of different persuasions. The point is rather that the phenomenology of partisanship—that is, of a willful commitment to substantive political objectives about what laws and policies a government should be instituting—necessarily marginalizes the concern for candor. Focused on victory, the partisan will understand the public appearances of leaders—and usually leadership itself—only as instruments for realizing the substantive outcomes that inspired the commitment to political advocacy in the first place. Even partisans unwilling to engage in cynical processes of political marketing and manipulation will still claim that the regulation of public appearances in accordance with the principle of candor pales in comparison to the solution of the "real" issues and problems facing any modern polity.

With one exception, the plebiscitarian perspective I have defended does not disrespect the participatory focus of the partisan. Certainly any republic depends on the vitality of those energized citizens who seek to write laws, solve problems, and contest those whose perspectives they deem wrong, harmful, or otherwise objectionable. While it is true that substantive decision making about laws and policies remains out of the reach of most citizens, it is nonetheless an applaudable feature of democratic institutions that the well-organized, well-funded, and otherwise committed have superior opportunities, relative to citizens of other regimes, to be heard and shape policies. My argument does not aim to dissuade partisans from their political activity. But I do insist on one important distinction: that partisans be understood as making use of democracy, not serving democracy itself. The partisan's substantive agenda ought not be confused with what the People wants or, by extension, with what is in accordance with the realization of popular sovereignty. In certain special cases, like humanitarian rights, one might be confident that the policies one seeks are not just for oneself or one's group but for the People. But the issues that make up the vast bulk of political debate in contemporary democracies— taxes, foreign affairs, public health, religious matters, the environment, economic incentives, and the allocation of limited resources—do not admit of purely rational or universalistic solutions. This means that the laws that are made will benefit some and hurt others. And it means those who win and those who lose a given political contest can both plausibly claim that their sides have the People's interest at heart. This state of affairs ought to be familiar to any student of politics. And it ought to demonstrate the wisdom of locating the People's interest not in this or that set of policies, decision, or election of candidates, but in the conditions that regulate how those who are separated from the People—leaders who decide how governmental power is to be used and as a result are empowered vis-à-vis the People—are to have their public lives conducted and organized. Participants can and must participate. But the goods they serve are never quite common, never the People's.

It is here as a theory of what it would mean to serve democracy itself— what it would mean for the People to be sovereign and rule in a given instance—that the plebiscitary ethics I have defended make their most radical move, *supplanting* familiar notions of sovereignty as self-legislation with the novel, ocular principle of candor. This logic of supplantation applies first and foremost, not to the spectator who lacks a prior political ethics nor to the partisan activist who seeks electoral and legislative victory, but to the *democrat* who wants only that the People itself be made to rule. I have objected to the air of inevitability with which it is assumed that if popular sovereignty is to exist at all, then it must be interpreted as a decisional power synonymous with self-legislation. Indeed, it is just this conflation of sovereignty with autonomous decision making that an ocular model of democracy calls into question. In its most basic and elemental sense, popular sovereignty means simply that the People rule. But the manner of how to define the People and the nature of its rule are hardly straightforward and certainly not predetermined by the concept of popular sovereignty itself. Accordingly, what I have insisted upon is the possibility of finding a new understanding of popular sovereignty over and against the usual—and indeed almost universal—conceptualization of popular sovereignty in terms of self-legislation.

But why? Why should the notion of popular sovereignty as self-legislation be overcome? My claim throughout these pages has been that intellectual honesty and a progressive consciousness both demand a deep skepticism toward any understanding of popular sovereignty as self-legislation. The existing methods of collective authorship in contemporary mass democracy—whether elections or public opinion—fall well short of the collectivity they promise. A genuinely collective process would appeal to everyday citizens in their everyday lives. But elections are too infrequent to empower ordinary citizens in anything but an exceedingly rare and exceptional way. They have only the slightest bearing on the ordinary citizen's passive experience of the political events that make up everyday political life—events that, from the ordinary citizen's perspective, affect but do not include and, therefore, reinforce rather than reduce a profound sense of distance from the contexts of actual decision making. Furthermore, even if one rejects this claim and insists that collective experiences can and ought to be exceptional, there is still the more trying problem that elections rarely register a genuine voice from below (an articulate and expressive decision about policies) but usually only a binary verdict on leadership. This verdict belongs not to the People, but only a majority—or perhaps even a minority if nonvoters are included. While all citizens in a democracy share the collective right to speak electorally, the actual use of this electoral right does not lead to a genuine sense of peoplehood. Whenever the People speaks in the form of a contested election, it dissolves its collectivity and thereby ceases to function as a People. With regard to public opinion, what was argued in chapter 3 should be reiterated: namely, that public opinion,

which promises a more nuanced and omnipresent reflection of the popular
voice, not only remains unreflective of the lack of clear opinions and preferences that characterizes so much of everyday political experience, but has
yet to prove itself an effective regulator of more than a fraction of the issues
and policies on the political agenda at any given time. Such claims are not
meant to deny that democratic polities must often bend to a majority's will,
that well-organized groups successfully compete and cooperate for a share
of a government's decision-making power, and that, as a result of these
factors, power in contemporary mass democracy tends to be pluralistic and
to some degree self-checking. What I object to is the characterization of
these otherwise praiseworthy features of the governmental process as acts
of popular sovereignty. The People does not elect candidates; the electorate does. Likewise, the People does not author norms and policies; only the
minority of active and well-organized citizens contributes to this process.
As Dahl famously said, in a modern democracy *minorities* rule. On the basis
of these considerations, I have insisted that a genuinely collective experience must be normal not exceptional, shared not partial—and this means
that it be passive not active, spectatorial rather than decisional.[1]

Plebiscitarians are not alone in the call for a more accurate and precise invocation of the People. Pluralists have long sought to rid democratic
theory of such notions as the People and popular sovereignty for their
apparent lack of rigor. Deliberative democrats have tended to follow suit,
focusing their theories on face-to-face discursive practices, rather than
elections and other institutions of mass politics, and thereby circumvent-
ing imprecise claims about the People as a collective entity. And there are
certainly numerous honest and responsible political journalists who cringe
when politicians and pundits indiscriminately invoke the People as a way
to justify their programs and appeals. But whereas these other approaches
can speak precisely about the People only by not speaking about it at all,
the plebiscitarian perspective I have defended refuses to abandon such
foundational democratic concepts as the People and popular sovereignty.
The plebiscitarian insists that there is such a thing as the People—that
is, ordinary citizens conceived in their collective capacity—and that this
entity needs to be maintained and indeed revived against rampant pluralism. The notion that this collective ought to *rule*—ought to have its interest imposed onto the political system—is likewise retained and celebrated
by the plebiscitarian as the quintessence of democracy. But the plebiscitarian perspective I have endorsed interprets the concept of rule differently
from standard usage. It is not conceived in terms of the People's capacity to author norms and laws. It is not defined as something the People
does, says, or accomplishes—as if the People were, but for its number,
precisely like a sovereign monarch. Thus the plebiscitarian notion of rule
is disconnected from any notion of the popular will. Rather than adopt an

anthropomorphic concept of rule, the plebiscitarian conceives of popular sovereignty as *the rule of a principle*: specifically the principle of candor. That is to say, the plebiscitarian understands the People as realizing its sovereignty to the extent leaders and other high officials are compelled to appear in public under conditions they do not control.

This reconceptualization of sovereignty as the rule of a principle is no doubt counter to common intuitions about sovereignty which assume that it must refer back to some personalistic dynamic of voice: whether in the form of the People's preferences, judgments, electoral choices, or some other kind of intention-based expression. Yet it is important to note that the theorization of popular sovereignty in terms of a principle is not altogether anomalous in recent democratic theory. It can be found, albeit in partial form, among influential French writers like Claude Lefort and more recently Pierre Rosanvallon, who have argued that strictly speaking the People is an empty space and that, consequently, it is never adequately represented by governments that claim to speak on its behalf.[2] While Lefort and Rosanvallon never let go of the assumption that the People's sovereignty is still to be realized, however futilely, in the enactments of government, it is nonetheless the case that a principle emerges here: the antitotalitarian principle that government can never unproblematically speak on behalf of the People and that therefore a government's legitimacy is always only provisional and in doubt. This principle is limited, however, since it renders popular sovereignty a self-refuting and paradoxical practice: the People can never have its voice represented in government, yet never ceases to demand precisely such a representation as a condition of its sovereignty. An even more promising theorization of popular sovereignty in terms of the rule of a principle comes from Jürgen Habermas. In his later writings especially, Habermas has argued against an embodied conceptualization of sovereignty, in which the People self-legislates in accordance with a unified will, on the grounds that both the complexity and the pluralism of modern societies make such a notion highly implausible.[3] However, rather than jettison the concept of popular sovereignty, Habermas proposes to redefine it in procedural terms as the *principle* that deliberative procedures govern decision-making processes to the greatest extent possible. In its most radical formulation, Habermas's reconceived notion of popular sovereignty becomes entirely "anonymous" and "subjectless," so that a citizen committed to popular sovereignty would seek not this or that substantive objective, but only the maximization of deliberative decision-making procedures: "Read in procedural terms, the idea of popular sovereignty refers to a context that, while enabling the self-organization of a legal community, is not at the disposal of the citizens' will in any way."[4] The suggestion, in other words, would be that in any given instance the People's sovereignty is realized not in the content of the decision, but in the degree to which decision-making processes cohere with deliberative principles of fairness, inclusivity, civility, reasonableness, and so forth. But this principled notion of popular sovereignty never entirely escapes the personated notion to which it is initially opposed. On the one hand, Habermas sometimes reverts to an embodied notion of popular sovereignty, locating the popular sovereign in the content of opinions deliberatively wrought in civil society.[5] On the other hand, Habermas's rationalism means that the ultimate promise of these deliberative procedures is that they produce results that, while fallible and provisional, nonetheless enjoy a presumptive validity as an indication of what all citizens *would agree to* had they been party to the deliberations.[6] Like Lefort and Rosanvallon, therefore, Habermas's reconceptualization of popular sovereignty in terms of a principle is partial and incomplete.

Grounded on an ocular model of popular empowerment, the theory of plebiscitary democracy I have outlined and defended aims to refine and more explicitly thematize an account of popular sovereignty in terms of the rule of a principle. A plebiscitarian claims that in the context of any political event the People is sovereign—that is, the People will have its collective interest realized—to the extent that candor governs the public presentation at hand. Popular sovereignty thus withdraws from the content of what is decided to the conditions under which decision makers appear on the public stage. This move respects Lefort and Rosanvallon's argument that the People, as a legitimator of governmental decision making, is an empty space, without being confined by such an acknowledgment. Rather than have the call for popular sovereignty oscillate endlessly between the familiar wish that government reflect the People's voice and the unhappy acknowledgment that such a state of affairs will always have been impossible, plebiscitarianism resituates sovereignty on an ocular terrain where it can have a stable and effective, rather than empty, significance. Defining popular sovereignty in terms of the principle of candor likewise shares Habermas's ambition to achieve a subjectless, anonymous, and disembodied account of sovereignty. But whereas Habermas's deliberative principle falls short of these goals to the extent it promises a modulated form of self-legislation, the plebiscitarian principle of candor is entirely outside of the inherently subject-laden (and speculative) rubric of representation and autonomy. Indeed, popular sovereignty on the plebiscitarian account has nothing to do with citizens' preferences and opinions—and, in fact, can exist even in the absence of them. This does not mean that citizens committed to the goal of popular sovereignty as such can contribute nothing to this goal (since they can seek various reforms that would place leaders' public appearances out of the full control of the leaders themselves), but only that such contributions are fully divorced from citizens' own substantive views regarding policies, candidates, and ideological agendas.

   Some no doubt will say that in abandoning popular sovereignty as self-legislation, a theory of plebiscitary democracy is both sad and grim. The control of the means of publicity via a principle of candor is no substitute, it will be objected, for the historic goal that a People author the laws under which it lives and, through such authorship, achieve the highest goal political life can afford: autonomous freedom. But redefining popular sovereignty in terms of candor is only as sad and as grim as the degree to which the ideal of a self-legislating People is in fact genuinely believed in. A key fact informing my argument has been that the figure of a self-legislating People has largely vanished from the contemporary study of politics. Either the notion of the People is condemned for being vague, imprecise, fictitious, or (as the agent of referenda) too prone to irrationality and totalitarian abuse. Or, when the People is invoked, as it is after all by journalists and within popular culture, it is identified with the electorate that votes on election day and responds to opinion polls—a usage that is triply alienating vis-à-vis the everyday citizen insofar as it refers to the extraordinary and rare moment of election rather than the everyday, *silent* experience of politics; assumes that the citizen is part of the majority that wins elections rather than the minority that loses; and presupposes that the citizen identify with substantive opinions and decisions, even though on most particular issues citizens do not possess clear or stable preferences. Thus, the tendency in political theory is either to dissolve the concept of the People on the grounds of its fictiveness or dangerousness, or to articulate it in a way that is so far removed from everyday political experience that it cannot be something that includes the citizen in any meaningful way.

   Given, then, that the concept of a People—a collective, inclusive entity to which all citizens belong, irreducible to the aggregation of individuals who form it—is not currently a very important figure in contemporary democratic thought, plebiscitary democracy's redefinition of popular sovereignty in terms of candor is less an attenuation of the historic wish that the People be made to rule than a *revival* of this ideal. Understood as an ocular entity rather than a vocal one, the People can once again be considered as a single and unified collective. Whereas most citizens do not use their political voices, and when they do, as in elections, there is not a unity of voice but multiplicity and division, the ocular experience of political spectatorship is both pervasive and inclusive. This is not to say that all citizens simultaneously watch the same political events—although certain political occurrences like presidential debates approximate this state of affairs and a plebiscitarian might seek the proliferation of such occurrences—but only that it is reasonable to consider the People's *interest* in terms of the interest all citizens have by virtue of their spectatorship. Two citizens might watch two different political events, yet both are linked by the fact that they relate to politics through their eyes, not their voice, and that the phenomenology of their political experience is therefore shaped by hierarchy, nondecision, and often nonpreference. It is this similarity in the *form* of political experience shared by political spectators and the possibility of grounding a political ideal (i.e., candor) on spectatorship—and not any assumption about the unity or singularity of the *content* that is being watched—that is designated by the plebiscitarian redefinition of the People as an ocular being.

As part of rendering the collective notion of the People more real, plebiscitarianism's redefinition of sovereignty also makes the People more relevant. If elections occur only once every few years, political images are constantly disseminated. As a result, a political principle like candor that regulates such images will have its applicability not limited to exceptional occasions, but rather extended to the regular functioning of ordinary political life. In linking the People's interest to the interest in candor, then, plebiscitarianism holds out the promise that the everyday citizen will routinely see proof of the People's existence and, through the control of the means of publicity, continually have evidence that the People's interest is being imposed onto political life. Moreover, not only will the People's impact— defined in terms of the principle of candor—be regular and discernible, but it will also be much more susceptible to measurement and evaluation. One knows whether leaders are appearing under conditions they control with much greater certainty and precision than whether leaders are implementing the People's alleged will. Defining popular sovereignty as the control of the means of publicity overcomes the mysticism and profound unverifiability that have undermined notions of sovereignty centered on self-legislation, at least insofar as these have played a role in modern mass representative democracy. Finally, there is no danger of demagogic or tyrannical abuse of the People when is defined ocularly. It is impossible for the malevolent demagogue or dictator to claim the support of the People, since, understood from a plebiscitarian perspective, the People does not give support (i.e., voice) but rather sight. Plebiscitarianism thereby calls for a welcome cleansing of political rhetoric: leaders should not be able to exploit the People by appealing to it as an endorser of their policies or decisions, but should have to stand on their own support—not that of a phantasmic popular will. Defining popular sovereignty in terms of the principle of candor, therefore, would make both the concept of the People and the ideal of popular sovereignty real, relevant, measurable, and safe— results that can hardly be viewed as melancholic. To reiterate it once more, the plebiscitarian ethics I have defended do not deny that certain individuals and groups can make a difference through active use of the political process. The claim is rather that the notion of popular sovereignty ought to be reserved for—and revitalized through—the eyes of the People.

Given that there are three distinct modes whereby the plebiscitarian principle of candor contributes to the ethical horizon of the citizen—

supply, supplementation, and supplantation—my argument ought to be shielded from any simple charge of outright irresponsibility. It is not irresponsible to provide an ethical framework for ordinary citizens in their ordinary lives, something democratic theory has not yet done, nor is it irresponsible to revive such notions as the People and popular sovereignty. But in defending myself I do not mean to suggest a dogged insistence on my own argument. Perhaps there are ways to seek progress and empowerment for the citizen-spectator besides the control of the means of publicity. And perhaps the nature of this control might be defined in a manner distinct from the principle of candor. My hope is not to settle the moral meaning of democracy once and for all, but the opposite: to make the question of democracy's meaning once more an urgent concern and the reformulation of political principles once more an essential task. Complacence with democracy, whether on the level of theory or practice, is hostile to democracy. Any confidence that democratic theory is complete, that the history of political concepts has thereby ended, would only mark the exhaustion of democratic energies that are, in their essence, progressive and critical. Democracy is the historical form of government par excellence because it seems to have been the flower of world history but also, just as much, because it insists that there is always history left to be made. Some will object to my particular proposals for the future of democracy. But if the intellectual and moral crises these proposals are intended to rectify are themselves recognized as such, and as justifying a fundamental rethinking of democratic ideals, this book at least can serve as a beginning if not an end.

NOTES

Chapter 1

1. Richard Bernstein, "Judging—the Actor and the Spectator," in *Philosophical Profiles: Essays in a Pragmatic Mode* (Cambridge, UK: Polity Press, 1986), 222.

2. To avoid misunderstanding, let me indicate at the outset that the *eyes of the People* is intended to designate not just the visual dimension of political spectatorship, but also importantly the audio one. If this synecdoche by which vision refers to the audiovisual field is not entirely precise, neither is it at all uncommon. Both in ordinary parlance and in philosophical discourse, visual processes are invested with an extravisual significance. When Kant, for example, refers to the world of appearances (*Erscheinungen*), he means to indicate a world accessed not simply by vision, but by any of the five senses. The important thing is to distinguish the passive, spectatorial processes of vision and hearing (both of which are intended by the expression "eyes of the People") from active processes of voice, participation, and decision making.

3. Norberto Bobbio, *The Future of Democracy: A Defence of the Rules of the Game*, trans. Roger Griffen (Minneapolis: University of Minneapolis Press, 1987), 27–39.

4. Thomas Jefferson, letter to John Adams, April 11, 1823, in Lester J. Cappon, ed., *The Adams-Jefferson Letters: The Complete Correspondence* (Chapel Hill: University of North Carolina Press, 1987), 592.

5. See, e.g., David L. Holmes, *Faiths of the Founding Fathers* (Oxford: Oxford University Press, 2006), ch. 3, esp. 46–47.

6. These can be the same—so that I may want to be rock star but also condemn myself when, not yet a rock star, I imagine how a rock star would view me—but they can also be different. See, e.g., Sigmund Freud, "On Narcissism: An Introduction," in James Strachey, ed., *The Standard Edition of the Complete Psychological Works of Sigmund Freud* (London: Hogarth Press, 1953), vol. 14, 67–102; Jacques Lacan, *The Four Fundamental Concepts of Psychoanalysis*, trans. Alan Sheridan (New York: Norton, 1998), 61, 130, 144–146, 155, 256–258, 272.

7. Sartre's treatment of the gaze is extremely varied and complex, but in general Sartre understands the gaze as a nonreciprocal intrusion that cancels the observed individual's capacity to act: "I grasp the Other's look at the very center

of my *act* as the solidification and alienation of my own possibilities....The Other as a look is only that—my transcendence transcended. Of course I still *am* my possibilities in the mode of non-thetic consciousness (of) these possibilities. But at the same time the look alienates them from me." Jean-Paul Sartre, *Being and Nothingness: An Essay on Phenomenological Ontology*, trans. Hazel E. Barnes (New York: Philosophical Library, 1956), 263.

8. Michel Foucault, *Discipline and Punish: The Birth of the Prison*, trans. Alan Sheridan (New York: Pantheon, 1977), 187–188.

9. Laura Mulvey, "Visual Pleasure and Narrative Cinema," *Screen* 16 (Autumn 1975): 6–18, 10.

10. For the folkloric tradition, see Tobin Siebers, *The Mirror of Medusa* (Berkeley: University of California Press, 1983), x. For discussion of the contemporary relevance of the evil eye, see Margaret Olin, "Gaze," in Robert S. Nelson and Richard Schiff, eds., *Critical Terms for Art History* (Chicago: University of Chicago Press, 1996), 212, 214.

11. Banned in the sense that the Commission on Presidential Debates (CPD) prohibited it. See, e.g., George Farah, *No Debate: How the Republican and Democratic Parties Secretly Control the Presidential Debates* (New York: Seven Stories, 2004), 7, 10, passim. The CPD changed its policy in 2008, but neither candidate took advantage of the opportunity to cross-examine the other.

12. Debord's polemical reaction to a society infused with spectacles is but the most virulent expression of political theory's broader tendency to oppose political imagery as such, rather than cultivate distinctions between morally better and worse forms of spectacles: "The spectacle is by definition immune from human activity, inaccessible to any projected review or correction. It is the opposite of dialogue. Wherever representation takes on an independent existence, the spectacle reestablishes its rule....[It] is the bad dream of modern society in chains, expressing nothing more than its wish for sleep. The spectacle is the guardian of that sleep....By means of the spectacle the ruling order discourses endlessly upon itself in an uninterrupted monologue of self-praise." Guy Debord, *Society of the Spectacle*, trans. Donald Nicholson (New York: Zone, 1994), 17, 18, 19. Other important studies that also include a wholesale negative interpretation of the spectacle include Jürgen Habermas, *Structural Transformation of the Public Sphere: An Inquiry into the Category of Bourgeois Society*, trans. Thomas Burger (Cambridge, Mass.: MIT Press, 1991), chs. 20–24; Daniel Boorstin, *The Image: A Guide to Pseudo-Events in America* (New York: Harper and Row, 1964). For a partial exception to this trend, see Joseph LaPalombara, *Democracy Italian Style* (New Haven, Conn.: Yale University Press, 1987).

13. See, e.g., Karl-Otto Apel, *The Response of Discourse Ethics to the Moral Challenge of the Human Situation as Such and Especially Today* (Leuven: Peters, 2001), 45–48.

14. For the importance of personality in the contemporary political scene, see Anthony King, ed., *Leaders' Personalities and the Outcomes of Democratic Elections* (Oxford: Oxford University Press, 2002); Bruce Cain, John Ferejohn,

and Morris Fiorina, *The Personal Vote: Constituency Service and Electoral Independence* (Cambridge, Mass.: Harvard University Press, 1987); Bernard Manin, *The Principles of Representative Government* (Cambridge: Cambridge University Press, 1997), 220, 221.

15. Pauline Marie Rosenau, *Post-modernism and the Social Sciences* (Princeton, N.J.: Princeton University Press, 1992), esp. 93. For a competing view, it is important to recognize that some defenders of representation have stressed that political representation does not require mimesis, but in fact depends on the distinction between the represented and representative. See, e.g., F. R. Ankersmit, *Aesthetic Politics: Political Philosophy beyond Fact and Value* (Stanford, Calif.: Stanford University Press, 1996), 39–51; Nadia Urbinati, *Mill on Democracy: From the Athenian Polis to Representative Government* (Chicago: University of Chicago Press, 2002). However, the overdetermined quality of the concept of representation (its capacity to mean so many different things to so many different interpreters) is another potential objection to it.

16. Jean-Jacques Rousseau, *The Social Contract*, trans. Maurice Cranston (Penguin: London, 1968), 3.15.

17. François Guizot, *Histoire des Origins du Gouvernement Représentatif en Europe* (Paris: Didier, 1851), 82, 83. Also see Alfred de Grazia, "Representation: Theory," in David L. Sills, ed., *International Encyclopedia of the Social Sciences* (New York: Macmillan, 1968), vol. 13, 462.

18. Ankersmit, *Aesthetic Politics*, 23.

19. Kenneth Arrow, *Social Choice and Individual Values* (New Haven, Conn.: Yale University Press, 1973); William Riker, *Liberalism against Populism: A Confrontation between the Theory of Democracy and the Theory of Social Choice* (San Francisco: Freeman, 1982); Kenneth Shepsle, *Analyzing Politics: Rationality, Behavior, and Institutions* (New York: Norton, 1997). The findings of social choice are controversial and have been subject to criticism. See, e.g., Gerry Mackie, *Democracy Defended* (Cambridge: Cambridge University Press, 2003).

20. See, e.g., Philip Converse, "The Nature of Belief Systems in Mass Publics," in David Apter, ed., *Ideology and Discontent* (London: Free Press of Glencoe, 1964), 206–261; John Zaller, *The Nature and Origins of Mass Opinion* (New York: Cambridge University Press, 1992).

21. See, e.g., Lawrence R. Jacobs and Robert Y. Shapiro, *Politicians Don't Pander: Political Manipulation and the Loss of Democratic Responsiveness* (Chicago: University of Chicago Press, 2000); Adam Przeworski, Susan Stokes, and Bernard Manin, eds., *Democracy, Accountability, and Representation* (Cambridge: Cambridge University Press, 1999), chs. 3, 7, 11; Martin Gilens, "Inequality and Democratic Responsiveness," *Public Opinion Quarterly* 69 (2005): 778–796; John D. Griffen and Brian Newman, "Are Voters Better Represented?" *Journal of Politics* 67 (2005): 1206–1227.

22. Joseph Schumpeter, *Capitalism, Socialism, and Democracy* (New York: Harper and Brothers, 1942), 242. I will argue in chapter 5, however, that Schumpeter ought to be recognized as standing for the ideal of competition among elites. Competition is not just a fact, but a moral restraint that can be more

or less maximized. Nonetheless, the interpretation of Schumpeter as standing for an amoral conception of democracy is widespread and has proved influential.

23. Przeworski, for example, defines democracy as "a system in which parties lose elections." Adam Przeworski, *Democracy and the Market* (Cambridge: Cambridge University Press, 1991), 10.

24. Thus in Riker's well-known critique of what he calls the "populist" theory of government, there is profound confusion regarding the so-called liberal alternative he sketches. It is not clear, for example, whether the liberal theory means that the People still chooses leaders but without any instruction as to what the leaders should accomplish, or that even the selection of leaders is not genuinely chosen by the People (i.e., that voting is random). Riker further complicates matters when he says that the liberal account fully satisfies traditional democratic values of participation, liberty, and equality. See Riker, *Liberalism against Populism*, ch. 10.

25. See, e.g., Benjamin Barber, *Strong Democracy: Participatory Politics for a New Age* (Berkeley: University of California Press, 1984), 146, 205–206. Barber reviews a variety of problems undermining the capacity of existing governments to represent the People—including social choice issues that prevent the rational aggregation of collective preferences as well as the profound limitations of voting as a form of political expression—but his strategy is to affirm a participatory ideal in which a future political society might somehow attain the same popular sovereignty that a representative system advertises but fails to provide.

26. Boorstin, *The Image*, esp. ch. 1.

27. Hannah Arendt, *The Human Condition* (Chicago: University of Chicago Press, 1958), 197.

28. Thus Arendt could write: "Our political life,...despite its being the realm of action, also takes place in the midst of processes which we call historical and which tend to become as automatic as natural or cosmic processes....The truth is that automatism is inherent in all processes, no matter what their origin may be." Hannah Arendt, *Between Past and Future: Eight Exercises in Political Thought* (New York: Penguin, 1977), 168–169.

29. See Arendt, *Human Condition*, 175–181.

30. As I discuss more fully in chapter 2, the spectating citizen can be considered interestless in the sense either of being without interests (not having a clear opinion on a matter), or of having interests but knowing that these will play no direct role in determining or affecting the political event being watched.

31. See Immanuel Kant, *The Contest of Faculties*, in *Political Writings*, ed. Hans Reiss, trans. H. B. Nisbet (Cambridge: Cambridge University Press, 1991), 182.

32. T. S. Eliot, *The Family Reunion* (Orlando, Fla.: Harvest Books, 1964), 19.

33. Schmitt expresses the modernist standpoint with his dictum: "All genuine political theories presuppose man to be evil, i.e., by no means an unproblematic but a dangerous and dynamic being." Carl Schmitt, *The Concept of the Political*, trans. George Schwab (Chicago: University of Chicago Press, 1996), 61.

34. What is objectionable about an idealistic approach, writes Machiavelli, is that one is always surrounded by enemies ready to do evil: "For a man who wants to make a profession of good in all regards must come to ruin among so many who are not good." Niccolò Machiavelli, *The Prince*, trans. Harvey C. Mansfield (Chicago: University of Chicago Press, 1998), 61. What makes Machiavelli different from others who recognize this fact—whether Plato (whose theory of justice takes as its starting point a feverish city overrun by avarice) or Hobbes (who reasons from a brutish state of nature)—is that Machiavelli presents his notion of *virtù* not as something that will overcome the prior state of evil, but only as an imperfect set of practices for wrestling with and containing evil. Hence, rather than link his project to final goals like harmony or peace, Machiavelli's political ethics must continually be renewed in such fraught practices as war, cruelty that is "well used," and the drive for expansion.

35. Niccolò Machiavelli, *Discourses on Livy*, trans. Harvey C. Mansfield and Nathan Tarcov (Chicago: University of Chicago Press, 1998), I, 55; II, preface; III, 1, 17. Thus Mansfield can write that for Machiavelli the People is the bastion of traditional morality, in the sense that "moral qualities are qualities 'held good' by the People." Harvey C. Mansfield, *Machiavelli's Virtue* (Chicago: University of Chicago Press, 1996), 179.

36. Claude Lefort, for example, describes the transition from monarchy to democracy as one in which power, formerly residing in the monarch, becomes an "empty place." Claude Lefort, *Democracy and Political Theory*, trans. David Macey (Minneapolis: University of Minnesota Press, 1988), 17.

37. Jean François Lyotard, *The Postmodern Condition: A Report on Knowledge*, trans. Geoff Bennington and Brian Massumi (Minneapolis: University of Minnesota Press, 1984), 30.

38. See, e.g., Iris Marion Young, *Inclusion and Democracy* (Oxford: Oxford University Press, 2000), 126; Pierre Bourdieu, *Language and Symbolic Power*, trans. Gino Raymond and Matthew Adamson (Cambridge, UK: Polity Press, 1991), chs. 7–9.

39. Consider Hitler's claim: "I have come from the people. In the course of fifteen years I have slowly worked my way up from the people, together with this movement. No one has set me above this people. I have grown from the people, I have remained in the people, and to the people I shall return. It is my ambition not to know a single statesman in the world who has a better right than I to say that he is a representative of the people." J. P. Stern, *Hitler: The Führer and the People* (Berkeley: University of California Press, 1975), 18. Or, consider the Argentine dictator Peron in 1950: "If my government is to have merit it must interpret completely the wishes of my people. I am no more than the servant. My virtue lies in carrying out honestly and correctly the popular will." Frank Owen, *Peron: His Rise and Fall* (London: Cresset Press, 1957), 168.

40. Jürgen Habermas, *Between Facts and Norms: Contributions to a Discourse Theory of Law and Democracy*, trans. William Rehg (Cambridge, Mass.: MIT Press, 1996), 463–491.

41. Recent developments suggest that the presence of a single public stage—already illusory for the commonsensical reason that it is unrealistic to expect the same political events to be seen by all citizens simultaneously—has been further disaggregated by the tendency of leaders to appear differently in front of different mass publics within the larger electorate. To the extent this practice is a device by which leaders control and minimize the risk of their public appearances (as it certainly seems to be), then a plebiscitarian, as a way to oppose this tendency, would favor public appearances simultaneously broadcast to the *largest possible* audience.

Chapter 2

1. See, e.g., Benjamin Constant, "The Liberty of the Ancients Compared with That of the Moderns," in Biancamaria Fontana, ed., *Political Writings* (Cambridge: Cambridge University Press, 1988), 316–317: "We can no longer enjoy the liberty of the ancients, which consisted in an active and constant participation in collective power. Our freedom must consist of peaceful enjoyment and private independence."

2. Important postwar studies detailing the apolitical nature of ordinary citizens include Bernard R. Berelson, Paul F. Lazarsfeld, and William N. McPhee, *Voting: A Study of Opinion Formation in a Presidential Campaign* (Chicago: University of Chicago Press, 1954); Angus Campbell et al., *The American Voter* (New York: Wiley, 1960); and Philip Converse, "The Nature of Belief Systems in Mass Publics," in David Apter, ed., *Ideology and Discontent* (London: Free Press of Glencoe, 1964), 206–261. For the argument that apoliticism is a necessary relaxant on the political system, see, e.g., Samuel Huntington, "The United States," in Michael Crozier, Samuel Huntington, and Joji Watanuki, eds., *The Crisis of Democracy* (New York: New York University Press, 1975), 113–115. The recovery of the rationality of the apathetic or minimally participatory citizen has many sources. See, e.g., Arthur Lupia, "Short-Cuts versus Encyclopedias: Information and Voting Behavior in California Insurance Reform Elections," *American Political Science Review* 88 (1994): 63–76; Samuel Popkin, *The Reasoning Voter: Communication and Persuasion in Presidential Campaigns* (Chicago: University of Chicago Press, 1991); Paul M. Sniderman, Richard A. Brody, and Philip. E. Tetlock, *Reasoning and Choice: Explorations in Political Psychology* (Cambridge: Cambridge University Press, 1991), 18; Donald A. Wittman, *The Myth of Democratic Failure* (Chicago: University of Chicago Press, 1995), esp. ch. 2; Franz Urban Pappi, "Political Behavior: Reasoning Voters and Multi-party Systems," in Robert Goodin and Hans-Dieter Klingemann, eds., *The New Handbook of Political Science* (Oxford: Oxford University Press, 1996), 255–275; and Shanto Iyengar, "Shortcuts to Political Knowledge: Selective Attention and the Accessibility Bias," in John Ferejohn and James Kuklinski, eds., *Information and Democratic Processes* (Urbana: University of Illinois Press, 1990), 160–185.

3. Aristotle, *Politics*, 1277a26–27: "The excellence of a citizen consists in the capacity both to rule and be ruled well"; also see *Politics*, 1277b14–15: "The good citizen must have ability and knowledge in regard to both ruling and being ruled."

4. There is of course a conceptual difference between obeying and listening, but for Aristotle these largely overlap.

5. Aristotle treats being-ruled in book 3 of the *Politics*, which examines ideal forms of citizenship and state, and not in book 4, which examines what is merely best under the circumstances or what is most easily attained by all states.

6. Aristotle, *Politics*, 1277b26–30.

7. Aristotle, *Politics*, 1277b22–24.

8. Aristotle, *Politics*, 1277b9–13. Aristotle, *The Politics and The Constitution of Athens*, trans. Stephen Everson (Cambridge: Cambridge University Press, 1996), 67.

9. Alford summarizes research on the "extraordinary facts" of the inclusiveness of the Athenian political system: "Virtually every citizen would serve as a magistrate, about half would sit on the council, and of those who sat on the council better than 70 percent (roughly 365 of 500) would serve as President of Athens for a day." C. Fred Alford, "The 'Iron Law of Oligarchy' in the Athenian Polis ... and Today," *Canadian Journal of Political Science* 1985 (1985): 302.

10. See, e.g., Josiah Ober, *The Athenian Revolution: Essays on Ancient Greek Democracy and Political Theory* (Princeton, N.J.: Princeton University Press, 1996). While Ober argues against considering Athens as an oligarchy, his analysis nonetheless relies on the distinction between *mass* (citizens who sat in the Assembly and the law courts but generally did not speak) and *elite* (citizens who did rise up as speakers and litigators before the People).

11. Ibid., 18–31.

12. Robert Morstein-Marx, *Mass Oratory and Political Power in the Late Roman Republic* (Cambridge: Cambridge University Press, 2004).

13. Even a century later, in 1900, a relatively democratic country like the United Kingdom had an electorate that was not even 7 million (about one-fifth of the total population). See F. W. S. Craig, *British Electoral Facts, 1932–1987* (Brookfield. VT: Gower, 1989).

14. Peter Bachrach, *The Theory of Democratic Elitism: A Critique* (Boston: Little, Brown, 1967), 1.

15. C. Wright Mills, *The Power Elite* (New York: Oxford University Press, 1956), 304.

16. In other words, there are discontinuities between Aristotle's notion of being-ruled and my own invocation of the concept to describe citizenship in mass democracy. While both refer to citizens in their passive capacities, Aristotle's version emphasizes obedience, whereas my usage focuses on spectatorship. The difference between obedience and spectatorship is hardly absolute, however, and thus Aristotle does indeed serve as a partial grounding of the citizen-being-ruled in the modern sense that I employ it.

17. Pluralists are perhaps relatively more skeptical about ideals of authorship and popular autonomy, but they still tend to uphold the capacity of representative government to successfully transmit the diffuse interests and preferences of the citizenry (see section 2.7).

18. Paine claimed that the American struggle for democracy "is in great measure the cause of all mankind ... [and] the Concern of every Man to whom Nature hath given the Power of feeling." Thomas Paine, *Common Sense* (London: Penguin, 1982), 63–64.

19. Within normative conceptions of citizenship, the citizen-governor predominates not only vis-à-vis the citizen-spectator, but also in relation to the citizen as a depoliticized economic agent. This latter figure, though prominent when democracy is treated in a realist or value-neutral fashion, cannot compete with the citizen-governor when a moralized account of democracy is at stake.

20. As Schumpeter argues, "Everyone is free to compete for political leadership.... Free, that is, in the same sense in which everyone is free to start another textile mill." Joseph Schumpeter, *Capitalism, Socialism, and Democracy* (New York: Harper and Brothers, 1942), 272.

21. Kay Schlozman, "Citizen Participation in America: What Do We Know? Why Do We Care?" in Ira Katznelson and Helen V. Milner, eds., *Political Science: State of the Discipline* (New York: Norton, 2002), 434, 436. Also see Verba et al., whose seven-nation study of political participation found that "voting is the only political act that a large part of the citizenry engages in." Sidney Verba, Norman H. Nie, and Jae-On Kim, *Participation and Political Equality: A Seven-Nation Comparison* (Cambridge: Cambridge University Press, 1978), 61.

22. See, e.g., Converse, "Nature of Belief Systems in Mass Publics"; Christopher H. Achen, "Mass Political Attitudes and the Survey Response," *American Political Science Review* 69 (1975): 1218–1231; Gillian Dean and Thomas Moran, "Measuring Mass Political Attitudes: Change and Uncertainty," *Political Methodology* 4 (1977): 383–424; Robert Erikson, "The SRC Panel Data and Mass Political Attitudes," *British Journal of Political Science* 9 (1979): 89–114; John Zaller, "Political Awareness, Elite Opinion Leadership, and the Mass Survey Response," *Social Cognition* 8 (1990): 125–130.

23. Converse, "Nature of Belief Systems in Mass Publics," 245.

24. For a general overview, see Donald Kinder and David Sears, "Public Opinion and Political Action," in Gardner Lindzey and Elliot Aronson, eds., *Handbook of Social Psychology* (New York: Random House, 1985), 659–741; and Tom W. Smith, "Non-attitudes: A Review and Evaluation," in Charles Turner and Elizabeth Martin, eds., *Surveying Subjective Phenomena* (New York: Russell Sage Foundation, 1984), 215–255.

25. John Zaller, *The Nature and Origins of Mass Opinion* (New York: Cambridge University Press, 1992), 34; W. Russell Neuman, *The Paradox of Mass Politics: Knowledge and Opinion in the American Electorate* (Cambridge, Mass.: Harvard University Press, 1986), 48, 64.

26. See, e.g., Timothy D. Wilson and Sara D. Hodges, "Attitudes as Temporary Constructions," in Leonard Martin and Abraham Tesser, eds., *The Construction of Social Judgments* (Hillsdale, N.J.: Erlbaum, 1992).

27. Tourangeau and Rasinksi, for example, argue for a model of public opinion as a "question-answering" process. Roger Tourangeau and Kenneth Rasinksi, "Cognitive Processes Underlying Context Effects in Attitude Measurement," *Psychological Bulletin* 103 (1988): 299–314. John Zaller has shown that individuals do not typically have well-developed preferences but answer questions spontaneously and with a certain variability, as their encounter with each new issue depends to a significant extent on whatever is most salient in their minds at that time. Zaller, "Political Awareness, Elite Opinion Leadership, and the Mass Survey Response."

28. As Kinder and Sanders conclude: "Those of us who design surveys find ourselves in roughly the same position as do those who hold and wield real power: public officials, editors and journalists, newsmakers and all sorts. Both choose how the public issues are to be framed, and in both instances, the choices seem to be consequential." Donald Kinder and Lynn Sanders, "Mimicking Political Debate with Survey Questions: The Case of White Opinion of Affirmative Action for Blacks," *Social Cognition* 8 (1990): 99.

29. For the concept of issueless politics, see, e.g., Neuman, *Paradox of Mass Politics*, 25–26, 38, 68, 73, 107, 180. For accounts of the tendency to vote on personality, see Michael Margolis, "From Confusion to Confusion: Issues and the American Voter (1956–1972)," *American Political Science Review* 71 (1977): 31–43; Manin, *The Principles of Representative Government* (Cambridge: Cambridge University Press, 1997), 220, 221; Bruce Cain, John Ferejohn, and Morris Fiorina, *The Personal Vote: Constituency Service and Electoral Independence* (Cambridge, Mass.: Harvard University Press, 1987).

30. Zaller, *Nature and Origins of Mass Opinion*, 79–80.

31. Ibid., 93, 95.

32. Ibid., 74–75, 76.

33. Ibid., 55.

34. Achen, "Mass Political Attitudes and the Survey Response," 1227.

35. For a thorough overview of these and other formulations, see Neuman, *Paradox of Mass Politics*, 192; also see Zaller, *Nature and Origins of Mass Opinion*, 333.

36. Zaller, *Nature and Origins of Mass Opinion*, 333.

37. Verba, Nie, and Kim, *Participation and Political Equality*, 71.

38. On the uniqueness of the vote as a political activity, see Sidney Verba, Kay Lehman Schlozman, and Henry E. Brady, *Voice and Equality: Civic Voluntarism in America* (Cambridge, Mass.: Harvard University Press, 1995).

39. See, e.g., Robert D. Putnam, "Tuning In, Tuning Out: The Strange Disappearance of Social Capital in America," *PS: Political Science and Politics* 28 (1995): 664–683; Lester W. Milbrath, *Political Participation: How and Why Do People Get Involved in Politics?* (Chicago: Rand McNally, 1965); and Neuman, *Paradox of Mass Democracy*, 11.

40. Evidence of this hard-core apathetic stratum goes back to Herbert H. Hyman and Paul B. Sheatsley, "Some Reasons Why Information Campaigns Fail," *Public Opinion Quarterly* 11 (1947): 412–423; also see Neuman (*Paradox of Mass Politics*, 170–174), who estimates this apathetic segment to be about 20 percent of the population.

41. Milbrath, *Political Participation*, 16–17.

42. Ibid., 22, 39.

43. In the concluding chapter, Milbrath does recognize a nonparticipatory civic ethics—based on loyalty and obedience, but also on maintaining minimal surveillance of power, passive attentiveness to political events, and an "open communications system" within the polity—yet this aspect of Milbrath's account is not extensively pursued (Milbrath, *Political Participation*, 145–154). What prevents exploration of this alternate set of civic ethics is Milbrath's primary focus on how spectator activities are predictive of gladiator activities; his tendency to identify with the burden elites bear in such a system; and his view that most citizens still manage to get what they want from a stratified political system.

44. See, e.g., Schlozman, "Citizen Participation in America," 439; Verba, Schlozman, and Brady, *Voice and Equality*, 269–287, 346; Campbell et al., *American Voter*, ch. 5. Even Zaller, whose analysis of ambivalence marks a real contribution to the everyday experience of citizenship, still treats political awareness as a predictor of response stability and, thus, as something likely to encourage a more active and ideologically informed political life (Zaller, *Nature and Origins of Mass Opinion*, 65).

45. Neuman, *Paradox of Mass Politics*, 86.

46. The locus classicus of the discovery of disappointingly low civic engagement is Berelson, Lazarsfeld, and McPhee, *Voting*.

47. Neuman, *Paradox of Mass Politics*, 3, 6–7. Also see Philip Converse, "Public Opinion and Voting Behavior," in Fred I. Greenstein and Nelson W. Polsby, eds., *Handbook of Political Science* (Reading, Mass.: Addison-Wesley, 1975), 79: "Surely the most familiar fact to arise from sample surveys in all countries is that popular levels of information about public affairs are, from the point of view of the informed observer, astonishingly low."

48. In Fukuyama's (in)famous triumphalization of Western representative institutions as defining the end point of political history, for example, *liberal democracy* is the key term used to describe the victorious political ideal. Within this hybrid, the protection of individuals from governmental power in the form of well-defined and well-entrenched rights is not seriously distinguished from the specifically democratic ideal that the governed also understand themselves as the governors. It is assumed, uncritically, that the replacement of authoritarian regimes with electoral institutions is sufficient to realize the Hegelian-Kojèvian end state of universal recognition. Francis Fukuyama, *The End of History and the Last Man* (New York: Free Press, 1992).

49. See, e.g., Emmanuel Joseph Sieyès, "Views on the Executive Means Available to the Representatives of France in 1789," in Michael Sonenscher, ed.,

Emmanuel Joseph Sieyès: Political Writings (Indianapolis: Hackett, 2003), 48;
Benjamin Constant espoused a similar view. See, e.g., Constant, *Political
Writings*, 23.

50. See, e.g., Nancy Rosenblum, *Membership and Morals: The Personal Uses
of Pluralism in America* (Princeton, N.J.: Princeton University Press, 1998).

51. For one thing, membership in voluntary organizations is increasingly
a passive, check-writing experience and decreasingly an active, participatory
one. See, e.g., Theda Skocpol, *Diminished Democracy: From Membership to
Management in American Civic Life* (Norman: University of Oklahoma Press,
2003); Schlozman, " Citizen Participation in America," 454. Furthermore, some
of the most common forms of membership—such as membership in churches
or self-help and recovery groups—cannot be seen primarily as a political form
of engagement, but are in fact consistent (although not necessarily so) with a
complete passivity or even apathy toward politics. Finally, any celebration of
civil society's capacity to exert a quasi-political or advocacy function runs the
risk of an overly Americanized conception of democracy. Outside of the United
States, civil society is often much thinner when it comes to national organizations
devoted to political advocacy. In Europe, for example, civil society mainly takes
the form of transnational organizations. See, e.g., Emanuela Lombardo, "The
Participation of Civil Society in the European Constitution-Making Process," in
Justus Schönlau et al. eds., *The Making of the European Constitution* (New York:
Palgrave, 2006).

52. As Robert Dahl, one of the classical pluralists, demonstrated in his
Preface to Democratic Theory, on particular issues and decisions representative
democracy most of the time does not reflect the will of the majority, but rather a
specific minority that is able to attract other groups to form a temporary
coalition. In *Who Governs?* Dahl found that public policy in New Haven,
Connecticut, was a product of numerous coalitions, rather than something
emanating from a single power-holding elite. Robert Dahl, *A Preface to
Democratic Theory* (Chicago: University of Chicago Press, 1956); Dahl, *Who
Governs? Democracy and Power in an American City* (New Haven, Conn.: Yale
University Press, 1961).

53. For the claim that majoritarian tyranny is a myth, see Dahl, *Preface to
Democratic Theory*, 133.

54. As Dahl observed, it is rarely useful "to construe [the numerical
majority at election time] as more than an arithmetic expression....[T]he
numerical majority is incapable of undertaking any co-ordinated action. It is the
various components of the numerical majority that have the means for action"
(ibid., 146).

55. As Held states the problem: "The existence of many power centers
hardly guarantees that government will (a) listen to them all equally; (b) do
anything other than communicate with leaders of such centers; (c) be susceptible
to influence by anybody other than those in powerful positions; (d) do anything
about the issues under discussion, and so on." David Held, *Models of Democracy*,
3rd edition (Stanford, Calif.: Stanford University Press, 2006), 169.

56. For a penetrating critique of the relevance of issue publics for most citizens, see Neuman, *Paradox of Mass Politics*, 38, 68, 73, 107, 180. For a more recent statement, see Scott L. Althaus, *Collective Preferences in Democratic Politics: Opinion Surveys and the Will of the People* (Cambridge: Cambridge University Press, 2003), 19.

57. Dahl writes: "I am inclined to think that it is in this characteristic of elections—not minority rule but minorities rule—that we must look for some of the essential differences between dictatorships and democracies" (Dahl, *Preface to Democratic Theory*, 132).

58. According to Dahl, pluralist groups are important for ensuring that representatives will be "somewhat responsive to the preferences of the ordinary citizens" (Dahl, *Preface to Democratic Theory*, 131). Also see Held, *Models of Democracy*, 187.

59. See, e.g., Held, *Models of Democracy*, 194.

60. Dahl thought control over leaders could be maintained indirectly through regular elections and political competition among parties and groups. These do not embody government by majority in any real way, but "they vastly increase the size, number, and variety of minorities whose preferences must be taken into account by leaders in making policy choices" (Dahl, *Preface to Democratic Theory*, 132).

61. See, e.g., Dahl, *A Preface to Economic Democracy* (Berkeley: University of California Press, 1985). For a recent neopluralist account, attuned to the poor resource base of many underrepresented groups, see Andrew S. McFarland, *Neopluralism: The Evolution of Political Process Theory* (Lawrence: University Press of Kansas, 2004).

62. Held, *Models of Democracy*, 165.

63. David B. Truman, *The Governmental Process: Political Interests and Public Opinion* (New York: Knopf, 1951), 503–516.

64. In their introduction to a collection of essays on deliberative democracy, Bohman and Rehg write: "The idea that legitimate government should embody the 'will of the people' has a long history and appears in many variants. As the beneficiary of this rich heritage, the concept of deliberative democracy that has emerged in the last two decades represents an exciting development in political theory....As a normative account of legitimacy, deliberative democracy evokes ideals of rational legislation, participatory politics, and civic self-governance." James Bohman and William Rehg, eds., *Deliberative Democracy: Essays on Reason and Politics* (Cambridge, Mass.: MIT Press, 1997), ix. Amy Gutmann defends education that cultivates deliberative capacities because children "must learn not just to behave in accordance with authority but to think critically about authority if they are to live up to the democratic ideal of sharing political sovereignty as citizens." Gutmann, *Democratic Education* (Princeton, N.J.: Princeton University Press, 1987), 299. James Fearon provides a variety of arguments for deliberation, but bases the moral arguments on the ideology of popular self-rule. Fearon, "Deliberation as Discussion," in Jon Elster, ed., *Deliberative Democracy* (Cambridge: Cambridge University Press, 1998), 44–68.

65. See, e.g., David Estlund, "Beyond Fairness and Deliberation: The Epistemic Dimension of Democratic Authority," in Bohman and Rehg, *Deliberative Democracy*, 173–204.

66. The latter option in all three cases is defended by Amy Gutmann and Dennis Thompson, *Democracy and Disagreement* (Cambridge, Mass.: Belknap Press of Harvard University Press, 1996).

67. John Rawls, "The Idea of Public Reason," in *Political Liberalism* (New York: Columbia University Press, 1996), 216–220.

68. Ibid., 213.

69. Ibid., 218.

70. Ibid., 215.

71. Rawls, "Introduction to the Paperback Edition," in *Political Liberalism*, lv.

72. Ibid., xlv.

73. Amy Gutmann and Dennis Thompson, *Why Deliberative Democracy?* (Princeton, N.J.: Princeton University Press, 2004), 30.

74. Thus, an interesting suggestion is not pursued: namely, that there is a secondary, nondeliberative set of moral interests likely to apply to citizens-being-ruled. Instead, Gutmann and Thompson define *all* democratic citizens as "autonomous agents who take part in the governance of their own society, directly or through their representatives. In deliberative democracy an important way these agents take part is by presenting and responding to reasons, *or by demanding that their representatives do so*, with the aim of justifying the laws under which they must live together" (Gutmann and Thompson, *Why Deliberative Democracy?* 3–4, emphasis added). The *demand* for giving reasons is no longer within the rubric of deliberation. It reflects the lack of reciprocity, symmetry, and equality required by deliberative settings. Although Gutmann and Thompson acknowledge this alternate form of civic ethics, they do not pursue it directly, but collapse it within the overarching deliberative model.

75. Ibid., 141.

76. Bruce Ackerman and James S. Fishkin, *Deliberation Day* (New Haven, Conn.: Yale University Press, 2004).

Chapter 3

1. Robert Filmer, *Patriarcha and Other Political Writings*, ed. Peter Laslett (Oxford: Basil Blackwell, 1949), 252.

2. For a recent contribution to this debate, see Philip Pettit, "Rawls's Political Ontology," *Politics, Philosophy, and Economics* 4 (2005): 157–174. Pettit asks whether the People has a corporate or aggregative will—or a third option, a combination of these that Pettit calls *civicity*. However, whether the People is one or many, there is still the key issue of the *medium* wherein popular power reveals itself. But Pettit overlooks this question. Instead, Pettit himself implicitly acknowledges that all three possibilities he outlines share the same commitment to the vocal, legislative ontology of popular power: i.e., all three assume that the

objects of popular power are the norms, laws, and policies governing public life
and that the mechanism of popular power is the People's vocal decision.

   3. Hansen writes that "in a democratic *polis*, especially Athens, government
and citizens largely coincided, primarily through the institution of the Assembly
of the People, and the dominant ideology was that the *polis* was the people
(*demos*): it manifests itself, for example, in all surviving treaties, where the state
of *Athens* is called *ho demos ho Athenaion*, 'the people of the Athenians.'" Mogens
Herman Hansen, *The Athenian Democracy in the Age of Demosthenes*, trans. J. A.
Crook (Oxford: Blackwell, 1991), 59.

   4. Gordon S. Wood, *The Radicalism of the American Revolution* (New York:
Knopf, 1992), 25–26, 598–599; Margaret Canovan, *The People* (Cambridge, UK:
Polity Press, 2005), 23; Edmund S. Morgan, *Inventing the People: The Rise of
Popular Sovereignty in England and America* (New York: Norton, 1988), esp.
chs. 1–3.

   5. See, e.g., Wood, *Radicalism of the American Revolution*, 365–376.

   6. James Madison, "Federalist No. 63," in Jacob E. Cooke, ed., *The
Federalist* (Middletown, Conn.: Wesleyan University Press, 1961), 428.

   7. James Madison, "Federalist No. 10," in Cooke, *The Federalist*, 61.
Madison's understanding of representative government as popular government
is also evinced when he says that the device of representation, though a
European institution, is being given a "wholly popular" usage in America
(Madison, "Federalist No. 14," in Cooke, *The Federalist*, 84). Likewise, in
"Federalist No. 39," Madison writes of "that honorable determination which
animates every votary of freedom, to rest all our political experiments on the
capacity of mankind for self-government" (Madison, "Federalist No. 39," in
Cooke, *The Federalist*, 250). Hamilton, too, refers to the "fundamental maxim
of republican government which requires that the sense of the majority should
prevail" (Alexander Hamilton, "Federalist No. 22," in Cooke, *The Federalist*,
139).

   8. Early interpreters of representative government were struck by this
tension between exclusion and empowerment and saw it as a real conundrum.
Guizot, for example, one of the first to thematize modern representative
government and examine it in a scholarly fashion, wondered what kind of system
representative democracy was, according to which "there is a sovereign who
does not rule, but obeys; and a government that rules but is not the sovereign?"
François Guizot, *Histoire des origines du gouvernement représentatif en Europe* (Paris:
Didier, 1851), 88. More recently, Pocock has described the problematic nature
of popular power in representative democracy this way: "It could be argued both
that all government was the people's and that the people had withdrawn from
government altogether." J. G. A. Pocock, *The Machiavellian Moment* (Princeton,
N.J.: Princeton University Press, 1975), 517.

   9. See, e.g., Christopher Hill, "The Many-Header Monster in Late
Tudor and Early Stuart Political Thinking," in Charles H. Carter, ed., *From
the Renaissance to the Counter-Reformation: Essays in Honor of Garrett Mattingly*
(New York: Random House, 1965), 296–324.

10. See, e.g., Warren Montag, *Bodies, Masses, Power: Spinoza and His Contemporaries* (London: Verso, 1999), 77: "One of the most common figures through which the nature and power of the masses is explicated is that of the ocean (the metaphor found in Tacitus and Quintius Curtius), usually an unnoticed backdrop to the business of the state but capable, during troubled times, of unleashing a force that nothing can withstand. The least fissure in the state, whether a death (e.g. Augustus for Tacitus or Alexander for Quintius Curtius) or dissension (Cataline's conspiracy for Sallust), may provoke mass action and the breakdown of order." A similar metaphor is used by Xun Zi, a second-century Confucian philosopher: "The ruler is the boat and the common people are the water. It is the water that holds the boat up, and the water that capsizes it." Quoted in Masayuki Sato, *The Confucian Quest for Order: The Origin and Formation of the Political Thought of Xun Zi* (Leiden: Brill, 2003), 262.

11. According to Hobbes, it is only with the leadership of the sovereign that a multitude becomes a people and, thus, attains a political existence with all its attendant possibilities for agency and expression. In *De Cive*, for example, Hobbes argues that the multitude—i.e., the mass of the people without the ordering of a state—is incapable of action and that, accordingly, the People ought to be redefined to refer to the organs of government, such as the monarch or legislative assembly, which are actually capable of making political decisions. Thomas Hobbes, *On the Citizen*, trans. Richard Tuck (New York: Cambridge University Press, 1998), XII.8; also see VI. The early Locke, too, evinced a similar theory as well as a serious fear of the multitude. John Locke, *The Political Writings of John Locke*, ed. David Wootton (New York: Mentor, 1993), 142.

12. As Spinoza argues in the *Tractatus Politicus* (ch. 7, par. 11): a king intent on preserving his right "whether led by fear of the multitude or by a wish to bind them to him, or whether he is led by a generous spirit, a desire to consult the public good [*utilitati*], will always support the majority opinion" (here I follow the translation of Montag, *Bodies, Masses, Power*, 80). A similar argument has been made, in more recent times, by Paolo Virno in his study of the multitude. Virno, *A Grammar of the Multitude* (Cambridge, Mass.: Semiotext(e), 2004). Michael Hardt and Antonio Negri likewise invoke and develop the concept of multitude, arguing for its relevance to the postmodern practice of democracy. They present the multitude as a "multiplicity that acts"—distinguishing it both from a violent and destructive *mass*, on the one hand, and from a unified, contracting, sovereign (what they call the *People*), on the other. Hardt and Negri, *Multitude: War and Democracy in the Age of Empire* (New York, The Penguin Press 2004).

13. Mosca makes a similar argument. Gaetano Mosca, *The Ruling Class*, trans. Hannah D. Kahn (New York: 1939), 155–56.

14. For this latter, see Canovan, *The People*, 17; Anthony Black, "Society and the Individual from the Middle Ages to Rousseau: Philosophy, Jurisprudence, and Constitutional Theory," *History of Political Thought* 1 (1980): 145–166; David Wootton, ed., *Divine Right and Democracy: An Anthology of Political Writing in Stuart England* (New York: Penguin, 1986), 49.

15. John Locke, *The Two Treatises of Government*, ed. Peter Laslett (Cambridge: Cambridge University Press, 1988), II: esp. secs. 149, 168.

16. Bruce Ackerman, *We the People*, 2 vols. (Cambridge, Mass.: Belknap Press of Harvard University Press, 1991, 1998).

17. Sheldon Wolin, "Fugitive Democracy," in Seyla Benhabib, ed., *Democracy and Difference: Contesting the Boundaries of the Political* (Princeton, N.J.: Princeton University Press, 1996), 31–45.

18. The most important exception of which I am aware is Montesquieu, who appears to have articulated a notion of popular power that would be limited to leadership selection and explicitly excluded from legislation. Montesquieu, *The Spirit of the Laws*, trans. Anne M. Cohler, Basia Carolyn Miller, and Harold Samuel Stone (Cambridge: Cambridge University Press, 1989), bk. 2.2, 12; bk. 11.6, 160. This was an unusual theory, however, and ought not be conflated with the traditional republican doctrine that the People was expert at judgment, but not at execution and administration. Whereas earlier republican theorists affirming the People's talent for judgment included judgments about *both* leadership and policies, Montesquieu was different in suggesting a strict distinction between these two spheres and argued for limiting popular power to leadership selection. For the traditional republican view, see Bernard Manin, *The Principles of Representative Government* (Cambridge: Cambridge University Press, 1997), 62. But Montesquieu is not altogether consistent on this point. Nor does he develop it. In any case, Montesquieu's theory needs to be distinguished from the plebiscitarian alternative I defend, which revises not simply the object of popular power (taking it to be the leader rather than the law), but the organ of popular empowerment (taking it to be the People's *gaze* rather than the People's decision). In other words, in calling into question the People's status as a decisional force, the plebiscitarian standpoint looks to understand the People as something other than a chooser of laws *or* leaders.

19. Carole Pateman, *Participation and Democratic Theory* (Cambridge: Cambridge University Press, 1970), 20–21. Also see John Medearis, *Joseph Schumpeter's Two Theories of Democracy* (Cambridge, Mass.: Harvard University Press, 2001), 129–133; Emilio Santoro, "Democratic Theory and Individual Autonomy: An Interpretation of Schumpeter's Doctrine of Autonomy," *European Journal of Political Research* 23 (1993): 122–123; C. B. Macpherson, *The Life and Times of Liberal Democracy* (Oxford: Oxford University Press, 1977), 85; David Held, *Models of Democracy* (Stanford, Calif.: Stanford University Press, 1987), 178–179.

20. Rousseau endorsed representation in *Discourse on Political Economy* (1755) but in that same year appears to have begun to change his mind, as evidenced in the *Second Discourse*. While the *Social Contract* (1762) marked Rousseau's most adamant opposition to representation, in *Constitutional Project for Corsica* (1765), Rousseau supported delegation with the imperative mandate. There is much debate as to Rousseau's final verdict on representation, but some have argued that Rousseau came to endorse representation, not just as a practical necessity in large states, but as a matter of principle insofar as it

would underwrite an elective aristocracy. See, e.g., Roger Masters, *The Political Philosophy of Rousseau* (Princeton, N.J.: Princeton University Press, 1968), 402; Robert Derathé, *Jean-Jacques Rousseau et la science politique de son temps* (Paris: J. Vrin, 1970), 279–280; Nadia Urbinati, "Continuity and Rupture: The Power of Judgment in Democratic Representation," *Constellations* 12 (2005): 219 n. 46.

21. Jean-Jacques Rousseau, *The Social Contract*, trans. Maurice Cranston (London: Penguin, 1968), 2.6; 82.

22. Ibid.

23. Ibid., 3.12; 136.

24. That Rousseau understood popular assemblies to be regularly meeting bodies that would legislate (or at least ratify) not just fundamental constitutional questions, but also more mundane statutes can be seen, for example, from his exhortation: "It is not enough that the assembled people should have once determined the constitution of the state by giving sanction to a body of laws; it is not enough that it should set up a perpetual government, or that it should have provided once and for all the election of magistrates. In addition to the extraordinary assemblies that unforeseen events may necessitate, there must be fixed and periodic assemblies which nothing can abolish or prorogue, so that on the appointed day the people is rightfully summoned by the law itself without any further convocation being needed.... The more strength the government has, the more frequently the sovereign should meet in assemblies" (ibid., 3.13; 137). The People's contribution to nonconstitutional lawmaking (if only as a ratifier) is also strongly suggested by claims in the *Social Contract* that "the legislative power belongs, and can only belong, to the people" (3.1; 101) and that "any law which the people has not ratified in person is void; it is not law at all" (3.15; 141).

25. Ibid., 3.14; 139: "The moment the people is lawfully assembled as a sovereign body all jurisdiction of the government ceases; the executive power is suspended, and the person of the humblest citizen is as sacred and inviolable as the highest magistrate, for in the presence of the represented there is no longer any representation."

26. Ibid., 3.11; 135: "The principle of political life dwells in the sovereign authority. The legislative power is the heart of the state, the executive is the brain, which sets all parts in motion. The brain may become paralysed and the individual still live. A man can be an imbecile and survive, but as soon as his heart stops functioning, the creature is dead."

27. See, e.g., ibid., 2.6; 80–83. Thus, Rousseau can say that one of Peter the Great's mistakes was to try to model the Russians on Germans or Englishmen, rather than have them use their political freedom to become distinctly Russian (ibid., 2.9; 88–90).

28. Ibid., 2.6; 82.

29. Madison, "Federalist No. 63," in Cooke, *The Federalist*, 428.

30. Madison, "Federalist No. 10," in Cooke, *The Federalist*, 62.

31. Thus, Madison opposes direct democracy because "the *passions*, [and] not *the reason*, of the public, would sit in judgment" (Madison, "Federalist

No. 50," in Cooke, *The Federalist*, 343). In a similar vein, Hamilton writes in defense of a strong executive: "The republican principle ... does not require an unqualified complaisance to every sudden breeze or passion, or to every transient impulse which the people may receive from the arts of men, who flatter their prejudices to betray their interests....[T]hey sometimes err" (Hamilton, "Federalist No. 71," in Cooke, *The Federalist*, 482).

32. Hamilton, "Federalist No. 68," in Cooke, *The Federalist*, 458; Madison, "Federalist No. 63, in Cooke, *The Federalist*, 425.

33. Hamilton, "Federalist No. 35," in Cooke, *The Federalist*, 219.

34. The merchants have "influence and weight and superior acquirements," which enable them to be the most effective advocates of the common interests merchants share with mechanics and manufacturers: "They [mechanics and manufacturers] are aware that however great the confidence they may justly feel in their own good sense, their interests can be more effectually promoted by the merchant than by themselves. They are sensible that their habits in life have not been such as to give them those acquired endowments, without which in a deliberative assembly the greatest natural abilities are for the most part useless" (ibid.).

35. Ibid., 220: "Every land-holder will therefore have a common interest to keep the taxes on the land as low as possible; and common interest may always be reckoned upon as the surest bond of sympathy."

36. Ibid., 222.

37. John Jay, "Federalist No. 2," in Cooke, *The Federalist*, 9. Madison, too, tended to collapse the People into a corporate entity, referring to citizens as living together "as members of the same family" and as "fellow citizens of one great respectable and flourishing empire" (Madison, "Federalist No. 14," in Cooke, *The Federalist*, 88).

38. As a matter of terminology, representative democracy goes at least as far back as Hamilton. See, e.g., Alexander Hamilton, *The Papers of Alexander Hamilton*, ed. Jacob E. Cooke (New York: Columbia University Press, 1961), I: 225. Yet democracy was still a bad word throughout most of the eighteenth century. With Mill and Bentham and their generation, an important shift takes place.

39. Jeremy Bentham, "Of Publicity," *Public Culture* 6 (1994): 581.

40. Jeremy Bentham, *The Works of Jeremy Bentham*, ed. J. Bowring. (New York: Russell & Russell, 1962), IX: 42.

41. Jeremy Bentham, *Constitutional Code*, ed. F. Rosen and J. H. Burns (Oxford: Clarendon Press, 1983), 35–36. Also see Fred Cutler, "Jeremy Bentham and the Public Opinion Tribunal," *Public Opinion Quarterly* 63 (1999): 329.

42. Bentham, *Constitutional Code*, 37, 39.

43. Bentham, "Of Publicity," 584; also see Cutler, "Bentham and the Public Opinion Tribunal," 325.

44. As Bentham writes, "The universal interest requires that, in regard to subsistence, abundance, security, and equality, the aggregate mass in the community in question, be maximized: and that in particular the shares, which

are the result of the first three, be as near to equality as consistently with security in all other shapes they can be" (Bentham, *Works*, IX: 127). Also see Bentham, *First Principles Preparatory to a Constitutional Code*, ed. Philip Schofield (Oxford: Clarendon Press, 1989), 153.

45. Gerald Postema, "Interests, Universal and Particular: Bentham's Utilitarian Theory of Value," *Utilitas* 18 (2006): 129.

46. Nancy Rosenblum, *Bentham's Theory of the Modern State* (Cambridge, Mass.: Harvard University Press, 1978), 82.

47. Thus in his *Introduction to the Principles of Morals and Legislation*, Bentham defines the universal interest as the "sum of the interests of the several members who compose it." Bentham, *An Introduction to the Principles of Morals and Legislation*, ed. J. H. Burns and H. L. A. Hart (London: Athlone, 1970), 12.

48. See, e.g., Bentham, *Constitutional Code*, 51, 63: Bentham now speaks of a person's share of "the universal interest—that interest which is common to himself and every other member of the community." This transition from an aggregative model of the universal interest to an inclusive model (in which the universal interest is the subset of overlapping interests) is not without exception, and Postema is no doubt correct to acknowledge "the confusion that a certain inconstancy of Bentham's language may generate" (Postema, "Interests, Universal and Particular," 122).

49. See, e.g., Michael James, "Public Interest and Majority Rule in Bentham's Democratic Theory," *Political Theory* 9 (1981): 49: "Bentham normally conceived of democracy as a set of institutions designed, not to discover the preponderant aggregate of individual interests, but to promote only the common interests of all the members of the community."

50. As James summarizes Bentham's rationale: "To stand the chance of being elected, each candidate would have to promise to support the common interests of the electors—i.e. the public interest. The elector would therefore calculate that his interest would be best served if he voted for the candidate who seemed likely to promote the public interest most effectively. The secret ballot was, then, a means of neutralizing the normal predominance of the individual's particular interest over his share of the public interest and of ensuring that he would vote to promote the latter." Ibid., 55, 50. See Bentham, *Works*, III: 452. Also see Rosenblum, *Bentham's Theory of the Modern State*, 85: "What popular elections can do is ensure that the governors chosen are at least capable of securing the universal interest."

51. Bentham, *Constitutional Code*, 36; also see Bentham, *First Principles Preparatory to a Constitutional Code*, 76, 186, 241, 286; Cutler, "Bentham and the Public Opinion Tribunal," 327.

52. For Bentham's challenge to the idea of a single public, see Bentham, *Securities against Misrule and Other Constitutional Writings for Tripoli and Greece*, ed. Philip Schofield (Oxford: Clarendon Press, 1990), 54. For Bentham's various doubts about the use of the term *public opinion*, see Bentham, *Securities against Misrule*, 54; Bentham, *First Principles Preparatory to the Constitutional Code*, 56, 283. Also see Cutler, "Bentham and the Public Opinion Tribunal," 325, 329.

53. Bentham, *Securities against Misrule*, 56; also see Cutler, "Bentham and the Public Opinion Tribunal," 327.

54. Bentham, *Works*, IX: 450.

55. As Mill writes, the People "must entrust [governmental power] to some one individual, or set of individuals, and such individuals will infallibly have the strongest motives to make a bad use of them." James Mill, *Essay on Government*, in Jack Lively and John Rees, eds., *Utilitarian Logic and Politics: James Mill's "Essay on Government," Macaulay's Critique, and the Ensuing Debate* (Oxford: Clarendon Press, 1978), 72.

56. Ibid., 87.

57. Ibid., 74.

58. Ibid., 73.

59. Ibid., 78.

60. On the one hand, Mill suggests that the People are incapable of actual governing—"a community in mass is ill adapted for the business of Government" (ibid., 59) so that "the people, as a body, cannot perform the business of Government for themselves" (ibid., 72)—and that, accordingly, the People will be content simply with "a general control" (ibid., 59). On the other hand, it is clear that Mill conceives of this control in legislative terms. What the People controls above all is that the substantive content of the state's legislative decision making coheres with its own opinions, preferences, and values.

61. Pateman, *Participation and Democratic Theory*, 18.

62. Bentham, *Works*, III: 452.

63. Dennis F. Thompson, *John Stuart Mill and Representative Government* (Princeton, N.J.: Princeton University Press, 1976).

64. For example, in one passage Mill refers to these activities as institutions "whereby not merely a few individuals in succession, but the whole public, are made, to a certain extent, participants in the government, and sharers in the instruction and mental exercise from it." Yet in another Mill writes of these same activities that with the exception of jury service and possibly also local government, "the practice which they give is more in thinking than in action, and in thinking without the responsibilities of action; which with most people amounts to little more than passively receiving the thought of some one else." Likewise while Mill argued for universal participation, he admitted that for most such participation would be limited to "some very minor portions of the public business." *Considerations on Representative Government*, in John Gray, ed., *John Stuart Mill: On Liberty and Other Essays* (Oxford: Oxford University Press, 1998), 286, 413, 255–256.

65. Ibid., 269.

66. Ibid., 270.

67. Ibid., 271.

68. Ibid., 282.

69. Ibid., 284.

70. Mill's conceptualization of popular power as a quasi-legislative force ought not be obscured on the basis of certain remarks Mill sometimes makes

about the separation of Parliament (or the popular assembly in a representative democracy) from a legislative chamber—or about Parliament being a body devoted to talking, not acting. While it is true that Mill expected that the actual drafting of the laws would take place in a separate committee of legal experts, the ratification of the laws was still something to be performed by the representative assembly (ibid., 282–283).

71. Ibid., 329.

72. Ibid., 330, 332.

73. Ibid., 358.

74. Ibid., 374.

75. Ibid., 347.

76. Ibid., 282–283, 378, 380.

77. Robert Weibe, *Self-Rule: A Cultural History of American Democracy* (Chicago: University of Chicago Press, 1995), 66.

78. Quoted in Alexander Keyssar, *The Right to Vote: The Contested History of Democracy in the United States* (New York: Basic Books, 2000), 190.

79. Ibid., 183.

80. Ibid., 189.

81. See, e.g., ibid., 218: "It is a well-known irony in American history that politics did not change very dramatically after women were enfranchised. The electorate nearly doubled in size between 1910 and 1920, but voting patterns and partisan alignments were little affected."

82. See, e.g., ibid., 48.

83. Charles Francis Adams Jr., "The Protection of the Ballot in National Elections," *Journal of Social Science* 1 (1869): 108–109; also see Keyssar, *Right to Vote*, 122–123.

84. See, e.g., Francis Parkman, "The Failure of Universal Suffrage," *North American Review* 127 (July–August 1878): 1–20; "Limited Sovereignty in the United States," *Atlantic Monthly*, February 1979, 184–192; Keyssar, *Right to Vote*, 79, 122.

85. William B. Munro, "Intelligence Test for Voters," *Forum* 80 (1928): 823–830.

86. Of course, this is not to say that there are not still those who contend that voting in its current form—i.e., *without* poll taxes, literacy tests, pauper restrictions, excessive voting ages, understanding clauses, or property and tax requirements—is unfair. See, e.g., Lani Guinier, *The Tyranny of the Majority: Fundamental Fairness in Representative Democracy* (New York: Free Press, 1994).

87. V. O. Key, *Public Opinion and American Democracy* (New York: Knopf, 1961), 536.

88. Frederick Grimke, *The Nature and Tendency of Free Institutions* (Cambridge, Mass.: Belknap Press of Harvard University Press, 1968), 136.

89. Speech of October 23, 1850, in Henry M. Flint, ed., *Life of Stephen A. Douglas* (Philadelphia: Keystone, 1890), 27.

90. Usher F. Linder, *Reminiscences of the Early Bench and Bar of Illinois*, 2nd ed. (Chicago: Chicago Legal News, 1879), 87.

91. For example, Mill could say of public opinion: "Every one now sees that it is ... the ruling power in the last resort." Mill, *Considerations on Representative Government*, 361; also see 242.

92. Ibid., 71. Mill thought that "free and public conferences" between representatives and their constituents, and the regular participation of the latter in local government would help everyday citizens exercise control over the most politically active and thereby reduce the difference between active and passive citizens. Mill, *Considerations on Representative Government*, 370. Also see Nadia Urbinati, *Mill on Democracy: From the Athenian Polis to Representative Government* (Chicago: University of Chicago Press, 2002), 73.

93. Mill, *Collected Works of John Stuart Mill* (Toronto: University of Toronto Press, 1963), XVIII: 165. Finley has noted the fantastical aspect of this wish, rightly pointing out that the agora cannot be virtual or symbolic. M. I. Finley, *Democracy Ancient and Modern* (New Brunswick, N.J.: Rutgers University Press, 1973), 36. Mill, however, made the case that the vote and certain informal conferences likely to take place during campaigns were sufficient, when combined with communication and transportation technologies of the mid-nineteenth century, to draw all elements of political society—elected officials and everyday citizens—into a reciprocal and equal deliberative context.

94. As Urbinati summarizes Mill's argument in this regard: "What makes modern democracy unique is the intermediary network of communication that ... Mill believed could reunite the *actual assembly* (Parliament) and *deferred assembly* (electors) so that representative democracy could reproduce the distinctive feature of Athenian democracy." Urbinati, *Mill on Democracy*, 73.

95. Mill, like so many political observers of the nineteenth century, made repeated use of the notion of the "tyranny of the majority." See, e.g., Mill, *Considerations on Representative Government*, 442.

96. Mill, *On Liberty*, in John Gray, ed., *John Stuart Mill: On Liberty and Other Essays* (Oxford: Oxford University Press, 1998), 7. Also see Mill, *Considerations on Representative Government*, 299–302.

97. Mill, *On Liberty*, 7.

98. Ibid., 7.

99. Ibid., 8, 7.

100. Mill, *Considerations on Representative Government*, 299–302.

101. Ibid., 303.

102. Ibid., 318.

103. Ibid., 328.

104. See ibid., 305–312. Mill claimed that Britain was not ruled by a minority, because if it were, then "the discordance of the House with the general sentiment of the country would soon become evident" (ibid., 305). This argument, however dubious, is important because it is another indication of Mill's assumption that the People, the great many not empowered to make actual decisions, should be conceived as the possessors of a will (or opinions, interests, and values) ready to be translated into governmental policy.

105. Alexis de Tocqueville, *Democracy in America*, ed. J. P. Mayer; trans. George Lawrence (New York: HarperPerennial, 1988), 722–723.

106. Ibid., 254, 58.

107. Ibid., 246–250.

108. Ibid., 60.

109. For a review, see Lawrence R. Jacobs and Robert. Y. Shapiro, "Studying Substantive Democracy: Public Opinion, Institutions, and Policymaking," *PS: Political Science and Politics* 27 (1994): 9–16. Also see Sidney Verba, "The Citizen as Respondent: Sample Surveys and American Democracy," *American Political Science Review* 90 (1996): 1–7; James A. Stimson, Michael B. MacKuen, and Robert S. Erikson, "Dynamic Representation," *American Political Science Review* 89 (1995), 543–565.

110. See, e.g., James Fishkin's aptly titled book, *The Voice of the People: Public Opinion and Democracy* (New Haven, Conn.: Yale University Press, 1995).

111. Paul Burstein, "The Impact of Public Opinion on Public Policy: A Review and an Agenda," *Political Research Quarterly* 56 (2003): 36.

112. Lawrence R. Jacobs and Robert Y. Shapiro, *Politicians Don't Pander: Political Manipulation and the Loss of Democratic Responsiveness* (Chicago: University of Chicago Press, 2000).

113. Kant refers to the "very wretched and harmful pretext of . . . impracticability. . . .For nothing is more harmful and less worthy of a philosopher than the vulgar appeal to allegedly contrary experience, which would not have existed at all if institutions had been established at the right time according to the ideas, instead of frustrating all good intentions by using crude concepts in place of ideas, just because these concepts were drawn from experience." Immanuel Kant, *Critique of Pure Reason*, ed. Paul Guyer and Allen W. Wood (Cambridge: Cambridge University Press, 1997), 397 (A316/B373—A317/B374).

114. V. O. Key, *The Responsible Electorate: Rationality in Presidential Voting, 1936–1960* (Cambridge, Mass.: Belknap Press of Harvard University Press, 1966); Morris Fiorina, *Retrospective Voting in American National Elections* (New Haven, Conn.: Yale University Press, 1981); Manin, *Principles of Representative Government*.

115. Key, *Responsible Electorate*, 2; see also 61.

116. See, e.g., Manin, *Principles of Representative Government*, 224. Also see John Ferejohn, "Incumbent Performance and Electoral Control," *Public Choice* 50 (1986): 5–25.

117. For the notion of "crafted talk," see Jacobs and Shapiro, *Politicians Don't Pander*, esp. ch. 2.

118. Fiorina, *Retrospective Voting*, 11.

119. This occurred, for example, in recent elections in Germany (2005) and Sweden (2006).

120. Max Weber, "Parliament and Government in Germany," in Peter Lassman and Ronald Speirs, eds., *Political Writings* (Cambridge: Cambridge University Press, 1994), 226–227.

121. See, e.g., James A. Stimson, *Public Opinion in America: Moods, Cycles, and Swings* (Boulder, Colo.: Westview, 1991); Stimson, MacKuen, and Erikson, "Dynamic Representation." For a recent discussion of standard methods of gauging ideology on a conservatism-liberalism scale, see Larry M. Bartels, *Unequal Democracy: The Political Economy of the New Gilded Age* (Princeton, N.J.: Princeton University Press, 2008), 254–257.

122. Adam J. Schiffer, "I'm Not *That* Liberal: Explaining Conservative Democratic Alignment," *Political Behavior* 22 (2000): 293–310. For analysis of the trend toward greater ideological homogeneity within the two major American parties, see Matthew Levendusky, *The Partisan Sort: How Liberals Became Democrats and Conservatives Became Republicans* (Chicago: University of Chicago Press, 2009).

123. Teresa E. Levitin and Warren E. Miller, "Ideological Interpretations of Presidential Elections," *American Political Science Review* 73 (1979): 751–771.

124. Ibid., 769; also see Philip E. Converse, "Comments on Davis's 'Changeable Weather in a Cooling Climate atop the Liberal Plateau,'" *Public Opinion Quarterly* 56 (1992): 308–309.

125. William Haltom, "Liberal-Conservative Continua: A Comparison of Measures," *Western Political Quarterly* 43 (1990): 387–401.

126. Manin, *Principles of Representative Government*, 233.

127. Ibid., 224, 179, 183.

128. Ibid., 225–226.

129. James Bryce, *The American Commonwealth* (New York: Macmillan, 1933), vol. 2, 267.

130. For an excellent overview, see Burstein, "Impact of Public Opinion on Public Policy."

131. Page and Shapiro's influential 1983 article, for example, which did assert a meaningful level of responsiveness, nonetheless included the caveat that without further research it would be "unwise to draw normative conclusions about the extent of democratic responsiveness in policymaking." Benjamin I. Page and Robert Y. Shapiro, "Effects of Public Opinion on Policy," *American Political Science Review* 77 (1983): 189.

132. See, e.g., John Zaller, *The Nature and Origins of Mass Opinion* (New York: Cambridge University Press, 1992); Jacobs and Shapiro, *Politicians Don't Pander*, 64; Key, *Public Opinion and American Democracy*.

133. Key, *Public Opinion and American Democracy*, 8.

134. William G. Domhoff, *Who Rules America: Power and Politics in the Year 2000* (Mountain View, Calif.: Mayfield, 1998); Graham K. Wilson, *Interest Groups* (Cambridge, Mass.: Basil Blackwell, 1990); John R. Wright, *Interest Groups and Congress* (Needham Heights, Mass.: Allyn and Bacon, 1996).

135. Burstein, "Impact of Public Opinion on Public Policy," 30.

136. Gabriel A. Almond, *The American People and Foreign Policy* (New York: Praeger, 1950), 53.

137. Key, *Public Opinion and American Democracy*, 284–285, 90–91, 286, 267.

138. Ibid., 409–410, 555.

139. Ibid., 7. Key argues that although there might be significant time lags and disjunctions between opinion and output, "in the long run majority purpose and public action tend to be brought into harmony" (ibid., 553).

140. Ibid., 32, 283.

141. Ibid., 284.

142. Ibid., 538, 547.

143. Ibid., 454–455, 412.

144. Ibid., 558, 412.

145. Ibid., 412.

146. Benjamin I. Page and Robert Y. Shapiro, *The Rational Public: Fifty Years of Trends in Americans' Policy Preferences* (Chicago: University of Chicago Press, 1992).

147. Just as scientific pollsters in the 1930s, like Gallup, dismissed prescientific polling as an inaccurate assessment of the popular will only to defend their own innovations as a true gauge of the People's voice, so do the recent deliberative reformers critique scientific polling only to uphold their own method for uncovering what the People really has to say. See, e.g., Fishkin, *Voice of the People*, esp. chs. 3 and 5. This is not to deny that deliberative polling, or similar procedures, have not been used to good effect in exceptional circumstances. See, e.g., Mark E. Warren and Hilary Pearse eds., *Designing Deliberative Democracy: The British Columbia Citizens' Assembly* (Cambridge: Cambridge University Press, 2008).

148. "Burstein, "Impact of Public Opinion on Public Policy," 36.

Chapter 4

1. The locus classicus of this interpretation of the plebiscitary is Jürgen Habermas, *Structural Transformation of the Public Sphere: An Inquiry into the Category of Bourgeois Society*, trans. Thomas Burger (Cambridge, Mass.: MIT Press, 1989).

2. On the basis of the historical linkage between the plebiscite, on the one hand, and tyranny and totalitarianism, on the other, some authors have used the term *plebiscitary* as synonymous with a democracy that violates liberal protections. See Richard S. Hillman, John A. Peeler, and Elsa Cardozo, *Democracy and Human Rights in Latin America* (Westport, Conn.: Praeger, 2002), 78; J. Roland Pennock, *Liberal Democracy: Its Merits and Prospects* (New York: Rinehart, 1950); J. L. Talmon, *The Origins of Totalitarian Democracy* (London: Secker and Warburg, 1952), 104–105, 203–207, 250–251.

3. See, e.g., John P. McCormick, ed., *Confronting Mass Democracy and Industrial Technology: Political and Social Theory from Nietzsche to Habermas* (Durham, N.C.: Duke University Press, 2002); Bruce Ackerman, *The Failure of the Founding Fathers: Jefferson, Marshall, and the Rise of Presidential Democracy* (Cambridge, Mass.: Belknap Press of Harvard University Press, 2005); Theodore J. Lowi, *The End of Liberalism: The Second Republic of the United States* (New York: Norton, 1979). Carl Schmitt does of course provide an account of

plebiscitary democracy, but, as I shall argue in chapter 5, in an unpalatable (and not entirely rigorous) manner.

4. Weber ushers in this meaning when he defines his theory of "plebiscitary leader democracy" in terms of a *merely apparent* element of popular self-rule: "'Plebiscitary democracy'—the most important type of leadership democracy [*Führerdemokratie*]—is in its genuine sense a kind of charismatic domination which conceals itself under the form of legitimacy which is derived from the will of the ruled and only sustained by them." Max Weber, *Economy and Society: An Outline of Interpretative Sociology*, ed. Guenther Roth and Claus Wittich (Berkeley: University of California Press, 1978), 268.

5. In a dictatorship or one-party state, the plebiscite appears more as a vehicle of manipulation and oppression than a genuine exercise of democratic will formation. Consider, for example, that Napoleon, who revived the practice, was confirmed as first consul by a vote of 3,011,007 to 1,562. Hitler's Nazi regime won its four major plebiscites by similarly lopsided support: the withdrawal from the Geneva Disarmament Conference in 1933 (95 percent), the merging of the offices of Reich president and chancellor in 1934 (90 percent), the military occupation of the Rhineland in 1936 (99 percent), and the annexation of Austria in 1938 (99 percent). Recent works that have challenged the plebiscite for its propensity for irrationality and manipulation, even within liberal multiparty states, include David S. Broder, *Democracy Derailed: The Initiative Movement and the Power of Money* (New York: Harcourt, 2000); Richard J. Ellis, *Democratic Delusions: The Initiative Process in America* (Lawrence: University Press of Kansas, 2002).

6. See, e.g., Bruce Ackerman and James S. Fishkin, *Deliberation Day* (New Haven, Conn.: Yale University Press, 2004), 199–200.

7. The concept of the plebiscitary president is employed by Theodore J. Lowi, *The Personal President: Power Invested, Promise Unfulfilled* (Ithaca, N.Y.: Cornell University Press, 1985); Stephen Skowronek, *The Politics Presidents Make: Leadership from John Adams to George Bush* (Cambridge, Mass.: Belknap Press of Harvard University Press, 1993); Colleen Shogan, "Rhetorical Moralism in the Plebiscitary Presidency: New Speech Forms and Their Ideological Entailments," *Studies in American Political Development* 17 (2003): 149–167; Andrew Arato, "Post-election Maxims," *Constellations* 12 (2005): 182–193. Other studies using different terminology to describe similar processes include Samuel Kernell, *Going Public: New Strategies of Presidential Leadership* (Washington, D.C.: CQ Press, 1986); Jeffrey Tulis, *The Rhetorical Presidency* (Princeton, N.J.: Princeton University Press, 1987); Richard Rose, *The Post-modern President* (Chatham, N.J.: Chatham House, 1988); Ryan J. Barilleaux, *The Post-modern Presidency: The Office after Reagan* (New York: Praeger, 1988). There is admittedly some debate as to whether the plebiscitary presidency has the pathological meaning I have attributed to it (i.e., that it stands for the neutralization or manipulation of popular decision making) or, more sanguinely, it refers only to presidents finding their support in public opinion rather than in parliament or other formal governmental bodies.

Exponents of the former usage include Lowi (who can be most credited with developing the notion of the plebiscitary president), Shogan, and Arato, whereas Skowronek and Tulis veer toward the latter rendering.

8. Skowronek, for example, employs the term *plebiscitary* to refer to the fourth and latest historical stage of resources by which presidents can secure power and bestow their leadership with legitimacy (*The Politics Presidents Make*, 52–55). Likewise, Manin, whose concept of "audience democracy" must be seen as a synonym for plebiscitary politics, posits audience democracy as the third and most contemporary phase of representative government. Bernard Manin, *The Principles of Representative Government* (Cambridge: Cambridge University Press, 1997), ch. 6.

9. See, e.g., Joe McGinniss, *The Selling of the President 1968* (New York: Trident Press, 1969); Gene Wyckoff, *The Image Candidates* (New York: Macmillan, 1968); Dan Nimmo, *The Political Persuaders: The Techniques of Modern Electoral Campaigns* (Englewood Cliffs, N.J.: Prentice-Hall, 1970); Harold Mendelsohn and Irving Crespi, *Polls, Television, and the New Politics* (Scranton, Pa.: Chandler, 1970); Shawn W. Rosenberg, Lisa Bohan, Patrick McCafferty, and Kevin Harris, "The Image and the Vote: The Effect of Candidate Presentation on Voter Preference," *American Journal of Political Science* 30 (1986): 108–127.

10. Kernell, *Going Public*; Richard S. Katz and Peter Mair, "Changing Models of Party Organization and Party Democracy: The Emergence of the Cartel Party," *Party Politics* 1 (1995): 5–28.

11. András Körösényi, "Political Representation in Leader Democracy," *Government and Opposition* 40 (2005): 358–378.

12. Manin, *Principles of Representative Government*, 220.

13. Ibid., 221. Also see Martin P. Wattenberg, *The Rise of Candidate-Centered Politics: Presidential Elections of the 1980s* (Cambridge, Mass.: Harvard University Press, 1991); Bruce Cain, John Ferejohn, and Morris Fiorina, *The Personal Vote: Constituency Service and Electoral Independence* (Cambridge, Mass.: Harvard University Press, 1987).

14. For a critical overview of (and important contribution to) the difficult task of determining just how much personality matters in determining elections, see Anthony King, ed., *Leaders' Personalities and the Outcomes of Democratic Elections* (Oxford: Oxford University Press, 2002).

15. Theodore J. Lowi, "Presidential Democracy in America: Towards the Homogenized Regime," *Political Science Quarterly* 109 (1994): 401–415; Körösényi, "Political Representation in Leader Democracy," 358–359; Michael Foley, *The Rise of the British Presidency* (Manchester: Manchester University Press, 1993); Thomas Poguntke and Paul Webb, *The Presidentialization of Politics: A Comparative Study of Modern Democracies* (Oxford: Oxford University Press, 2005); Wattenberg, *Rise of Candidate-Centered Politics*.

16. Körösényi, "Political Representation in Leader Democracy," 358.

17. There is debate as to how pernicious creative leadership is. In her work on political parties, for example, Rosenblum offers a positive view of political

leaders creating both policy and comprehensive frameworks for governing. Nancy Rosenblum, "Primus Inter Pares: Political Parties and Civil Society," *Chicago-Kent Law Review* 75 (2000): 493–529; Rosenblum, "Political Parties as Membership Groups," *Columbia Law Review* 3 (2000): 813–844. Others, however, have understood the creative function of leadership in mass democracy in more pathological terms. See, e.g., William Riker, *The Art of Political Manipulation* (New Haven, Conn.: Yale University Press, 1986); José Maria Maravall, "Accountability and Manipulation," in Adam Przeworski, Susan Stokes, and Bernard Manin, eds., *Democracy, Accountability, and Representation* (Cambridge: Cambridge University Press, 1999).

18. Adam Przeworski, Susan Stokes, and Bernard Manin, "Elections and Representation," in Przeworski, Stokes, and Manin, *Democracy, Accountability, and Representation*, 29.

19. Manin, *Principles of Representative Government*, 218; Gerald M. Pomper, *Voters' Choice: Varieties of American Electoral Behavior* (New York: Dodd, Mead, 1975); Norman H. Nie, Sidney Verba, and John R. Petrocik, *The Changing American Voter* (Cambridge, Mass.: Harvard University Press, 1976); Morris P. Fiorina, *Retrospective Voting in American National Elections* (New Haven, Conn.: Yale University Press, 1981), x.

20. See, e.g., Scott L. Althaus, *Collective Preferences in Democratic Politics: Opinion Surveys and the Will of the People* (Cambridge: Cambridge University Press, 2003), 19: "Although there is some support for the 'issue publics' hypothesis, which suggests that people may be highly informed about the few issues that are important to them and ignorant of others, researchers tend to conclude that people are generalists rather than specialists when it comes to knowledge about politics." Also see Angus Campbell et al. (*The American Voter* [New York: Wiley, 1960]), who found that across sixteen policy domains, only 20 to 33 percent of the electorate satisfied the necessary conditions to be considered issue-based voters.

21. Manin argues that the complexity of government enables discretion: "It is more difficult for candidates to make detailed promises: such platforms would become unwieldy and unreadable" (Manin, *Principles of Representative Government*, 220).

22. Körösényi, "Political Representation in Leader Democracy," 364.

23. As Manin describes the way in which plebiscitary democracy undercuts the economic theory of democracy: "The only valid element in the metaphor of the market is the notion that the initiating of the terms of choice belongs to actors who are distinct and relatively independent of those who finally make the choice" (*Principles of Representative Government*, 226).

24. In addition to such concerns about the reality or effectiveness of the popular voice, there is also the problem that any voice from below is not truly that of the People, but only some fraction thereof: the majority of those who vote, for example.

25. Joseph Schumpeter, *Capitalism, Socialism, and Democracy* (New York: Harper and Brothers, 1942), 269, 271, 282, 283, 287, 290.

26. The biblical prophets, Weber's prototype of charismatic authority, made public appearances in which they lacked control, behaved unpredictably, and subjected themselves to contestation, risk, and even physical abuse. Max Weber, *Ancient Judaism*, trans. H. H. Gerth and Don Martindale (Glencoe, Ill.: Free Press, 1952), 267–296. Likewise, Weber argues that what distinguishes the modern democratic politician (the inheritor of the charismatic, prophetic legacy) from other types of political elites (like monarchs and bureaucrats) is precisely a willingness and capacity to enter into candid forms of publicity. See, e.g., Max Weber, "Parliament and Government in Germany," in Peter Lassman and Ronald Speirs, eds., *Political Writings* (Cambridge: Cambridge University Press, 1994), 218–219.

27. Max Weber, *Briefe, 1909–1910*, ed. Rainer Lepsius and Wolfgang J. Mommsen (Tübingen: Mohr, 1994), 576–578.

28. See, e.g., Allan Bloom, *Shakespeare's Politics* (New York: Basic Books, 1964), 75–112; Dennis Bathory, "With Himself at War: Shakespeare's Roman Hero and the Republican Tradition," in Joseph Alulis and Victoria Sullivan, eds., *Shakespeare's Political Pageant: Essays in Literature and Politics* (Lanham, Md.: Rowman and Littlefield, 1996); Anne Barton, "Livy, Machiavelli, and Shakespeare's *Coriolanus*," in Catherine M. S. Alexander, ed., *Shakespeare and Politics* (Cambridge: Cambridge University Press, 2004), 67–90.

29. William Shakespeare, *Julius Caesar*, ed. David Daniell (London: Arden, 1998), I.ii.245, 248; Shakespeare, *Coriolanus*, ed. Philip Brockbank (London: Arden, 1996), I.i.59; II.i.233; III.iii.120–121.

30. The People's ineffectuality as a decisional and expressive force is well described by a paradoxical remark of a citizen in *Coriolanus* who observes in regard to the question of whether the People might be able to choose whether Coriolanus becomes consul: "We have power in ourselves to do it, but it is a power that we have no power to do" (*Coriolanus*, II.ii.164–165).

31. See, e.g., *Julius Caesar*, I.ii.286.

32. Ibid., I.ii.216–286.

33. Also see *Coriolanus*, III.ii.130–145.

34. For the suggestion that the People potentially have a special ability to decipher a false appearance, see *Coriolanus*, II.ii,156.

35. See, e.g., *Coriolanus*, II.iii.156–214.

Chapter 5

1. At the beginning of the twentieth century, elite theorists such as Vilfredo Pareto, Gaetano Mosca, and Roberto Michels emphasized the persistence of oligarchic structures within representative systems. See Eva Etzioni-Halevy, ed., *Classes and Elites in Democracy and Democratization* (New York: Garland, 1997), 47–62, 243–250. A generation later, Lionel Robbins's demonstration that interpersonal comparisons of cardinal utility are impossible seemed to invalidate any Benthamite attempt to aggregate diverse utility functions and thereby scientifically calculate the common good. Robbins, "Interpersonal Comparisons

of Utility: A Comment," *Economic Journal* 43 (1938): 635–641. In the second half
of the twentieth century, social choice theory, especially Arrow's impossibility
theorem, McKelvey's chaos theorem, and Riker's application of these to political
science, has taken aim at the capacity of voting to rationally aggregate individual
preferences to form a meaningful and nonarbitrary collective preference. See,
e.g., William Riker, *Liberalism against Populism: A Confrontation between the
Theory of Democracy and the Theory of Social Choice* (San Francisco: Freeman,
1982). Finally, over the last sixty years, research in political behavior has
demonstrated that only a small minority of citizens takes on the kind of political
activism associated with classical notions of democratic life. Key postwar studies
revealing civic behavior inconsistent with traditional democratic expectations
include Bernard R. Berelson, Paul F. Lazarsfeld, and William N. McPhee,
Voting: A Study of Opinion Formation in a Presidential Campaign (Chicago:
University of Chicago Press, 1954); Angus Campbell et al., *The American Voter*
(New York: Wiley, 1960); and Philip Converse, "The Nature of Belief Systems
in Mass Publics," in David Apter, ed., *Ideology and Discontent* (London: Free
Press of Glencoe, 1964), 206–261. These contributions, while valuable as potent
challenges to the viability of any simplistic conception of democracy in terms of
popular self-rule, are hampered by their negativity. Their normative meaning
consists mostly in their disruption of familiar ideals rather than in the articulation
of new ones.

    2. See, e.g., Wolfgang J. Mommsen, *The Political and Social Theory
of Max Weber* (Cambridge, UK: Polity Press, 1989), 31; Robert Tucker, "The
Theory of Charismatic Leadership," *Daedalus* 97 (1968): 753; Peter Breiner, *Max
Weber and Democratic Politics* (New York: Cornell University Press, 1996).

    3. Max Weber, *Economy and Society: An Outline of Interpretative Sociology*,
ed. Guenther Roth and Claus Wittich (Berkeley: University of California Press,
1978), 241.

    4. As Weber explains, "Pure charisma does not know any 'legitimacy'
other than that flowing from personal strength, that is, one which is constantly
being proved." Max Weber, "The Sociology of Charismatic Authority," in
H. H. Gerth and C. Wright Mills, eds., *From Max Weber: Essays in Sociology*
(New York: Oxford University Press, 1946), 248.

    5. Weber, *Economy and Society*, 243.

    6. As Weber writes of the charismatic leader, "If proof and success elude
the leader for long, if he appears deserted by his god or his magical or heroic
powers, above all, if his leadership fails to benefit his followers, it is likely that his
charismatic authority will disappear. This is the true meaning of the divine right
of kings (*Gottesgnadentum*)" (ibid., 242).

    7. Thus, as I mentioned in chapter 1, Weber could speak of plebiscitary
leadership democracy in terms of a *merely apparent* element of popular self-rule:
"'Plebiscitary democracy'—the most important type of leadership democracy
[*Führerdemokratie*]—is in its genuine sense a kind of charismatic domination
which conceals itself under the form of legitimacy which is derived from the will
of the ruled and only sustained by them" (ibid., 268–269).

8. Ibid., 1129–1130.

9. Max Weber, "Parliament and Government in Germany," in Peter Lassman and Ronald Speirs, eds., *Political Writings* (Cambridge: Cambridge University Press, 1994), 228.

10. Max Weber, "The President of the Reich," in Lassman and Speirs, *Political Writings*, 304–305.

11. While Weber's proposals for plebiscitary leader democracy did include referenda and recalls, he did not think these would play more than a minor role, because of both their infrequency and their tendency toward irrationality. See, e.g., Weber, "Parliament and Government in Germany," 226–227.

12. For a classic statement of this understanding of the plebiscitary, see Jürgen Habermas, *Structural Transformation of the Public Sphere: An Inquiry into the Category of Bourgeois Society*, trans. Thomas Burger (Cambridge, Mass.: MIT Press, 1989), 66–67, 201, 207, 217–218. Also see Bruce Ackerman and James Fishkin, "Deliberation Day," *Journal of Political Philosophy* 10 (2002): 151; Anthony G. Wilhelm, *Democracy in the Digital Age: Challenges to Political Life in Cyberspace* (New York: Routledge, 2000), 45; John C. Ranney, "Do the Polls Serve Democracy?" *Public Opinion Quarterly* 10 (1946): 350.

13. Max Weber, *Wirtschaft und Gesellschaft: Grundriss der Verstehenden Soziologie*, ed. Johannes Winckelmann (Tübingen: Mohr, 1956), 558.

14. Rather, such constraint would be supplied by Parliament, an independent judiciary, the administrative bureaucracy, and a political culture that accepted basic human rights.

15. While Weber occasionally supported democratization for a variety of local, contingent reasons—for example, that it would be unseemly and impolitic for the mass of German citizens fighting and dying in World War I to be denied the vote, or that universal suffrage, and the mass parties it engendered, would weaken the political power of the Prussian aristocracy whose ineffective hegemony in Germany Weber despised—at the heart of Weber's justification of plebiscitary leader democracy was the expectation that this regime would produce charismatic leaders with strength, vision, and a sense of responsibility. See, e.g., Weber, *Economy and Society*, 1449–1453; Weber, "The President of the Reich," 304; Max Weber, "Politics as a Vocation," in Gerth and Mills, *From Max Weber*, 113–114.

16. See, e.g., Kurt Becker, *"Der Römische Cäsar mit Christi Seele": Max Webers Charisma-Konzept* (Frankfurt am Main: P. Lang, 1988). However, as numerous commentators have observed, there is much that is unfair with such a linkage. Weber preceded the rise of fascism. He identified himself as a liberal. See, e.g., letter to Lujo Bretano, February 20, 1893, in Eduard Baumgarten, ed., *Max Weber: Werk und Person* (Tübingen: Mohr, 1964), 85. And Weber argued that "it is primitive self-deception to imagine that we today (even the most conservative among us) would be able to live without these achievements dating from the period of 'the rights of man.'" Max Weber, *Gesammelte Politische Schriften*, ed. Johannes Winckelmann (Tübingen: Mohr, 1971), 312; cited and

translated by Karl Loewenstein, *Max Weber's Political Ideas in the Perspective of Our Time* (Amherst: University of Massachusetts Press, 1966), 23.

17. See, e.g., Georg Lukács, *Die Zerstörung der Vernunft* (Berlin: Aufbau-Verlag, 1954), 488; Mommsen, *Max Weber and German Politics*, 395.

18. David Beetham, *Max Weber and the Theory of Modern Politics* (London: Allen and Unwin, 1974), 112, 101–102, 239.

19. Max Weber, "Between Two Laws," in Lassman and Speirs, eds., *Political Writings*, 75.

20. Weber, "The President of the Reich," 308.

21. By the last decade of his life, Weber was an adamant supporter of democratic institutions such as universal suffrage, a democratically elected and free parliament, and direct elections for executive leadership in the state. In his occasional writings as a political advocate, Weber argued forcefully for these institutions as ethical and pragmatic necessities for Germany. Moreover, Weber contributed as a framer of the Weimar Constitution, which institutionalized democracy within postwar Germany, and Weber was himself allied with the Democratic Party on behalf of which he very nearly served as a representative in Parliament.

22. Lindholm, however, does appreciate this relational aspect of charisma: "Unlike physical characteristics, charisma appears only in interaction with others who lack it. In other words, even though charisma is thought of as something intrinsic to the individual, a person cannot reveal this quality in isolation. It is only evident in interaction with those who are affected by it. Charisma is, above all, *a relationship*, a mutual mingling of the inner selves of leader and follower.... Understanding charisma thus implies not only a study of the character of the charismatic and the attributes that make any particular individual susceptible to the charismatic appeal, but an analysis as well of the dynamic of the group itself in which the leader and follower interact." Charles Lindholm, *Charisma* (Cambridge, Mass.: Blackwell, 1990), 7.

23. Weber, "Sociology of Charismatic Authority," 246.

24. Ibid., 246–247. Also see Weber, *Economy and Society*, 242.

25. Thus, even in Weber's discussion of the routinization of charisma in a democratic direction, charisma stands to a large extent opposed to elections. If the People engages in elections that really reflect its will, then the charismatic element drops out and the authority in question approaches legal-rational authority (*Economy and Society*, 218, 267, 293).

26. Weber, "Sociology of Charismatic Authority," 249.

27. See, e.g., Weber, "Parliament and Government in Germany," 225–226: "In a mass state the specific instrument of purely plebiscitary democracy, namely direct popular elections and referenda, and above all the referendum on removal from office, are completely unsuited to the task of selecting *specialist* officials or of criticizing their performance.... The selecton of *specialist* officials and the selection of *political leaders* are simply *two* quite different things."

28. Weber, *Economy and Society*, 1128.

29. Ibid.

30. See Weber, "Politics as a Vocation," 83–84.

31. Thus Weber could claim, "Nowhere in the world, not even in England, can the parliamentary body as such govern and determine policies. The broad mass of deputies functions only as a following for the leader or the few leaders who form the government, and it blindly follows them *as long as* they are successful. *This is the way it should be*" (Weber, *Economy and Society*, 1414; also see, 289–292, 1128).

32. See Weber, *Wirtschaft und Gesellschaft*, 558.

33. See, e.g., Michels's "iron law of oligarchy," specifically his claim that the very effort of mass-based parties to seek democratic ends produced organizations that reinforced hierarchical political structures. Robert Michels, *Political Parties: A Sociological Study of Oligarchical Tendencies of Modern Democracy* (Gloucester, Mass.: P. Smith, 1978), viii. Likewise, Mosca, especially in his earlier writings, downplayed any distinctiveness of democracy: "What happens in other forms of government—namely, that an organized minority imposes its will on the disorganized majority—happens also and to perfection, whatever the appearances to the contrary, under the representative system." Gaetano Mosca, *The Ruling Class*, trans. Hannah D. Kahn (New York: McGraw-Hill, 1967), 154. Pareto, too, minimized the difference that democratic institutions made and could therefore liken modern democracy to the very feudal order it supposedly supplanted: "'Democratic' countries might be defined as a sort of feudalism that is primarily economic and in which the principal instrument of governing is the manipulation of political followings, whereas the military feudalism of the Middle Ages used force primarily as embodied in vassalage." Vilfredo Pareto, *Mind and Society: A Treatise on General Sociology* (New York: Dover, 1935), 1422–1432, 1568–1592.

34. For Mosca and Pareto especially, there is a notion of natural elite types, possessing superior amounts of talent and political expertise, who monopolize all power and instrumentalize the great many who are not elite. See, e.g., Mosca, *Ruling Class*, 50.

35. Thus, Weber could criticize Michels, writing to him: "The *concept* of 'domination' is not clarified in your work. Your analysis [of it] is too *simple*." Cited in Lawrence Scaff, *Fleeing the Iron Cage: Culture, Politics, and Modernity in the Thought of Max Weber* (Berkeley: University of California Press, 1989), 155.

36. Thus, Weber could write in a private letter: "The governmental form is all the same to me, if only politicians govern the country and not dilettantish fops like Wilhelm II and his kind....As far as I'm concerned, forms of government are techniques like any other machinery." Letter to Ehrenberg, July 16, 1917; trans. Mommsen, *Max Weber and German Politics*, 396.

37. See, e.g., Francesco Guicciardini, *"Del modo di eleggere gli uffici nel Consiglio Grande,"* in *Dialogo e Discoursi del Reggimento di Firenze* (Bari: G. Laterza, 1932), 178–179; James Harrington, *The Prerogative of Popular Government*, in J. G. A. Pocock, ed., *The Political Works of James Harrington*

(Cambridge: Cambridge University Press, 1977), 477; Harrington, *Oceania*, in Pocock, *Political Works of James Harrington*, 172; Montesquieu, *The Spirit of the Laws*, trans. Anne M. Cohler, Basia Carolyn Miller, and Harold Samuel Stone (Cambridge: Cambridge University Press, 1989), 2.2; 12.

38. Montesquieu, *Spirit of the Laws*, 11.6; 160: "A great vice in most ancient republics was that the people had the right to make resolutions for action, resolutions which required some execution, which altogether exceeds the people's capacity. *The people should not enter the government except to choose their representatives*; this is quite within their reach" (emphasis added).

39. Niccolò Machiavelli, *The Prince*, trans. Harvey C. Mansfield (Chicago: University of Chicago Press, 1998), 4.

40. Thus, in an oft-quoted letter to Michels, Weber dismissed Michels's worries about how the popular will might somehow be recovered: "But, oh, how much resignation you will still have to face! Such notions as the 'will of the people,' the true will of the people, ceased to exist for me years ago; they are fictions." Letter to Michels, August 4, 1908; trans. Mommsen, *Max Weber and German Politics*, 395.

41. Crucial to Weber's critique of the vocal ontology of popular power was his insistence that most instances of popular expression—such as occasional referenda and recalls—would be confined by a binary, yes-no structure that limited their articulacy, rationality, and usefulness. See Weber, "Parliament and Government in Germany," 226–227; Weber, *Economy and Society*, 1455). If Weber's overall critique of the vocal ontology of popular power has not been shared by most political scientists working in the century since his death, Weber's suspicion of the referendum is in fact repeated by many contemporary observers, including those otherwise committed to the notion of popular autonomy. See, e.g., David S. Broder, *Democracy Derailed: The Initiative Campaign and the Power of Money* (New York: Harcourt, 2000); Richard J. Ellis, *Democratic Delusions: The Initiative Process in America* (Lawrence: University Press of Kansas, 2002).

42. Weber, *Economy and Society*, 1128.

43. Michel Foucault, *Discipline and Punish: The Birth of the Prison*, trans. Alan Sheridan (New York: Pantheon, 1977), 170–171, 187.

44. There are two main differences, however. First, whereas Foucault understands the state as the *observer* of disciplinary power, under the Weberian model the state—or at least individual political leaders and officials of great power—are the *observed*. For Weber, it is the People—and not the doctor, teacher, or prison warden—who monitors and surveys with a disciplinary gaze. This alternate disciplinary process—whereby Foucault's own emphasis on the capacity of the few to see the many is paralleled by an attunement to the capacity of the many to see the few—is pursued in Thomas Mathiesen, "The Viewer Society: Michel Foucault's 'Panopticon' Revisited," *Theoretical Criminology* 1 (1997): 215–234. Second, if the disciplinary gaze generates docility for Foucault, in the Weberian case the popular gaze helps to produce the very different, almost opposite trait of charisma.

45. The precise nature of the charisma of the modern democratic political leader—and specifically its relation to other forms of routinized charisma—is one of the most complex features of Weber's theory of charisma. On the one hand, the charisma of the democratically elected leader is not pure, but manufactured. On the other hand, unlike other forms of manufactured charisma, which entirely displace charisma from the individual to the office he or she occupies, the charisma of the democratic leader is still tied to personal qualities and characteristics. Of the various forms of routinized charisma that Weber treats in a systematic way, it is not office charisma, but *charismatic education*, that best typifies how charismatic authority is produced in the democratic leader within mass democracy. While it is true of charisma that it cannot be taught in the manner of rational or empirical instruction, it can be awakened or tested: "The real purpose of charismatic education is regeneration, hence the development of the charismatic quality, and the testing, confirmation and selection of the qualified person" (Weber, *Economy and Society*, 1143; also see 249).

46. Weber writes: "This is the decisive psychological quality of the politician: his ability to let realities work upon him with inner concentration and calmness. Hence his *distance* to things and men" (Weber, "Politics as a Vocation," 115).

47. Weber, *Economy and Society*, 1456.

48. Weber, "Between Two Laws," 76.

49. While it is true that in his inaugural lecture Weber spoke of political education for the bourgeois, this is still an exclusive class differentiated from the mass of everyday citizens (Weber, "The Nation State and Economic Policy," in Lassman and Speirs, *Political Writings*, 1–28). Moreover, Weber developed the idea of political education in an increasingly elitist way, as it came to refer to educating a few select leaders for political power, rather than a whole class or group. See Stephen P. Turner and Regis A. Factor, *Max Weber and the Dispute over Reason and Value: A Study in Philosophy, Ethics, and Politics* (London: Routledge and Kegan Paul, 1984), 87–89.

50. In "Politics as a Vocation," Weber refers to the *geistige Proletarisierung* and the *seelische Proletarisierung* of the masses (Weber, *From Max Weber*, 113, 125; Weber, *Gesammelte Politische Schriften*, 532, 545).

51. Weber, "Between Two Laws," 75.

52. Moreover, Weber's most adamant support of the ideal of a nation possessing world-historical power precedes his proposals for plebiscitary leader democracy—as it does Germany's defeat in World War I. As Beetham points out, "Weber's strongest insistence on a plebiscitary type of leadership came after the point of Germany's defeat, when Weber himself recognized that a world-political role was no longer possible for his country" (Beetham, *Max Weber and the Theory of Modern Politics*, 237). Indeed, Weber argued that the Weimar Constitution must presuppose a "clear renunciation of imperialist dreams" (Weber, *Gesammelte Politische Schriften*, 443).

53. Not only were the prophets one of three ideal types of pure charisma (the other two being demagogues and magicians), but they can be credited as

the master type in the sense that they share elements of the other two. Thus, independent of the prophets' role as messengers of religious salvation, they were also, like demagogues, *speakers* who "addressed their audiences in public" and had to be capable of winning over a mass audience. Max Weber, *Ancient Judaism*, trans. H. H. Gerth and Don Martindale (Glencoe, Ill.: Free Press, 1952), 268. And like magicians, the prophets were also obligated to perform miracles. It is not surprising, then, that of the three ideal types, the prophet receives the most attention from Weber and, thus, is most useful in trying to understand the bidirectional power dynamics between charismatic leader and charismatic community.

54. Ibid., 269, 273, 286; also see 271.

55. For example, the ancient warrior kings who ruled by charisma were often thrown into a state of manic passion before battle. Weber also refers to the "magician who in the pure type has to be subject to epileptoid seizures as a means of falling into trances" (Weber, *Economy and Society*, 242).

56. Weber, *Ancient Judaism*, 272–273.

57. See, e.g., Tucker, "Theory of Charismatic Leadership," 736: "A leader can be both charismatic and contested on specific points....We should not, therefore, envisage the charismatic authority-relation as one that necessarily involves automatic acquiescence of the followers in the leader's views or excludes the possibility of their disagreeing with him on occasion and up to a point."

58. Weber, *Ancient Judaism*, 292–294. It is also relevant that, according to Weber, the prophet Jeremiah experienced his prophetic gifts as a "horrible fate" and that, more generally, Weber can refer to the prophets' "constant state of tension and of oppressive brooding" (ibid., 287, 291; see Jer. 17:16).

59. See, e.g., Weber, "Sociology of Charismatic Authority," 245, 249.

60. Weber, *Ancient Judaism*, 286–287.

61. Weber, "Parliament and Government in Germany," 218–222, 228–232.

62. Ibid., 220.

63. It is said of Gladstone: "Mr. Gladstone never wrote a line of his speeches, and some of his most successful ones have been made in the heat of debate and necessarily without preparation." Quoted by Henry Hardwicke, *History of Oratory and Orators: A Study of the Influence of Oratory upon Politics and Literature* (New York: Putnam's, 1896), 289; see also John Morley, *The Life of William Ewart Gladstone* (London: Macmillan, 1903).

64. In public appeals, Johnson would disclaim any interest in his dignity. See Eric L. McKitrick, *Andrew Johnson and Reconstruction* (Chicago: University of Chicago Press, 1960), 438; Jeffrey Tulis, *The Rhetorical Presidency* (Princeton, N.J.: Princeton University Press, 1987), 90; Lloyd Paul Stryker, *Andrew Johnson* (New York: Macmillan, 1929), 341–372; and James E. Sefton, *Andrew Johnson and the Uses of Constitutional Power* (Boston: Little, Brown 1980), 140.

65. Tulis, *Rhetorical Presidency*, 88, 90.

66. U.S. Senate, *Proceedings in the Trial of Andrew Johnson* (Washington, D.C., 1869), 5–6.

67. See, e.g., Weber, *Economy and Society*, 1450: "The decisive point is that for the tasks of national leadership only such men are prepared who have been selected in the course of political struggle, since the essence of all politics is struggle. It simply happens to be a fact that such preparation is, on the average, accomplished better by the much-maligned 'craft of demagoguery' than by the clerk's office, which in turn provides an infinitely superior training for efficient administration. Of course, political demagoguery can lead to striking misuses."

68. Weber, "Parliament and Government in Germany," 218–219.

69. Thus Weber argued that democracy could be made to improve demagoguery (ibid., 220).

70. See Mommsen, *Max Weber and German Politics*, 361; also see 360–370.

71. Aberbach gestures toward this recognition when he observes: "Does crisis create charisma? Is it not also true that charisma provokes crisis? . . . Charisma and crisis are dynamic, interlocking forces, feeding on and manipulating each other." David Aberbach, *Charisma in Politics, Religion, and the Media: Private Trauma, Public Ideals* (New York: New York University Press, 1996), 5, 7.

72. Habermas, for example, argued in the 1960s: "If we are to judge Weber here and now, we cannot overlook the fact that Carl Schmitt was a 'legitimate pupil' of Weber's." Quoted in Otto Stammer ed., *Max Weber and Sociology Today*, trans. Kathleen Morris (Oxford: Blackwell, 1971), 66. As I suggested earlier (see note 16), however, any insinuations about Weber's complicity with National Socialism are misguided.

73. Carl Schmitt, *The Crisis of Parliamentary Democracy*, trans. Ellen Kennedy (Cambridge, Mass.: MIT Press, 1985), 33–50. For an overview of Schmitt's critique of the rationality of the parliamentary state, see William Scheuerman, *Carl Schmitt: The End of Law* (Lanham, Md.: Rowman and Littlefield, 1999), chs. 1–6; Ellen Kennedy, *Constitutional Failure: Carl Schmitt in Weimar* (Durham, N.C.: Duke University Press, 2004), 135–137.

74. Carl Schmitt, "Juristische Fiktionen," *Deutsche Juristen-Zeitung* 18, no. 2 (1913): 805.

75. See, e.g., Schmitt's lament that voting processes in Weimar could be considered neither elections (a genuine selection of particular leadership as opposed to the rubberstamping of a preselected set of party lists) nor plebiscites (a validation of a particular course of action). Carl Schmitt, *Legality and Legitimacy*, trans. Jeffrey Seitzer (Durham, N.C.: Duke University Press, 2004), 89–90. Also see Schmitt, *Constitutional Theory*, trans. Jeffrey Seitzer (Durham, N.C.: Duke University Press, 2008), 273, 274; Kennedy, *Constitutional Failure*, 140–148.

76. Schmitt, *Legality and Legitimacy*, 27, 28, 30, 56.

77. See, e.g., Schmitt, *Constitutional Theory*, 289, 292, 303; Schmitt, *Legality and Legitimacy*, 42; Kennedy, *Constitutional Failure*, 123–125.

78. Schmitt, *Constitutional Theory*, 271; also see Carl Schmitt, *Volksentscheid und Volksbegehren; ein Beitrag zur Auslegung der Weimarer Verfassung und zur Lehr von der unmittelbaren Demokratie* (Berlin: W. de Gruyter, 1927), 33–34.

79. See, e.g., Schmitt, *Legality and Legitimacy*, 24, 61; also see Schmitt, *Constitutional Theory*, 301, where Schmitt refers to the "legal sensibility of the People."

80. See, e.g., Schmitt, *Constitutional Theory*, 255: "Democracy is a state form that corresponds to the principle of identity (in particular, the self-identity of the concretely present people as a political unity)." Also see, ibid., 264: "*Definition of Democracy*. As a state form as well as a governmental or legislative form, democracy is the identity of ruler and ruled, governing and governed, commander and follower.... This definition results from the substantial equality that is the essential presupposition of democracy. It precludes the possibility that inside the democratic state the distinction of ruler and being ruled, governor and governed expresses or produces a *qualitative* difference. In democracy, dominance or government may not rest on inequality, therefore, not on the superiority of those ruling or governing, nor on the fact that those governing are qualitatively better than the governed. They must agree substantively in terms of democratic equality and homogeneity. Hence, when one rules or governs, he may not deviate from the general identity and homogeneity of the people.... The word 'identity' is useful for the definition of democracy, because it denotes the comprehensive identity of the homogenous people.... In this regard, it is noteworthy that the difference between representing and being represented does not come into consideration, for that which is being represented is not those governing, but instead the political unity of the whole." For other important statements about *Artgleichhheit* and the authentic political community's alleged self-identity, see ibid., 239, 247, 259, 262, 263. The concept of substantive equality would come to play a crucial role in Schmitt's argument that an authoritarian plebiscitary regime would not be tyrannical, because leaders and led would share in the same foundational self-identity (see, e.g., Schmitt, *Staat, Bewegung, Volk: Die Dreigliederung der Politischen Einheit* [Hamburg: Hanseatische Verlagsanstalt, 1933], 42, 45, 46; also see Kennedy, *Constitutional Failure*, 128–130).

81. Schmitt, *Volksentscheid und Volksbegehren*, 3; Schmitt, *Constitutional Theory*, 130, 239; Kennedy, *Constitutional Failure*, 126.

82. See, e.g., Schmitt, *Constitutional Theory*, 272; Schmitt, *Volksentscheid und Volksbegehren*, 34.

83. Schmitt, *Constitutional Theory*, 286.

84. Ibid., 273: "Genuine popular assemblies and acclamations are entirely unknown to the constitutional regime of contemporary bourgeois democracy."

85. For the claim that public opinion, generated through a plebiscite, is the modern form of acclamation, see Schmitt, *Constitutional Theory*, 275, 287, 302; also see George Schwab, *The Challenge of the Exception: An Introduction to the Political Ideas of Carl Schmitt between 1921 and 1936* (New York: Greenwood Press, 1970), 64.

86. Schmitt, *Legality and Legitimacy*, 90; Schmitt, *Staat, Bewegung, Volk*, 42. Schmitt insisted that a purer and more genuine form of popular opinion

would be generated by plebiscites managed by an authoritarian leader as opposed to a parliament (*Legality and Legitimacy*, 61–62).

87. Schmitt, *Volksentscheid und Volksbegehren*, 35–37; Schmitt, *Constitutional Theory*, 302–304; Schmitt, *Legality and Legitimacy*, 90.

88. Schmitt, *Constitutional Theory*, 304; also see 269: "the value of the answer depends entirely on the posing of the question."

89. See, e.g., Schmitt, *Staat, Bewegung, Volk*, 12: the People is the "nonpolitical part [of the state], keeping watch in the protection and shadow of political decisions."

90. Nazi theorists who interpreted the regime in terms of an ultrarobust form of popular sovereignty include Reinhard Höhn, *Rechtsgemeinschaft und Volksgemeinschaft* (Hamburg: Hanseatische Verlagsanstalt, 1935), 79; Otto Koellreutter, *Grundriss der Allgemeinen Staatslehr* (Tübingen: Mohr, 1933), 164; Gottfried Neesse, *Partei und Staat* (Hamburg: Hanseatische Verlagsanstalt, 1936), 21. Also see Schwab, *Challenge of the Exception*, 112.

91. Schmitt, *Constitutional Theory*, 264; also see 266: "A democracy must not permit the inevitable *factual* difference between governing and being governed to become a qualitative distinction and to distance governing persons from those governed."

92. Schmitt, *Legality and Legitimacy*, 90. Also see ibid., 69, where Schmitt refers to the leader as the "special commissioner of the abnormal situation."

93. Carl J. Friedrich and Zbigniew K. Brzezinski, *Totalitarian Dictatorship and Autocracy* (Cambridge, Mass.: Harvard University Press, 1965), 163–165.

94. See Schmitt, *Staat, Bewegung, Volk*, 42, 45, 46

95. For a more thorough discussion of the linkage between Schumpeter and Weber, see Jürgen Osterhammel, "Varieties of Social Economics: Joseph A. Schumpeter and Max Weber," in Wolfgang Mommsen, ed., *Max Weber and His Contemporaries* (London: German Historical Institute, 1987); Mommsen, *Max Weber and German Politics*, 406; Scheuerman, *Carl Schmitt*, ch. 7; Tamsin Shaw, "Max Weber on Democracy: Can the People Have Political Power in Modern States?" *Constellations* 15 (2008): 38.

96. Downs credits Schumpeter: "Schumpeter's profound analysis of democracy forms the inspiration and foundation of our whole thesis, and our debt and gratitude to him are great indeed" Anthony Downs, *An Economic Theory of Democracy* (New York: Harper, 1967), 29 n. 11. This credit is inappropriate because, as I explain, Schumpeter's account undercuts the definition of the People as consumers with exogenous demands.

97. Thus, Plamenatz, perhaps the most severe and uncharitable of the critics, writes of Schumpeter's account of the classical doctrine that it is "ignorant and inept, and is worth discussing only because it has been taken seriously. It is uncertain whom he is attacking, and even what beliefs he is ascribing to them." John Plamenatz, *Democracy and Illusion: An Examination of Certain Aspects of Modern Democratic Theory* (London: Longman, 1973), 96. Also see John Medearis, *Schumpeter's Two Theories of Democracy* (Cambridge,

Mass.: Harvard University Press, 2001), 129; Carole Pateman, *Participation and Democratic Theory* (Cambridge: Cambridge University Press, 1970), 17; David Held, *Models of Democracy* (Stanford, Calif.: Stanford University Press, 1987), 178–179; C. B. Macpherson, *The Life and Times of Liberal Democracy* (Oxford: Oxford University Press, 1977), 85; David Miller, "The Competitive Model of Democracy," in Graeme Duncan, ed., *Democratic Theory and Practice* (Cambridge: Cambridge University Press, 1983), 137; Emilio Santoro, "Democratic Theory and Individual Autonomy: An Interpretation of Schumpeter's Doctrine of Autonomy," *European Journal of Political Research* 23 (1993): 122–123.

98. Joseph Schumpeter, *Capitalism, Socialism, and Democracy* (New York: Harper and Brothers, 1942), 250.

99. Miller, for example, writes that the classical doctrine is "an unwieldy composite of Enlightenment rationalism, utilitarianism, and Rousseauvian ideas" (Miller, "Competitive Model of Democracy," 137). The straw-man accusation stems not only from Schumpeter's unrigorous treatment of authors, but from the fact that he denies what most students of politics would allow: the capacity of the political process to *form* a provisional conception of the common good in the absence of a preestablished one. Schumpeter, however, argues that in the absence of a preexisting common good, the result of the democratic process "lacks not only rational unity but also rational sanction" (Schumpeter, *Capitalism, Socialism, and Democracy*, 253).

100. Medearis, *Schumpeter's Two Theories of Democracy*, 130–131.

101. Pateman, *Participation and Democratic Theory*, 17–21; Medearis, *Schumpeter's Two Theories of Democracy*, 131–133.

102. Medearis, *Schumpeter's Two Theories of Democracy*, 129, 133.

103. Schumpeter, *Capitalism, Socialism, and Democracy*, 250.

104. Bernard Manin, *The Principles of Representative Government* (Cambridge: Cambridge University Press, 1997), 161–162, 225–226. Also see Gerry Mackie, "Schumpeter's Leadership Democracy" *Political Theory* 37 (2009): 141.

105. Schumpeter, *Capitalism, Socialism, and Democracy*, 261.

106. Schumpeter approvingly quotes a politician who says: "What businessmen do not understand is that exactly as they are dealing in oil so I am dealing in votes" (ibid., 285). This *nondecisional* account of electoral power—in which what is emphasized is the *process* and *experience* of elections and the effect these have on leaders, rather than the ultimate decision that is reached—parallels Weber's theory of plebiscitary leader democracy and goes right to the heart of plebiscitarianism.

107. It is of course possible to imagine a more partial critique of the vocal ontology of popular power that challenges only the legislative *object* of popular power and leaves unquestioned the decisional *organ*. The model of personality politics, for example, which holds that voters and elections are concerned more with the personality of leaders than the determination of policies, can be seen as precisely such a partial critique of the vocal model. For a critical overview of

the relevance of personality to contemporary democratic politics, see Anthony King, ed., *Leaders' Personalities and the Outcomes of Democratic Elections* (Oxford: Oxford University Press, 2002).

108. See chapter 2, note 2.

109. Schumpeter, *Capitalism, Socialism, and Democracy*, 254.

110. Ibid., 261.

111. John Zaller, *The Nature and Origins of Mass Opinion* (New York: Cambridge University Press, 1992), 74–76.

112. David Miller, for example, treats Schumpeter and Downs as exponents of the same economic model (Miller, "Competitive Model of Democracy"); for another instance, see Amy Gutmann and Dennis Thompson, *Why Deliberative Democracy?* (Princeton, N.J.: Princeton University Press, 2004), 14.

113. Schumpeter, *Capitalism, Socialism, and Democracy*, 242. Of course, even if it were possible to separate fact from value, a nonnormative account of democracy would fail in its very objective of being descriptive, since part of what democracy signifies is precisely a regime widely understood to be morally superior to its rivals and something that injects moral ideals into political life.

114. Ibid., 295.

115. Ian Shapiro, for example, drawing explicitly on Schumpeter, looks to maximize competition within contemporary democracy, but in a way that serves "consumer sovereignty." He favors devices for making political contests more competitive—such as extending antitrust legislation to make elections less duopolistic—so that political institutions might better serve the underlying, objective interests of the electorate. The goal, Shapiro says, is "enhancing the voice of critically weakened democratic participants." What Shapiro overlooks is the way competition might regulate and discipline leaders in the absence of underlying preferences, opinions, or well-established interests on the part of the electorate. Given his consumerist, economics-based understanding of competition, it is not surprising that only a policy-based politics—and not also a politics of personality (in the sense of placing individuals under strenuous conditions of public presentation)—is validated within Shapiro's account of competition and, more generally, within his view of democracy: "Competition is the engine that provides politicians the reason to be responsive to voters, but for it to work well, they must have the incentive to compete over policies rather than personalities." Ian Shapiro, *The State of Democratic Theory* (Princeton, N.J.: Princeton University Press, 2003), 58, 74–76.

Chapter 6

1. For a critical overview of the importance of candor (or sincerity) to deliberative democracy, see Elizabeth Markovits, "The Trouble with Being Earnest: Deliberative Democracy and the Sincerity Norm," *Journal of Political Philosophy* 14 (2006): 249–269, esp. n. 12.

2. For the tendency to see the British practice of forbidding prepared speeches as indicative of a commitment to deliberation (rather than also to

candor), see Robert E. Goodin, "Democratic Deliberation Within," *Philosophy and Public Affairs* 29 (Winter 2000): 91.

3. See, e.g., W. Russell Neuman, *The Paradox of Mass Politics: Knowledge and Opinion in the American Electorate* (Cambridge, Mass.: Harvard University Press, 1986); Lester W. Milbrath, *Political Participation: How and Why Do People Get Involved in Politics?* (Chicago: Rand McNally, 1965), 16–17, 22, 39.

4. Kate Connolly, "Hungarian Leader Defies Resignation Calls Despite Second Night of Protests," *Daily Telegraph*, September 20, 2006, news section, 14. One could also conceive, in a more positive light, that the candor which reveals an uncommonly noble or heroic nature might also inspire the wider citizenry to take political action. I owe this point to Nancy Rosenblum.

5. See, e.g., Jürgen Habermas, *Structural Transformation of the Public Sphere: An Inquiry into the Category of Bourgeois Society*, trans. Thomas Burger (Cambridge, Mass.: MIT Press, 1989), chs. 6–7.

6. The concept of nondeliberative discourse—or the talking that occurs between adversaries without motivation to reach agreement—is not usually recognized by deliberative democrats, who tend to link discourse with consensus or the cooperative management of conflict. Adversarial discourse is recognized, however, in Susan Bickford, *The Dissonance of Democracy: Listening, Conflict, Citizenship* (Ithaca, N.Y.: Cornell University Press, 1996), esp. 16–19.

7. The Supreme Court has described the presidential debates as the "only occasion during a campaign when the attention of a large portion of the American public is focused on the election." *Arkansas Education Television Commission v. Forbes*, 118 Sup. Ct. 1633, 1640 (1998).

8. Alan Schroeder, *Presidential Debates: Forty Years of High-Risk TV* (New York: Columbia University Press, 2000), 45–46, 95.

9. Robert G. Meadow, "Televised Campaign Debates as Whistle-Stop Speeches," in William C. Adams, ed., *Television Coverage of the 1980 Presidential Campaign* (Norwood, N.J.: Ablex, 1983), 91: the debates "offer the viewers a chance to observe 'history,' be it the event itself as history or the possibility that a candidate will make a verbal error, stumble, or otherwise appear less than presidential." For a review of memorable moments generated by presidential debates, see Schroeder, *Presidential Debates*, 39–40.

10. George Farah, *No Debate: How the Republican and Democratic Parties Secretly Control the Presidential Debates* (New York: Seven Stories, 2004), 7, 10, passim. That the CPD is beholden to the candidates is well reflected by Scott Reed, chairman of Bob Dole's 1996 presidential campaign: "The commission does what you tell them to do" (quoted in ibid., 10).

11. See Sidney Kraus, *Televised Presidential Debates and Public Policy* (Mahwah, N.J.: Erlbaum, 2000), 43, 142; Farah, *No Debate*.

12. Lou Cannon, *Reagan* (New York: Putnam, 1982), 297.

13. Kraus reports, "The candidates did not want to question each other. The risk of being perceived as badgering the opponent, and the impression that the President was being attacked, were two of the reasons offered for not debating head-to-head" (*Televised Presidential Debates and Public Policy*, 42).

14. Farah, *No Debate*, 85–86; Schroeder, *Presidential Debates*, 131.

15. Farah, *No Debate*, 86.

16. See, e.g., Daniel Boorstin *The Image: A Guide to Pseudo-events in America* (New York: Harper and Row, 1964), 41; Kraus, *Televised Presidential Debates and Public Policy*, 147; Schroeder, *Presidential Debates*, 22–23.

17. As Farah summarizes the deliberative position, which is after all a key aspect of most critiques of the debates: "Academics, pundits, civic leaders, and journalists recognize that permitting follow-up questions, increasing response times, prohibiting candidate selection of moderators, requiring candidate-to-candidate questioning, and employing a mixed array of formats would greatly enhance the quality of the debate discourse" (Farah, *No Debate*, 90).

18. Sidney Kraus, for example, argues that the promotion of truth is and ought to be the orienting ideal for the debates (*Televised Presidential Debates and Public Policy*, 31).

19. Typical is the political scientist Samuel Popkin's remark: "Debates are to elections what treatises are to wars. They ratify what has already been accomplished on the battlefield." Quoted in Ronald Brownstein, "Pressure Is on Bush for First Debate," *Los Angeles Times*, October 11, 1992, news section, A1.

20. Schroeder expresses a similar sentiment when he writes: "Alone among television spectaculars, debates carry an aura of civic virtue" (Schroeder, *Presidential Debates*, 206; also see Farah, *No Debate*, 1).

21. On the nonrepresentative character of town hall audiences, see Schroeder, *Presidential Debates*, 146.

22. On the importance of listening as a more realistic, less consensual goal of deliberation, see Bickford, *Dissonance of Democracy*. For the conceptualization of deliberation as a way to manage disagreement, rather than reach consensus, see Amy Gutmann and Dennis Thompson, *Democracy and Disagreement* (Cambridge, Mass.: Belknap Press of Harvard University Press, 1996).

23. Thus, in reflecting on the nature of the debates, presidential candidate Walter Mondale could insist that they were not akin to a deliberative discourse. Rather, the debates exist in a "kind of environment that people remember: combat. It's not giving a speech. This was real war" (Walter Mondale, interview by Kevin Sauter, March 31, 1999; cited in Schroeder, *Presidential Debates*, 202).

24. Henry Steele Commager, "Washington Would Have Lost a TV Debate," *New York Times Magazine*, October 30, 1960, VI-13. Also see Boorstin, *The Image*, 43–44; Harvey Wheeler, "The Great Debates," in Earl Mazo et al., eds., *The Great Debates* (Santa Barbara, Calif.: Center for the Study of Democratic Institutions, 1962), 15.

25. See Schroeder, *Presidential Debates*, 202, 205, 210, 211.

26. See Wolfgang Mommsen, *Max Weber and German Politics, 1890–1920*, trans. Michael Steinberg (Chicago: University of Chicago Press, 1984), 361; also see 360–370.

27. There is an exception to this norm: the congressional committee that investigates ethics is bipartisan, giving each party equal representation. See House Rule V(a)(3)(A). In the Senate, parity is maintained by convention.

28. In Germany, it is customary for the ruling party to control only a minority of committee chairs. And in the United Kingdom, even though the House of Commons grants considerable power to the majority, it is common for the government to grant approximately ten committee chairs to the minority. See Bruce Ackerman, *Before the Next Attack: Preserving Civil Liberties in an Age of Terrorism* (New Haven, Conn.: Yale University Press, 2006), 85, 190.

29. Ibid., 85.

30. See Mary S. Hartman, "Benjamin Constant and the Question of Ministerial Responsibility in France, 1814–1815," *Journal of European Studies* 6 (1976): 249: "For such a clear writer and avid admirer of the English system, Constant seems to have been almost willfully obscure in his analysis of ministerial responsibility."

31. Benjamin Constant, *Principles of Politics Applicable to All Representative Governments*, in *Political Writings*, ed. Biancamaria Fontana (Cambridge: Cambridge University Press, 1988), 239.

32. Ibid., 241.

33. Ibid., 240.

34. Ibid., 235, 240.

35. Ibid., 230.

36. Ibid., 240.

37. Ibid., 233.

38. Ibid., 239.

39. Ibid., 239: "The mildness in the practical application of responsibility is merely a necessary and just consequence of the principle upon which my whole theory rests. I have shown that responsibility can never be free from a certain degree of arbitrariness."

40. Ibid., 235–240.

41. Ibid., 239.

42. Ibid. There was also an epistemological basis for considering the purpose of the trials in terms not limited to culpability: Constant admitted that "in questions of this nature crime and innocence are seldom entirely evident" (ibid., 239).

43. Thus, Constant could invoke famous trials in which the defendant was acquitted or only very mildly punished—such as those of Hastings, Melville, or the persecutors of Wilkes—as examples of investigations whose ultimate purpose was not the remediation of wrongdoing, but the vivid presentation of a leader under hostile attack. So, for example: "Lord Melville was not punished, and I do not wish to question his innocence. But the example of a man, grown old in the habit of dexterity and the skill of speculation, yet denounced despite his adroitness, accused notwithstanding his many connections, has reminded those who followed the same career that there is a value in disinterestedness and security in rectitude" (ibid., 240).

44. Carolyn D. Smith, *The Presidential Press Conference: A Critical Approach* (New York: Praeger, 1990), 116; W. Dale Nelson, *Who Speaks for the President?*

The White House Press Secretary from Cleveland to Clinton (Syracuse, N.Y.: Syracuse University Press, 1998), 42, 51.

45. Nelson, *Who Speaks for the President?* 155–56; Smith, *Presidential Press Conference*, 39; Helen Thomas, *Watchdogs of Democracy? The Waning Washington Press Corps and How It Has Failed the Public* (New York: Scribner, 2006), 62.

46. Nelson, *Who Speaks for the President?* 73, 226; Smith, *Presidential Press Conference*, 71, 114.

47. Commission on Presidential Press Conferences, *Report of the Commission on Presidential Press Conference* (Washington, D.C.: University Press of America, 1981); Marvin Kalb and Frederick Mayer, eds., *Reviving the Presidential News Conference: Report of the Harvard Commission on the Presidential News Conference* (Cambridge, Mass.: Harvard University, Kennedy School of Government, Joan Shorenstein Barone Center on the Press, Politics, and Public Policy, 1988); also see Smith, *Presidential Press Conference*, xviii.

48. To cite one example, the 1981 Commission on Presidential Press Conferences focused primarily on practical concerns like making the conferences less unruly, proposing to this end that the president take fuller control over whom to call on—thereby taking for granted, and indeed further strengthening, the president's management of the conditions of publicity (Commission on Presidential Press Conferences, *Report*, 8).

49. Kalb and Mayer, *Report of the Harvard Commission*, 52–54; Smith, *Presidential Press Conference*, xviii.

50. Blaire A. French, *The Presidential Press Conference* (Washington, D.C.: University Press of America, 1982), 33.

51. Gutmann and Thompson (*Democracy and Disagreement*), for example, explicitly theorize their version of deliberative democracy around the standards of publicity and accountability.

52. Thus, the 1981 Commission on Presidential Press Conferences proposed getting away from the adversarial, "circus-like atmosphere" of the formal press conference by having the president meet informally with reporters outside of the public view in a setting more conducive to a deliberative discussion (Commission on Presidential Press Conferences, *Report*, 8, 9).

53. In the United States, the first person to formally hold the position was Stephen T. Early under FDR, but in fact the office can be traced back to George Bruce Cortelyou, who served during Grover Cleveland's second term (Nelson, *Who Speaks for the President?* 12–23).

54. Beginning in the 1990s, the press secretary held televised press conferences, sometimes two per day. See ibid., 245–256.

Chapter 7

1. As I acknowledged in chapter 1, ocular power dynamics in mass democracy, while separate from vocal ones, are still beholden to the vocal practice of elections: without the risk of electoral defeat, politicians might not feel compelled to appear in public at all, let alone under conditions of candor.

But that candor requires elections does not mean that the commitment to candor is not distinct and separate from traditional vocal concerns like autonomy and representation.

2. Claude Lefort, *The Political Forms of Modern Society* (Cambridge, Mass.: MIT Press, 1986), 302–306; Pierre Rosanvallon, *Democracy Past and Future* (New York: Columbia University Press, 2006), 79–114.

3. See, e.g., Jürgen Habermas, "Further Reflections on the Public Sphere," in Craig Calhoun, ed., *Habermas and the Public Sphere* (Cambridge, Mass.: MIT Press, 1992), 439, 440, 443; Habermas, *Between Facts and Norms: Contributions to a Discourse Theory of Law and Democracy*, trans. William Rehg (Cambridge, Mass.: MIT Press, 1996), 468.

4. Jürgen Habermas, "Three Normative Models of Democracy," in Seyla Benhabib, ed., *Democracy and Difference: Contesting the Boundaries of the Political* (Princeton, N.J.: Princeton University Press, 1996), 30. Also see Habermas, *Between Facts and Norms*, 489: "Once the subject is removed from practical reason, the progressive institutionalization of procedures of rational collective will-formation can no longer be conceived as purposive action, as a kind of sublime process of production.... The sole substantial aim of the project is the gradual improvement of institutionalized procedures of rational collective will-formation, procedures that cannot prejudge the participants' concrete goals." Also see Habermas, "Further Reflections on the Public Sphere," 451.

5. See, e.g., Habermas, "Further Reflections on the Public Sphere," 452: "This sovereignty turned into a flow of communication comes to the fore in the power of public discourses that uncover topics of relevance to all of society, interpret values, contribute to the resolution of problems, generate good reasons, and debunk bad ones." On the basis of such passages, some critics have interpreted Habermas's account of a subjectless and anonymous form of popular sovereignty to mean only that the content of the sovereign will results from an intersubjective process and is therefore distinct from the will of any specific citizen or group and not the more radical claim that popular sovereignty be conceived as something other than a willful, decisional force. See, e.g., James Bohman, *Public Deliberation: Pluralism, Complexity, and Democracy* (Cambridge, Mass.: MIT Press, 1996), 178. Habermas lends credence to such an interpretation when he presents his reconfigured notion of sovereignty as being in accordance with the traditional norm of popular self-legislation: "This is not to denounce the [common] intuition connected with the idea of popular sovereignty but to interpret it in intersubjective terms" (Habermas, "Three Normative Models of Democracy," 29).

6. Certainly both Habermas and his critics understand him to be espousing the traditional ideal of autonomy: that the law's addressees also understand themselves to be the law's authors. See, e.g., Habermas, *Between Facts and Norms*, 120; Lasse Thomassen, *Deconstructing Habermas* (New York: Routledge, 2008), 44–46; Martin Morris, *Rethinking the Communicative Turn: Adorno, Habermas, and the Problem of Communicative Freedom* (Albany: State University of New York Press, 2001), 80.

BIBLIOGRAPHY

Aberbach, David. *Charisma in Politics, Religion, and the Media: Private Trauma, Public Ideals.* New York: New York University Press, 1996.

Achen, Christopher H. "Mass Political Attitudes and the Survey Response." *American Political Science Review* 69 (1975): 1218–1231.

Ackerman, Bruce. *Before the Next Attack: Preserving Civil Liberties in an Age of Terrorism.* New Haven, Conn.: Yale University Press, 2006.

———. *The Failure of the Founding Fathers: Jefferson, Marshall, and the Rise of Presidential Democracy.* Cambridge, Mass.: Belknap Press of Harvard University Press, 2005.

———. *We the People.* 2 vols. Cambridge, Mass.: Belknap Press of Harvard University, 1991, 1998.

Ackerman, Bruce, and James S. Fishkin. "Deliberation Day." *Journal of Political Philosophy* 10 (2002): 129–152.

———. *Deliberation Day.* New Haven, Conn.: Yale University Press, 2004.

Adams, Charles Francis, Jr. "The Protection of the Ballot in National Elections." *Journal of Social Science* 1 (1869): 91–111.

Alexander, Catherine M. S., ed. *Shakespeare and Politics.* Cambridge: Cambridge University Press, 2004.

Alford, C. Fred. "The 'Iron Law of Oligarchy' in the Athenian Polis ... and Today." *Canadian Journal of Political Science* 1985 (1985): 295–312.

Almond, Gabriel A. *The American People and Foreign Policy.* New York: Praeger, 1950.

Althaus, Scott L. *Collective Preferences in Democratic Politics: Opinion Surveys and the Will of the People.* Cambridge: Cambridge University Press, 2003.

Alulis, Joseph, and Victoria Sullivan, eds. *Shakespeare's Political Pageant: Essays in Literature and Politics.* Lanham, Md.: Rowman and Littlefield, 1996.

Ankersmit, F. R. *Aesthetic Politics: Political Philosophy beyond Fact and Value.* Stanford, Calif.: Stanford University Press, 1996.

Apel, Karl-Otto. *The Response of Discourse Ethics to the Moral Challenge of the Human Situation as Such and Especially Today.* Leuven: Peters, 2001.

Arato, Andrew. "Post-election Maxims." *Constellations* 12 (2005): 182–193.

Arendt, Hannah. *Between Past and Future: Eight Exercises in Political Thought.* New York: Penguin, 1977.

———. *The Human Condition.* Chicago: University of Chicago Press, 1958.

Aristotle. *The Politics and the Constitution of Athens*. Translated by Stephen Everson. Cambridge: Cambridge University Press, 1996.

Arrow, Kenneth. *Social Choice and Individual Values*. New Haven, Conn.: Yale
University Press, 1973.

Bachrach, Peter. *The Theory of Democratic Elitism: A Critique*. Boston: Little,
Brown, 1967.

Barber, Benjamin. *Strong Democracy: Participatory Politics for a New Age*. Berkeley:
University of California Press, 1984.

Barilleaux, Ryan J. *The Post-modern Presidency: The Office after Reagan*. New
York: Praeger, 1988.

Baker, Ed. "Campaign Expenditures and Free Speech." *Harvard Civil Rights–
Civil Liberties Law Review* 33 (Winter 1998): 1–56.

Bartels, Larry M. *Unequal Democracy: The Political Economy of the New Gilded
Age*. Princeton, N.J.: Princeton University Press, 2008.

Bathory, Dennis. "With Himself at War: Shakespeare's Roman Hero and the
Republican Tradition." In *Shakespeare's Political Pageant: Essays in Literature
and Politics*, edited by Joseph Alulis and Victoria Sullivan. Lanham, Md.:
Rowman and Littlefield, 1996.

Becker, Kurt. *"Der Römische Cäsar mit Christi Seele": Max Webers Charisma-
Konzept*. Frankfurt am Main: P. Lang, 1988.

Beetham, David. *Max Weber and the Theory of Modern Politics*. London: Allen and
Unwin, 1974.

Bentham, Jeremy. *Constitutional Code*. Edited by F. Rosen and J. H. Burns.
Oxford: Clarendon Press, 1983.

———. *First Principles Preparatory to a Constitutional Code*. Edited by Philip
Schofield. Oxford: Clarendon Press, 1989.

———. *An Introduction to the Principles of Morals and Legislation*. Edited by
J. H. Burns and H. L. A. Hart. London: Athlone, 1970.

———. "Of Publicity." *Public Culture* 6 (1994): 579–595.

———. *Securities against Misrule and Other Constitutional Writings for Tripoli
and Greece*. Edited by Philip Schofield. Oxford: Clarendon Press, 1990.

———. *The Works of Jeremy Bentham*. Edited by John Bowring. New York:
Russell and Russell, 1962.

Berelson, Bernard R., Paul F. Lazarsfeld, and William N. McPhee. *Voting: A
Study of Opinion Formation in a Presidential Campaign*. Chicago: University
of Chicago Press, 1954.

Bernstein, Richard. *Philosophical Profiles: Essays in a Pragmatic Mode*. Cambridge,
UK: Polity Press, 1986.

Bickford, Susan. *The Dissonance of Democracy: Listening, Conflict, Citizenship*.
Ithaca, N.Y.: Cornell University Press, 1996.

Black, Anthony. "Society and the Individual from the Middle Ages to Rousseau:
Philosophy, Jurisprudence, and Constitutional Theory." *History of Political
Thought* 1 (1980): 145–166.

Bloom, Allan. *Shakespeare's Politics*. New York: Basic Books, 1964.

Bobbio, Norberto. *The Future of Democracy: A Defence of the Rules of the Game*. Translated by Roger Griffen. Minneapolis: University of Minneapolis Press, 1987.

Bohman, James. *Public Deliberation: Pluralism, Complexity, and Democracy*. Cambridge, Mass.: MIT Press, 1996.

Bohman, James, and William Rehg. *Deliberative Democracy: Essays on Reason and Politics*. Cambridge, Mass.: MIT Press, 1997.

Boorstin, Daniel. *The Image: A Guide to Pseudo-events in America*. New York: Harper and Row, 1964.

Bourdieu, Pierre. *Language and Symbolic Power*. Translated by Gino Raymond and Matthew Adamson. Cambridge, UK: Polity Press, 1991.

Breiner, Peter. *Max Weber and Democratic Politics*. New York: Cornell University Press, 1996.

Broder, David S. *Democracy Derailed: The Initiative Movement and the Power of Money*. New York: Harcourt, 2000.

Brownstein, Ronald. "Pressure Is on Bush for First Debate." *Los Angeles Times*, October 11, 1992, news section, A1.

Bryce, James. *The American Commonwealth*. Vol. 2. New York: Macmillan, 1933.

Buisine, Alain. *Laideurs de Sartre*. Lille: Presses Universitaires de Lille, 1986.

Burstein, Paul. "The Impact of Public Opinion on Public Policy: A Review and Agenda." *Political Research Quarterly* 56 (2003): 29–40.

Cain, Bruce, John Ferejohn, and Morris Fiorina. *The Personal Vote: Constituency Service and Electoral Independence*. Cambridge, Mass.: Harvard University Press, 1987.

Campbell, Angus, et al. *The American Voter*. New York: Wiley, 1960.

Cannon, Lou. *Reagan*. New York: Putnam, 1982.

Canovan, Margaret. *The People*. Cambridge, UK: Polity Press, 2005.

Cappon, Lester J., ed. *The Adams-Jefferson Letters: The Complete Correspondence*. Chapel Hill: University of North Carolina Press, 1987.

Commager, Henry Steele. "Washington Would Have Lost a TV Debate." *New York Times Magazine*, October 30, 1960, VI-13.

Commission on Presidential Press Conferences. *Report of the Commission on Presidential Press Conference*. Washington, D.C.: University Press of America, 1981.

Connolly, Kate. "Hungarian Leader Defies Resignation Calls Despite Second Night of Protests." *Daily Telegraph*, September 20, 2006, news section, 14.

Constant, Benjamin. *Political Writings*. Edited by Biancamaria Fontana. Cambridge: Cambridge University Press, 1988.

Converse, Philip. "Comments on Davis's 'Changeable Weather in a Cooling Climate atop the Liberal Plateau.'" *Public Opinion Quarterly* 56 (1992): 308–309.

———. "The Nature of Belief Systems in Mass Publics." In *Ideology and Discontent*, edited by David Apter. London: Free Press of Glencoe, 1964.

————. "Public Opinion and Voting Behavior." In *Handbook of Political Science*, edited by Fred I. Greenstein and Nelson W. Polsby. Reading, Mass.: Addison-Wesley, 1975.

Craig, F. W. S. *British Electoral Facts, 1932–1987*. Brookfield: Gower, 1989.

Creed, Barbara. *The Monstrous-Feminine: Film, Feminism, Psychoanalysis*. London: Routledge, 1993.

Cutler, Fred. "Jeremy Bentham and the Public Opinion Tribunal." *Public Opinion Quarterly* 63 (1999): 321–346.

Dahl, Robert. *A Preface to Democratic Theory*. Chicago: University of Chicago Press, 1956.

————. *A Preface to Economic Democracy*. Berkeley: University of California Press, 1985.

————. *Who Governs? Democracy and Power in an American City*. New Haven, Conn.: Yale University Press, 1961.

Dean, Gillian, and Thomas Moran. "Measuring Mass Political Attitudes: Change and Uncertainty." *Political Methodology* 4 (1977): 383–424.

Debord, Guy. *Society of the Spectacle*. Translated by Donald Nicholson. New York: Zone, 1994.

Derathé, Robert. *Jean-Jacques Rousseau et la science politique de son temps*. Paris: J. Vrin, 1970.

Didion, Joan. *Political Fictions*. New York: Knopf, 2001.

Domhoff, William G. *Who Rules America: Power and Politics in the Year 2000*. Mountain View, Calif.: Mayfield, 1998.

Downs, Anthony. *An Economic Theory of Democracy*. New York: Harper, 1967.

Eden, Robert. *Political Leadership and Nihilism: A Study of Weber and Nietzsche*. Tampa: University Presses of Florida, 1983.

Eliot, T. S. *The Family Reunion*. Orlando, Fla.: Harvest Books, 1964.

Elkins, James. "The End of the Theory of the Gaze." Unpublished manuscript, available online at jameselkins.com/Texts/visualculturegaze.pdf.

Ellis, Richard J. *Democratic Delusions: The Initiative Process in America*. Lawrence: University Press of Kansas, 2002.

Erikson, Robert. "The SRC Panel Data and Mass Political Attitudes." *British Journal of Political Science* 9 (1979): 89–114.

Estlund, David. "Beyond Fairness and Deliberation: The Epistemic Dimension of Democratic Authority." In *Deliberative Democracy*, edited by James Bohman and William Rehg. Cambridge, Mass.: MIT Press, 1997.

Etzioni-Halevy, Eva, ed. *Classes and Elites in Democracy and Democratization*. New York: Garland, 1997.

Fan, David P. *Predictions of Public Opinion from the Mass Media*. New York: Greenwood Press, 1988.

Farah, George. *No Debates: How the Republican and Democratic Parties Secretly Control the Presidential Debate*. New York: Seven Stories, 2004.

Fearon, James. "Deliberation as Discussion." In *Deliberative Democracy*, edited by Jon Elster. Cambridge: Cambridge University Press, 1998.

The Federalist. Edited by Jacob E. Cooke. Hanover, N.H.: Wesleyan University Press, 1961.

John Ferejohn, "Incumbent Performance and Electoral Control." *Public Choice* 50 (1986): 5–25.

Filmer, Robert. *Patriarcha and Other Political Writings.* Edited by Peter Laslett. Oxford: Basil Blackwell, 1949.

Finley, M. I. *Democracy Ancient and Modern.* New Brunswick, N.J.: Rutgers University Press, 1973.

Fiorina, Morris P. *Retrospective Voting in American National Elections.* New Haven, Conn.: Yale University Press, 1981.

Fishkin, James. *The Voice of the People: Public Opinion and Democracy.* New Haven, Conn.: Yale University Press, 1995.

Flint, Henry M., ed. *Life of Stephen A. Douglas.* Philadelphia: Keystone, 1890.

Foley, Michael. *The Rise of the British Presidency.* Manchester: Manchester University Press, 1993.

Foucault, Michel. *Discipline and Punish: The Birth of the Prison.* Translated by Alan Sheridan. New York: Pantheon, 1977.

French, Blaire A. *The Presidential Press Conference.* Washington, D.C.: University Press of America, 1982.

Freud, Sigmund. "Medusa's Head." In *The Standard Edition of the Complete Psychological Works of Sigmund Freud,* vol. 18, edited by James Strachey. London: Hogarth Press, 1953.

———. "On Narcissism: An Introduction." In *The Standard Edition of the Complete Psychological Works of Sigmund Freud,* vol. 14, edited by James Strachey. London: Hogarth Press, 1953.

Friedrich, Carl J., and Zbigniew K. Brzezinski. *Totalitarian Dictatorship and Autocracy.* Cambridge, Mass.: Harvard University Press, 1965.

Fukuyama, Francis. *The End of History and the Last Man.* New York: Free Press, 1992.

Gilens, Martin. "Inequality and Democratic Responsiveness." *Public Opinion Quarterly* 69 (2005): 778–796.

Goodin, Robert E. "Democratic Deliberation Within." *Philosophy and Public Affairs* 29 (Winter 2000): 81–109.

Gravel, Pierre Bettez. *The Malevolent Eye: An Essay on the Evil Eye, Fertility, and the Concept of Mana.* New York: P. Lang, 1995.

Grazia, Alfred de. "Representation: Theory." In *International Encyclopedia of the Social Sciences,* vol. 13, edited by David L. Sills. New York: Macmillan, 1968.

Griffen, John D., and Brian Newman. "Are Voters Better Represented?" *Journal of Politics* 67 (2005): 1206–1227.

Grimke, Frederick. *The Nature and Tendency of Free Institutions.* Cambridge, Mass.: Belknap Press of Harvard University Press, 1968.

Guicciardini, Francesco. *Del modo di eleggere gli uffici nel Consiglio Grande.* In *Dialogo e Discorsi del Reggimento di Firenze.* Bari: G. Laterza, 1932.

Guinier, Lani. *The Tyranny of the Majority: Fundamental Fairness in Representative Democracy*. New York: Free Press, 1994.

Guizot, François. *Histoire des origins du gouvernement représentatif en Europe*. Paris: Didier, 1851.

Gutmann, Amy. *Democratic Education*. Princeton, N.J.: Princeton University Press, 1987.

Gutmann, Amy, and Dennis Thompson. *Democracy and Disagreement*. Cambridge, Mass.: Belknap Press of Harvard University Press, 1996.

———. *Why Deliberative Democracy?* Princeton, N.J.: Princeton University Press, 2004.

Habermas, Jürgen. *Between Facts and Norms: Contributions to a Discourse Theory of Law and Democracy*. Translated by William Rehg. Cambridge, Mass.: MIT Press, 1996.

———. "Further Reflections on the Public Sphere." In *Habermas and the Public Sphere*, edited by Craig Calhoun. Cambridge, Mass.: MIT Press, 1992.

———. "Popular Sovereignty as Procedure." In *Between Facts and Norms: Contributions to a Discourse Theory of Law and Democracy*, translated by William Rehg. Cambridge, Mass.: MIT Press, 1996.

———. *Structural Transformation of the Public Sphere: An Inquiry into the Category of Bourgeois Society*. Translated by Thomas Burger. Cambridge, Mass.: MIT Press, 1989.

———. "Three Normative Models of Democracy." In *Democracy and Difference: Contesting the Boundaries of the Political*, edited by Seyla Benhabib. Princeton, N.J.: Princeton University Press, 1996.

Haltom, William. "Liberal-Conservative Continua: A Comparison of Measures." *Western Political Quarterly* 43 (1990): 387–401.

Hamilton, Alexander. *The Papers of Alexander Hamilton*. Edited by Jacob E. Cooke. New York: Columbia University Press, 1961.

Hansen, Mogens Herman. *The Athenian Democracy in the Age of Demosthenes*. Translated by J. A. Crook. Oxford: Blackwell, 1991.

Hardt, Michael, and Antonio Negri. *Multitude: War and Democracy in the Age of Empire*. New York: The Penguin Press, 2004.

Hardwicke, Henry. *History of Oratory and Orators: A Study of the Influence of Oratory upon Politics and Literature*. New York: Putnam's, 1896.

Harrington, James. *The Political Works of James Harrington*. Edited by J. G. A. Pocock. Cambridge: Cambridge University Press, 1977.

Hartman, Mary S. "Benjamin Constant and the Question of Ministerial Responsibility in France, 1814–1815." *Journal of European Studies* 6 (1976): 248–261.

Held, David. *Models of Democracy*, 3rd edition. Stanford, Calif.: Stanford University Press, 2006.

Hill, Christopher. "The Many-Headed Monster in Late Tudor and Early Stuart Political Thinking." In *From the Renaissance to the Counter-Reformation: Essays in Honor of Garrett Mattingly*, edited by Charles H. Carter. New York: Random House, 1965.

Hillman, Richard S., John A. Peeler, and Elsa Cardozo. *Democracy and Human Rights in Latin America*. Westport, Conn.: Praeger, 2002.

Hobbes, Thomas. *On the Citizen*. Translated by Richard Tuck. New York: Cambridge University Press, 1998.

Höhn, Reinhard. *Rechtsgemeinschaft und Volksgemeinschaft*. Hamburg: Hanseatische Verlagsanstalt, 1935.

Holmes, David L. *Faiths of the Founding Fathers*. Oxford: Oxford University Press, 2006.

Huntington, Samuel. "The United States." In *The Crisis of Democracy*, edited by Michael Crozier, Samuel Huntington, and Joji Watanuki. New York: New York University Press, 1975.

Hyman, Herbert H., and Paul B. Sheatsley. "Some Reasons Why Information Campaigns Fail." *Public Opinion Quarterly* 11 (1947): 412–423.

Iyengar, Shanto. "Shortcuts to Political Knowledge: Selective Attention and the Accessibility Bias." In *Information and Democratic Processes*, edited by John Ferejohn and James Kuklinski. Urbana: University of Illinois Press, 1990.

Iyengar Shanto, and Donald Kinder. *News That Matters: Television and American Public Opinion*. Chicago: University of Chicago Press, 1987.

Jacobs, Lawrence R., and Robert Y. Shapiro. *Politicians Don't Pander: Political Manipulation and the Loss of Democratic Responsiveness*. Chicago: University of Chicago Press, 2000.

———. "Studying Substantive Democracy: Public Opinion, Institutions, and Policymaking." *PS: Political Science and Politics* 27 (1994): 9–16.

James, Michael. "Public Interest and Majority Rule in Bentham's Democratic Theory." *Political Theory* 9 (1981): 49–64.

Jay, Martin. *Downcast Eyes: The Denigration of Vision in the Twentieth Century*. Berkeley: University of California Press, 1993.

Jefferson, Thomas. *The Writings of Thomas Jefferson*. Edited by Andrew A. Lipscomb. Washington, D.C.: Thomas Jefferson Memorial Association, 1903.

Kagay, Michael R., and Greg A. Caldeira. "'I Like the Looks of His Face': Elements of Electoral Choice, 1952–1972." presented at the annual meeting of the American Political Science Association, San Francisco, California, September 2–5, 1975.

Kalb, Marvin, and Frederick Mayer, eds. *Reviving the Presidential News Conference: Report of the Harvard Commission on the Presidential News Conference*. Cambridge, Mass.: Harvard University, Kennedy School of Government, Joan Shorenstein Barone Center on the Press, Politics, and Public Policy, 1988.

Kant, Immanuel. *Critique of Pure Reason*. Edited and translated by Paul Guyer and Allen W. Wood. Cambridge: Cambridge University Press, 1997.

———. *Political Writings*. Edited by Hans Reiss and translated by H. B. Nisbet. Cambridge: Cambridge University Press, 1991.

Katz, Richard S., and Peter Mair. "Changing Models of Party Organization and Party Democracy: The Emergence of the Cartel Party." *Party Politics* 1 (January 1995): 5–28.

Kennedy, Ellen. *Constitutional Failure: Carl Schmitt in Weimar*. Durham, N.C.: Duke University Press, 2004.

Kernell, Samuel. *Going Public: New Strategies of Presidential Leadership*. Washington, D.C.: CQ Press, 1986.

Key, V. O. *Public Opinion and American Democracy*. New York: Knopf, 1961.

———. *The Responsible Electorate: Rationality in Presidential Voting, 1936–1960*. Cambridge, Mass.: Belknap Press of Harvard University Press, 1966.

Keyssar, Alexander. *The Right to Vote: The Contested History of Democracy in the United States*. New York: Basic Books, 2000.

Kinder, Donald, and Lynn Sanders. "Mimicking Political Debate with Survey Questions: The Case of White Opinion of Affirmative Action for Blacks." *Social Cognition* 8 (1990): 73–103.

Kinder, Donald, and David Sears. "Public Opinion and Political Action." In *Handbook of Social Psychology*, edited by Gardner Lindzey and Elliot Aronson. New York: Random House, 1985.

King, Anthony, ed. *Leaders' Personalities and the Outcomes of Democratic Elections*. Oxford: Oxford University Press, 2002.

Koellreutter, Otto. *Grundriss der Allgemeinen Staatslehr*. Tübingen: Mohr, 1933.

Körösényi, András. "Political Representation in Leader Democracy." *Government and Opposition* 40 (2005): 358–378.

Kraus, Sidney. *Televised Presidential Debates and Public Policy*. Mahwah, N.J.: Erlbaum, 2000.

Lacan, Jacques. *Four Fundamental Concepts of Psychoanalysis*. Translated by Alan Sheridan. New York: Norton, 1998.

LaPalombara, Joseph. *Democracy Italian Style*. New Haven, Conn.: Yale University Press, 1987.

Lefort, Claude. *Democracy and Political Theory*. Translated by David Macey. Minneapolis: University of Minnesota Press, 1988.

———. *The Political Forms of Modern Society*. Cambridge, Mass.: MIT Press, 1986.

Levendusky, Matthew. *The Partisan Sort: How Liberals Became Democrats and Conservatives Became Republicans*. Chicago: University of Chicago Press, 2009.

Levitin, Teresa E., and Warren E. Miller. "Ideological Interpretations of Presidential Elections." *American Political Science Review* 73 (1979): 751–771.

Linder, Usher F. *Reminiscences of the Early Bench and Bar of Illinois*. Chicago: Chicago Legal News, 1879.

Lindholm, Charles. *Charisma*. Cambridge, Mass.: Blackwell, 1990.

Locke, John. *The Political Writings of John Locke*. Edited by David Wootton. New York: Mentor, 1993.

———. *The Two Treatises of Government*. Edited by Peter Laslett. Cambridge: Cambridge University Press, 1988.

Loewenstein, Karl. *Max Weber's Political Ideas in the Perspective of Our Time.* Amherst: University of Massachusetts Press, 1966.

Lombardo, Emanuela. "The Participation of Civil Society in the European Constitution-Making Process." In *The Making of the European Constitution,* edited by Justus Schönlau et al. New York: Palgrave, 2006.

Lowi, Theodore J. *The End of Liberalism: The Second Republic of the United States.* New York: Norton, 1979.

———. *The Personal President: Power Invested, Promise Unfulfilled.* Ithaca, N.Y.: Cornell University Press, 1985.

———. "Presidential Democracy in America: Towards the Homogenized Regime." *Political Science Quarterly* 109 (1994): 401–415.

Lukács, Georg. *Die Zerstörung der Vernunft.* Berlin: Aufbau-Verlag, 1954.

Lupia, Arthur. "Short-cuts versus Encyclopedias: Information and Voting Behavior in California Insurance Reform Elections." *American Political Science Review* 88 (1994): 63–76.

Lyotard, Jean François. *The Postmodern Condition: A Report on Knowledge.* Translated by Geoff Bennington and Brian Massumi. Minneapolis: University of Minnesota Press, 1984.

Machiavelli, Niccolò. *Discourses on Livy.* Translated by Harvey C. Mansfield and Nathan Tarcov. Chicago: University of Chicago Press, 1998.

———. *The Prince.* Translated by Harvey C. Mansfield. Chicago: University of Chicago Press, 1998.

Mackie, Gerry. *Democracy Defended.* Cambridge: Cambridge University Press, 2003.

———. "Schumpeter's Leadership Democracy." *Political Theory* 38 (2009): 128–153.

Macpherson, C. B. *The Life and Times of Liberal Democracy.* Oxford: Oxford University Press, 1977.

Manin, Bernard. *The Principles of Representative Government.* Cambridge: Cambridge University Press, 1997.

Mansfield, Harvey C. *Machiavelli's Virtue.* Chicago: University of Chicago Press, 1996.

Maravall, José Maria. "Accountability and Manipulation." In *Democracy, Accountability, and Representation,* edited by Adam Przeworski, Susan Stokes, and Bernard Manin. Cambridge: Cambridge University Press, 1999.

Margolis, Michael. "From Confusion to Confusion: Issues and the American Voter (1956–1972)." *American Political Science Review* 71 (1977): 31–43.

Markovits, Elizabeth. "The Trouble with Being Earnest: Deliberative Democracy and the Sincerity Norm." *Journal of Political Philosophy* 14 (2006): 249–269.

Masters, Roger. *The Political Philosophy of Rousseau.* Princeton, N.J.: Princeton University Press, 1968.

Mathiesen, Thomas. "The Viewer Society: Michel Foucault's 'Panopticon' Revisited." *Theoretical Criminology* 1 (1997): 215–234.

McCormick, John P., ed. *Confronting Mass Democracy and Industrial Technology: Political and Social Theory from Nietzsche to Habermas.* Durham, N.C.: Duke University Press, 2002.

McFarland, Andrew S. *Neopluralism: The Evolution of Political Process Theory.* Lawrence: University Press of Kansas, 2004.

McGinniss, Joe. *The Selling of the President 1968.* New York: Trident Press, 1969.

McKitrick, Eric L. *Andrew Johnson and Reconstruction.* Chicago: University of Chicago Press, 1960.

Meadow, Robert G. "Televised Campaign Debates as Whistle-Stop Speeches." In *Television Coverage of the 1980 Presidential Campaign*, edited by William C. Adams. Norwood, N.J.: Ablex, 1983.

Medearis, John. *Joseph Schumpeter's Two Theories of Democracy.* Cambridge, Mass.: Harvard University Press, 2001.

Mendelsohn, Harold, and Irving Crespi. *Polls, Television, and the New Politics.* Scranton, Pa.: Chandler, 1970.

Michels, Robert. *Political Parties: A Sociological Study of Oligarchical the Tendencies of Modern Democracy.* Gloucester, Mass.: P. Smith, 1978.

Milbrath, Lester W. *Political Participation: How and Why Do People Get Involved in Politics?* Chicago: Rand McNally, 1965.

Mill, James. *Essay on Government.* In *Utilitarian Logic and Politics: James Mill's "Essay on Government," Macaulay's Critique, and the Ensuing Debate*, edited by Jack Lively and John Rees. Oxford: Clarendon Press, 1978.

Mill, John Stuart. *Collected Works of John Stuart Mill.* Toronto: University of Toronto Press, 1963.

———. *Considerations on Representative Government.* In *John Stuart Mill: On Liberty and Other Essays*, edited by John Gray. Oxford: Oxford University Press, 1998.

———. *On Liberty.* In *John Stuart Mill: On Liberty and Other Essays*, edited by John Gray. Oxford: Oxford University Press, 1998.

Miller, David. "The Competitive Model of Democracy." In *Democratic Theory and Practice*, edited by Graeme Duncan. Cambridge: Cambridge University Press, 1983.

Mills, C. Wright. *The Power Elite.* New York: Oxford University Press, 1956.

Mommsen, Wolfgang J. *Max Weber and German Politics, 1890–1920.* Translated by Michael Steinberg. Chicago: University of Chicago Press, 1984.

———, ed. *Max Weber and His Contemporaries.* London: German Historical Institute, 1987.

———. *The Political and Social Theory of Max Weber.* Cambridge, UK: Polity Press, 1989.

Montag, Warren. *Bodies, Masses, Power: Spinoza and His Contemporaries.* London: Verso, 1999.

Montesquieu. *The Spirit of the Laws.* Translated by Anne M. Cohler, Basia Carolyn Miller, and Harold Samuel Stone. Cambridge: Cambridge University Press, 1989.

Morgan, Edmund S. *Inventing the People: The Rise of Popular Sovereignty in England and America*. New York: Norton, 1988.

Morley, John. *The Life of William Ewart Gladstone*. London: Macmillan, 1903.

Morris, Martin. *Rethinking the Communicative Turn: Adorno, Habermas, and the Problem of Communicative Freedom*. Albany: State University of New York Press, 2001.

Morstein-Marx, Robert. *Mass Oratory and Political Power in the Late Roman Republic*. Cambridge: Cambridge University Press, 2004.

Mosca, Gaetano. *The Ruling Class*. Translated by Hannah D. Kahn. New York: McGraw-Hill, 1967.

Mulvey, Laura. "Visual Pleasure and Narrative Cinema." *Screen* 16 (Autumn 1975): 6–18.

Munro, William B. "Intelligence Test for Voters." *Forum* 80 (1928): 823–830.

Neesse, Gottfried. *Partei und Staat*. Hamburg: Hanseatische Verlagsanstalt, 1936.

Nelson, W. Dale. *Who Speaks for the President? The White House Press Secretary from Cleveland to Clinton*. Syracuse, N.Y.: Syracuse University Press, 1998.

Neuman, W. Russell. *The Paradox of Mass Politics: Knowledge and Opinion in the American Electorate*. Cambridge, Mass.: Harvard University Press, 1986.

Nie, Norman H., Sidney Verba, and John R. Petrocik. *The Changing American Voter*. Cambridge, Mass.: Harvard University Press, 1976.

Nimmo, Dan. *The Political Persuaders: The Techniques of Modern Electoral Campaigns*. Englewood Cliffs, N.J.: Prentice-Hall, 1970.

Ober, Josiah. *The Athenian Revolution: Essays on Ancient Greek Democracy and Political Theory*. Princeton, N.J.: Princeton University Press, 1996.

Olin, Margaret. "Gaze." In *Critical Terms for Art History*, edited by Robert S. Nelson and Richard Schiff. Chicago: University of Chicago Press, 1996.

Osterhammel, Jürgen. "Varieties of Social Economics: Joseph A. Schumpeter and Max Weber." In *Max Weber and His Contemporaries*, edited by Wolfgang Mommsen. London: German Historical Institute, 1987.

Owen, Frank. *Peron: His Rise and Fall*. London: Cresset Press, 1957.

Page, Benjamin I., and Robert Y. Shapiro. "Effects of Public Opinion on Policy." *American Political Science Review* 77 (1983): 175–190.

———. *The Rational Public: Fifty Years of Trends in Americans' Policy Preferences*. Chicago: University of Chicago Press, 1992.

Paine, Thomas. *Common Sense*. London: Penguin, 1982.

Pappi, Franz Urban. "Political Behavior: Reasoning Voters and Multi-party Systems." In *The New Handbook of Political Science*, edited by Robert Goodin and Hans-Dieter Klingemann. Oxford: Oxford University Press, 1996.

Pareto, Vilfredo. *Mind and Society: A Treatise on General Sociology*. New York: Dover, 1935.

Parkman, Francis. "The Failure of Universal Suffrage." *North American Review* 127 (July–August 1878): 1–20.

Pateman, Carole. *Participation and Democratic Theory*. Cambridge: Cambridge University Press, 1970.

Pennock, J. Roland. *Liberal Democracy: Its Merits and Prospects*. New York: Rinehart, 1950.

Pettit, Philip. "Rawls's Political Ontology." *Politics, Philosophy, and Economics* 4 (2005): 157–174.

Plamenatz, John. *Democracy and Illusion: An Examination of Certain Aspects of Modern Democratic Theory*. London: Longman, 1973.

Pocock, J. G. A. *The Machiavellian Moment*. Princeton, N.J.: Princeton University Press, 1975.

Poguntke, Thomas, and Paul Webb. *The Presidentialization of Politics: A Comparative Study of Modern Democracies*. Oxford: Oxford University Press, 2005.

Pomper, Gerald M. *Voters' Choice: Varieties of American Electoral Behavior*. New York: Dodd, Mead, 1975.

Popkin, Samuel. *The Reasoning Voter: Communication and Persuasion in Presidential Campaigns*. Chicago: University of Chicago Press, 1991.

Postema, Gerald. "Interests, Universal and Particular: Bentham's Utilitarian Theory of Value." *Utilitas* 18 (2006): 109–133.

Postman, Neil. *Amusing Ourselves to Death*. New York: Viking, 1985.

Przeworski, Adam. *Democracy and the Market*. Cambridge: Cambridge University Press, 1991.

Przeworski, Adam, Susan Stokes, and Bernard Manin, eds. *Democracy, Accountability, and Representation*. Cambridge: Cambridge University Press, 1999.

Putnam, Robert D. "Tuning In, Tuning Out: The Strange Disappearance of Social Capital in America." *PS: Political Science and Politics* 28 (1995): 664–683.

Ranney, John C. "Do the Polls Serve Democracy?" *Public Opinion Quarterly* 10 (1946): 349–360.

Rawls, John. *Political Liberalism*. New York: Columbia University Press, 1996.

Riker, William. *The Art of Political Manipulation*. New Haven, Conn.: Yale University Press, 1986.

———. *Liberalism against Populism: A Confrontation between the Theory of Democracy and the Theory of Social Choice*. San Francisco: Freeman, 1982.

Robbins, Lionel. "Interpersonal Comparisons of Utility: A Comment." *Economic Journal* 43 (1938): 635–641.

Rosanvallon, Pierre. *Democracy Past and Future*. New York: Columbia University Press, 2006.

Rose, Richard. *The Post-modern President*. Chatham, N.J.: Chatham House, 1988.

Rosenau, Pauline Marie. *Post-modernism and the Social Sciences*. Princeton, N.J.: Princeton University Press, 1992.

Rosenberg, Shawn W., Lisa Bohan, Patrick McCafferty, and Kevin Harris. "The Image and the Vote: The Effect of Candidate Presentation on Voter Preference." *American Journal of Political Science* 30 (1986): 108–127.

Rosenblum, Nancy L. *Bentham's Theory of the Modern State*. Cambridge, Mass.: Harvard University Press, 1978.

———. *Membership and Morals: The Personal Uses of Pluralism in America*. Princeton, N.J.: Princeton University Press, 1998.

————. *On the Side of the Angels: An Appreciation of Parties and Partisanship.* Princeton, N.J.: Princeton University Press, 2008.

————. "Political Parties as Membership Groups." *Columbia Law Review* 3 (2000): 813–844.

————. "Primus Inter Pares: Political Parties and Civil Society." *Chicago-Kent Law Review* 75 (2000): 493–529.

Rousseau, Jean-Jacques. *The Social Contract.* Translated by Maurice Cranston. London: Penguin, 1968.

Santoro, Emilio. "Democratic Theory and Individual Autonomy: An Interpretation of Schumpeter's Doctrine of Autonomy." *European Journal of Political Research* 23 (1993): 121–143.

Sartre, Jean-Paul. *Being and Nothingness: An Essay on Phenomenological Ontology.* Translated by Hazel E. Barnes. New York: Philosophical Library, 1956.

————. *Black Orpheus.* Translated by S. W. Allen. Paris: Présence Africaine, 1963.

Sato, Masayuki. *The Confucian Quest for Order: The Origin and Formation of the Political Thought of Xun Zi.* Leiden: Brill, 2003.

Scaff, Lawrence. *Fleeing the Iron Cage: Culture, Politics, and Modernity in the Thought of Max Weber.* Berkeley: University of California Press, 1989.

Scheuerman, William. *Carl Schmitt: The End of Law.* Lanham, Md.: Rowman and Littlefield, 1999.

Schiffer, Adam J. "I'm Not *That* Liberal: Explaining Conservative Democratic Alignment." *Political Behavior* 22 (2000): 293–310.

Schlozman, Kay. "Citizen Participation in America: What Do We Know? Why Do We Care?" In *Political Science: State of the Discipline*, edited by Ira Katznelson and Helen V. Milner. New York: Norton, 2002.

Schmitt, Carl. *The Concept of the Political.* Translated by George Schwab. Chicago: University of Chicago Press, 1996.

————. *Constitutional Theory.* Translated by Jeffrey Seitzer. Durham, N.C.: Duke University Press, 2008.

————. *The Crisis of Parliamentary Democracy.* Translated by Ellen Kennedy. Cambridge, Mass.: MIT Press, 1985.

————. "Juristische Fiktionen," *Deutsche Juristen-Zeitung* 18, no. 2 (1913): 804–816.

————. *Legality and Legitimacy.* Translated by Jeffrey Seitzer. Durham, N.C.: Duke University Press, 2004.

————. *Staat, Bewegung, Volk: Die Dreigliederung der Politischen Einheit.* Hamburg: Hanseatische Verlagsanstalt, 1933.

————. *Volksentscheid und Volksbegehren; ein Beitrag zur Auslegung der Weimarer Verfassung und zur Lehr von der unmittelbaren Demokratie.* Berlin: W. de Gruyter, 1927.

Schroeder, Alan. *Presidential Debates: Forty Years of High-Risk TV.* New York: Columbia University Press, 2000.

Schroeder, Ralph, ed. *Max Weber, Democracy, and Modernization.* New York: St. Martin's Press, 1998.

Schumpeter, Joseph. *Capitalism, Socialism, and Democracy.* New York: Harper and Brothers, 1942.

Schwab, George. *The Challenge of the Exception: An Introduction to the Political Ideas of Carl Schmitt between 1921 and 1936.* New York: Greenwood Press, 1970.

Sefton, James E. *Andrew Johnson and the Uses of Constitutional Power.* Boston: Little, Brown, 1980.

Shakespeare, William. *Coriolanus.* Edited by Philip Brockbank. London: Arden, 1996.

——. *Julius Caesar.* Edited by David Daniell. London: Arden, 1998.

Shapiro, Ian. *The State of Democratic Theory.* Princeton, N.J.: Princeton University Press, 2003.

Shaw, Tamsin. "Max Weber on Democracy: Can the People Have Political Power in Modern States?" *Constellations* 15 (2008): 38–45.

Shepsle, Kenneth. *Analyzing Politics: Rationality, Behavior, and Institutions.* New York: Norton, 1997.

Shogan, Colleen. "Rhetorical Moralism in the Plebiscitary Presidency: New Speech Forms and Their Ideological Entailments." *Studies in American Political Development* 17 (2003): 149–167.

Siebers, Tobin. *The Mirror of Medusa.* Berkeley: University of California Press, 1983.

Sieyès, Emmanuel Joseph. *Political Writings.* Edited by Michael Sonenscher. Indianapolis: Hackett, 2003.

Skocpol, Theda. *Diminished Democracy: From Membership to Management in American Civic Life.* Norman: University of Oklahoma Press, 2003.

Skowronek, Stephen. *The Politics Presidents Make: Leadership from John Adams to George Bush.* Cambridge, Mass.: Belknap Press of Harvard University Press, 1993.

Smith, Carolyn D. *The Presidential Press Conference: A Critical Approach.* New York: Praeger, 1990.

Smith, Rogers M. *Stories of Peoplehood: The Politics and Morals of Political Membership.* New York: Cambridge University Press, 2003.

Smith, Tom W. "Non-attitudes: A Review and Evaluation." In *Surveying Subjective Phenomena,* edited by Charles Turner and Elizabeth Martin. New York: Russell Sage Foundation, 1984.

Sniderman, Paul M., Richard A. Brody, and Philip. E. Tetlock. *Reasoning and Choice: Explorations in Political Psychology.* Cambridge: Cambridge University Press, 1991.

Stammer, Otto, ed. *Max Weber and Sociology Today.* Translated by Kathleen Morris. Oxford: Blackwell, 1971.

Stern, J. P. *Hitler: The Führer and the People.* Berkeley: University of California Press, 1975.

Stimson, James A. *Public Opinion in America: Moods, Cycles, and Swings.* Boulder, Colo.: Westview, 1991.

Stimson, James A., Michael B. MacKuen, and Robert S. Erikson. "Dynamic Representation." *American Political Science Review* 89 (1995): 543–565.

Stryker, Lloyd Paul. *Andrew Johnson.* New York: Macmillan, 1929.

Talmon, J. L. *The Origins of Totalitarian Democracy*. London: Secker and Warburg, 1952.

Thomas, Helen. *Watchdogs of Democracy? The Waning Washington Press Corps and How It Has Failed the Public*. New York: Scribner, 2006.

Thomassen, Lasse. *Deconstructing Habermas*. New York: Routledge, 2008.

Thompson, Dennis F. *John Stuart Mill and Representative Government*. Princeton, N.J.: Princeton University Press, 1976.

Tocqueville, Alexis de. *Democracy in America*. Edited by J. P. Mayer and translated by George Lawrence. New York: HarperPerennial, 1988.

Tourangeau, Roger, and Kenneth Rasinksi. "Cognitive Processes Underlying Context Effects in Attitude Measurement." *Psychological Bulletin* 103 (1988): 299–314.

Truman, David B. *The Governmental Process: Political Interests and Public Opinion*. New York: Knopf, 1951.

Tucker, Robert. "The Theory of Charismatic Leadership." *Daedalus* 97 (1968): 731–756.

Tulis, Jeffrey. *The Rhetorical Presidency*. Princeton, N.J.: Princeton University Press, 1987.

Turner, Stephen P., and Regis A. Factor. *Max Weber and the Dispute over Reason and Value: A Study in Philosophy, Ethics, and Politics*. London: Routledge and Kegan Paul, 1984.

Urbinati, Nadia. *Mill on Democracy: From the Athenian Polis to Representative Government*. Chicago: University of Chicago Press, 2002.

U.S. Senate. *Proceedings in the Trial of Andrew Johnson*. Washington, D.C., 1869.

Verba, Sidney. "The Citizen as Respondent: Sample Surveys and American Democracy." *American Political Science Review* 90 (1996): 1–7.

Verba, Sidney, and Norman H. Nie. *Participation in America: Political Democracy and Social Equality*. New York: Harper and Row, 1972.

Verba, Sidney, Norman H. Nie, and Jae-On Kim. *Participation and Political Equality: A Seven-Nation Comparison*. Cambridge: Cambridge University Press, 1978.

Verba, Sidney, Kay Lehman Schlozman, and Henry E. Brady. *Voice and Equality: Civic Voluntarism in America*. Cambridge, Mass.: Harvard University Press, 1995.

Virno, Paolo. *A Grammar of the Multitude*. Cambridge, Mass.: Semiotext(e), 2004.

Warren, Mark, and Hilary Pearse, eds. *Designing Deliberative Democracy: The British Columbia Citizens' Assembly*. Cambridge: Cambridge University Press, 2008.

Wattenberg, Martin P. *The Rise of Candidate-Centered Politics: Presidential Elections of the 1980s*. Cambridge, Mass.: Harvard University Press, 1991.

Weber, Max. *Ancient Judaism*. Translated by H. H. Gerth and Don Martindale. Glencoe, Ill.: Free Press, 1952.

———. *Briefe, 1909–1910.* Edited by M. Rainer Lepsius and Wolfgang J. Mommsen. Tübingen: Mohr, 1994.

———. *Economy and Society: An Outline of Interpretative Sociology.* Edited by Guenther Roth and Claus Wittich. Berkeley: University of California Press, 1978.

———. *From Max Weber: Essays in Sociology.* Edited by H. H. Gerth and C. Wright Mills. New York: Oxford University Press, 1946.

———. *Gesammelte Politische Schriften.* Edited by Johannes Winckelmann. Tübingen: Mohr, 1971.

———. *Max Weber: Werk und Person.* Edited by Eduard Baumgarten. Tübingen: Mohr, 1964.

———. *Political Writings.* Edited by Peter Lassman and Ronald Speirs. Cambridge: Cambridge University Press, 1994.

———. *Wirtschaft und Gesellschaft: Grundriss der Verstehenden Soziologie.* Edited by Johannes Winckelmann. Tübingen: Mohr, 1956.

Weibe, Robert. *Self-Rule: A Cultural History of American Democracy.* Chicago: University of Chicago Press, 1995.

Wheeler, Harvey. "The Great Debates." In *The Great Debates,* edited by Earl Mazo et al. Santa Barbara, Calif.: Center for the Study of Democratic Institutions, 1962.

Wilhelm, Anthony G. *Democracy in the Digital Age: Challenges to Political Life in Cyberspace.* New York: Routledge, 2000.

Wilson, Graham K. *Interest Groups.* Cambridge, Mass.: Basil Blackwell, 1990.

Wilson, Timothy D., and Sara D. Hodges. "Attitudes as Temporary Constructions." In *The Construction of Social Judgments,* edited by Leonard Martin and Abraham Tesser. Hillsdale, N.J.: Erlbaum, 1992.

Wittman, Donald A. *The Myth of Democratic Failure.* Chicago: University of Chicago Press, 1995.

Wolin, Sheldon. "Fugitive Democracy." In *Democracy and Difference: Contesting the Boundaries of the Political,* edited by Seyla Benhabib. Princeton, N.J.: Princeton University Press, 1996.

Wood, Gordon S. *The Radicalism of the American Revolution.* New York: Knopf, 1992.

Wootton, David, ed. *Divine Right and Democracy: An Anthology of Political Writing in Stuart England.* New York: Penguin, 1986.

Wright, John R. *Interest Groups and Congress.* Needham Heights, Mass.: Allyn and Bacon, 1996.

Wyckoff, Gene. *The Image Candidates.* New York: Macmillan, 1968.

Young, Iris Marion. *Inclusion and Democracy.* Oxford: Oxford University Press, 2000.

Zaller, John. *The Nature and Origins of Mass Opinion.* New York: Cambridge University Press, 1992.

———. "Political Awareness, Elite Opinion Leadership, and the Mass Survey Response." *Social Cognition* 8 (1990): 125–153.

INDEX